A
BIBLICAL
THEOLOGY
OF
MATERIAL
POSSESSIONS

A BIBLICAL THEOLOGY OF MATERIAL POSSESSIONS

by

GENE A. GETZ

FOREWORD BY
JOSEPH M. STOWELL

MOODY PRESS

CHICAGO

ISBN: 0-8024-0891-5

1 2 3 4 5 6 Printing/AK/Year 95 94 93 92 91 90

Printed in the United States of America

To a group of eleven Christian men who serve as leaders
at Fellowship Bible Church North in Plano, Texas,

Eddie Burford
Jack Cole
Mike Cornwall
Bill Fackler
Jim Harris
Earl Lindgren
Don Logue
Steve Meyer
Richard Pascuzzi
Stan Potocki
Jim Wilson

men who are godly models of how Christians should view and use
their material possessions and whose input was invaluable in
both interpreting and applying scriptural truth in this book.

Contents

Index of Graphics

Index of Maps

Foreword

Since, as someone has well said, you can tell more about a person's spiritual life by reading through his checkbook ledger than by almost any other means, it is paramount that we Christians instruct each other in regard to the biblical management of our resources. From that standpoint at least, this study is long overdue.

As I read through *A Biblical Theology of Material Possessions*, I was struck immediately by the balance and the direct-rootedness in the biblical data of this study. Dr. Getz avoids all the traps of recent forays into this topic. He neither bashes the blessed nor burdens the bereft. There is no hint of the extremes we often hear about: that voluntary simplicity of life is what God demands of all of us or that abundant prosperity is a direct sign of God's blessing and of our personal faith.

When a pastor I often shied away from teaching principles of stewardship for several reasons. First, in no way did I want to give the impression to those who were seekers that all the church was interested in was their money. Nor did I wish to seem manipulative in seeking financial income for the plans and programs we had drawn up for the ministry of the church. It seemed a very touchy thing to talk to people about their money. Perhaps my feeling was that messages of this sort would create a great amount of discomfort in many people's hearts, and, after all, shouldn't the gospel bring peace and comfort instead?

While I struggled with some of these feelings, I knew deep down that I was called to preach the whole counsel of God. So at times I would awkwardly enter this arena, often creating a serious sense of imbalance. I remember one wealthy deacon who came to me after a message on money. He said that he didn't think it was right for me to make him "feel guilty" that God had blessed him with an abundant supply of goods. This man had been faithful to and generous toward God's work, and I knew right away that something had been wrong with the way I presented the material.

I remember preaching on another occasion a rather hard-hitting sermon on biblical stewardship. At the end of my message, I essentially apologized for having to preach on money. I said something like, "I know this is a hard topic, and I wish we didn't have to talk about it, but, nevertheless, it is important." A dear friend of mine, whose life was characterized by consistent commitment to the biblical principles of stewardship, approached me afterwards. He began by saying that he thought it had been a good sermon. Then he reproved me, saying, "Don't ever apologize for preaching God's truth about money!"

I don't think I would have suffered such examples of ministerial awkwardness if I had had Gene Getz's well thought through and carefully organized treatment of the biblical material. No one's ministry, and certainly no one's life and perspectives, will be the same after honestly interacting with the truth in this book.

The strength of this volume is that Dr. Getz has been careful to cite only *biblical* truth about money, material possessions, and giving. This truth is framed in clear principles, leaving the reader to apply these principles in each given situation. Thankfully the author has refused to give the impression that in every life situation and in every culture these principles will be applied uniformly. He has emphasized the priority of giving to the local church and yet outlined a good list of guidelines for those who give additional resources to parachurch ministries.

The value of this book is that it calls us nonnegotiably to obedience in terms of our possessions. It shows us what is right and qualifies our excuses and rationalizations in terms of our ultimate accountability to God.

You'll be surprised, as I was, at how much Christ, the apostles, and Scripture in general has to say about money. God obviously knows that one of the major struggles in life is the task of sorting out, prioritizing, and resisting the pressures that personal gain engenders in our existence.

One thing becomes clear, however: God is interested first and foremost in our *hearts.* The biblical management of our money and possessions is actually a reflection of our love for God, His cause, the gospel, and each other. Once our hearts are right, the management of our treasures will reflect our love for God and others.

Time and time again, the exposition of these relevant passages demonstrate the truth that it's not so much *what you have* but, rather, *what has you* that makes all the difference. You can tell a lot about the heart of a person by looking at the allocation of his treasures. As Christ said, "Where your treasure is, there will your heart be also" (Luke 12:34).

JOSEPH M. STOWELL
PRESIDENT, MOODY BIBLE INSTITUTE

Preface

Researching and writing on what the Bible says about material possessions has brought back many singular memories of the cultural events that played a part in my research and writing of a previous book on the biblical theology of the church. In the late 60s and early 70s, I was catapulted into a fresh study of the New Testament Scriptures to determine what God says about the Body of Christ. Challenged by the anti-institutional trends and forces in society generally, I explored the Word of God with my students at Dallas Theological Seminary.

Eventually, I wrote a book entitled *Sharpening the Focus of the Church.* For several years I interacted with seminarians and with Christian leaders already in full-time ministry. From what I learned I outlined a number of scriptural supracultural principles for creating forms and structures for the church in any particular society in the world and at any moment in history. Looking through the "lens of Scripture," the "lens of history," and the "lens of culture," I attempted to formulate principles that are normative and enduring.

MOVING FROM PRINCIPLIZING TO CHURCH PLANTING

Little did I realize that this effort would eventually lead me out of the seminary classroom as a professor to become a church-planting pastor. Several of my students at Dallas Theological Seminary challenged me to test these principles in a real-life situation. This was followed by an invitation from several families in Dallas to launch a new church. They were keenly interested in utilizing the principles outlined in *Sharpening the Focus of the Church* to develop new forms and structures that were based upon scriptural foundations but that were also culturally relevant. Consequently, we launched the first Fellowship Bible Church in the fall of 1972, determined not to do things differently just to be different but committed not to do things the same way just because they have always been done that way.

Since that time, I have been personally involved in launching new churches. After twenty years of teaching (thirteen years at Moody Bible Institute and seven years at Dallas Theological Seminary), I gave up my full-time professor role in 1973. Needless to say, the next twenty years have become a great learning experience.

UNIQUE SIMILARITIES BUT SIGNIFICANT DIFFERENCES

Several unique similarities, but also some significant differences, existed between researching and writing *A Biblical Theology of Material Possessions* and *Sharpening the Focus of the Church*. Both projects were precipitated by circumstances in the larger cultural setting. But rather than the anti-institutionalism trends in the late 60s and early 70s that launched my study of the New Testament church, the materialistic trends of the 80s have created the setting for this study on what the Bible says about material possessions.

Ironically, many young people who were part of the earlier movement, with its criticism of what they called the "plastic culture," have now created one of their own—a superficial society permeated with self-preoccupation and self-advancement. Often designated as "baby boomers"—people born during the ten-to-twelve-year period following World War II—they have probably become the most materialistically oriented group of people in the two hundred years of American history. For instance, researchers have discovered that baby boomers give almost nothing to any form of charity.[1]

Needless to say, this mentality has also become a part of the Christian community. Some estimate that evangelical Christians give an average of only 2 percent of their income to further the kingdom of God.[2] Since this statistic includes approximately 15 percent of those in the evangelical community who give at least 10 percent or more of their income, it is easy to conclude that Christian "baby boomers" differ very little from their secular counterparts. They too give next to nothing.

The second similarity is that researching and writing *A Biblical Theology of Material Possessions* has been a group process. But there is a singular difference. The first book grew out of the seminary classroom. Though the initial results of that process were shared again and again with pastors and Christian leaders before they were refined and put into permanent book form (including the extensive revision in 1984), the bulk of the research and work was forged out of an academic setting—and then tested and applied in various church planting situations.

A Biblical Theology of Material Possessions, however, has grown directly out of the local church setting itself. Rather than a group of seminarians, those involved in this process were primarily lay elders/pastors and leaders who serve with me at Fellowship Bible Church North in Plano, Texas. For a number of months we researched and studied in-depth what the

Scriptures have to say about material possessions. Such study resulted in this present volume.

AN ECONOMIC CRISIS AND CULTURAL SPILLOVER

Although various economic crises have plagued our country over the last several years, no recession has had more wide-ranging effects than what has happened in the Southwestern part of the United States. Texas particularly has been hard hit by the oil crisis, which in turn devastated the real estate market. And once the real estate market began to crater, an unusual domino effect took place that has impacted the banking industry. Failures, particularly among savings and loan institutions in Texas, have made world news.

Pastoring a church in the Dallas Metroplex brought me face-to-face with the results of this economic recession and the way it impacted Christians in their patterns of giving. Frankly, I had not given much attention to this area of Christian living in my pastoral experience, primarily because we had not faced any serious budget deficits—until the recession hit.

What was a hidden reality suddenly became quite visible. Because economic times had been very good over the years, many Christians had been giving—primarily when the need arose—out of what was "left over," rather than out of what was set aside regularly as "firstfruits." To be more specific, the majority of Christians attending our church (and other churches) were not regular, systematic, and proportional givers. God's work was not a budget item—and, generally speaking, had never been. Consequently, when they felt the economic crunch, they had very little left over—virtually no excess to give. It took everything they were earning to handle their indebtedness—on their homes and their cars—and, in many instances, on a number of items that were considered investments in the pure enjoyment in life.

The effect on the financial needs of churches all over Texas was felt immediately. Even though some churches were growing numerically, giving was declining. Had Christians been giving God their firstfruits all along and making these monies a part of their personal budgets the ministry would not have been the first place to feel the financial crunch. But now it took most, if not all, of their income to make their payments on their debts to the world system and to maintain the life-style they were used to. Their indebtedness to God was the first to go by the wayside. This is not surprising since God's work was not a priority item.

But this economic dynamic was a blessing in disguise. It brought into sharp focus a spiritual problem in our own congregation and in churches in most areas of the Western world. Most Christians are not putting God first in the financial area of their lives. Materialism has taken its toll and impacted believers. The world has pressed us into its mold, and the majority of evangelical believers in our society are not walking in the will of God in relationship to their material possessions (Rom. 12:1-2).

A Closer Look at the Process

Sensing my own personal concern about the way this cultural crisis was impacting believers in our own church, a good friend approached me one day and offered to do what he could to help me and our other church leaders address this need. When I shared the results of this conversation with my fellow elders, they agreed we should take action.

AN "ACTS 6 GROUP"

They asked my friend and six others to form a special task force to study this issue. We identified these men as our "Acts 6 Group," based upon the example of the seven men in Jerusalem who were appointed by the apostles to resolve the economic problems in the church at that time. These men took this assignment very seriously. They met weekly for several months, devoting a lot of time to prayer as they began to seek the will of God. This process resulted in a number of recommendations to the elders. However, one proposal that relates directly to this book was that I—as senior pastor—bring a series of messages to the total congregation concerning what the Bible says about material possessions. Impressed with this suggestion, the elders charged me with this responsibility.

AN EXPANDED TASK FORCE

I responded to this challenge by asking my fellow elders, as well as the members of the Acts 6 Group, to join me in a detailed study of the Word of God to gather basic information that would enable me to prepare this series of messages. They all agreed, and we began the study.

Initially, few of us realized the gigantic task we had tackled. We met weekly in my home on Wednesday evenings for a number of months, looking carefully at *every* reference in the Bible to material possessions. Beginning in the book of Acts, we moved to the gospels and then to the epistles. From there we turned to Genesis and ended our study with the book of Malachi. To our surprise, we found more detailed information on the subject of material possessions than nearly any other subject in the Bible— outside of what Scripture says about God Himself.

OBSERVING AND INTERPRETING

Reading ahead, I compiled every biblical reference to material possessions I could find. Using a computer program that contained the whole Bible, we printed these biblical texts on separate sheets, leaving space to make specific observations. During those Wednesday evening studies, each man in the group took his turn reporting what he had observed from his own personal study, resulting in some dynamic interaction and discussion.

We attempted to interpret what these biblical events and teachings meant in their historical and cultural context. We also read selected extra-biblical literature, including the early church Fathers, attempting to discover how Christians over the years have interpreted and applied what they believed were the basic principles in these passages.

SYNTHESIZING AND PRINCIPLIZING

Once we had completed the observation and interpretation phase, we began the process of principlizing—discovering the supracultural teachings in these biblical accounts. At this point, I took the major responsibility of synthesizing a vast amount of biblical data, following the historical flow of events as they unfolded during the New Testament era. (This process is explained in detail in the Introduction.) I brought this synthesized material to the group each week for discussion, evaluation, and refinement.

Our next step was to present the material to our total leadership team—well over one hundred lay leaders, many of whom pastor small groups we call minichurches. Then I prepared the material in sermonic form and brought a series of messages to the total congregation.

The final step was to carefully rework the manuscript material after delivering a series of messages. The end result of this total process is *A Biblical Theology of Material Possessions.* The series of messages presented to the congregation took on an entirely different form and structure than the format in this book. It is one thing to formulate a biblical theology of material possessions for an in-depth study in manuscript form. It is yet another thing to develop and organize the material to teach these concepts to the church at large on a weekly basis. Both approaches call for distinctive patterns and methodology (see graphic on p. 18).

This book outlines passages of Scripture as they appear chronologically in various units of thought in the New Testament. These specific passages are then interpreted in their historical and cultural context. From these observations, a number of supracultural principles are outlined that grow directly out of Scripture.

The outlines used in preaching and teaching this biblical information are quite different. Rather, various supracultural principles were stated as biblical propositions. Following each proposition, selected biblical material was used to support and verify the supracultural nature of each principle.

PRACTICAL RESULTS

At the time of this writing, many people at Fellowship Bible Church North have begun to respond in a wonderful way to the Word of God. Pre-

"BOOK FORM" COMPARED WITH "SERMONIC FORM"

BOOK FORM
or Classroom Discussions

SERMONIC FORM
or Pulpit Presentations

Biblical Exposition
(Observations & Interpretation)

Supracultural Principles

Biblical Propositions
(Supracultural Principles)

Biblical Passages to Support Propositions
(Principles)

dictably, many are still struggling to make changes. Understandably, it takes time to break old patterns and restructure one's economic life. And as in every church, some have chosen, at least outwardly, to ignore the principles of Scripture. We are convinced, however, that God is at work in their hearts, and eventually His Word will not return void.

Only time and especially eternity will tell the whole story. But for now, those of us in leadership in our church are very encouraged with the response to the principles that are outlined in this volume. Hopefully they will help you, not only to conform your own life to the will of God in this matter, but to help others do so as well.

One final thought: statements that are formulated by any biblical interpreter and presented as scriptural principles and propositional truths, and that are supposedly accurate reflections of the meaning of scriptural writings, whether in narrative or command form, are certainly subject to human error. These principles and propositions should be carefully evaluated in light of the actual scriptural record and subjected to proper exegetical scrutiny. As a student of Scripture, I humbly present the principles in this volume, hopefully as an accurate reflection of biblical truth, but certainly subject to further evaluation by scriptural exegetes who may be more exact and thorough than I.

Notes

1. *The Yankelovich Monitor Report*, 1987.

2. Unfortunately, research demonstrates that, out of the total number of Christians in America, though many give at least 10 percent, this number probably represents only about 10-15 percent. On average, the remaining 85-90 percent give much less than 10 percent. E. Calvin Beisner, "How Much for How Many?" *Discipleship Journal* 49:20, states that "average churchgoers' giving today is only about 1.8 to 2.2 percent of income (depending on whose estimates and assumptions you accept)."

Acknowledgments

I would like to express special appreciation to my wife, Elaine, who graciously hosted the special research team that met weekly in our home to assist me with this study. Her consistent encouragement was a primary source of motivation to persevere in this project. Most important, Elaine has been a model to me in the use of our material possessions. Over the years she has taught me to be a regular and systematic giver. Though we are still working on the "proportional" aspect of giving (a lifetime goal), our objective has always been to give at least 10 percent of our gross income to God's work. Because of Elaine's careful planning and frugal approach to home and money management, we have often been able to exceed a tithe. Her unselfish and generous spirit has deeply impacted my life and ministry.

A special word of acknowledgment is also due Iva Morelli, my executive assistant. Her expert skills on the computer facilitated both the research and writing phases of this book. Her personal dedication to this task, involving many hours of time and effort beyond the call of duty, was a constant source of encouragement.

I am grateful to the total staff at Fellowship Bible Church North and the Center for Church Renewal. These committed men and women provided me with inner strength, often taking on extra responsibilities to free up my time for manuscript preparation. I would also like to express appreciation to the whole church body at FBCN, with special acknowledgment to our lay leadership team, which ministers to people in our small groups. Their positive response to the principles outlined in this book greatly motivated me to prepare this material for publication.

Finally, I am indebted to the leadership at Moody Bible Institute for their keen interest in this project. Special thanks is due President Joseph Stowell for writing the Foreword and to former Senior Vice President of Media Don Johnson, who contacted me about this material. It has been a delight to work with Greg Thornton, general manager and executive editor of Moody Press. His enthusiasm has been a constant source of motivation.

Introduction: Gaining Perspective

In his penetrating historical analysis of faith and wealth during the centuries immediately following the New Testament era, Justo Gonzalez draws some rather startling conclusions. He notes that these issues were never separated in the minds of the church Fathers. Yet he concludes that current theologians and church historians give very little attention to economic issues as they relate to the Christian faith.

Gonzalez questions why this is true. "One obvious answer," he says, "is that matters such as the origin, nature, and use of wealth are not considered theological issues, and therefore when historians of doctrine have read these texts in the past they have not been looking for such matters."[1] This leads Gonzalez to ask, "Why have such matters not been considered properly theological issues, when it is clear that the ancient writers themselves considered them of great theological significance?" There is, he continues, "the inescapable conclusion that they [faith and wealth] have not been considered theological issues because the church at large has avoided them."[2]

Whatever one's theological persuasion, Gonzalez poses questions that cannot be circumvented by Bible-believing Christians who are serious about knowing and doing the will of God. The facts are that the church Fathers were concerned about these issues because they were considered important by Jesus Christ and those who followed Him. How believers are to view and use their material possessions is a pervasive theme throughout the Word of God.

To understand our Christian faith and how it relates to material possessions will require more than merely studying the history of theology. Rather, we must focus initially on *biblical* theology. According to George Ladd biblical theology "is that discipline which sets forth the message of the books of the Bible in their historical setting."[3] Charles Ryrie defines it as "that branch of theological science which deals systematically with the his-

21

torically conditioned process of the self-revelation of God as deposited in the Bible."[4]

BIBLICAL THEOLOGY IN THIS VOLUME

Regarding a study on material possessions, we need to amend these definitions as follows: *A Biblical Theology of Material Possessions* is a progressive study of what the Bible teaches regarding how New Testament Christians viewed and used their material possessions so as to determine principles that are supracultural and normative. This particular study follows the "historically conditioned process of the self-revelation of God," beginning with the founding of the church as recorded by Luke (the book of Acts) and tracing the unfolding of God's revelation as it is recorded in the rest of the New Testament. "Biblical theology," as Paul Enns asserts, "traces that *progress of revelation*, noting the revelation concerning Himself that God has given in a *particular era* or through a *particular writer.*"[5]

Christians tend to forget that what is now a complete volume—what we call the Holy Bible—was not written in one brief period of time. Rather, the truth of Scripture "was unfolded in a *long series of successive acts* and through the minds and hands of many men of varying backgrounds."[6] This study, then, follows the unfolding of God's work in history.[7]

Luke's historical record in the book of Acts is used as the basic structure for this biblical research. Simultaneously we will study the literature that was written as a result of the church planting efforts of the apostles and other New Testament Christians. This interrelated process will help us understand more clearly how the specific references to material possessions in the rest of the New Testament relate to the events described by Luke in the epistle-like narrative addressed to his friend Theophilus (Acts 1:1-2).[8]

In doing biblical theology, we must, as Ladd reminds us, "expect progression" in God's revelation. Though "the various stages of the prophetic interpretation of redemptive history are equally inspired and authoritative . . . they embody differing degrees of apprehension [comprehension] of the meanings involved."[9] These degrees of understanding are particularly obvious when it comes to what God says about material possessions.

God's will unfolded as the church expanded throughout the New Testament world. The Holy Spirit (through various authors of Scripture) clarified and built on basic truths as one event followed another. What initially appears as a foundational and basic concept is often refined and expanded as New Testament history progresses. Furthermore, these developments appear directly related to geographical, cultural, ethnic, economic, and political factors involved over a period of time. Relative to the way Christians should view and use their material possessions, these factors created new challenges and necessitated clarification and correctives as the church grew and expanded throughout the Roman Empire.

What happened in the New Testament era did not take place in isolation from God's revelation in the Old Testament. As in any history, there is progression and continuity. It is important to study this continuity to understand all aspects of Bible doctrine, but it is particularly important to understand this connection as we attempt to formulate a body of truth regarding how a Christian should view and use material possessions. The Old Testament has a great deal to say about how God's people dealt with possessions under the Old Testament covenant (the law of Moses especially). Consequently, we will look at the unfolding of God's revelation regarding material possessions in the Old Testament and evaluate and integrate that revelation with the unfolding of God's revelation in the New Testament.

SUPRACULTURAL PRINCIPLES

As we progress through this study and complete each part, we will delineate biblical principles that emerge from each unit of study. Since one of our major goals is to determine from Scripture a *body of principles* to guide twentieth-century Christians in the use of their material possessions, it is important, first of all, to define what is meant by a *principle.*

DEFINITIONS

Webster defines a *principle* as "a comprehensive and fundamental law, doctrine, or assumption" or as "a rule or code of conduct." Applied to principles based upon supracultural truth, this becomes a helpful definition—particularly since the term "principle" is used in this study. We are looking for basic "laws" or "doctrines" or "assumptions" that reveal God's will for Christians regarding how they should view and use their material possessions. In that sense, these principles become a "code of conduct" to guide Christians in their living. If rightly stated, these principles are applicable to believers who live in every culture of the world and at any moment in history.[10]

DIFFERENTIATIONS

Principles per se do not include the *way* in which a principle is applied in any given cultural situation. Principles relate to activities (functions) and directives (teachings), not to forms, patterns, and methodology. Though it is impossible to engage in *functions* (the application of principles) without some kind of formal methodology and structure, it *is* possible to state a principle that describes a function without describing the *form* that principle takes when it is applied.

This is what makes a biblical principle truly supracultural. If it is, indeed, a correctly worded biblical principle, it can be applied anywhere in the world, no matter what the cultural conditions. Furthermore, it is applicable at any moment in history—in the first century as well as in the twentieth century, anytime in-between, and in the future.[11]

APPLICATIONS

Understanding the supracultural nature of these principles is important in helping Christians apply them. For example, being able to apply these principles does not depend on the existence of certain economic structures in a particular society. Furthermore, being able to apply them is not dependent on one's economic status in that society, either as an individual Christian or as a group of Christians. In fact, being able to apply these principles is not dependent upon *any* cultural factors. Though it may be more difficult to apply them because of certain cultural restrictions and pressures, their *supracultural* nature makes it possible for these principles to work in some form or fashion.

In some social environments in the world, of course, practicing certain biblical principles may be so threatening that it leads to persecution. In rare instances, this persecution has caused some Christians to pay the ultimate price in order to obey God—death through martyrdom. Stephen's death illustrates this in graphic fashion (Acts 7:54-60).

Fortunately, Christians are not severely persecuted in most cultures of the world—particularly in terms of how they use their material possessions. In fact, when these principles are applied properly, it usually does not alienate non-Christians or make them angry; rather, it contributes to peaceful relationships with unbelieving governmental authorities, employers, and employees. For example, when Christians pay their taxes regularly, it demonstrates that they are good citizens and loyal to the government, which in turn usually helps make it possible for believers to live "peaceful and quiet lives" (1 Tim. 2:2).

INTERPRETATIONS

How do we determine a biblical principle from the study of God's unfolding revelation? First, we must look carefully at the totality of Scripture. Biblical principles can be determined only in the context of God's complete written revelation. To attempt to principlize without the total context of Scripture can lead to statements that are only partially true or even untrue and inaccurate.

Second, we must look at all the *actions* and *functions* of God's people as they are described in Scripture and interpret these events in the light of what was happening in the culture of the time. It is especially important to look at what transpired during New Testament days, for it is in this historical context that the New Testament describes our New Covenant relationships with God and one another.

Narrowing our sphere of existence still further, we are all citizens of the kingdom of God, if we know Jesus Christ personally as Lord and Savior. But more specifically, we are members of Christ's Body, the church. Therefore, it is vitally important that we interpret Scripture and develop principles in the light of an adequate *ecclesiology*—an accurate perspective on what the Bible teaches about the church.

Third, we must look at all the *teachings* and *directives* of Scripture (e.g., the teachings of Jesus Christ and the teachings of the apostles). We must interpret these exhortations through careful grammatical and contextual analysis, attempting to understand what these teachings mean in their original historical and cultural context. To ignore this important principle of hermeneutics (the science of biblical interpretation) can lead to serious error.

One teaching that has become a serious problem in today's culture is the doctrine of prosperity theology. This so-called "principle," which teaches that God will multiply Christians' earthly possessions if they tithe (give 10 percent of their income) regularly, has become popular for several reasons. For one thing, certain Bible teachers have taken scriptural statements out of context. They have made biblical teachings and illustrations say things that the authors did not intend. Some Bible teachers fail to recognize (or admit) that this doctrine tends to produce results only in capitalistic societies where it is possible to better oneself financially due to the free enterprise system.

Unfortunately, some media evangelists and Bible teachers as well as other high-powered preachers are very much aware that this false doctrine is a successful way to generate money. Consequently, some use it as a manipulative means to carry on dishonest and fraudulent activities. And they do this in the name of Jesus Christ. Unbiblical teaching like this shows why this biblical study is so necessary.[12]

Fourth, in order to determine supracultural principles from Scripture, we must observe the extent to which New Testament "activities" and "teachings" are repeated, verified, expanded, and reinforced throughout the whole counsel of God, including *both* the Old and New Testaments. This process helps avoid taking Scripture out of context to support our own "personal agendas." Looking carefully at God's truth as it is unfolded *throughout Scripture* will help us understand *God's* agenda, not ours.

THE STRUCTURE FOR THIS STUDY

This study begins with the founding of the church in the book of Acts. As God's revelational history unfolds in Luke's historical account, the remainder of the books and letters in the New Testament are studied and evaluated in chronological order. Following each series of events and major teachings, *principles* are stated that are defined as *supracultural.* It is at this

A Historical and Chronological Structure for Determining God's Will Regarding Material Possessions

PART I
THE CHURCH IN JERUSALEM

Acts 1:1–Acts 7:60

Supracultural Principles

PART II
THE TEACHINGS OF JESUS CHRIST

The Four Gospels

Matthew (60's A.D.)
Mark (50's A.D.)
Luke (60 A.D.)
John (85-90 A.D.)

Supracultural Principles

PART III
MOVING BEYOND JERUSALEM

Acts 8:1–11:30

Supracultural Principles

PART IV
THE GENTILE CHURCH & ITS EXPANDED MISSION

Acts 13:1–15:35

James (45-50 A.D.)
Galatians (49-55 A.D.)

Supracultural Principles

PART V
PAUL'S MISSION

Acts 15:36–18:22

1 Thessalonians (51 A.D.)
2 Thessalonians (51 A.D.)
1 Corinthians (56 A.D.)
2 Corinthians (57 A.D.)

Supracultural Principles

PART VI
PAUL'S MISSION CONTINUED & HIS ROMAN IMPRISONMENT

Acts 18:23–28:31

Romans (58 A.D.)
Philemon (61 A.D.)
Ephesians (61 A.D.)
Colossians (61 A.D.)
Philippians (61 A.D.)

Supracultural Principles

PART VII
FINAL YEARS OF THE NEW TESTAMENT ERA

Beyond the Book of Acts

1 Timothy (63 A.D.), Titus (65 A.D.)
2 Timothy (66 A.D.), 1 Peter (63 A.D.)
Hebrews (64-68 A.D.), Jude (70-80 A.D.)
2 Peter (66 A.D.), 1,2,3 John (90 A.D.)
Revelation (90's A.D.)

Supracultural Principles

PART VIII
APPLYING BIBLICAL PRINCIPLES

Practical methodology applying supracultural principles in our church, our families and our personal lives juncture, particularly, that Old Testament insights and teachings are utilized to explain and reinforce these supracultural principles. This structure is visualized on page 26.

NOTES

1. Justo L. Gonzalez, *Faith and Wealth: A History of Early Christian Ideas on the Origin, Significance, and Use of Money* (San Francisco: Harper & Row, 1990), p. 230.

2. Ibid., pp. 230-31.

3. George Elton Ladd, *A Theology of the New Testament* (Grand Rapids: Eerdmans, 1974), p. 25.

4. Charles C. Ryrie, *Biblical Theology of the New Testament* (Chicago: Moody, 1959), p. 12.

5. Paul Enns, *The Moody Handbook of Theology* (Chicago: Moody, 1989), p. 20.

6. Ryrie, *Biblical Theology*, p. 13.

7. Enns, *Handbook of Theology*, p. 20, writes, "Biblical theology pays attention to the important historical circumstances in which the biblical doctrines were given. What can be learned from the Old Testament era of revelation? What were the circumstances in the writing of Matthew or John? What were the circumstances of the addressees of the letter to the Hebrews? These are important questions that help resolve the doctrinal emphasis of a particular period or of a specific writer."

8. At the outset of this study, I would like to pay tribute to the late Dr. Merrill Tenney, who served for many years as dean of the Wheaton College Graduate School and professor of New Testament literature. It was my privilege to study under Dr. Tenney. More than any other professor, both in his classroom teaching and through his writings, he introduced me to the process of understanding the New Testament in its historical, cultural, and chronological context. His classic volume, *New Testament Survey* (Grand Rapids: Eerdmans, 1953), has been of immeasurable help in providing a unique research model and design for structuring and pursuing this study on how Christians in the New Testament era viewed and used their material possessions.

9. Ladd, *A Theology of the New Testament*, pp. 32-33.

10. Enns, *Handbook of Theology*, p. 21, explains the importance of exegesis to biblical theology:

    Biblical theology has a direct relationship to exegesis ("to explain; to interpret"), inasmuch as biblical theology is the result of exegesis. Exegesis lies at the foundation of biblical theology. Exegesis calls for an analysis of the biblical text according to the literal-grammatical-historical methodology. (1) The passage under consideration should be studied according to the normal meaning of language. How is the word or statement normally understood? (2) The passage should be studied according to the rules of grammar; exegesis demands an examination of the nouns, verbs, prepositions, etc., for a proper understanding of the passage. (3) The passage should be studied in its historical context. What were the political, social, and particularly the cultural circumstances surrounding it? Biblical theology does not end with exegesis, but it must begin there. The theologian must be hermeneutically exacting in analyzing the text to properly understand what Matthew, Paul, or John wrote.

11. Henry A. Virkler, *Hermeneutics: Principles and Processes of Biblical Interpretation* (Grand Rapids: Baker, 1981), especially chap. 8, "Applying the Biblical Message: A Proposal for the Transcultural Problem," pp. 211-31; also see Roy B. Zuck, "Applications in Biblical Hermeneutics and Exposition," in *Walvoord: A Tribute*, ed. by Donald K. Campbell (Chicago: Moody, 1982).

12. See Michael Horton, ed., *The Agony of Deceit: What Some TV Preachers Are Really Teaching* (Chicago: Moody, 1990); Bruce Barron, *The Health and Wealth Gospel: A Fresh Look at Healing, Prosperity & Positive Confession* (Downers Grove, Ill.: Inter-Varsity, 1987).

Part 1
THE CHURCH IN JERUSALEM

Part 1 describes the activities and functions of the church in Jerusalem during the first five years. It covers the time from its inception on the Day of Pentecost to when it was scattered after Stephen's trial and martyrdom. The totality of the events described by Luke form a singular segment in the history of the church, and, viewed together, they give us an illuminating profile of how the New Testament believers in Jerusalem viewed their material possessions. It is significant that approximately *half* of these events focus on the way the first Christians used their material possessions to further the work of God's kingdom.

1. Setting the Stage

2. Identifying with the Jewish Community

3. The Church in Action

4. Supracultural Principles

1

Setting the Stage

Following Christ's ascension, the apostles "returned to Jerusalem" as they had been told (Acts 1:12). They joined more than one hundred other followers of Christ in the upper room, where they had been staying. Then they waited for the Holy Spirit to come as Jesus Christ said He would. In the meantime, "they all joined together constantly in prayer" (Acts 1:14).

This small band of disciples could only respond to what they knew and understood. One major fact was clear—particularly in the minds of the eleven apostles: *Jesus had been resurrected.* Jesus "showed himself to these men and gave many convincing proofs *that he was alive*" (Acts 1:3a). Even Thomas, the most skeptical of the apostles, had stopped doubting and now believed (John 20:24-29).

At some point during those days of waiting, Peter remembered two statements from the Psalms that he now understood as applying directly to Judas Iscariot (Acts 1:20). These two prophecies predicted *his betrayal* (Ps. 69:25) and *his replacement* (Ps. 109:8). Peter knew that they must choose another man to join them—a man who had been with the other eleven apostles from the time John came baptizing. "One of these," Peter shared with the whole group, "must become a witness with us of his resurrection" (Acts 1:21-22). Consequently, Matthias "was added to the eleven apostles" (Acts 1:26).

THE SETTING IN JERUSALEM: ACTS 2:1

Three times a year, faithful Jews participated in three special events in the holy city. Jeremias observes that "on three occasions during these months the number of visitors increased by leaps and bounds to a prodigious height, at the three great festivals when pilgrims came from all over the world: Passover, Pentecost and Tabernacles (Deut. 16:1-16). The annual peak was reached at Passover."[1]

The special celebration that was in progress when Jesus ascended was the Feast of Pentecost. More precisely, scholars tell us that this special festival began on the same day Jesus rose from the grave and culminated fifty days later on the Day of Pentecost. This was the day the Holy Spirit descended on the 120 believers gathered in the upper room (2:1-4).

If these calculations are correct, this means that ten days transpired between the time Jesus ascended and the Holy Spirit came. This calculation is based upon Luke's observation that Christ "appeared to them over a period of forty days" (1:3). Since the Feast of Pentecost lasted fifty days and culminated on the Day of Pentecost, we can assume that the disciples waited ten days for the Holy Spirit to come. It was during this ten-day period that the 120 gathered in the upper room and joined together in prayer. It was also during this period that Peter took the lead in replacing Judas Iscariot with Matthias.

At the time the Holy Spirit descended on this small band of believers, thousands of faithful pilgrims from all over the Roman Empire were present in Jerusalem. Luke identified them as *"God-fearing Jews* from every nation under heaven" (2:5, italics added*). Many had no doubt come earlier to also participate in the Passover celebration, which means that they were there during the time of the crucifixion. Most of those present at Passover probably stayed for the Feast of Pentecost. Jeremias estimates that the permanent inhabitants of Jerusalem totaled about 55,000 and that there were approximately 125,000 visitors, the "God-fearing Jews" Luke refers to in Acts 2:5.[2]

THE GIFT OF THE HOLY SPIRIT: ACTS 2:2-39

The coming of the Holy Spirit was a total surprise, not only to the inhabitants of Jerusalem but to all of the visitors who had come from all over the New Testament world. The only ones who were actually looking for this event composed the little band gathered in the upper room. And even they did not know specifically what was going to happen.

Evidently, the sound that seemed to be "like the blowing of a violent wind" (2:2) could be heard throughout Jerusalem: when the people in Jerusalem heard this sound, they "came together in bewilderment" (2:6b). When they gathered at the location in Jerusalem where the 120 had been staying, they were "utterly amazed" in that they heard the apostles speaking in their own languages. "Are not all these men who are speaking Galileans?" they asked (2:7).

Luke provides us with a descriptive list of the language groups represented. There were "Parthians, Medes and Elamites; residents of Mesopotamia, Judea and Cappadocia, Pontus and Asia, Phrygia and Pamphylia, Egypt

*In future Scripture quotations, all italics have been added for the sake of emphasis and will not be noted.

and the parts of Libya near Cyrene; visitors from Rome (both Jews and converts to Judaism); Cretans and Arabs" (2:9-11). All of these visitors heard the apostles speaking the Word of God in their own languages.

This phenomenon was so unusual that some of the onlookers accused the apostles of being drunk. Peter responded by quoting from the prophet Joel, who prophesied that this event would take place (2:17-21). He explained that Jesus of Nazareth whom they had crucified was now the resurrected Christ. He was indeed the promised Messiah that David had referred to in Psalm 16:8-11 (Acts 2:25-28).

Christ had been raised from the dead and had also been "exalted to the right hand of God" and "had received from the Father the promised Holy Spirit." Consequently, Peter concluded, Jesus Christ Himself was the one who had "poured out" what they could now "see and hear" (2:33). Peter culminated his initial message with a firm conclusion: "Therefore," he said, "let all Israel be assured of this: God has made this Jesus, whom you crucified, both Lord and Christ" (2:36).

A NEW ERA FOR GOD'S PEOPLE: ACTS 2:40-41

We are not told how many people were actually gathered together when Peter preached this message. However, we are told that three thousand responded to his invitation to "repent and be baptized" (2:38). Though we do not know how many genuine believers this three thousand represents, many of these individuals were probably heads of households. This means that the actual number of believers far exceeded the initial number referred to in Acts 2:41.

Though most Bible teachers pinpoint this event as the beginning of the church, those who believed and were baptized that day did not fully understand the concept of the church. This was true of the apostles as well. However, this was definitely the moment in history when God began a new era in His relationship with His people the Jews. The sacrificial system, established at Mt. Sinai many years before, had pointed to the cross where the Lamb of God would be slain for the sins of the world. The Jews who had responded to Peter's message were now looking back to the cross and the resurrection, and with their faith were acknowledging that Christ had become the once-for-all Passover Lamb who would never be sacrificed again.

NOTES

1. Joachim Jeremias, *Jerusalem in the Time of Jesus*, trans. F. H. and C. H. Kay (London: SCM, 1969), p. 58.
2. Ibid., p. 83.

2

Identifying with the Jewish Community

Imagine the setting! Thousands of Jews had come from all over the Roman Empire—and beyond. Most were "faithful" and "God-fearing" Jews. Otherwise, they would not have come to offer sacrifices at the Temple, to pay their Temple tax, and to use their "second tithe" to participate in this great festival (Deut. 14:22-27). Together with the residents of Jerusalem and those who had come from the outlying districts of Jerusalem, they were expressing their Jewish faith.

While there, the unexpected happened. Many had witnessed the crucifixion of a man who claimed to be the Messiah. Later, many heard reports that those who had followed Him before His death stole His body during the night. Matthew recorded that this story "was widely circulated" among the Jews. His account helps us understand the mentality of the majority of the Jews (Matt. 28:11-15).

PERSONALIZING THE DAY OF PENTECOST: A POSSIBLE SCENARIO (ACTS 2)

What would you have done if you had been a God-fearing Grecian Jew—a father of a large family—let us say from Rome? All of you had come to worship God in the Temple in Jerusalem. You had traveled by ship to Caesarea and from there by foot to Jerusalem. While there, you witnessed the crucifixion. In fact, you got caught up in the mob psychology that permeated the atmosphere. Though you did not fully understand why you were doing it, you even joined the crowd and shouted, "Crucify him! Crucify him!" You were convinced that this Jesus of Nazareth was guilty of blasphemy. After all, some of your best friends who were members of the Sanhedrin told you they heard Jesus claim to have existed before Abraham was born (John 8:58).

YOUR ENLIGHTENMENT

Now you realize that Jesus *was* the Messiah. The rumors you had heard about a "supposed resurrection" were true! You heard the sound like a mighty rushing wind that swept through Jerusalem. Once again, you followed the crowd, this time to a location where you heard twelve men from Galilee speaking in various languages—languages they had never learned. In fact, you recognized most of them as uneducated men. And one of them spoke your Latin dialect, "declaring the wonders of God" (2:11).

Then you heard Peter speak. You found out that he was a former fisherman who had left his boats and nets nearly three and a half years ago to follow Christ. You were utterly amazed when he stood and quoted a lengthy section from the prophet Joel, explaining that the disciples were speaking by the influence and power of the Holy Spirit (2:17-18). He further explained that the man you had helped crucify was indeed the Messiah.

You then heard the same man quote from a psalm written by David. You had heard this psalm read many times before—and it always puzzled you. Who was David speaking about (2:25-28)? That day you heard Peter explain the meaning of this psalm. David could not have been speaking of himself because he died and was buried. "His tomb," Peter stated, "is here to this day" (2:29).

Peter explained that David was a prophet. He knew God's promise that He would place one of David's descendants on his throne. He explained that David was looking ahead and, through the power of the Holy Spirit, had predicted the resurrection of Christ. Furthermore, David had predicted that this Christ would ascend to heaven. Peter reminded you—and the crowd—that

> David did not ascend to heaven, and yet he said,
> "'The Lord said to my Lord:
> "Sit at my right hand
> until I make your enemies
> a footstool for your feet."'"
>
> (2:34; cf. Psalm 110:1)

YOUR CONVERSION

At that moment you were overwhelmed with conviction—"cut to the heart." With a number of other listeners, you cried out, "Brothers, what shall we do?" (2:37).

"Repent and be baptized . . . in the name of Jesus Christ for the forgiveness of your sins," Peter responded. Peter promised that you would then "receive the gift of the Holy Spirit" just as they had (2:38).

After you heard this message, you rushed back to where you were staying—one of the inns of Jerusalem where your family was eagerly awaiting a report of this unusual disturbance. You immediately shared what you had seen and heard. Because your wife and your sons and daughters (and their spouses) respected you as their spiritual leader, your total family, including your servants, eagerly responded to the truth.

Together, all of you elbowed your way back through the crowds where the apostles were already baptizing thousands of people. You and your extended family joyfully joined in this experience to demonstrate to your fellow Jews that you were now acknowledging Christ as the true Messiah. With this act of public confession, you let everyone know that you had joined the ranks of those who were disciples of Christ.

YOUR CRITICAL DECISION

Since this was the final day of the festival of Pentecost you had a critical decision to make. The fifty-day celebration had come to a close. The money and food (your second tithe) you had saved for the trip was nearly depleted with just enough resources to travel back to your home in Rome.

You soon found out that thousands of other Grecian Jews, including numerous widows, were facing the same decision. Should you return home or stay in Jerusalem? You were aware, of course, that the Old Testament prophets predicted that the Messiah would indeed occupy the throne of David and reign as king in Jerusalem. It would be a perfect kingdom. As you retired that night, you shared with your family the words of Isaiah:

> Behold, I will create
> new heavens and a new earth.
> The former things will not be remembered,
> nor will they come to mind.
> But be glad and rejoice forever
> in what I will create,
> for I will create Jerusalem to be a delight
> and its people a joy.
> I will rejoice over Jerusalem
> and take delight in my people;
> the sound of weeping and of crying
> will be heard no more.
>
> (Isa. 65:17-19)

YOUR REFLECTIONS

You could hardly sleep that night thinking about Isaiah's words. You thought about the Roman emperor, Tiberius, whose throne was just a few miles from your home in Rome. He was a godless man. Though he had made some good decisions and had established some helpful policies in the Roman Empire, he was an arrogant leader. The experience just two years ago (A.D. 31) when Aelius Sejanus, the captain of the praetorian guard, had tried to seize his throne had left Tiberius extremely paranoid and even more cruel than he had been before.

You also thought of Herod Antipas, the tetrarch of Galilee and Perea. Though a Jew by religion, he was an insensitive and immoral leader. You heard about what he had allowed to happen to John the Baptist—how he had him beheaded to placate his wife Herodias, who was intensely angry at John for accusing both of them of having an adulterous relationship (Matt. 14:1-12).

You saw him nearly two months ago when he arrived in Jerusalem for the Passover celebration. As usual, he had entered this holy city with pomp and circumstance—actually pride and arrogance. You had also heard about the way he treated Jesus when Pilate sent Him to his quarters for a hearing—how he and his soldiers had "ridiculed and mocked him, dressing him in an elegant robe" (Luke 23:11).

And then, of course, there was Pontius Pilate, who was appointed by the Roman emperor as procurator of Judea. You had seen him in action the day Christ was sentenced to death. In some respects, you felt sorry for him because he wrestled with the decision, knowing full well that Christ was innocent of the charges brought against Him.

But you could not, as you reflected on the day's events, forget what Pilate had done several years before when he took office in Jerusalem. He had insisted that his troops carry into the Holy City banners bearing the image of the Roman emperor. The news of the violent reaction among your Jewish brethren had traveled all the way to Rome in a matter of days and had reached the ears of Tiberius. Pilate had yielded only when he saw that his actions would lead to bloodshed.

But Pilate's move still made political hay in Rome. He had ingratiated himself with the emperor but, at the same time, demonstrated wisdom by changing his actions so as to placate the Jews. You had always been thankful that most of the Roman emperors did not wish to interfere with the religious views and practices of the people in various provinces in the Empire. Nevertheless, you were well aware of the pressures your fellow Jews felt, particularly in Jerusalem.

As all of these events churned and then congealed in your thoughts, the reality of what may be happening kept your mind racing most of the night. You finally drifted off to sleep reflecting on Peter's sermon earlier that day when he quoted the prophet Joel. Your mind jumped ahead to the next section of the prophecy:

> In those days and at that time,
>   when I restore the fortunes of *Judah* and *Jerusalem*,
> I will gather all nations
>   and bring them down to the Valley of Jehoshaphat.

There I will enter into judgment against them
  concerning my inheritance, my people Israel,
for they scattered my people among the nations
  and divided up my land. . . .
Then you will know that I, the Lord your God,
  dwell in Zion, my holy hill.
Jerusalem will be holy;
  never again will foreigners invade her.
                                            (Joel 3:1-2, 17)

Did not Zechariah prophesy the same future for Jerusalem? "On that day," Zechariah wrote, "living water will flow out from *Jerusalem*. . . . The Lord will be king over the whole earth. On that day *there will be one Lord, and his name the only name*" (Zech. 14:8-9).

At that moment, your mind was in a state of limbo—half conscious and half unconscious. But you never forgot the visual picture imprinted on your heart, for in your dreams you saw Herod—and Pilate—and yes, even the Roman emperor Tiberius, all bowing low and kneeling before Jesus Christ who was sitting on the throne in Jerusalem. And beyond, you saw people coming from all parts of the world to pay homage to the King of kings, the one and final and great King of the Jews.

THE SCENE IN PERSPECTIVE

Though this is an imaginary scenario, it fits what was happening in Jerusalem. It reconstructs what may have been the thinking of many God-fearing Jews who came from all over the New Testament world to worship God. Those who were relatively wealthy had been in Jerusalem for at least two months. They had witnessed the crucifixion and now had been confronted with their sin of rejecting the Messiah. Others had come for a shorter period of time. Though their knowledge of everything that had transpired was more limited, they were able to very quickly get an update. The Jewish residents in Jerusalem would have filled them in on the details, for many of them had actually heard Jesus teach and had seen Him work miracles. They would have felt the impact of their sin more forcefully since they had witnessed and participated in His life as well as His death.

Evidently, most of the Grecian Jews who responded to Peter's message decided to stay in Jerusalem so as not to miss the next chapter in this exciting story. After all, the last words the apostles received directly from the Lord came via the two men dressed in white. These heavenly messengers had appeared to the twelve apostles as they "were looking intently up into the sky" as Christ was disappearing from sight. "Men of Galilee," they said, "why do you stand here looking into the sky? The same Jesus, who has been taken from you into heaven, will come back in the same way you have seen him go into heaven" (Acts 1:11).

THEIR VIEW OF THE FUTURE

There is no historical evidence that the Holy Spirit expanded, at this time, on this eschatological perspective in the minds and hearts of the apostles. In fact, some of the specific details regarding the return of Christ to earth following His ascension have never been revealed—even to this day. The totality of Scripture testifies to this reality.

The apostles, then, did not have a total perspective on what was to transpire in the days to come, even though Jesus Christ had given them some very specific information about their responsibility. When they asked Him if He was "going to restore the kingdom to Israel" at this time, Jesus responded by saying, "It is not for you to know the times or dates the Father has set by his own authority. *But* you will receive power when the Holy Spirit comes on you; and you will be my witnesses in Jerusalem, and in all Judea and Samaria, and to the ends of the earth" (Acts 1:6-8).

With this explanation and directive, Jesus Christ made clear that He would not return to restore the kingdom to Israel until these men had at least *begun* the process of being witnesses of Christ's death and resurrection to the "ends of the earth." The apostles did not fully understand what this meant nor did they give much attention to it initially. But in God's sovereign plan, the Holy Spirit began to unfold the future in broad brush strokes, enabling Peter to interpret the prophecies of Joel and David but without a specific understanding of that great era of which he was now a part—the age of the church. Peter did not even understand at this moment in his life that Gentiles would be "a part of the kingdom." This insight did not come until at least five years later when he was confronted with the task of witnessing to a Gentile named Cornelius. At that time he confessed, "I now realize how true it is that God does not show favoritism but accepts men from every nation who fear him and do what is right" (Acts 10:34-35).

SOME QUESTIONS

Why did God choose to reveal His message in this way? Why did He not make it all clear immediately? When it comes to God's plans for future events, Scripture reveals that He has purposely kept these theological realities somewhat nebulous. For example, on one occasion, several of Christ's disciples tested Him about the future. "What will be the sign of your coming and of the end of the age?" they queried. Though Jesus related some specific signs that would take place before He returned, He stated, "No one knows about that day or hour, not even the angels in heaven, nor the Son, but only the Father" (Matt. 24:36). If the Son of God Himself, who was God in the flesh, did not know the specifics relative to the future, who are we to question God's decision to keep these realities veiled in mystery?

Another important factor helps us understand God's unfolding revelation. The children of Israel have always played a very significant role in God's redemptive plan and continue to do so until this very day. They *are* His chosen people—chosen not to show favoritism, but to reveal Himself to the whole world. Through His divine wisdom, He chose to make this a lengthy process. And as Gentiles, we are "wild olive shoots" that "have been grafted" among the "original olive shoots" in the "cultivated olive tree"— which Paul made clear is Israel (Rom. 11:17-24). God chose to unveil these truths a step at a time, which is what we see happening in the opening chapters of the book of Acts.

As we observe this process unfolding, we will see some important supracultural principles that span the transitional nature of Jewish-Christian history. I am speaking of those principles that relate to how we, as Christians, are to view and use our material possessions. These principles are clear in the opening chapters of Acts, even though those who practiced them did not understand what we now understand from the perspective of Christian history. And though the forms and structures of the early church changed dramatically, particularly as the gospel spread out and beyond Jerusalem, the principles remain the same. In fact, they are foundational principles that create a framework for additional principles, which will emerge as we see God's revelation unfold.

3
The Church in Action: Acts 2:42–6:7

When the church was born in Jerusalem, it appears that the majority of those Jews who had come from distant places and who responded to the gospel decided to stay and wait for Christ to return and to restore the earthly kingdom to Israel. In view of what they knew from the Old Testament, and in view of the Holy Spirit's lack of specificity at this moment in history, we cannot blame them. Because God, in His sovereign plan, had not fully revealed the future, they were not yet ready to leave. As God intended, the church would grow quantitatively and qualitatively and become a dynamic force that would in God's own time be scattered to the ends of the then known world.

THE FELLOWSHIP OF THE BELIEVERS (ACTS 2:42-47)

These new Jewish believers immediately "devoted themselves to the apostles' teaching" (2:42). Though we cannot prove what the apostles actually taught, we know that the Holy Spirit reminded them of everything Jesus had taught them (John 14:26). We can also speculate, on the basis of the believers' attitudes and actions, that the Holy Spirit must have reminded the apostles of some of the truths Christ had taught about material possessions.

This was necessary because of what was happening in Jerusalem. Thousands of families decided to stay. Many had already used up their surplus of money and food. Those who were staying in public inns would need to pay their rent, and everyone needed food daily. To solve this problem, the believers decided to "have everything in common." This included both those who lived in Jerusalem and those who lived in other parts of the Roman Empire. But the residents of Jerusalem had to take the initial steps in solving the problem. This they did—willingly and unselfishly.

"Selling their possessions and goods, they gave to anyone as he had need" (2:45). Those who owned homes in Jerusalem opened their doors to those from other places in the world, and "they broke bread in their homes and ate together with glad and sincere hearts." Through this great demonstration of love and unselfishness, these new believers were "enjoying the favor of all the people." More and more Jews recognized that Jesus Christ was the true Messiah, and "the Lord added to their number daily those who were being saved" (2:47).

Two primary factors were used by the Holy Spirit to cause the growth of the church in Jerusalem. First, the love and unity expressed by these believers, especially as it was reflected in the way they shared their material possessions, had a profound impact on the unbelieving community. The unconverted people saw them not only *talking* about love, but *demonstrating* love (2:46-47). The second factor God used in a mighty way to bring growth to the church was the divine power released by the Holy Spirit. This involved the signs and wonders and miracles that were evident in a special way through the ministry of the apostles (2:43).

Peter Heals the Crippled Beggar (Acts 3:1-10)

Following the experience at Pentecost, the first miracle recorded by Luke involved Peter and John as they were going up to the Temple to pray. It was about three o'clock in the afternoon. As they were approaching the Temple gate called Beautiful, they encountered a man who had been crippled from birth. He was being carried by some of his friends to a place inside the Temple courts where he was allowed to beg. It is doubtful he knew who Peter and John were, so he went about his daily routine and "asked them for money." Luke recorded that "Peter looked straight at him, as did John. Then Peter said, 'Look at us!'"

Because of Peter's command, the man evidently assumed that they were going to give him money. So he gave them his full attention. Peter's response is significant. He said, "Silver or gold I do not have, but what I have I give you. In the name of Jesus Christ of Nazareth, walk" (3:6).

Predictably, this miracle had a tremendous impact on the Jewish community. Many people had seen this man over a lengthy period of time sitting at the Temple gate begging for money and food. When they saw him "walking and jumping and praising God . . . they were filled with wonder and amazement at what had happened to him" (3:8, 10).

This miraculous healing gave Peter and John an opportunity to preach the gospel of Jesus Christ. But the religious leaders were "greatly disturbed because the apostles were teaching the people and proclaiming in Jesus the resurrection of the dead" (4:2). Their message also affected the Sadducees, particularly since they did not believe in resurrection. Consequently, Peter and John were seized and put in jail. However, the results of this miracle and the message that was proclaimed already had a profound impact on the people: "many who heard the message believed, and the number of men grew to about five thousand" (4:4).

Peter's words to the crippled man are significant. The man was begging for money, but Peter and John were unable to respond; they had no "silver and gold." Rather, they could share the power God had bestowed upon them to heal. Subsequently, they shared the message of eternal life in Christ that could be received as a free gift—apart from money.

God wants us to learn a specific message from this passage. The religious leaders in Jerusalem were the rich people. In many instances, their wealth was overwhelming. And many of the poor people felt that this wealth was a result of God's special blessing on their leaders.

By contrast, here were two former fishermen with very little but who had the power to heal and the message of salvation that could give eternal life. The contrast had to be startling in the eyes of those who observed this event. For the first time, many moved from a purely human perspective on religion to a divine perspective and responded to the gospel. It is understandable why this antagonized the religious leaders in Jerusalem.

THE BELIEVERS SHARE THEIR POSSESSIONS (ACTS 4:32-35)

As the church continued to grow and expand, the Christians' unselfish attitudes toward material possessions continued to permeate the total community. Consequently, "all the believers were one in heart and mind. No one claimed that any of his possessions were his own, but they shared everything they had." As a result, "there were no needy persons among them. For from time to time those who owned houses or lands sold them, brought the money from the sales and put it at the apostles' feet, and it was distributed to anyone as he had need" (4:32, 34-35).

When Luke recorded that people "shared everything they had," he did not mean to imply that *everyone* sold *everything* and put the total proceeds in a common fund. Rather, he clarified this statement when he said, "There were no *needy* persons among them. For *from time to time* those who owned lands or houses sold them" (4:34). As the needs of people became obvious, people who could, and desired to do so, responded by liquidating their property in order to provide money to meet these people's needs. This was a voluntary system, which must have greatly impacted the "God-fearing" but non-Christian Jews who were used to a rather rigid, legalistic approach to giving. The believers shared their materials possessions out of hearts of love, both because of their commitment to Jesus Christ and because of human needs.

BARNABAS'S ACT OF UNSELFISHNESS (ACTS 4:36-37)

The Holy Spirit inspired Luke to record one specific instance to illustrate what was happening in Jerusalem. Joseph was a Levite from Cyprus who evidently had been in Jerusalem for some time. Either he had moved to

Jerusalem and invested in properties or he operated his business from his home in Cyprus. In view of the number of times that some of the more wealthy Jews visited Jerusalem, this would be a conceivable arrangement. Whatever, he owned property in Jerusalem, and when the need arose, he "sold a field that he owned and brought the money and put it at the apostles' feet" (4:37).

Though this man's name was Joseph, the apostles called him Barnabas, which means "Son of Encouragement." Though briefly stated, these facts tell us a great deal about how Barnabas viewed and used his material possessions. Luke's account also demonstrates the open and public way these believers shared their material possessions with others.

Obviously, a special relationship had already developed between this man and the apostles. Perhaps this was not the first field that Barnabas had sold in order to meet the needs of the church. It is also possible that Barnabas had traveled with the apostles prior to the crucifixion. In fact, some believe that "Joseph called Barsabbas," whom the apostles had considered as a possibility to replace Judas Iscariot, may have been Barnabas (Acts 1:23). In both instances, the name Joseph is used to describe these men (cf. 1:23 and 4:36). The apostles may have changed the name "Barsabbas" to "Barnabas," giving him a name that actually reflected his generous lifestyle.

ANANIAS'S AND SAPPHIRA'S ACT OF PRIDE (ACTS 5:1-11)

The next major event involving material possessions is in stark contrast to those recorded earlier. One similarity is that both involved the liquidating of property and giving the proceeds to meet the needs of the church. Another significant similarity relates to the fact that specific individuals are identified by name—just as Barnabas was in the previous event. At this point, however, the similarities end.

The two people mentioned are a husband and wife named Ananias and Sapphira. Like Barnabas, they were probably well-to-do business people who "*also* sold a piece of property." However, Ananias and Sapphira had agreed together to keep back part of the money they received from the sale and to bring the remainder of the amount and put it at the apostles' feet.

The results were devastating. Both Ananias and Sapphira were severely judged for their wrongdoing. When Ananias brought the money, Peter knew within himself (through the power of the Holy Spirit) that this man was lying about the gift. Both Ananias and Sapphira wanted to give the impression to the apostles and to the rest of the church that they were giving the total sum from the sale of the property.

"Didn't it belong to you before it was sold?" Peter asked. "And after it was sold, wasn't the money at your disposal? What made you think of doing such a thing?" At once, Ananias "fell down and died" (5:4-5). Sapphira arrived on the scene about three hours later, still unaware of what had happened to her husband (5:7). Peter, giving her an opportunity to right the wrong, asked her if the amount of money given by Ananias earlier was indeed the price of the land. Sapphira also lied, and she too fell down and died. Predictably, "great fear seized the whole church and all who heard about these events" (5:11).

This story was not recorded to demonstrate that Ananias and Sapphira were out of the will of God when they gave this money publicly. Many others throughout Jerusalem were doing the same thing. Neither was it wrong to keep back part of the money. There was no obligation either to sell the land or to give the money. Peter made that point clear. The sin that brought death was not even in giving a false impression to other believers—though this was certainly involved. The essence of the sin was in lying to God (5:3-4) and in testing the Holy Spirit (5:9).

This story is meant to be read and interpreted as a back-to-back contrast to the Barnabas story. The two events together demonstrate dramatically how important our material possessions are in reflecting our relationship to God and to Jesus Christ. They are inseparable concepts, particularly as they relate to honesty and integrity.

Furthermore, these stories reflect how important is the way we view and use our material possessions in maintaining a proper witness for Jesus Christ, both to our fellow Christians and to the unbelieving world. The way these Christians used their money was a highly visible activity, and God did not want to give false impressions to those who were looking on.

MEETING THE NEEDS OF WIDOWS (ACTS 6:1-7)

As the church grew in numbers, the predictable happened. Certain individuals were neglected in this semi-communal system. We read that "the Grecian Jews among them complained against the Hebraic Jews because their widows were being overlooked in the daily distribution of food" (6:1).

As a result of mass conversions to Jesus Christ, the widows who would ordinarily be taken care of through the Jewish social system were now cut off. And those who were neglected first were the Grecian widows who had come as visitors to Jerusalem. It is only logical to conclude that they would run out of resources before those Hebrew widows who were part of the "Aramaic-speaking community" in Jerusalem and the surrounding areas. These people would also be better taken care of because their own families and relatives were residing there.

Some suggest that this neglect was a *cultural problem* involving prejudice. It is true that Judaism could be very stringent in the way different classes of people were treated. But if there was prejudice involved, it would certainly be contradictory to everything that had happened in the church to this point. There seemed to be too much love, unity, and concern for this to be the case. It simply happened because of the vast number of people involved. It was basically an organizational problem. The church was multiplying by leaps and bounds. In fact, it is conceivable that by now the number of Christians in Jerusalem totaled anywhere from fifty to a hundred thousand.

This projection is based upon the number of family units that had become Christians. In Acts 4 we are told that the number of *men* who became Christians "grew to about five thousand." Many believe that this refers to heads of households. If each of these men, or even half of them, represented extended families, the total number would be multiplied many times. Even those who were visitors in Jerusalem often included whole households, since one of the purposes of these festivals was to worship God *as a family.*

The apostles responded to this organizational problem immediately. Luke recorded that they "gathered all the disciples together and proposed a solution"—which probably involved only those who were Grecian Jews. In other words, only those who were nonresidents in Jerusalem were invited to this "congregational" meeting. There would be no need to invite the Aramaic-speaking community because their widows were evidently not neglected. Furthermore, the reference to "all the disciples" may have been only those among the Grecian Jews who brought the complaint. This would be a more logical conclusion from an administrative and organizational point of view. Pragmatically, it would be difficult at this juncture in the church's history to have a public meeting involving thousands of people. Christians were, by this time, deeply resented by the religious leaders and not even allowed to meet in the Temple courts.

The first part of the apostles' solution involved their own *priorities.* They made clear that the work was getting too complex for them to take time "to wait on tables." They in no way negated the importance of this ministry to the widows, but it would not be appropriate for them to "neglect the ministry of the Word of God," which was their primary calling. Neither were they saying that they were not willing to be involved in resolving the problem. Earlier, they were responsible for distributing the money to the people. Evidently, they still maintained this responsibility. However, the problem now involved the distribution of the food. They needed an effective system to make sure it was distributed fairly and in an equitable fashion.

Consequently, the apostles instructed the Grecian brothers to select seven men that were highly qualified—men who were known to be full of the Holy Spirit and wisdom (6:3). When they were selected, they turned "this responsibility over to them" and gave their own "attention to prayer and the ministry of the word" (6:3-6). The results of this organizational step were evident immediately in that "the word of God spread" and "the number of disciples in Jerusalem increased rapidly." Even more significantly, "a large number of priests [the elite among the Jews] became obedient to the faith" (6:7).

What does this unique event in the history of the Jerusalem church teach us? First, meeting the material needs of these people was very important. The system was no longer fair and equitable, which created unhappiness and led to a lack of unity.

Second, as the number of believers increased in the Jerusalem church, so did the need to have more organizational efficiency to meet the material needs of these people. Consequently, the apostles had to take steps to make sure this was done.

Third, as the number of people increased and as their needs increased, the spiritual leaders (in this case the apostles) had to delegate the responsibility to other qualified leaders—men who were also "full of the Holy Spirit and wisdom." These qualifications in themselves underscore and demonstrate the importance of this task.

4

Supracultural Principles

The principles outlined and described in this chapter relate to events as they took place day by day and week by week during the first five years of the church's existence in Jerusalem.[1] Though these principles have emerged from activities and functions that took place nearly two millennia ago in the city of Jerusalem, they are presented as truths that are supracultural and normative. They are affirmed throughout Scripture and have been verified in history. When applied consistently by Christians in all parts of the world, they will bring blessings, not only to believers but to unbelievers as well. (See the Introduction for an explanation regarding the importance of subjecting propositional statements, such as the principles outlined in this volume, to constant evaluation in the light of exegetical study of Scripture itself.)

THE FIRST SUPRACULTURAL PRINCIPLE

As Christians use their material possessions in harmony with the will of God, it will encourage people to believe in Jesus Christ (Acts 2:47).

When Jesus spent His final days with the apostles in the upper room, He gave them a new commandment: "love one another." He demonstrated and illustrated His love in the middle of the Passover meal when He washed the disciples' feet. Christ said, "As I have loved you, so you must love one another." Then Jesus proceeded to state what would result from this kind of love: "All men will know that you are my disciples if you love one another" (John 13:34-35).

The Christians in Jerusalem began immediately to practice this new commandment. Consequently, they were "enjoying the favor of all the people." Those who were still unsaved responded positively to the unselfish and generous attitudes and actions of these New Testament Christians. We read that "the Lord added to their number daily *those who were being saved*" (Acts 2:45-47).

What happened in Jerusalem happened in other places and at other times. When we come to Part 3, we will see that the story of Dorcas is an illustration of the way God used her effort "in always doing good and helping the poor" to eventually influence people to respond to the gospel of Jesus Christ (Acts 9:32-42). It is, and always has been, God's plan that believers be attracted to Jesus Christ by the way Christians use their material possessions in unselfish and benevolent ways.

THE SECOND SUPRACULTURAL PRINCIPLE

As Christians use their material possessions to meet one another's needs, it will create love and unity in the Body of Christ (Acts 4:32).

The way Christians in Jerusalem used their material possessions reflected their love and unity. Conversely, these acts of kindness created *more* love and unity. Thus, Luke recorded that "all the believers were *one* in heart and mind" (Acts 4:32). Selfishness regarding the way we use our material possessions breeds disunity. Paul had to deal with this problem in the Corinthian church regarding the "agape" or "love feast" (Jude 12). This special meal was an extension of what Jesus instituted in the upper room and what the Jerusalem Christians practiced daily as "they broke bread in their homes and ate together with glad and sincere hearts" (Acts 2:46*b*).

As the Corinthians came together to share in this common meal and to remember the broken body and shed blood of Christ, some—particularly the more well-to-do—brought extensive portions of food and drink and proceeded to partake before others arrived. When the poor arrived with their more limited contributions, most of the food and drink had already been consumed. In fact, some of the more indulgent Corinthians were actually drunk (1 Cor. 11:21).

Thus, Paul began his instructions regarding this issue by saying, "In the following directives I have no praise for you, for your meetings do more harm than good. In the first place, I hear that when you come together as a church, there are *divisions among you*" (1 Cor. 11:17-18). Here is a specific illustration that stands out in sharp contrast to what was happening in the first church. Believers in Jerusalem were "one in heart and mind." A strong contributing factor was their *unselfish* behavior when they shared their material possessions with one another. By contrast, the Corinthians were divided and carnal because of their *selfishness*.

THE THIRD SUPRACULTURAL PRINCIPLE

Spiritual leaders should model the way all Christians ought to use their material possessions (Acts 2:42).

The apostles stood out immediately among the Jerusalem Christians as men who were willing to give up the accumulation of material possessions in order to serve Jesus Christ and His kingdom. In fact, Peter, when asked for a contribution by the crippled beggar in the Temple, responded by saying that he and John had no "silver or gold" (Acts 3:6). This was literally true. Both men had given up what was probably a rather productive fishing business to follow Christ and "fish for men" instead. All of the other apostles, in one way or another, had followed suit. Their example was dynamic and powerful. They were not asking others to do something they had not done themselves.

Barnabas stands out as a specific example in Luke's historical record. Although he may not have given up his material possessions to the same degree as the twelve men designated "apostles" (Christ did not ask him to), he stands out as a leader who paved a way for others to follow by unselfishly demonstrating at least one way a Christian can use his material possessions to further Christ's work.

Modeling in the area of giving is not only a *New* Testament principle. David shared specifically with "the whole assembly" what he had decided to give to the Temple (1 Chron. 28:1), from both his corporate resources as king of Israel (1 Chron. 29:2-3) as well as from his personal resources (1 Chron. 29:3-5). Consequently, those listening were so encouraged that they, in turn, "gave willingly . . . toward the work of the temple of God" (1 Chron. 29:7). This "leadership model" impacted all Israel, for "the people rejoiced at the *willing response of their leaders*, for they had given freely and wholeheartedly to the Lord" (1 Chron. 29:9).

God's people need visible leadership models in terms of what God expects regarding the use of material possessions. How this "fleshes out" methodologically will vary greatly in different cultural circumstances. What must be consistent in every situation, however, is the model itself.

THE FOURTH SUPRACULTURAL PRINCIPLE

Christians should be willing to make special sacrifices in order to meet special material needs within the Body of Christ (Acts 4:34-35).

The circumstances in Jerusalem were unique and unusual. The Christians had special needs, and because of this "from time to time those who owned lands or houses sold them, brought the money from the sales and put it at the apostles' feet, and it was distributed to anyone as he had need" (Acts 4:34-35). This New Testament example illustrates an ongoing phenomenon throughout church history.

There are always special circumstances that create special needs among God's people. In New Testament days, it was sometimes a famine, such as the one faced by the Jerusalem Christians several years later. In this case, the church in Antioch came to the rescue (Acts 11:25-30; see discussion in Part 3). Later, Paul faced special needs because of his imprisonment in Rome, and it was the Philippian church who rose to the occasion and met his needs (Phil. 4:10-20). And so it is today. Special needs emerge, and when they do, God's people should respond to meet those needs. Not to respond when it is possible to do so is to violate the will of God.

THE FIFTH SUPRACULTURAL PRINCIPLE

A primary motivating factor for consistent Christian giving should be to meet others' needs, particularly within the Body of Christ (Acts 4:34-35).

The Jerusalem Christians stand out in the pages of Scripture and throughout the annals of church history as believers who demonstrated this biblical truth in an unprecedented way. Their love for God was demonstrated by their love for one another.

Throughout Scripture, we see that human needs continue to be a primary factor for Christian giving. Frequently, we see directives to meet the physical needs of the poor. We see exhortations to care for the needs of those who minister to us in the Word of God. And we are commanded to show hospitality to friends and strangers alike.

Following the first two centuries of church history, Christians were eventually allowed to purchase property. They constructed buildings to provide a place for the church to gather and worship God, just as God's Old Testament people did when they built the Temple and later the synagogues. This too was meeting a significant human need—a need for a permanent place to gather together on a regular basis to "encourage one another" (Heb. 10:25).

THE SIXTH SUPRACULTURAL PRINCIPLE

It is the will of God that Christians share their material possessions in order to encourage others in the Body of Christ (Acts 4:36).

The key word in this principle is *encourage.* And Barnabas, the "Son of Encouragement," is an example of this in the Jerusalem church (Acts 4:36). Anyone who has ever been in Christian leadership and responsible for meeting the physical needs of others can identify with the reason the apostles changed Joseph's name to Barnabas. People who are generous are special encouragers, not only to other Christians but to God Himself.

This principle is illustrated frequently throughout the New Testament. For example, when Paul wrote to the Philippians from a Roman prison after he had received their special gift, he said, "*I rejoice greatly* in the Lord that at last you have renewed your concern for me" (Phil. 4:10; see chap. 33).

THE SEVENTH SUPRACULTURAL PRINCIPLE

Christians who are faithful in sharing their material possessions should be shown special appreciation (Acts 4:36).

Again, this principle can be demonstrated throughout the New Testament, both in showing appreciation to *individuals* as well as to *groups* of Christians. Paul wrote to Philemon and said, "Your love has given me great joy and encouragement, because you, brother, *have refreshed the hearts of the saints*" (Philem. 7). Most Bible interpreters agree that Paul was referring to the way Philemon utilized his wealth, and particularly his home, to show Christian hospitality (see chap. 31). Paul showed appreciation to a group of Christians when he wrote to the Corinthians. Referring to the Macedonian churches, he said, "We want you to know about the grace that God has given" to these churches. "Out of the most severe trial, their overflowing joy and their extreme poverty welled up in rich generosity. For I testify that they gave as much as they were able, and even beyond their ability" (2 Cor. 8:2-3; see chap. 24).

Today, Christian leaders need to develop sensitive but specific ways to show appreciation to Christians, both in a personal and a corporate way, for being faithful in giving of their time and their talents, as well as of their treasures. All Christians need this kind of encouragement if they are expected to encourage others by being generous.

THE EIGHTH SUPRACULTURAL PRINCIPLE

Christians need to be able to observe other believers who are faithful in sharing their material possessions (Acts 4:36-37).

This principle runs counter to the strong emphasis on confidentiality that often accompanies Christian giving today. An insistence on total confidentiality contradicts the examples in the Word of God. No one can deny that what Barnabas did was visible, not only to the apostles, but to other Christians in Jerusalem. Otherwise, Ananias and Sapphira would not have attempted to do the same thing, but with wrong motives.

Paul used the generosity of the Christians in Achaia to motivate the Macedonian believers to be generous as well. Consequently, Paul wrote that their enthusiastic desire to give had motivated most of the Macedonian Christians to do the same thing (2 Cor. 9:1-2; see chap. 25).

Christians today—just as the Christians of the New Testament era—need personal and corporate models to inspire them to use their material possessions to further the work of the kingdom of God. Mere verbal teaching alone will not motivate this action. It is true that Jesus said on one occasion, "But when you give to the needy, do not let your left hand know what your right hand is doing, so that your giving may be in secret" (Matt. 6:3-4). We will see, however, that this statement in no way contradicts the principle we have just discussed. We will look carefully at what Jesus really meant in our next unit of study (see chap. 9).

THE NINTH SUPRACULTURAL PRINCIPLE

What Christians give should always be given to honor God and not themselves (Acts 4:34-36; 5:1-10).

This principle points to at least one major reason Luke recorded the story of Ananias and Sapphira immediately following Barnabas's generous act of love. They too wanted to sell a piece of property that they owned and to give the proceeds to help others. However, their motive was entirely wrong. They wanted self-glory, so much so that they gave a false impression and actually lied to the Holy Spirit. Glorifying God relates to everything a Christian does. Paul underscored this point when he wrote, "So whether you eat or drink or whatever you do, *do it all for the glory of God*" (1 Cor. 10:31).

THE TENTH SUPRACULTURAL PRINCIPLE

God detests dishonesty, lack of integrity, and hypocrisy when it comes to giving (Acts 5:1-10).

Though serious punishment is not God's normal way of dealing with sin in the lives of His children, the Ananias and Sapphira story illustrates this principle in dramatic fashion. Periodically in Scripture, God judges sins severely in the lives of His children. Ananias and Sapphira lost their lives. On another occasion, God severely judged some of the Corinthian Christians in the same way because they had so flagrantly abused the Lord's Supper (1 Cor. 11:27). Paul explained that was why many of these believers were "weak and sick," and a number of them had actually died (1 Cor. 11:30).

Fortunately, this is not a common way God deals with His children when they sin. On these rare occasions God is reminding all believers how serious it is to ignore His instructions and to purposely walk out of His will—especially when we know what His will is. It is only because of His grace and love that we are not always disciplined severely for our deliberate disobedience. Therefore, let us not ignore His love and abuse His grace. As Paul taught the Roman Christians, so let these words teach us: "Shall we go on sinning so that grace may increase? By no means! We died to sin; how can we live in it any longer?" (Rom. 6:1-2).

THE ELEVENTH SUPRACULTURAL PRINCIPLE

Though God wants all of His children to be generous, what Christians give should always be voluntary and from a heart of love and concern (Acts 5:4).

Peter made this point clear when he addressed Ananias. Referring to both his property and the money that he had received from the sale, Peter asked, "Didn't it belong to you before it was sold? And after it was sold, wasn't the money at your disposal?" (Acts 5:4). God *wants* our gifts. If we do not give generously in relationship to our resources, we are out of His will. Conversely, however, He wants our gifts to come from generous hearts. Paul affirmed this principle in the context of some of his strongest exhortations to be generous when he wrote to the Corinthians (see chap. 24): "Each man should give what he has decided in his heart to give, not reluctantly or under compulsion, for God loves a cheerful giver" (2 Cor. 9:7).

THE TWELFTH SUPRACULTURAL PRINCIPLE

It is God's will that every church have an efficient system for helping to meet the true material needs of others in the Body of Christ (Acts 6:1-7).

Though the church in Jerusalem was unique in its structure, what they did in meeting the needs of widows illustrates this principle. When there is a true need among Christians that cannot be met in other ways, that need should be met by members of the Body of Christ. Consequently, any given church in any given cultural situation should develop a proper system to determine what that need is and then how to meet that need.

This is particularly important in a church that is growing rapidly, since, as in Jerusalem, the larger the church becomes, the easier it becomes to neglect people. On the other hand, church size also adds to the probability that there will be those who attempt to take financial advantage of the church. Paul addressed these issues in some of his later letters (see chaps. 22 and 34). He outlined some specific guidelines for determining whether or not the church is meeting real needs and at the same time not allowing people to abuse this principle.

THE THIRTEENTH SUPRACULTURAL PRINCIPLE

Spiritual leaders in the church must at times delegate the administrative responsibilities to other qualified people who can assist them in meeting material needs (Acts 6:2-4).

It is not the will of God for those responsible for teaching the Word of God to be burdened with the responsibility of administering programs that meet the material needs of people. This principle was clearly illustrated in the Jerusalem church. True, the apostles were responsible for making sure that the widows' needs were met by setting up a proper system. But they were not responsible for the actual distribution of food. The reason for this principle is quite simple. God does not want those designated primarily as teachers and pastors in the local church to become sidetracked from fulfilling this ministry. Though social work is very important, it should be done by other qualified leaders.

The apostle Paul reinforced this principle in his first letter to Timothy. First, he outlined the qualifications for elders (1 Tim. 3:1-7)—those who are responsible to manage and shepherd God's people. Then, he outlined the qualifications for deacons (1 Tim. 3:8-13)—men and women who are to serve in various roles in the church in order to meet physical needs. Both elders and deacons who minister in these two areas of the church were to be *highly qualified people* (see chap. 34).

THE FOURTEENTH SUPRACULTURAL PRINCIPLE

Meeting the "spiritual needs" of people and meeting the "material needs" of people require the same high standards when selecting leaders to meet these needs (Acts 6:3).

The seven men who were appointed by the apostles to oversee the responsibility of meeting the needs of widows were to be "full of the Spirit and wisdom" (Acts 6:3). Furthermore, the men and women who were to occupy serving roles in the church in Ephesus were to also be highly qualified individuals. Paul repeated many of the same basic qualifications for them as he did for those who were to serve as elders (pastors and teachers) in the church.

This indicates the value that God places on this area of ministry. Meeting *spiritual* needs and meeting *material* needs are both important areas in doing the will of God. They should not be separate in terms of importance but, rather, in terms of how to make sure both are done properly.

NOTE

1. Harold Hoehner, *Chronology of the Apostolic Age* (doctoral diss. presented to faculty of the graduate school of Dallas Theological Seminary, 1975), pp. 156, 211, concludes that the Day of Pentecost could have occurred on May 27, A.D. 30, and that Stephen's martyrdom could have taken place in April of A.D. 35. Since the persecution that drove people out of Jerusalem occurred rather quickly after Stephen's death, we can conclude that the church in Jerusalem was approximately five years old at this time.

Part 2

THE TEACHINGS OF JESUS CHRIST

To understand more clearly the perspective New Testament Christians had regarding material possessions, we must understand what Jesus Christ taught on this subject. It is apparent that what Jesus taught the apostles during His earthly ministry influenced their thinking greatly and, in turn, gave specific direction to their message once the church was founded. What Jesus taught about material possessions gives insight for interpreting the activities and functions of the church as it was scattered and reestablished *beyond* Jerusalem: "in all Judea and Samaria, and to the ends of the earth" (Acts 1:8).

5. The Apostles' Teaching

6. Jesus' Perspective on Economic Structures

7. The Apostles' Personal Witness

8. Jesus' Teachings in Matthew 5

9. Jesus' Teachings in Matthew 6

10. Jesus' Teachings in Matthew 10, 15, 19, 23

11. Moving from Specific to General Principles

5

The Apostles' Teaching

The new Christians in Jerusalem "devoted themselves to the *apostles'
teaching*" (Acts 2:42*a*). But what was included in this body of information?
Luke did not give us a specific outline of what these twelve men taught
these new believers regarding how to live the Christian life. However, he did
record the basic content of their message to those who were still unconverted. It was a message of repentance, forgiveness of sins, the anticipated return of Christ, and the establishment of His kingdom (Acts 3:19-21).

But what was the apostles' continuing message to those who responded and joined those who had already become disciples of Jesus Christ?
What did these people learn regarding how to live the Christian life? More
specifically, what did the apostles communicate regarding how these new
believers should view and use their material possessions?

It is only logical to conclude that the apostles began their teaching
ministry in Jerusalem by, first of all, communicating to these new Christians
what Jesus had taught them over the past three and a half years. The vast
numbers of Grecian Jews visiting Jerusalem when the church was born had
never met Jesus and, consequently, had never heard Him teach. Furthermore, even those Jews who lived in Judea and Galilee where Jesus did most
of His teaching would have heard only bits and pieces of what He taught.
The thousands of people who had acknowledged Christ as their Messiah
would certainly want to know immediately what His will was for their lives.

Unknown to these new believers, God had designed a plan for this
communication to take place in a supernatural way. Though from a human
point of view these twelve men would have been able collectively to recall
and reconstruct from memory much of what Christ taught, God did not leave
this process to chance. Rather, He miraculously blended their natural abili-
ties to learn and remember with a divine process of Spirit-directed
revelation.

Before Jesus Christ was crucified, He gave a strong clue as to *what* the "apostles' teaching" would have included, particularly in the early days of the church. Furthermore, He was quite specific as to *how* it would happen. While gathered with these men to celebrate the Passover meal, He promised to send them "another Counselor . . . the *Spirit of truth*" (John 14:16-17). This Counselor, whom Jesus immediately identified as the Holy Spirit, would teach them all things. More specifically, Jesus said the Holy Spirit "will remind you of *everything I have said to you*" (John 14:26).

Later in this same passage, Jesus tells them that the "Spirit of truth" would guide them into "all truth." Elaborating on what He meant, Jesus said, "He will tell you *what is to come*" (John 16:12-13). In other words, not only would the Holy Spirit bring to their minds everything that Christ had taught them while the apostles traveled with Him from place to place but would also give them additional truth, particularly regarding future events. The book of Revelation, written by the apostle John, certainly illustrates this latter point.

It is significant, however, that one of the first areas of truth that the Holy Spirit would communicate to these disciples involved what Christ had already taught them the past three and a half years (John 14:26). The "apostles' teaching," then, would have included much of what Christ taught while He was with them. Fortunately, we have four separate historical accounts of what Christ taught. Two of these "gospels" were written by apostles themselves—Matthew and John. The other two were written by a Gentile doctor named Luke and a young man from Jerusalem named John Mark (Acts 12:1-2).

Out of all that is recorded in the four gospels, what biblical clue tells us what the Holy Spirit may have brought to the apostles' mind initially? That clue involves the immediate attitudes and actions of the new Christians in Jerusalem that are described by Luke: "all the believers were *together*"; they "had everything *in common*"; they sold "their possessions and goods"; they "gave to anyone as he had need" (Acts 2:44-45).

It does not seem coincidental that these new converts to Christianity immediately began to view their material possessions as belonging, not just to themselves, but to each other. Furthermore, this was not just an *attitude*. They demonstrated their belief with their *actions* by actually "selling their possessions and goods" and sharing the proceeds with people who had material needs.

In the midst of these social dynamics, it seems apparent that the Holy Spirit "reminded" the apostles of what Jesus had said about money and material possessions (John 14:26) and that they, in turn, shared these truths with the new believers. Here, of course, was an opportunity heretofore unparalleled in their experience to practice what Jesus taught.

In the four gospels—and particularly in Matthew—we have a specific written record of what Christ taught about material possessions. Before these things were ever written down, however, they were communicated on numerous occasions. Initially, these truths were spoken by the apostles as the Holy Spirit reminded them of everything Christ had taught them (John 14:26). These teachings were then communicated by word-of-mouth to others by those who heard the apostles' teaching during these early and monumental days in Jerusalem. Years later, this process was described by Paul when he wrote his final letter from a Roman prison: "And the things you have heard me say in the presence of many witnesses entrust to reliable men who will be qualified to teach others" (2 Tim. 2:2).

It may be that the reference to the "apostles' teaching" in Acts 2:42 is an initial reference to the New Testament *gift of teaching* mentioned in 1 Corinthians 12:27-31 and Ephesians 4:11. If this conclusion is correct, this gift was a "revelatory" gift and, in some respects, in the same category as the gifts of prophecy, wisdom, knowledge, and tongues. It would follow, then, that it was primarily the gift of teaching that enabled the apostles to later pen the New Testament, which is, in essence, the "apostles' teaching." In other words, the same miraculous blending of the human and divine process that enabled the apostles to preach and teach the Word of God orally also enabled them to author the New Testament literature.

We see this same process at work in the apostle Paul's life and ministry. He certainly had the *supernatural* gift of teaching enabling him to receive divine truth directly from God (Gal. 1:12; 1 Tim. 2:7; 2 Tim. 1:11). With this gift he taught many people, including Timothy. Timothy, in turn, seemingly used his *natural* teaching skills to communicate God's revealed truth to other "reliable men," who in turn also used their natural skills to "teach others" (2 Tim. 2:2). Evidently, like Peter, John, and Matthew, Paul (as an apostle as well) was inspired by the Holy Spirit to use his supernatural gift of teaching to put in writing what had initially been taught orally. This inspired content includes at least thirteen letters in the New Testament.

6

Jesus' Perspective on Economic Structures

Jesus' earthly father was a carpenter, a respectable trade, but one that would provide just the bare necessities of life. The lack of material resources in His family is clearly evident from the trip His parents made to Jerusalem to present Him to the Lord in the Temple. Mary's sacrifice involved "a pair of doves or two young pigeons," which was allowable when people could not afford to offer a lamb (Luke 2:21-24; cf. Lev. 12:1-8).

THE PARABLES AS ECONOMIC ILLUSTRATIONS

Evidently Jesus learned the carpenter trade from His father and maintained a relatively low profile in His hometown of Nazareth. However, when He began His ministry, He demonstrated an unusual awareness of all kinds of economic activity in Palestine. The main source for comprehending Jesus' knowledge of what kinds of business enterprises existed at that time is His parables, which He told to illustrate spiritual truth. In fact, a large number of these stories utilized various facets of economic life to make spiritual applications. More than a quarter of these parables (eleven out of thirty-nine) deal with finances and money directly:

- He referred to *investment* in jewels and treasures to illustrate the importance of investing in the kingdom of God (Matt. 13:44-45).

- He referred to *saving* new treasures as well as old treasures to illustrate the importance of storing up both old and new truth (Matt. 13:52).

- He used *indebtedness* to illustrate the importance of forgiveness (the parable of the unmerciful servant; Matt. 18:23-35).

- He referred to *hiring procedures* and *wage structures* to illustrate God's sovereignty and generosity in treating all with equality, forgiving sins, and rewarding people with eternal life (the parable of the workers in the vineyard; Matt. 20:1-16).

• He told a story about a fruit farmer who *leased* his property to illustrate the way the chief priests and Pharisees were rejecting God and His Son (the parable of the tenants; Matt. 21:33-46; Mark 12:1-12; Luke 20:9-19).

• He discussed *capital, investments, banking,* and *interest* to emphasize our human responsibility to utilize God's gifts in a prudent and responsible way (the parable of the talents, Matt. 25:14-30; the parable of the ten minas, Luke 19:11-27).

• He referred to *money lenders, interest,* and *debt cancellation* to illustrate the importance of love and appreciation to God for canceling our debt of sin (Luke 7:41-43).

• He spoke of building barns to *store grain* for the future while neglecting to store up spiritual treasures as a very foolish decision (the parable of the rich fool; Luke 12:16-21).

• He used *architectural planning, building construction,* and *cost analysis* to illustrate the importance of future planning and counting the cost before we make decisions in building our spiritual lives (Luke 14:28-30).

• He used the human joy that comes from *finding lost money* to illustrate the joy in the presence of angels when a lost soul believes in Christ (Luke 15:8-10).

• He used *wealth,* dividing up an *estate,* irresponsible *spending,* and a *change of heart* to illustrate repentance and forgiveness (the parable of the prodigal son; Luke 15:11-32).

• He used *bad financial management* and *dishonest debt reduction* to illustrate that dishonest business people are sometimes wiser in their worldly realm than honest followers of Christ in the spiritual realm (the parable of the shrewd manager; Luke 16:1-12).

• He contrasted a *rich man* who died and went to hell with a *poor beggar* who died and went to heaven to illustrate how wealth and what it can provide may harden our hearts against spiritual truth (the parable of the rich man and Lazarus; Luke 16:19-31).

• He contrasted the proud Pharisee who *fasted* and *tithed* regularly with the humble tax collector who acknowledged his sin of *dishonesty* and *greed* to illustrate that God acknowledges humility and rejects self-exaltation (the parable of the Pharisee and the tax collector; Luke 18:9-14).

• He used a *grain-ripened field* and *harvesters* to illustrate "spiritually ripened hearts" in Samaria and the part the apostles would have in "harvesting" people's souls (John 4:34-38).

When Jesus told these parables, His purpose was not to evaluate various aspects of the economic policies and procedures used in Palestine. Rather, He was using what was most familiar in order to teach spiritual truth. He was tapping into what was uppermost in people's minds at all economic levels in an effort to capture their attention. One of His target audiences, however, was the priests and scribes, who were very much involved in the economic situations illustrated by Jesus.

Because Jesus did not evaluate financial procedures and policies in His parables does not mean He condoned what His characters did and the way they did it. We must evaluate the parables in light of Christ's nonfigurative teachings regarding material possessions and about eternal values, honesty, integrity, and ethics. It is safe to assume, however, that Jesus accepted the basic economic policies and procedures at that time as normal for any society that is based upon free enterprise. His fellow Jews could own property, lease it, and sell it. They could borrow money, lend money, and invest. They could operate their own businesses, build buildings, hire employees, and determine salary structures. All of these business activities were prevalent throughout Palestine—as well as in many other locations. It was basically a free enterprise system of economics developed throughout the long and complex history of the Roman Empire.

How Jesus Handled Economic Structures

Before looking at the specific lessons Jesus taught about material possessions, we can initially learn a valuable lesson from Jesus by the way He handled economic policies and procedures in His own society. Though He was an itinerant teacher and healer who did not own property and certainly had nothing of this world's goods (Matt. 8:19-20), He did not go about attacking the economic systems per se. Rather, He taught spiritual truths and principles that His listeners could use as a means for evaluating these various practices.

Jesus was using an important supracultural approach when ministering to the Jews of His day. They did not possess the land of Palestine and had not done so for many years. They were a part of the Roman Empire and responsible to their local pagan kings and magistrates, and ultimately to the Roman emperor. Though they possessed a great deal of freedom to engage in free enterprise and to practice their religion, it was impossible for them to function as they once had when they possessed the land in Old Testament days and operated under leaders like Joshua—and later their own judges and kings. This is the reason Jesus instructed them to pay taxes to the Roman government—to "give to Caesar what is Caesar's, and to God what is God's" (Matt. 22:21).

This approach made many Jewish leaders angry, for they believed it was sacrilegious to give money to pagan kings. In actuality, their anger probably reflected their selfishness more than concern about violating God's will. They simply wanted more for themselves. Some of their other sinful activities—such as the way they circumvented the laws of God so they would not have to care for their parents (see chap. 10)—would make their resistance to paying taxes to the Roman government another glaring inconsistency. To quote Jesus, they would be straining "out a gnat" but swallowing "a camel" (Matt. 23:24).

7

The Apostles' Personal Witness

When the Holy Spirit first brought to the apostles' minds everything Christ had taught them, what would they have shared with these new believers in Jerusalem—especially in relation to how they should view and use their material possessions?

The Apostles' Testimony

The apostles would certainly share at some point in time what was very personal to them. After all, they had given up their former vocations to follow Christ. The two sets of brothers who were in the fishing business (Peter and Andrew, as well as James and John) had left their boats and nets on the Galilean shore (Matt. 4:18-22).

The decision these men made does not necessarily mean they left their boats and nets to rot or to be stolen by other fishermen. James and John left not only their boat but their father (Matt. 4:22). It was a family business that no doubt continued to operate without their involvement. This is probably true of the fishing business operated by Peter and Andrew as well. A careful look at the relationship between these four men indicates that all of them may have been in business together, with Peter as the primary leader.

The fact remains, however, that these men left their fishing business to follow Jesus. Whatever income they continued to have would have been minimal and probably just enough to care for their families. They willingly withdrew from what was probably a profitable enterprise when they joined Jesus' band of traveling disciples.

Matthew's Personal Experience

Matthew's testimony was probably the most well-known in view of his materialistically oriented vocation before he became an apostle of Christ. In fact, for this man to give up his money-making enterprise to follow Christ was so unusual that the Holy Spirit inspired Matthew (as well as Mark and Luke) to record the events surrounding his calling (Matt. 9:9-13; Mark 2:13-17; Luke 5:27-32). And even if Matthew hesitated to share his personal experience publicly, his change in life-style was so dramatic that it would have been a topic of conversation among many people.

When Christ called Matthew to follow Him, he was a tax collector, a despised profession in Jesus' day.[1] Identified as "publicans," they were hated by the Jews. One reason for this antagonism is that being a tax collector for the Roman government offered these individuals many opportunities to be dishonest and to extort money from people. John the Baptist put his finger on the major problem that created this hostility when "tax collectors also came to be baptized. 'Teacher,' they asked, 'what should we do?' 'Don't collect any more than you are required to,' he told them" (Luke 3:12-13).

Matthew, of all the apostles, could share firsthand how Christ changed his perspective on money. Before becoming a follower of Christ, he had lived totally for himself, accumulating his wealth in a dishonest fashion. But when he decided to give up tax collecting, he even invited Jesus to his house to have dinner with a number of his fellow "publicans" (Luke 5:29).

We are not told that Matthew sold his home in Capernaum when he decided to follow Christ. No doubt he had a family who continued to live there while he gave up his profession and followed Christ on His teaching and healing tours. Neither are we told how—or if—he followed Zacchaeus's example and returned money to those he knew he had cheated. Perhaps he did.

Not only Matthew, but all of the apostles could testify to God's continued provisions after giving up their businesses and following Christ. On one occasion, at least, the Lord sent them out to preach the gospel with nothing but a staff—"no bread, no bag, no money." They wore sandals but had no extra tunic (Mark 6:8-13; Luke 9:1-6). And just as Christ worked miracles through them and protected them from their enemies, He also used other people to provide for their physical needs.

The apostles also could have shared their experience when Christ sent out the seventy-two others. They were basically given the same instructions as the twelve apostles. As they went, they stayed in homes and ate and drank what was given to them. At that time, Jesus made clear that these people deserved shelter and food for their effort, for He said, "The worker deserves his wages" (Luke 10:7).

JUDAS ISCARIOT

What may have been the apostles' most dramatic communication to these new believers involved Judas Iscariot. His suicide was a topic of conversation in Jerusalem, even among those who had not responded to the gospel (Acts 1:19). Peter had already talked about Judas to the 120 in the upper room prior to the Day of Pentecost when they had cast lots to replace him with Matthias.

Judas's incredible betrayal would not be the only issue that the apostles could share with these new believers. Everyone must have been chagrined at what motivated this man. Even more unbelievable, Judas had delivered Jesus to the chief priests for thirty pieces of silver (Matt. 26:14-16; Mark 14:10-11; Luke 22:1, 6; John 13:18-30). *Greed* had been at the root of his downfall.

Years later in his gospel, the apostle John revealed that Judas had been a thief all along. On one occasion he had objected when Mary poured an expensive ointment on Jesus' feet. "Why wasn't this perfume sold and the money given to the poor? It was worth a year's wages," Judas complained. John explained that "he did not say this because he cared about the poor but because he was a thief; as keeper of the money bag, he used to help himself to what was put into it" (John 12:1-6).

Did the Holy Spirit reveal this information to John early in church history? Did he share it with the believers in Jerusalem? If he or any other apostle had shared this aspect of Judas's story with the multitudes in Jerusalem, it would have had a sobering effect on the church—just as it has had a sobering effect on believers of all time. This was probably one reason the Holy Spirit inspired all four gospel writers to record Judas's act of betrayal. Greed can cause people to make irrational decisions that almost defy explanation. History is filled with illustrations but none as self-centered as that of Judas Iscariot. His wicked deed stands out on the pages of Scripture as a warning to believers and unbelievers alike that the "love of money" is indeed "a root of all kinds of evil" (1 Tim. 6:10; see chap. 34).

PETER'S TESTIMONY

Peter's personal experiences with Jesus would have had the most impact on the believers in Jerusalem. The Lord made some incredible promises to him, one I am sure he would remember even apart from the Holy Spirit's having brought it to mind. Following the confrontation Jesus had with the rich young ruler, Peter asked Jesus what He would provide for him and the other apostles since they had left everything to follow Him. Jesus' response must have been overwhelming.

First, it involved an incredible promise of prestige and position for each of the twelve apostles. Second, Jesus promised them unusual material and spiritual blessings. "I tell you the truth," Jesus said to them,

> at the renewal of all things, when the Son of Man sits on his glorious throne, you who have followed me will also sit on twelve thrones, judging the twelve tribes of Israel. And everyone who has left houses or brothers or

sisters or father or mother or children or fields for my sake will receive a hundred times as much and will inherit eternal life. (Matt. 19:28-29)

If Peter had shared this promise of material and spiritual blessings for "everyone" with the believers in Jerusalem, it is not surprising that "all the believers" in Jerusalem in those early days "were together and had everything in common." Not only were they motivated to sell "their possessions and goods" and to give "to anyone as he had need" because of this new-found love and unity, but also because of the glorious promises that Jesus Christ had made to those who are willing to follow Him totally.

Is it feasible that Peter shared this promise? I believe it is. We must remember that neither Peter nor the other apostles understood fully what Jesus had in mind, even after the church was founded and even though the Holy Spirit was speaking through them. The "renewal of all things" would certainly have *immediate implications* involving the "twelve tribes of Israel." There could be only one interpretation in view of Old Testament and New Testament prophecies and promises (Isa. 65:17; 66:22; 2 Pet. 3:13; Rev. 21:1-5). Christ would be king and the twelve apostles would each have jurisdiction over a particular tribe. They would be completely restored to the land promised to Abraham centuries before (Gen. 12:1-3), and the kingdom would be an eternal one involving material abundance for everyone and eternal life as well.

Unanswered Questions

The unanswered questions in the minds of these new believers would be, *When* will these things take place? *When* would Jesus return as the "two men dressed in white" promised He would? (Acts 1:11). Their only clue related to Jesus' statement that they were to be His witnesses beginning "in Jerusalem" and then "in all Judea and Samaria, and to the ends of the earth" (Acts 1:8).

But even this statement by Jesus did not answer their specific questions as to when Jesus was "going to restore the kingdom to Israel" (Acts 1:6). Did this mean that Christ would return to establish His kingdom *after* they carried out His commission to be His witnesses "to the ends of the earth"? Would He return at some point *while* they were carrying out this commission?

Jesus did not make this point clear. Obviously, He did not want the twelve apostles or their followers to know the specific answers to these questions. He simply wanted them to be obedient to what they knew at that moment in their lives. One thing they knew and believed: Jesus would take care of them materially and spiritually if they sought first "Christ's kingdom and his righteousness." If they were obedient to this command, Jesus had promised that "all these things" would be given to them as well (Matt. 6:33).

THE BASIS OF THEIR MOTIVATION

Looking forward to both spiritual and material blessings most certainly would have been involved in the motivation that encouraged the apostles and others to place a low priority on their own material possessions. Since these New Testament Christians did not understand God's timetable, their motivation to serve Christ and one another in material ways would be related to the promises that Jesus had given them. And even though these Christians did not experience these blessings in their lifetime, they continued to serve Christ. And more and more, they understood that these promises, both material and spiritual, would be fulfilled at a future time when they were once again face-to-face with Jesus Christ in a totally new environment.

Peter certainly understood this concept more fully many years later, probably shortly before his own martyrdom:

> Since everything will be destroyed in this way, what kind of people ought you to be? You ought to live holy and godly lives as you look forward to the day of God and speed its coming. That day will bring about the destruction of the heavens by fire, and the elements will melt in the heat. But in keeping with his promise we are looking forward to *a new heaven and a new earth*, the home of righteousness. (2 Pet. 3:11-13)

The progressive and unfolding nature of Peter's own knowledge and understanding of God's will following Pentecost points to the importance of biblical theology. But this limited perspective in no way eradicates the supracultural principles inherent in these events. This fact alone points to the divine process God used in recording scriptural truth.

NOTE

1. D. Edmond Hiebert, *Wycliffe Bible Encyclopedia* (Chicago: Moody, 1975), 2:1427, gives the following helpful comment:

   Roman taxes were of two sorts, direct and indirect. By NT times the direct taxes, on land and persons, were no longer farmed out but were collected by the regular imperial officers. But the indirect taxes, import and export dues, road money, bridge tolls, harbor dues, etc., were still farmed out to the highest bidders. The actual collection was usually performed by native employees. Native subcontractors may have been used. Zacchaeus, called a "chief publican" . . . , may have been the contractor for the revenues of Jericho, having collectors under him. At least, he supervised a collecting district.

   Most of the NT publicans, like Levi [Matthew] . . . , were customhouse employees. They might have their "place of toll" (ASV) at city gates, on public roads, or bridges. Levi's post . . . at Capernaum apparently was near the sea on the important trade route entering Galilee from Damascus.

8
Jesus' Teachings in Matthew 5

Which of Jesus' teachings about material possessions might the Holy Spirit have first brought to the apostles' minds while they taught in Jerusalem (John 14:26)? To answer this question, we need first to look at what the Holy Spirit inspired the apostles to record in the gospels. We can then assume to have at least discovered the essence of the "apostles' teaching" as described in Acts 2:42-47, realizing of course that it would have been unnatural and impractical for these men to mention all of these things at one particular time.

Most of what Jesus taught about material possessions is recorded by Matthew. Did the Holy Spirit choose him to be the primary communicator of Christ's teachings on material possessions because he was previously a first-century materialist? Perhaps so. Before Matthew followed Christ, he probably violated the Lord's teachings more than any of the other men called to be apostles. After his conversion, he could probably write with more experiential conviction about these matters.[1] Following are some of Jesus' teachings that Matthew and the other apostles may have pointed out to New Testament Christians before they were ever recorded in Scripture. We will look first at Christ's historic "Sermon on the Mount."

MATTHEW 5:3

Blessed are the poor in spirit,
for theirs is the kingdom of heaven.

What did Jesus have in mind when He referred to the "poor in spirit"? Luke's record is more specific. He wrote "Blessed are you who are poor, for yours is the kingdom of God" (Luke 6:20).

Whatever Jesus had in mind when He included the word "spirit," one thing is clear from both the literary as well as the social context: He was addressing many people who had very little of this world's goods. Though they were "poor spiritually," Jesus was addressing people who were also "poor materially."

If these people responded to Christ's message of eternal life, He was assuring them that they would have a special place in God's kingdom. In fact, their lack of wealth probably helped them to recognize their "impoverished spirits," motivating them to respond to Christ's call to be His followers.[2]

THE BOTTOM LINE

This is one of the points Jesus was making to His disciples following His encounter with the rich young ruler (Matt. 19:16-26; Mark 10:17-27; Luke 18:18-27). He came to Jesus asking what "good thing" he must do to inherit eternal life (Matt. 19:16). To his surprise, Jesus told him to sell what he had and give the proceeds to the poor. Then he would "have treasure in heaven" (19:21). But "when the young man heard this, he went away sad, because he had great wealth" (19:22).

As those who heard this conversation watched the man turn and walk away, Jesus told them that it was very "hard for a rich man to enter the kingdom of heaven."

His disciples "were greatly astonished and asked, 'Who then can be saved?'

"With man this is impossible," Jesus responded, "but with God all things are possible" (19:23-26).

Jesus was not teaching this young man or those listening that they must sell everything and give away the proceeds in order to be saved. This would contradict the whole of Scripture—for no one can be saved by doing good works (Rom. 4:1-3; 5:1; Eph. 2:8-9). Jesus did not require this kind of sacrifice from other rich people who followed Him. Rather, He was dealing with a man who was in love with his material possessions. He had "great wealth," and it was his stumbling block. Though he did a lot of good things with his life, his love of money kept him from experiencing God's saving love and grace. Evidently, he was not even willing to discuss the matter further with Jesus. He simply walked away with a heavy heart.

And so, as Jesus taught that day on the mountain in Galilee, He was encouraging those who were poor, both materially and spiritually, to be encouraged. They had little of this world's goods. This in turn could serve as a means to open their hearts to God. The fact that they were "poor in a material sense" enabled them to be "poor in spirit." To be rich may have given them a feeling of being "rich in spirit," which tends to interfere with a person's response to God's invitation to be saved. Unfortunately, people often feel no need for God when they feel "rich" and self-satisfied in their inner beings.

REFLECTIONS OF JESUS' TEACHING

Did the apostles remind those gathered in Jerusalem for the Feast of Pentecost of this teaching? If so, many poor people would have been encouraged with this truth. Yes, there were many well-to-do people present—like Barnabas—but the "poor widow" Jesus referred to in the Temple may have been among those who first responded to the gospel. For the first time in their lives, they all witnessed an incredible miracle: "No one claimed that any of his possessions was his own, but they shared everything they had." Consequently, Luke recorded that "there were no needy persons among them" (Acts 4:32, 34). In a real sense, those who were "poor in spirit" were already experiencing what Jesus meant when He said, "For theirs is the kingdom of heaven" (Matt. 5:3). They had come to know Jesus Christ as personal Savior. The "kingdom of God" was already with them (Luke 17:21).

THE FIRST SUPRACULTURAL PRINCIPLE

Having a lot of material things often makes it difficult for people to recognize and acknowledge their need of God in salvation (Matt. 5:3).

This principle does not mean that well-to-do people cannot and will not respond to the gospel. Zacchaeus certainly illustrates this fact, and so do others who came to Christ when the church was born in Jerusalem. As we continue our study, we will encounter well-to-do people like the Ethiopian eunuch and Cornelius (chap. 14), Lydia (chaps. 16, 33), Priscilla and Aquila (chaps. 16, 21), and Philemon (chap. 31), all of whom responded to the gospel once the church expanded beyond Jerusalem.

The facts are, however, that an abundance of things and a desire to accumulate more and more can cause anyone to be self-satisfied, self-indulgent, and even cruel. All of this, James affirmed, can lead a person headlong into eternal hell (James 5:1-6). It is often the "poor in spirit" who more willingly respond to spiritual and eternal values and truths.

MATTHEW 5:24b

First go and be reconciled to your brother;
then come and offer your gift.

When Jesus was teaching on the mountain that day, He demonstrated the interrelatedness of the two great commandments, which are foundational for *all* the commandments. The "first and greatest" is that we should fervently love the Lord our God. The second greatest is that we should love our neighbors as ourselves (22:37-39).

Applied to giving, Jesus taught His followers that before they offered their material possessions to God, they must seek forgiveness from those they had wronged. To be out of harmony with their fellow Jews was to be out of harmony with God. Under these conditions, their gifts were not acceptable to God no matter what the size or how perfect. In other words, their "love for God" was marred because of their "lack of love for their neighbor."

Does this mean that the gifts these people offered at the altar were not acceptable to God unless they had righted *every* wrong they had ever committed toward others? That would have put them—and us—in an impossible situation. Rather, Jesus said, "If you are offering your gift at the altar and there *remember* that your brother has something against you" (5:23), *then* go and be reconciled before you continue to offer your gift. In other words, they were not to make offerings to God until they had made the things right that came to their conscious memory. Jesus probably also had in mind contemplated actions toward others that were *vindictive* (5:21-22). In such a case the thought and intent of the heart had become just as sinful as the action itself.

REFLECTIONS OF JESUS' TEACHING

Many in Jerusalem at the time the church was born had come from all over the New Testament world to offer gifts on the altar in the Temple. However, many were also there who lived in Jerusalem. Among all these people were those guilty of serious sins against their fellow Jews. Some had cheated in business—such as Matthew and Zacchaeus had done when they were still tax collectors. Others were guilty of covetousness or of lying. Or they had committed private sins involving intense hatred or even adultery.

To be reconciled to their fellow Christians before offering gifts to God (which would have been part of the "apostles' teaching") must have contributed significantly to the unity and love that first existed in the church in Jerusalem. Not only were these new Christians not cheating and mistreating one another, they were doing just the opposite: sharing what they had in order to meet one another's needs. In the midst of this community of love, those believers who had cheated or defrauded others in some way and had not yet righted these wrongs would certainly have been motivated to seek reconciliation.

THE SECOND SUPRACULTURAL PRINCIPLE

Material gifts are acceptable and "well pleasing" to God only when Christians have done their part to be in harmony with their brothers and sisters in Christ (Matt. 5:24*b*).

Christians who are harboring conscious memories of sinning against another Christian and have not asked forgiveness are to do all they can to be at peace with that person before continuing to offer material possessions to the Lord. Just as the apostle Paul exhorted the Corinthians to examine themselves before they participated in eating and drinking at the Lord's Supper (1 Cor. 11:27-29), so Christians should examine themselves when they worship God with their material gifts. If we discover sin in our lives, we should seek forgiveness from others as soon as possible.

The apostle Paul affirmed this principle in his letter to the Romans. When exhorting all Christians to pay whatever they owe people—taxes, revenue, respect, honor—Paul concluded with this specific, and yet general, admonition: "Let no debt remain outstanding, except *the continuing debt to love one another*" (Rom. 13:7-8).

MATTHEW 5:42

Give to the one who asks you,
and do not turn away from the one
who wants to borrow from you.

JESUS' USE OF HYPERBOLE

On several occasions in the Sermon on the Mount, Jesus used exaggerated and paradoxical statements to get the attention of His listeners and to make His points. Such is the case when He seemingly instructed His disciples to both give and loan money with indiscretion to people who asked for it. It may appear that Jesus was teaching His followers to be totally vulnerable to every individual who asked them for money—including thieves, robbers, cheats, selfish manipulators, and false teachers. But note that in the same immediate context, Jesus also commanded,

- "If someone strikes you on the right cheek, turn to him the other also" (5:39).

- "And if someone wants to sue you and take your tunic, let him have your cloak as well" (5:40).

- "If someone forces you to go one mile, go with him two miles" (5:41).

Jesus used this linguistic technique earlier in the Sermon on the Mount in dealing with other areas of sin. For example, when teaching against adultery, He said,

- "If your right eye causes you to sin, gorge it out and throw it away" (5:29).

- "And if your right hand causes you to sin, cut it off and throw it away" (5:30).

Obviously, Jesus did not mean for His followers to take these statements regarding physical mutilation literally. Neither did He mean for His followers to take all of His exhortations regarding material possessions literally. As in the case of the rich young ruler, He was attempting to deal with the major area of weakness in his life—his love of material possessions more than of God or anything else in this world.

What then was Jesus teaching when He said, "Give to the one who asks you, and do not turn away from the one who wants to borrow from you" (5:42)? The context demonstrates that Christ was dealing with basic attitudes toward those who are *our enemies*—those who hate us. We are not to demand an "eye for eye" and a "tooth for tooth" (5:38). William Hendriksen summarizes this passage with the following conclusion: "We have no right to hate the person who tries to deprive us of our possessions. Love even towards him should fill our hearts and reveal itself in our actions."[3]

REFLECTIONS OF JESUS' TEACHING

Though we do not have a specific illustration of the apostles or of any of the Christians in the Jerusalem church actually giving money, food, clothing, or shelter to their enemies, we do have a dynamic illustration of loving one's enemies as Christ loved His enemies. When Stephen was being stoned because of his witness for Christ, "he fell on his knees and cried out, 'Lord, do not hold this sin against them'" (Acts 7:60). In essence, this is exactly what Christ did when He died on the cross. Looking down on His enemies, He cried, "Father, forgive them, for they do not know what they are doing" (Luke 23:34).

We can certainly conclude that a Christian like Stephen, who loved those who were stoning him, would never hesitate to help meet his enemies' economic needs (5:42). This is also a remarkable demonstration of "turning the other cheek" (5:39), "giving your cloak as well as your tunic" (5:40), and going two miles when your enemy "forces you to go one mile" (5:41). Jerusalem was filled with Christians who were willing to practice these attitudes and actions toward their enemies—a marvelous demonstration of God's grace in enabling these believers to follow the teachings of Jesus Christ.

THE THIRD SUPRACULTURAL PRINCIPLE

Christians should not only give to those who love them and care for them but even to those who may resent them and even try to harm them (Matt. 5:42).

Jesus was certainly not teaching that we should allow people to manipulate and take advantage of us. If we do, we are contributing to their irresponsibility. Paul made this clear when he said that a person who purposely will not work should not be provided with food (2 Thess. 3:10). But it is possible to express, at least in a token way, the same love Christ demonstrated for His enemies when He gave His life for those who condemned

Him and nailed Him to the cross. We can do this by helping even our enemies when they have physical needs.

NOTES

1. William Hendriksen, *New Testament Commentary: Exposition of the Gospel According to Matthew* (Grand Rapids: Baker, 1973), pp. 95-97, outlines seven logical observations to demonstrate why Matthew was probably the author of the gospel that traditionally bears his name. I would like to add an eighth. Since Matthew was a tax collector and understood personally the effects of greed on a man's life, it is logical that the Holy Spirit would choose him to be the apostle who would record what Jesus taught about material possessions. Very little is recorded in the other three gospels about this subject. And what the other three gospel writers recorded, in the most part, was also recorded by Matthew.

2. R. V. G. Tasker, *The Gospel According to St. Matthew: An Introduction and Commentary,* vol. 2 of *The Tyndale New Testament Commentaries* (Grand Rapids: Eerdmans, 1961), p. 61, states, "The *poor in spirit* are not the 'poor spirited' as this somewhat unfortunate English translation might suggest. There are those who recognize in their hearts that they are 'poor' in the sense that they can do no good thing without divine assistance, and that they have no power in themselves to help them do what God requires them to do. The *kingdom of heaven* belongs to such, for from that kingdom the proudly self-sufficient are inevitably excluded."

3. Hendriksen, *New Testament Commentary*, p. 310. Note further the author's explanation of this total passage:

> What then did Jesus mean when he said, "Do not resist the evil-doer; but to him that slaps you," etc.? When Christ's words (vv. 39-42) are read in the light of what immediately *follows* in vv. 43-48, and when the parallel in Luke 6:29-30 is explained on the basis of what immediately *precedes* in vv. 27-28, it becomes clear that the key passage, identical in both Gospels, is "Love your enemies" (Matt. 5:44; Luke 6:27). In other words, Jesus is condemning the spirit of lovelessness, hatred, yearning revenge. He is saying, "Do not resist the evil-doer with measures that arise from an unloving, unforgiving, unrelenting, vindictive disposition."

Tasker, in *The Gospel According to St. Matthew*, p. 70, gives the following explanation: "The following illustrations in [Matthew 5] 39b-42 are not to be taken literally; they serve to drive home the point (almost to the point of absurdity) that a Christian rather than avenging himself upon a brother who has done him a personal wrong had better go to the opposite extreme!" John Peter Lange, *The Gospel According to Matthew*, Lange's Commentary on the Holy Scriptures, trans. and ed. Philip Schaff (Grand Rapids: Zondervan, 1969), 8:117-18, makes a similar statement: "Of course, these expressions, in their paradox form, must not be taken literally. The fundamental idea of the passage is, that Christian love must make us willing to bear twice as much as the world, in its injustice, could demand."

9

Jesus' Teachings in Matthew 6

In Matthew 6 Jesus makes seven statements, each of which can be applied in the form of a supracultural principle.

MATTHEW 6:3-4

But when you give to the needy, do not let
your left hand know what your right hand is doing,
so that your giving may be in secret.

To understand what Jesus meant with this rather unusual exhortation, we must consider several important factors. First, the Lord was again using hyperbole to make a point. Not to allow the "left hand" to be aware of what the "right hand" is doing would mean that individuals themselves would not be able to know what they (themselves) were giving. As discussed in chapter 8, Jesus was not speaking literally in this case any more than when He said, "If your right hand causes you to sin, cut it off and throw it away" (5:30).

Second, we must interpret Jesus' exhortation to "give in secret" alongside another similar teaching in the very next paragraph: "When you pray, go into your room, close the door, and pray to your Father, who is unseen" (6:6a). If Jesus was teaching that all *giving* was to be private, we must also conclude that all *praying* must be private. Not only would we have to avoid "being heard" as we pray, but we would have to avoid "being seen." This would contradict the extensive emphasis on public and corporate prayer in the rest of the New Testament.

Third, we must look at what Jesus actually practiced and promoted. Generally speaking, Jesus never condemned people who gave publicly. In fact, as the poor widow put her gift in the Temple treasury, He used her public offering to illustrate sacrificial giving to those who were watching (Luke 21:1-4). Jesus would also be contradicting His own actions, for He prayed in public (e.g., Luke 23:34; John 11:41-42; 17) and in a public setting taught His disciples to pray (6:9-13).

Fourth, we must interpret Jesus' statement in view of what actually happened in the early church. Public giving, as well as public prayer and praise, was a vital part of the way in which Christians in Jerusalem demonstrated their love for one another and God. The Holy Spirit used both their personal and corporate witness in these areas to draw others into the kingdom of God (Acts 2:42-47).

Fifth, and perhaps most important, we must understand the historical and cultural setting. Many of the religious leaders and wealthy people within Judaism at the time of Christ were given to parading their good works before others. When they gave to the needy, they would "announce it with trumpets" (6:2*a*). Their motivation was "to be honored by men" (6:2*b*). By teaching that giving should be a private matter, Jesus was removing this wrong motivation. If they could not be seen by men, they would have felt no need whatsoever to give—or to pray. Their motivation to help the poor was 100 percent selfish; it did not spring from their love for God and a real concern for those who were needy. Motive, then, was the deeper issue. To give gifts to God and to others in order to glorify ourselves is a serious violation of the will of God.

REFLECTIONS OF JESUS' TEACHING

Ananias and Sapphira were guilty of violating Jesus' teaching. Their sole motivation for giving was self-glorification. Consequently they suffered extreme judgment (Acts 5:1-11). But the vast majority of Christians in Jerusalem had a true perspective on what Jesus was teaching when He said, "Do not let your left hand know what your right hand is doing." Their personal giving was public, but their hearts and motives were right and pure. They wanted to minister to one another and, in the process, to glorify God—not themselves.

THE FOURTH SUPRACULTURAL PRINCIPLE

Christians should periodically check their motives to see if they are giving to glorify God or to glorify themselves (Matt. 6:3-4).

To check our motives as Christians, we can stop and ask ourselves several questions: What if *no one* knew what we were giving? Would we give to the same degree? On the other hand, what if others did know what we were giving? Would we be embarrassed and ashamed?

If we look at the context of what Jesus taught, particularly in the light of the whole of Scripture, we will see that a "doctrine of public giving" per se (which is often promoted by religious groups that teach a works-oriented salvation) can lead to pride and self-glorification. Conversely, a "doctrine of private giving" per se can lead to another form of sin—"self-orientation." We are particularly vulnerable to this kind of sin when we are not being held accountable to be good stewards of what God has given us. In short, we may be using our personal "doctrine of privacy" to cover up our disobedience.

It is possible to blend and balance these extremes in our giving. Our motive for public giving should be God's glory. Once we understand God's perspective on this issue and once we are giving as God intended us to give, we will not be concerned that our giving be kept confidential. In fact, we will feel good (not proud) that we are obeying God and modeling God's will to others. Once we have a biblical perspective on the way God wants us to use our material possessions, we will not want to keep this aspect of our Christian lives private any more than we want to keep private our commitment to moral and ethical behavior.

MATTHEW 6:11

Give us today our daily bread.

The history of the Jewish people reveals that they often became incredibly independent and, often, unthankful and ungrateful. Moses warned them against this tendency before they even came into the Promised Land: "When you eat and are satisfied, be careful that you do not forget the Lord, who brought you out of Egypt, out of the land of slavery" (Deut. 6:11-12). Moses warned further that when they received cities, houses, wells, and many other good things they had not worked for, they must be on guard against the temptation to say to themselves, "*My power and the strength of my hands* have produced this wealth for me" (Deut. 8:17).

Unfortunately, the history of Israel is a story of disobedience. And even though they were not dwelling in the land in freedom as God had promised they would someday, they were still a self-sufficient people when Jesus walked among them. Seeking God's daily guidance for provisions was not a part of their mentality. Though they had their regular ritualistic prayer times in the Temple and in the synagogues, personal, intimate prayer with the heavenly Father was a foreign experience. This is why one of His disciples (no doubt one of the twelve apostles), who was watching Jesus pray, asked Him to teach them to pray as well (Luke 11:1). Among other things, Jesus taught them to pray for their "daily bread."

REFLECTIONS OF JESUS' TEACHING

Was the Lord's prayer for daily bread part of the message that the apostles shared with the believers in Jerusalem? I would think so. These new believers also learned that they did not have to go to the Temple or into a synagogue to pray. They could pray at any time and in any place. Jesus was their high priest, the only mediator between themselves and God (1 Tim. 2:5). This was a new experience.

Then, too, many of the visitors in Jerusalem were at that time "without daily bread." Their resources were depleted. As "they devoted themselves . . . to prayer," praying as Jesus had taught the apostles to pray (Acts 2:42), God moved especially upon the hearts of those who lived in Jerusalem to be a part of the answer to their request for "daily bread."

THE FIFTH SUPRACULTURAL PRINCIPLE

Christ wants Christians to pray for daily sustenance (Matt. 6:11).

The apostle Paul both affirmed and broadened Jesus' specific exhortation to pray for daily bread: "Do not be anxious about *anything*, but in *everything* by prayer and petition, with thanksgiving, present your requests to God" (Phil. 4:6). In Jesus' model prayer, He gave "specificity" to the "everything" that Paul mentioned in his exhortation to the Philippians.

In terms of our material needs, we should also remember that God in His sovereignty sometimes allows difficult economic situations to refocus our thinking from dependency on ourselves to dependency on Him. How easy it is during times of plenty to revert to Israel's behavior and say, "We did this ourselves" (Deut. 18:18).

It is our privilege, then, to ask God for "daily bread." God wants to bless us and provide us with the necessities of life. Though there are times when Christians suffer—along with all humanity—because of natural disasters and human frailty, God wants to encourage us whether we have little or much. We should never hesitate to ask God to meet our needs. Not to do so is to violate His will for our lives.

MATTHEW 6:19

Do not store up for yourselves treasures on earth . . .
but store up for yourselves treasures in heaven.

On one occasion, Jesus told the story of a wealthy farmer whose land was very productive, so much so that he decided to tear down his granaries and build larger ones. He was satisfied with his material accumulations and concluded that he had enough resources to retire. Unfortunately, he did not realize that he was going to suddenly die. He had made preparation for *this* life, but not for eternity. Jesus then made an application that is directly related to His teaching in the Sermon on the Mount: "This is how it will be with anyone who stores up *things for himself* but is not rich toward God" (Luke 12:21).

Many people in Jesus' day were storing up "treasures on earth," just as they are today. That Jesus made this statement to His listeners demonstrates that not only were there poor people listening to His message but many rich people as well.

REFLECTIONS OF JESUS' TEACHING

As the apostles met with the new believers in Jerusalem, they must have shared with them this perspective on material possessions. If so, many of those who had their focus on material things were evidently convicted of this particular sin in their lives. The property they had purchased and the houses they had built no longer had the same meaning. With love in their hearts produced by the Holy Spirit, they were able to relinquish these things in order to "store up for themselves treasures in heaven, where moth and rust do not destroy, and where thieves do not break in and steal" (6:20).

THE SIXTH SUPRACULTURAL PRINCIPLE

Whatever excess material possessions God enables Christians to accumulate should be used in creative ways to further the kingdom of God (Matt. 6:19-20).

Applying this principle in modern culture does not mean that it is wrong to plan ahead. Neither does it mean that it is wrong to accumulate material possessions or to have a plan to care for ourselves and our families in the future. Many teachings in the book of Proverbs affirm that we are to be responsible Christians:

> Go to the ant, you sluggard; consider its ways and be wise! It has no commander, no overseer or ruler, yet it stores its provisions in summer and gathers its food at harvest (6:6-8).
>
> He who gathers crops in summer is a wise son, but he who sleeps during harvest is a disgraceful son (10:5).
>
> A good man leaves an inheritance for his children's children (13:22*a*).
>
> The plans of the diligent lead to profit as surely as haste leads to poverty (21:5).
>
> Finish your outdoor work and get your fields ready; after that, build your house (24:27).
>
> Be sure you know the condition of your flocks, give careful attention to your herds (27:23).
>
> He who works his land will have abundant food, but the one who chases fantasies will have his fill of poverty (28:19).

When Jesus warned us not to store up "treasures on earth" but rather to store up "treasures in heaven," He never intended to give the impression that it is wrong to accumulate material possessions. Rather, He was teaching us that our focus should always be on eternal values and accomplishing the will of God by the way we *use* our material possessions. Those who have much should give much—as Paul says—in proportion to what they have. In this way, we are using our excess to accomplish God's will in the world.

WHAT IS EXCESS?

It is difficult to define *excess*. What is excessive in terms of the kinds of houses we live in, the kinds of cars we drive, or the clothes we wear? What is ample in terms of planning for future needs, including retirement? How much insurance should we have? How much should we plan to leave for our children or even for our grandchildren? In some cultures, these questions are answered automatically. People live and die with just enough to meet their needs. However, in affluent areas of the world, sincere Christians face these questions everyday.

There are no pat answers. These questions must be addressed at a personal level by every Christian or Christian couple. But the principles that emerge from this study should enable Christians in all cultural situations to answer these questions satisfactorily, assuming they take them seriously and providing they are honest with God and themselves. Each one should be able to develop a special approach for using, in creative ways, whatever excess material possessions God has given in order to further the kingdom of God without neglecting human responsibility. Most of all, we will find joy in this process because we are storing up for ourselves "treasures in heaven."

MATTHEW 6:21

For where your treasure is, there your heart will be also.

Though the Greek word *heart* (*kardia*) literally refers to the chief organ that gives life to the human body, in Scripture it refers to "man's entire mental and moral activity, both the rational and emotional elements. In other words, the heart is used figuratively for the hidden springs of the personal life."[1] *Treasures* refer to our dearest possessions—those things that occupy our minds and hearts, our total being. It is what we think about and what affects our emotions in the innermost recesses of our souls.

Jesus was teaching that you can test people's focus regarding material possessions by what occupies their attitudes and actions. If they are constantly concerned about their possessions on earth—thinking about them, worrying about them, demonstrating jealousy and greed, mistreating others to gain more or to keep what they have—their treasures are on earth. That is where their heart is. Conversely, if Christians are consistently thinking in terms of how they can use their material possessions to glorify God—how they can meet others' needs, how they can further God's work, how they can invest in eternal purposes—their treasure is in heaven because that is where their heart is.

REFLECTIONS OF JESUS' TEACHING

There is no question as to how to describe the hearts of most Jerusalem Christians. With the exception of a few, like Ananias and Sapphira, their focus was on eternal values. Rather than thinking about how much they could accumulate for themselves and how they could use their material possessions for self-gratification and self-glorification, they were thinking in terms of how to honor Jesus Christ and serve one another. What an incredible example this is for Christians of all time—no matter what their economic and social structures.

THE SEVENTH SUPRACULTURAL PRINCIPLE

Christians can determine their true perspective toward material possessions by evaluating the consistent thoughts and attitudes of their hearts (Matt. 6:21).

Consider the following questions:

What do I think about the most?

What occupies most of my emotional and physical energy?

How do I respond emotionally when I see human needs?

How do I respond emotionally when I hear biblical messages on what God says my attitudes and actions should be regarding material possessions?

How do I respond when I feel I may need to part with some material possessions so that they could be better used to meet someone else's needs or to help carry out the Great Commission?

What priorities do I have other than making money (such as worshiping God, learning the Word of God, spending quality time with my family, serving others in my church, bettering the community)?

What is my attitude when I do give?

These questions will help us determine if our treasures are on earth or in heaven. For where our treasure is, there our hearts will be also. We all react negatively at times to the way some Christian leaders attempt to raise money—with manipulation, guilt, and pressure tactics. However, this should not cause us to respond negatively to what God says about the way we should use our material possessions. Though some people use God's

Word in inappropriate ways, this does not give any one of us an excuse to ignore God's will for our lives. Perhaps we are feeling guilty because we are disobeying God. If so, we should listen to our conscience.

The best way to check our heart's attitudes regarding material possessions is to allow all of the principles of the Word of God to penetrate our innermost being. "The word of God is living and active. Sharper than any double-edged sword, it penetrates even to dividing soul and spirit, joints and marrow; *it judges the thoughts and attitudes of the heart*" (Heb. 4:12).

MATTHEW 6:24

You cannot serve both God and money.

This teaching is an extension of what Christ has just taught regarding the heart (6:21). Money can become our "master." Elaborating, Jesus stated that we "will hate the one and love the other," or we "will be devoted to the one and despise the other" (6:24).

This was the rich young ruler's tension. Money was his master. Jesus knew this to be true because He could penetrate the thoughts and intents of the man's heart. Unfortunately, the young man walked away sadly, not aware that He could master his money for the glory of God and experience great joy in doing so.

REFLECTIONS OF JESUS' TEACHING

It is quite conceivable that this subject came up for discussion on numerous occasions as the new church grew and flourished in Jerusalem. All around these new believers were Jews—including the religious leaders of their day—who were serving money. They claimed to know God, but by their actions they denied Him. In contrast, coming to know Christ had set many people free from their slavery to material possessions. They began to experience the joy of open hearts and open hands.

THE EIGHTH SUPRACULTURAL PRINCIPLE

It is possible for a Christian to be in bondage to material possessions (Matt. 6:24).

Not only was the rich young ruler in bondage to money, it also kept him from becoming a true disciple of Jesus Christ. In that sense, he had to make a choice between his material possessions and salvation in Jesus Christ. Paul agreed with Jesus when he stated that people who *consistently* engage in various acts of the sinful nature "will not inherit the kingdom of God" (Gal. 5:21). That is why it is important for people who claim to be Christians but who are in love with "things" to search their hearts to see if their relationship with Christ is personal and real.

Many Christians, however, have also allowed themselves to become slaves to materialism. In this sense, they are serving money—even as believers. Just as some Christians may be serving other carnal and sinful desires, as outlined by Paul in his letter to the Galatians (sexual immorality, impurity, jealousy; Gal. 5:19-20), some are guilty of being in bondage to their material possessions. If this is true of us, we must not allow God's grace and patience to cause us to go on sinning. If we do, at some point in time, He will discipline us as a loving father. If we "are not disciplined, then" we "are illegitimate children and not true sons" (Heb. 12:8).

How does God discipline His children when they serve their material possessions rather than Him? The most extreme form involves the way He dealt with Ananias and Sapphira. Fortunately, this is not God's normal form of discipline. But one aspect of God's discipline is certain: We will "reap what we sow" (Gal. 6:7). Though it may take years to harvest this painful crop, some materialistic parents experience it when their own children grow up and become even more materialistic than they are. What is worse, they may—following our example—become materialistic in the ultimate sense and, like the rich young ruler, reject Jesus Christ.

MATTHEW 6:33

But seek first His kingdom and His righteousness
and all these things will be given to you as well.

"Spiritual realities" and "material things" are not irreconcilable entities in our lives. They are a matter of our *priorities.* Jesus recognized that we live in the midst of a material world. We cannot live without food, clothing, and shelter. These things are necessary for life and sustenance and protection from the elements.

REFLECTIONS OF JESUS' TEACHING

The new believers in Jerusalem needed "these things" in order to survive. In fact, when material needs were not cared for, the Grecian widows became discontented, as well as others who knew them. Consequently, the apostles made sure their needs were met. But the fact remains that most of these new Christians were not placing a priority on material things. Rather than focusing on their own physical needs, they concentrated on seeking the will of God. In the process, the things they needed were given to them as well (6:33).

THE NINTH SUPRACULTURAL PRINCIPLE

If Christians put God first in all things, He has promised to meet their material needs (Matt. 6:33).

When Jesus taught this principle, He was not referring to eternity but to the physical world in which these people lived. Paul affirmed this promise to the Philippians when they had been faithful in sharing their material possessions to meet his needs: "And my God will meet all your needs according to His glorious riches in Christ Jesus" (Phil. 4:19).

Paul wrote similarly to the Corinthians when he was encouraging them to be generous in their giving. In order to reassure them, Paul followed his exhortation with this promise: "God is able to make all grace abound to you so that in all things at all times, having all that you need, you will abound in every good work. . . . You will be made rich in every way so that you can be generous on every occasion" (2 Cor. 9:8, 11).

It is important to note that neither Jesus nor Paul was teaching "prosperity theology"—that God guarantees to multiply our material possessions *if* we are faithful givers. God has never promised that He will give us *more* than we need. However, He has promised to give us *what* we need. This concept will become increasingly clear as we continue to study God's unfolding revelation.

This principle raises two important questions. Does God ever give Christians more than they need because they are faithful in using their material possessions to glorify God? It appears that He does. We will explore this more thoroughly in later chapters. On the other hand, are there ever Christians whose basic needs are not met even though they are faithful stewards of their material possessions? We must remember that God, in most circumstances, fulfills His divine promises through other Christians. Consequently, situations occur where people's needs are not met because followers of Christ have not been obedient in applying the principles that God has outlined in His Word. For instance, sometimes the basic needs of Christian workers (e.g., pastors, missionaries, teachers) are not met as they should be because the people they have ministered to have not responded and shared their material blessings as God intended. This issue is frequently addressed in the New Testament.

GOD'S PROVISIONS

Scripture presents several instances where God has at certain times and in special situations used supernatural means to meet people's needs, such as when He provided the children of Israel with water and food in the wilderness (Deut. 8:15-16). During the forty years that they wandered, He not only provided them with food and drink but their "clothes did not wear out," nor "did the sandals" on their feet (Deut. 29:5).

On another occasion, when Elijah was hiding from King Ahab in the Kerith ravine, "the ravens brought him bread and meat in the morning and bread and meat in the evening" (1 Kings 17:6). And when he went to live with a poor widow in Zarephath, God miraculously caused a jar of flour and a jug of oil to continue replenishing themselves until the Lord sent "rain on the land" (1 Kings 17:14).

We could cite numerous other examples where God miraculously provided sustenance for His children. However, under normal circumstances, the Lord has ordained that human needs be met in more natural ways. This we have already seen illustrated graphically in the church in Jerusalem. It was the Christians themselves who from "time to time" sold their houses and lands in order to generate money to meet others' needs (Acts 4:34). Though these believers' actions were certainly motivated supernaturally by the Holy Spirit, God used a very natural process to meet their human needs.

As God's revelation unfolds, we will also see that His normal plan is that believers, when possible, should meet their own needs through hard and diligent work. Some of the Thessalonian Christians violated this principle. Thus, Paul wrote that "if a man will not work, he shall not eat" (2 Thess. 3:10). These are strong words, but they demonstrate that God does not tolerate lazy Christians. When it is possible for us to provide for our own material needs, we are to do so.

MATTHEW 6:34*a*

Therefore do not worry about tomorrow,
for tomorrow will worry about itself.

Jesus was not teaching His followers to be unconcerned about their material needs. In fact, the very moment He was teaching these people not to "worry about tomorrow," His "earthly father" was probably hard at work in his carpenter shop earning a living in order to support the rest of the family. And as we have already observed, several of Jesus' parables emphasized diligent planning, hard work, and being responsible citizens.

Jesus was dealing with a human tendency—the tendency to devote all of our energies to worrying about our life on earth—what we "will eat or drink" or what we "will wear" (6:25). He encouraged His listeners to "look at the birds of the air" and to look at "the lilies of the field" (6:26, 28). If our Father in heaven takes care of the birds and if He takes care of the flowers, will He not take care of His own children? After all, Jesus said, "The pagans run after all these things, and your heavenly Father knows that you need them" (6:32).

REFLECTIONS OF JESUS' TEACHING

The new church in Jerusalem is a glowing example of practicing what Jesus taught. They did "not worry about tomorrow." And as they were obedient to what was being modeled, as well as taught directly by the apostles, they discovered that God did take care of them since "there were no needy persons among them" (Acts 4:34).

THE TENTH SUPRACULTURAL PRINCIPLE

It is not the will of God that Christians be absorbed with worry about the future and how their material needs will be met (Matt. 6:34a).

This principle does not conflict with Paul's exhortation to be a responsible Christian and to work for a living (2 Thess. 3:6-10). However, if we are *continually anxious*, we have probably not arrived at that important balance between trusting God to meet our needs and, at the same time, doing our part to be responsible Christians in the world. Or it may be that we are not applying another basic principle in Scripture—the principle of prayer. This is why Paul told the Philippians, "Do not be *anxious* about anything, but in everything, *by prayer and petition, with thanksgiving* present your requests to God." When we follow this principle and apply it in our lives, God promises that "the peace of God, which transcends all understanding, will guard" our "hearts and" our "minds in Christ Jesus" (Phil. 4:7).

There is another perspective regarding worry and concern that must be addressed at this point. There are times when Christian leaders become very anxious about meeting the needs of others (e.g., paying salaries, providing funds for needy people, paying operating expenses in the ministry). Oftentimes, the primary reason for this anxiety is that those who are being ministered to from the Word of God are not, in turn, responding generously, as God has instructed them. In this set of circumstances, such disobedience makes it very difficult for Christian leaders to avoid anxiety and concern.

Once again we see that God has ordained that all of His divine principles work in harmony. "As each part does its work," the Body of Christ "builds itself up in love" (Eph. 4:16). Certainly, Paul's words to the Ephesians include what God has said regarding the way we use our material possessions. When we do God's work in God's way, wonderful things can happen. The Jerusalem church illustrated this reality in a marvelous way.

NOTE

1. W. E. Vine, *An Expository Dictionary of New Testament Words* (Old Tappan, N.J.: Revell, 1940), pp. 206-7.

10

Jesus' Teachings in Matthew 10, 15, 19, 23

Most of what Jesus taught regarding how His disciples were to view and use material possessions are included in the Sermon on the Mount (Matt. 5:6). However, Matthew also recorded several other important statements Jesus made at other times and in other places.

MATTHEW 10:42

*And if anyone gives even a cup of cold water to one of these
little ones because he is my disciple, I tell you the truth,
he will certainly not lose his reward.*

The context for this teaching involves the charge that Jesus gave to the twelve disciples when He sent them out to teach, "to drive out evil spirits and to heal every disease and sickness" (10:1). Jesus had instructed them *not* to "take along any gold or silver or copper." They were to take "no bag for the journey, extra tunic, or sandals or a staff." Jesus made clear that "the worker is worth his keep" (10:9-10).

When Jesus taught that whoever gives a cup of cold water will be rewarded, He was referring to those who ministered to the apostles *materially* while they were ministering to these people *spiritually.* The reward would be given to God's people because they had not neglected His representatives—no matter how unimpressive they may have appeared. The apostles did not wear colorful robes like the religious leaders in Israel. Neither did they arrive in these cities with pomp and circumstance. They had no money in their pockets and did not even carry a suitcase with extra clothes. From the world's point of view, they were poor and unworthy. Thus, Jesus identified them as "little ones."

What a contrast compared with the priestly class in Israel. Jeremias, in his book *Jerusalem in the Time of Jesus*, describes "the various extravagances of the rich in Jerusalem in their houses, their clothing, their servants, as well as their rich offerings and bequests to the temple." More specifically, he relates,

> According to tradition, there was great luxury in the houses of the high-priestly families. It was reported that Martha of the high-priestly family of Boethus was so pampered that she carpeted the whole district from her house to the Temple gate because she wanted to see her husband Joshua B. Gamaliel officiate on the Day of Atonement, on which day everyone had to go barefoot.[1]

Jeremias cites many more illustrations of the great wealth that existed among the religious leaders in Jerusalem.[2]

REFLECTIONS OF JESUS' TEACHING

When the apostles were leading the new church in Jerusalem, their lack of prestige and wealth reflected a stark contrast to the religious leaders who graced the Temple courts in Jerusalem. This was dramatically illustrated the day Peter and John went up to the Temple to pray and met the poor beggar who asked them for money. They had "no silver or gold" (Acts 3:6).[3]

It seems clear that the new believers considered it a rare privilege to support the apostles and to meet their physical needs. These twelve men had no excess property to sell like Barnabas, or Ananias and Sapphira, and no padded bank accounts like their religious counterparts in the Temple. They were dependent from day to day on those who would provide them with daily sustenance. Indeed, it must have been the apostles' example of sacrifice that helped motivate these new believers to unselfishly make their resources available to carry out the work of the kingdom of God.

THE ELEVENTH SUPRACULTURAL PRINCIPLE

God honors Christians in a special way when they meet the material needs of those who truly serve God (Matt. 10:42).

This principle is frequently reinforced with illustrations and directives in the Scriptures. God designated the first tithe in Israel to be used to care for the physical needs of the Levites who ministered in the Tabernacle (Num. 18:21-29). Paul and other writers of the New Testament letters emphasized the importance of taking care of spiritual leaders who devote a lot of time and energy to the ministry. The specific principle to remember from Jesus' teaching, however, is that Christians who care for their spiritual leaders will not only encourage these people, they will also be blessed themselves—even if they can only give "a cup of cold water."

MATTHEW 15:4

Honor your father and mother.

Though this injunction, which was originally given by God at Mount Sinai, was comprehensive in terms of application (Ex. 20:12), Jesus' reiteration related to a certain way in which the Pharisees and teachers of the law were violating this commandment. Jesus followed this exhortation with the following explanation: "But you say that if a man says to his father or mother, 'Whatever help you might otherwise have received from me is a gift devoted to God,' he is not to 'honor his father' with it" (15:5-6).

The Pharisees and teachers of the law had devised a set of human rules whereby people could classify their material possessions as being "devoted to God." By making certain "religious decisions," the Jews were legally "freed up" from having to take care of their fathers and mothers. Sadly, the Pharisees developed these traditions to receive more money themselves.[4]

Jesus directed some of His sharpest barbs toward this kind of hypocrisy. He told them in no uncertain terms that they had violated the law of God—which says they must *honor their fathers and mothers.* By quoting Isaiah, Jesus applied these Old Testament words directly to the religious leaders: "These people honor me with their lips, but their hearts are far from me. They worship me in vain; their teachings are but rules taught by men" (15:8-9).

Tragically, it was the religious leaders in Jesus' day who violated the Word of God the most. When Jesus discovered that He had offended the Pharisees with His teachings, He told His disciples to "leave them; they are blind guides. If a blind man leads a blind man, both will fall into a pit" (15:14).

REFLECTIONS OF JESUS' TEACHING

If the apostles had reminded the new believers of these words, it must have given them unusual encouragement in the midst of the persecution that would eventually take place. And when the religious leaders "arrested the apostles and put them in the public jail" because of their teaching and healing ministry, it only motivated the followers of Christ to remain more steadfast in their faith—even though they had to take a stand against men they had previously looked to for spiritual guidance (see also Acts 4:23-31).

Furthermore, what Jesus taught about honoring father and mother would certainly have motivated these new believers to take care of their parents and other family members. But more generally, it would motivate these believers to view the church as an "extended family"—a larger body of believers where individual members should be concerned about one another's earthly welfare.

Christian children who are able should make sure that they care for their parents' physical needs (Matt. 15:4-6).

Paul enunciated this principle in his first letter to Timothy: "If anyone does not provide for his relatives, and especially for his immediate family, he has denied the faith and is worse than an unbeliever" (1 Tim. 5:8). The Pharisees and teachers of the law had violated this principle in an incredibly selfish way.

Cultures vary in terms of economic structures that have been devised to care for people who have reached old age. Today, in our American society, we have retirement pensions, unemployment benefits, Social Security, Medicare, and senior citizen discounts. These private and government programs must be factored into the way we apply this biblical principle. If our parents' needs are being met in other ways, this enables us to utilize excess funds more creatively in caring for needs within the larger family—the church. But these governmental provisions for the elderly must never be used as a rationalization to neglect parents or to keep more for ourselves when we could use these resources to further God's eternal work.

Conversely, applying this principle does not mean that we are to allow our parents to be selfish and to take advantage of us. But it does mean that we should assist our parents when they have bona fide needs—whether they are Christians or non-Christians. In fact, even if they are resentful of what we have and who we are, this should not be the deciding factor as to whether or not we help them.

MATTHEW 19:30

But many who are first will be last,
and many who are last will be first.

The context in which Jesus made this statement relates to the promise that those who have given up land, homes, and family for the sake of Christ will receive one hundredfold in God's eternal kingdom. Jesus was teaching that some of those who from a human perspective seemingly deserve to be honored first will be honored last.

Jesus' remarks regarding the extremely poor widow who put "two very small copper coins" into the Temple treasury describes this truth graphically. What she gave was "worth only a fraction of a penny" (Mark 12:42). Jesus, after observing what she gave in comparison to many of the rich, gathered His disciples around Him and used her gift as a visual demonstration. "I tell you the truth," He said, "this poor widow has put more into the treasury than all the others. They all gave out of their wealth; but she, out of her poverty, put in everything—all she had to live on" (Mark 12:43-44).

With this observation, Jesus explained what He meant when He said that many who have given much, even as believers, "will be last" while "many who are last will be first" (19:30). In God's scheme of things, "one hundredfold" in the eternal kingdom of God would be measured, not in terms of the *quantity* this widow gave, but in terms of the *proportional nature* of the gift. She would receive much more from the Lord, according to His accounting system, than those who gave a lot and had a lot left over. As Alan Cole states, "It is well to remember that the Lord measures giving, not by what we give, but by what we keep for ourselves; and the widow kept nothing, but gave all."[5]

REFLECTIONS OF JESUS' TEACHING

This experience impacted the apostles in an unusual way. They would never forget it. It would not be surprising if they had repeated this story often in Jerusalem during the early days of the church. Furthermore, before Christians were forbidden to meet in the Temple courts, they had probably seen this event reenacted many times as poor widows put their gifts into the Temple treasury.

This perspective on giving must have also given the apostles increased motivation to assure that the widows were cared for who were being neglected in the daily distribution of food. Though they could not get involved in the distribution itself, they developed a system to make sure the needs of these people were met.

THE THIRTEENTH SUPRACULTURAL PRINCIPLE

God will reward Christians in His eternal kingdom on the basis of the degree of sacrifice involved in their giving (Matt. 19:30).

To understand this principle and how it works from God's perspective, consider the following example. Many Christians tithe (that is, give at least 10 percent) regularly to their church. Some of these tithers give more "sacrificially." In other words, they give up some things they would like to have but cannot buy because of their financial commitment to God's work. Others who tithe could give much more in terms of material possessions. In order to give to the *same sacrificial degree*, these people would need to give a much higher percentage of their total income and resources.

The Bible calls this giving "in keeping with" one's income (1 Cor. 16:2), what many today call "proportional" giving. In fact, some Christians could easily give as much as 50 percent or more of their income and still be able to secure for themselves many luxuries that others who give 10 percent cannot.

These observations are not being used to determine what is proper or improper. In fact, twentieth-century American illustrations can be duplicated in many respects in the New Testament world. Compare, for example, the poor widow's resources to those of Philemon. It is clear that this very wealthy man did not give the same "proportion" as the widow. Jesus stated that "she, out of her poverty, put in everything—all she had to live on" (Mark 12:44). Not so with Philemon. And yet Paul commended him for his generous spirit (Philem. 7). He did not make this man feel guilty because of his abundance. The facts are, however, that the widow and others like her will probably be more greatly rewarded in God's eternal kingdom than Philemon and others like him.

EVALUATING OUR GIVING PATTERNS

Only God can judge the hearts of men and women who fall into the categories just discussed. We are responsible, however, to evaluate ourselves and the way in which we use our material possessions in the light of *all* of God's principles. Are we giving unselfishly? Are we giving proportionately? Are we giving generously? Are we truly ministering materially to those who are ministering to us spiritually?

Though we cannot provide definitive answers for all of these questions—particularly as they relate to others—one thing is sure: "many who are first will be last, and many who are last will be first." Compared to many American Christians, there will be believers from other cultures of the world and other moments in history (including New Testament Christians) who will be far more rewarded in God's kingdom. Put another way, many Christians in the kingdom of God, like the widow, have given out of their poverty. In some instances, they have given all they "had to live on."

Conversely, many American Christians have given out of *plenty* rather than *poverty.* This in no way means we have seriously violated the will of God. Rather, it simply means that there will be others inhabiting the kingdom who will be first and we will be last. All of us will have eternal life, but some Christians will have far more rewards and far greater prominence because of their sacrificial spirit. In certain situations, some of us will probably have had our rewards on earth (Matt. 6:2). Their rewards, however, will last throughout eternity.

MATTHEW 23:23b

You give a tenth of your spices—mint, dill and cummin.
But you have neglected the more important matters of the law—
justice, mercy and faithfulness. You should have practiced
the latter, without neglecting the former.

Once again Jesus directed His teaching at "the teachers of the law and Pharisees" (Matt.23:23*a*). Referring to the laws of God regarding tithing as outlined in the Old Testament (Deut. 14:22-29), He accused these men of straining "out a gnat" while swallowing "a camel" (23:24*b*; cf. Luke 11:42). These religious leaders were giving a tenth of the small aromatic herbs from their gardens—which actually was going beyond the requirements given in the law of Moses. As Hendriksen states, "Careful examination of *the context* shows that what the law really meant—at least emphasized—was that, as far as products of the field were concerned, the three 'great' crops of the land, namely, grain, wine, and oil, should be tithed." In other words, these religious leaders were "overextending or overstretching the law."[6]

Jesus' main point was that these men were giving to God what was *easy to grow* and *easy to give*—and even being arrogant about it. But at the same time, they were not practicing the more important aspects of the law—justice, mercy, and faithfulness (23:23*b*). There is some question as to whether or not Jesus affirmed in this statement God's Old Testament requirement to tithe.[7] However, there is no question regarding the way these religious leaders violated God's law. They were notoriously hypocritical, even in the way they treated their parents. They were overdoing the Old Testament tithe requirement ("you strain out a gnat") and were violating the law of love and concern for others ("but swallow a camel").

REFLECTIONS OF JESUS' TEACHING

Most of those who became Christians in Jerusalem were "God-fearing" Jews. Consequently, they would understand the "three tithe" system described in the Old Testament. In fact, most of them would probably have been very faithful in practicing this requirement. (The three tithe system is described in detail on p. 112.) However, many wealthy believers in Jerusalem did not allow the "three tithe" concept to restrict their giving. For example, when Barnabas "sold a field he owned and brought the money and put it at the apostles' feet" (Acts 4:37), he did not give a tenth of the proceeds. He gave it all. We can assume that many others who owned lands or houses, and who "from time to time . . . sold them," also brought the *entire amount* and laid it at the apostles' feet for distribution to those who had a need.

As we have learned from Ananias's and Sapphira's experience, they were certainly not obligated to bring the total amount from these sales. They had a choice. The example of the individuals who had previously given the total amount of their property sales apparently motivated Ananias and Sapphira to give the impression that they too had given the total price of their land.

The important point, however, is that many of these Christians in Jerusalem at times gave far beyond three tithes to carry on God's work. When the need was there, and when they had the resources to do so, many gave 100 percent of certain transactions. In a literal sense, "no one claimed that any of his possessions was his own, but they shared everything they had" (Acts 4:32). However, most of these believers were motivated to give because of their love for God and for their fellow Christians. They were not neglecting the more important matters of the law. They had only one "outstanding debt"—the "continuing debt to love one another" (Rom. 13:8).

THE FOURTEENTH SUPRACULTURAL PRINCIPLE

Christians who give regularly and faithfully are invalidating the acceptability of their gifts to God when they neglect to love God and one another (Matt. 23:23b).

Some Christians seem to believe that, if they give away a lot of money to God's work, this benevolent act compensates for the unethical way in which they have made that money. Not so, said Jesus. Being generous will never compensate for dishonesty and insensitivity. Furthermore, generous giving will never cancel out the results of a life-style that conforms to this world's system. God wants us to do His will *in all respects*—including the way we view and use our material possessions (Rom. 12:1-2).

Notes

1. Joachim Jeremias, *Jerusalem in the Time of Jesus*, trans. F. H. and C. H. Kay (London: SCM, 1969), pp. 92, 96-97. For a scholarly and thorough treatment of the economic status of many people in Jerusalem, see the following chapters in Jeremias's book: "Industries," pp. 3-30; "Commerce," pp. 31-57; "The Rich," pp. 87-99.

2. Following are additional illustrations recorded by Jeremias that describe the way in which the apostles stood out in contrast to the religious leaders in Israel:

    The priestly aristocracy belonged to the wealthy class. In the upper part of the city lived the high priest Ananias, Zadok the chief priest, and according to tradition Annas and Caiaphas. The house where lived the ex-high priest Annas, father-in-law of the officiating high priest, to whom John says Jesus was first taken after his arrest (John 18:13), had a spacious court (John 18:15). A woman doorkeeper (John 18:16) and other servants belonged to the household (John 18:18, where the group who took Jesus prisoner is no doubt included). Annas's grave, in the south-east of the city, must have been a large construction dominating the district. The officiating high priest Caiaphas, to whom Jesus was taken next, lived in a house large enough to accommodate an emergency session of the Sanhedrin (Matt. 26:57; Mark 14:53; Luke 22:66), and it apparently possessed a gatehouse (Matt. 26:71; Mark 14:68). He had in his household a fair number of servants, both men and women (pp. 96-97).

    The councillor Nicodemus (John 7:50; John 3:1; John 12:42) was wealthy. It is said that he brought a hundred Roman pounds' worth of ointments and spices for Jesus' burial (John 19:39). Jerusalem merchants dealing in grain, wine and oil, and wood, who belonged to the Counsel between A.D. 66-70, are mentioned in rabbinic literature. There is a great deal of tradition about one of them, the corn merchant Nicodemus (Naqdimon B. Gorion). We are told about the luxury that was prevalent in his household, and of the generous benefactions, not always free from ambition, and of the destruction of his wealth during the chaos which preceded the destruction of Jerusalem, when the mob fired his granaries full of wheat and barley in the winter of A.D. 69-70, according to Josephus (p. 96).

When Joseph of Arimathea, another member of the Sanhedrin, is described as [*uskee-mōn*] (Mark 15:43), the papyri make it clear that this means a wealthy landowner. He was a rich man (Matt. 27:57) and owned a garden to the north of the city with a family grave hewn from the rock (John 19:41; John 20:15). The main part of his property would probably be in his native city, since the Jerusalem site had evidently not been long in the possession of his family, for the grave was newly hewn (p. 96).

3. Most of these twelve men probably had houses in Galilee where their extended families resided. However, they had left the warmth and security of their homes to travel with Christ and to carry out His commission. It is clear that Jesus did not ask them to sell these dwellings that met the needs of their families. Neither was Jesus asking the believers in Jerusalem to give away the necessities of life. Rather, these people were sharing their excess with those whose needs were *not* being met.

4. William Hendriksen, *New Testament Commentary: Exposition of the Gospel According to Matthew* (Grand Rapids: Baker, 1973), p. 613, comments on this event:

> The Pharisees and scribes were telling the children that there was a way to get around the heavy burden of having to bestow honor upon their parents by supporting them. If either father or mother, noticing that a son had something which was needed by the parent, asked for it, all that was necessary was for this son to say, "It's *doron* (a gift)" or "*corban* (an offering)." Either way, whether the son uses the Greek word *doron* or the Hebrew *corban*, he is really saying, "It is consecrated to God," and by making this assertion or exclamation he, according to Pharisaic teaching based on tradition, had released himself from the obligation of honoring parents—here "father" is also representing the mother—by helping them in their particular need.

5. R. A. Cole, *The Gospel According to St. Mark: An Introduction and Commentary*, vol. 2 of *The Tyndale New Testament Commentaries* (Grand Rapids: Eerdmans, 1961), p. 196.

6. Hendriksen, *New Testament Commentary*, p. 831.

7. Some well-known commentators believe someone later added the following words to Matthew's original manuscript: "You should have practiced the latter, without neglecting the former." They argue that if Jesus stated this, He would be contradicting Himself when He called them "blind guides" (Matt. 23:23*b*-24*a*). For example, R. V. G. Tasker, *The Gospel According to Matthew: An Introduction and Commentary*, vol. 1 of *The Tyndale New Testament Commentaries* (Grand Rapids: Eerdmans, 1961), p. 221, states:

> It is very improbable that Jesus uttered these last words of this verse *these ought ye to have done, and not to leave the others undone*, for they contradict His argument. The point is that the Mosaic law enacted that "all the tithe of the land, whether of the seed of the land, or the fruit of the tree, is the Lord's" (Lev. 27:30), and the scribes *wrongly* extended this to the tiniest and commonest herbs. Although there is no manuscript evidence for the omission of these words, the rhythm of the passage is against them. . . . We may assume that the suspected words were originally a marginal comment made by a stringent Jewish Christian, which subsequently became inserted in the text.

Whether or not Tasker's observation is accurate does not really affect the interpretation outlined above. Jesus was affirming the Old Testament law. However, He was stating that it is possible to be meticulous and even go beyond what is required in the area of giving and at the same time neglect our relationships with people in the area of "justice, mercy and faithfulness."

11

Moving from Specific
to General Principles

We have looked at two important phases in early Christianity. First, we observed how Christians viewed and used their material possessions during the initial five years of the church's history. Second, we looked in detail at what Jesus taught about material possessions, assuming that the apostles and others taught these great truths during (and following) the first five years of the church's existence.

From these two sections of Scripture, we also outlined twenty-eight specific supracultural principles—fourteen from each unit. These principles are succinctly reviewed in this chapter. Then thirteen *general* principles are gleaned from the events recorded in the opening section of the book of Acts and from the teachings of Jesus as recorded by Matthew in his gospel.

SPECIFIC PRINCIPLES IN PERSPECTIVE FROM PART 1:
THE CHURCH IN JERUSALEM

1 As Christians use their material possessions in harmony with the will of God, it will encourage people to believe in Jesus Christ (Acts 2:47).

2. As Christians use their material possessions to meet one another's needs, it will create love and unity in the Body of Christ (Acts 4:32).

3. Spiritual leaders should model the way all Christians ought to use their material possessions (Acts 2:42).

4. Christians should be willing to make special sacrifices in order to meet special material needs within the Body of Christ (Acts 4:34-35).

5. A primary motivating factor for consistent Christian giving should be to meet others' needs—particularly within the Body of Christ (Acts 4:34-35).

6. It is the will of God that Christians share their material possessions in order to encourage others in the Body of Christ (Acts 4:36).

7. Christians who are faithful in sharing their material possessions should be shown special appreciation (Acts 4:36).

8. Christians need to be able to observe other believers who are faithful in sharing their material possessions (Acts 4:36-37).

9. What Christians give should always be given to honor God and not themselves (Acts 4:34-36; 5:1-10).

10. God detests dishonesty, lack of integrity, and hypocrisy when it comes to giving (Acts 5:1-10).

11. Though God wants all of His children to be generous, what Christians give should always be voluntary and from a heart of love and concern (Acts 5:4).

12. It is God's will that every church have an efficient system for helping to meet the true material needs of others in the Body of Christ (Acts 6:1-7).

13. Spiritual leaders in the church must at times delegate the administrative responsibilities to other qualified people who can assist them in meeting material needs (Acts 6:2-4).

14. Meeting the "spiritual needs" of people and meeting the "material needs" of people require the same high standard in terms of selecting leaders to meet these needs (Acts 6:3).

SPECIFIC PRINCIPLES IN PERSPECTIVE FROM PART 2:
THE TEACHINGS OF JESUS CHRIST

1. Having a lot of material things often makes it difficult for people to recognize and acknowledge their need of God in salvation (Matt. 5:3).

2. Material gifts are acceptable and "well pleasing" to God only when Christians have done their part to be in harmony with their brothers and sisters in Christ (Matt. 5:24b).

3. Christians should not only give to those who love them and care for them but even to those who may resent them and even try to harm them (Matt. 5:42).

4. Christians should periodically check their motives to see if they are giving to glorify God or to glorify themselves (Matt. 6:3-4).

5. Christ wants Christians to pray for daily sustenance (Matt. 6:11).

6. Whatever excess material possessions God enables Christians to accumulate should be used in creative ways to further the kingdom of God (Matt. 6:19-20).

7. Christians can determine their true perspective toward material possessions by evaluating the consistent thoughts and attitudes of their hearts (Matt. 6:21).

8. It is possible for a Christian to be in bondage to material possessions (Matt. 6:24).

9. If Christians put God first in all things, He has promised to meet their material needs (Matt. 6:33).

10. It is not the will of God that Christians be absorbed with worry about the future and how their material needs will be met (Matt. 6:34a).

11. God honors Christians in a special way when they meet the material needs of those who truly serve God (Matt. 10:42).

12. Christian children who are able should make sure that they care for their parents' physical needs (Matt. 15:4-6).

13. God will reward Christians in His eternal kingdom on the basis of the degree of sacrifice involved in their giving (Matt. 19:30).

14. Christians who give regularly and faithfully are invalidating the acceptability of their gifts to God when they neglect to love God and one another (Matt. 23:23b).

GENERAL PRINCIPLES FROM PART 1:
THE CHURCH IN JERUSALEM

THE FIRST GENERAL SUPRACULTURAL PRINCIPLE

The way Christians use their material possessions is an important criterion for determining whether or not they are living in the will of God (Acts 2–6).

This principle emerges immediately from the study of the New Testament church during its first five years of existence. Approximately *half of the events* described in the book of Acts following the founding of the church in Jerusalem and prior to Stephen's martyrdom have to do with how these people used their material possessions (2:42-47; 3:1-10; 4:32-35; 4:36-37; 5:1-10; 6:1-7). It is true that the Jerusalem church is unique in terms of its sociological status and climate at this moment in history. However, our study will demonstrate that how these believers in Jerusalem used their material possessions continued to be a vital part of the overall lifestyle of dedicated Christians throughout the rest of the New Testament era.

It may be startling for some Christians living in the midst of the twentieth-century world to realize that more is recorded in Scripture about material possessions and how Christians are to use them for the glory of God than any other aspect of Christian living—including principles for maintaining sexual purity. When the apostle Paul exhorted and pleaded with the Roman Christians to offer their bodies to Christ, he certainly had in mind how Christians are to use their material possessions. Paul affirmed this fact when he wrote to the Philippian Christians and thanked them for their gifts of money sent to sustain him in prison. Their material gifts to Paul were an extension of the gift of themselves to God. Compare Paul's statement to the Romans with what he says to the Philippians:

Romans 12:1	Philippians 4:18
"Therefore, I urge you, brothers, in view of God's mercy, to offer your bodies as living sacrifices, holy and pleasing to God—which is your spiritual worship."	"I have received full payment and even more; I am amply supplied, now that I have received from Epaphroditus the gifts you sent. They are a fragrant offering, an acceptable sacrifice, pleasing to God."

These verses contain the following specific comparisons:

Romans 12:1	Philippians 4:18
"Offer your bodies"	"The gifts you sent"
"Living sacrifices"	"An acceptable sacrifice"
"Pleasing to God"	"Pleasing to God"
"Your spiritual worship"	"A fragrant offering"

Writing to the Corinthians, Paul again underscored this correlation and sequence. Referring to the Christians in Macedonia (probably the Philippians or the Thessalonians), he wrote, "For I testify that they gave as much as they were able, and even beyond their ability. . . . *They gave themselves first to the Lord* and then to us [their material gifts] in keeping with *God's will*" (2 Cor. 8:3-5).

THE SECOND GENERAL SUPRACULTURAL PRINCIPLE

It is by divine design that local churches provide the primary context in which Christians are to use their material possessions to further the work of God's kingdom (Acts 2–6).

Much of the New Testament is the story of the church of Jesus Christ. Jesus stated that He would build His church upon the foundation of the apostles and prophets and the gates of Hades would not overcome it (Matt. 16:18; see also Eph. 2:19-22). It is true that the larger concept in the New Testament involves the kingdom of God (also identified as the kingdom of heaven), but the specific, unique, and visible expression of that kingdom—the church of Jesus Christ—occupies most of the New Testament.

As we have seen, the church began in Jerusalem. From there it spread around the world. Great sections of the New Testament involve letters written to local churches (localized expressions of the universal church) or to individuals (such as Timothy and Titus) who were involved in ministry in local churches.

Any view, then, of how Christians should use their material possessions must focus first and foremost on local churches. This is what we see in the Bible. To bypass this important concept in Scripture is, in essence, to ignore what is recorded by gifted men inspired by the Holy Spirit. Furthermore, as will be demonstrated in future chapters, if Christians bypass the concept of the local church, they will inevitably violate a number of other important supracultural principles.

Do not misunderstand. The fact that God allows "freedom in form" for the church has given birth to many legitimate ministries we call parachurch organizations. In many respects, these organizations perform the same functions as God intended for local churches, both in the areas of evangelism and edification. However, before we support any particular parachurch ministry financially, it is important to view that ministry through the lens of biblical ecclesiology. In other words, we must carefully evaluate the functions and goals of every parachurch ministry by what Scripture teaches about the local church. We must also look carefully at how particular ministries view the local church. Hopefully, this study will provide specific guidance for twentieth-century Christians in making these financial decisions wisely and, most of all, biblically. (This subject is developed more fully on pp. 242-44.)

THE THIRD GENERAL SUPRACULTURAL PRINCIPLE

Christians should respond immediately to whatever portion of God's truth they have received (Acts 2–6).

This principle applies to all areas of a Christian's life, but it applies particularly to the way we view and use our material possessions. The believers in Jerusalem did not understand many aspects of what would eventually emerge as a more stabilized economic situation. Initially they were expecting Jesus Christ to return to "restore the kingdom to Israel" (1:6), even though Christ had made clear that it was not for them "to know the times or dates the Father has set by his own authority" (1:7).

However, the motivation these Christians demonstrated to share their material possessions so liberally was not merely based upon their "expectancy" that Christ would soon return, but also upon what they knew of Jesus' teachings during the three and a half years prior to His crucifixion, resurrection, and ascension. They took Christ's teaching seriously, probably more so than any other group of Christians at any moment in history. They responded immediately to the knowledge they had received.

THE FOURTH GENERAL SUPRACULTURAL PRINCIPLE

The expectancy of the second coming of Jesus Christ should always be a strong motivational factor in the way Christians view and use their material possessions (Acts 2–6).

As time went on, Christians became more tentative regarding the immanency of Christ's return. Unfortunately, this affected the way they related to earthly possessions. On the one hand, they had to face the reality that they might live out their lives on earth before Christ returned and that they had to function as responsible citizens. On the other hand, their tendency was to begin to focus more on the security and status that comes from owning houses and lands and accumulating wealth. This tendency began to permeate Christianity soon after the first century—and has continued to this very day.

Those of us living in twentieth-century Western culture have probably been affected by materialism more significantly than any other group of Christians who have ever lived. It is easy to allow weeks, months, and even years to go by without even thinking about the possible return of Jesus Christ. The majority of us may seldom contemplate our eternal rewards and what Christ would say should we suddenly stand before His judgment seat to give an account of how we used our material possessions while on earth.

Paul pleaded for godly and righteous living "while we wait for the *blessed hope*—the glorious appearing of our great God and Savior, Jesus Christ" (Titus 2:13). Why this emphasis on holiness? Because Jesus Christ "gave himself for us to redeem us from all wickedness and to purify for himself a people that are his very own, *eager to do what is good*" (Titus 2:14).

How much does this phrase—"eager to do what is good"—characterize twentieth-century Christians when it comes to the way we use our material possessions? There are a number of statements in Scripture that encourage us to "do good" with the resources we have at our disposal. Part of the motivation for doing good while we have opportunity is that one day—perhaps soon—Jesus Christ will return and that opportunity will no longer exist. At that moment, we will reap what we have sown. Paul related this to material possessions: "Remember this: Whoever sows sparingly will also reap sparingly, whoever sows generously will also reap generously" (2 Cor. 9:6).

THE FIFTH GENERAL SUPRACULTURAL PRINCIPLE

As we obey God, He will clarify and help us understand His specific plans, enabling us to more and more live by faith and respond to His will (Acts 2–6).

We must realize that the knowledge Christians had from God's unfolding revelation in New Testament days was quite different from what we have in our twentieth-century setting. Many believers today have at their disposal the complete written revelation of God as it is recorded in both the Old and New Testaments. This fact is what enables us to develop a biblical theology of material possessions. However, biblical principles still apply to all Christians today—just as they applied in the first century. As we obey God, He honors obedience and increases faith.

In the book of Hebrews, one of the last books to be written and included in the New Testament, the author encourages Christians to obey God and walk by faith. After giving numerous Old Testament illustrations (11:1-40), he concludes, "Therefore, since we are surrounded by such a great cloud of witnesses, let us throw off everything that hinders and the sin that so easily entangles, and let us run with perseverance the race marked out for us" (12:1).

No sin entangles a Christian in the affairs of this life more quickly and subtly than materialism. Though temptations to be sexually immoral are a strong force in many people's lives, the lines between right and wrong are clear-cut. To be guilty of adultery and fornication are rather nondebatable issues among Christians who believe in the values recorded in Scripture.

But where are the clear-cut lines when it comes to materialistic behaviors? Perhaps no sin is rationalized away more quickly by twentieth-century Christians than greed. Hopefully, this study will help us determine where the lines between right and wrong really are so that we can truly obey God and learn to walk by faith in this area. As we do, God—as He always has—will honor that obedience, increase our faith, and meet our needs.

THE SIXTH GENERAL SUPRACULTURAL PRINCIPLE

God's plan for Israel in the Old Testament serves as a foundational model regarding the way Christians should view and use their material possessions today (Acts 2–6).

Those who composed the first church in Jerusalem were, for the most part, Jews who took their religion very seriously. This was particularly true of the visitors in Jerusalem at the time the church was founded. Luke states that those who "were staying in Jerusalem" at the time the Holy Spirit came on the Day of Pentecost were "God-fearing Jews from every nation under heaven" (2:5). Great numbers of these "Grecian Jews," along with the "Aramaic-speaking community" (residents of Jerusalem and Judea), became believers (6:1).

To be "God-fearing Jews" simply meant that these people were committed to doing everything they could to keep the Old Testament laws. We can certainly assume that most of them, before they became Christians, practiced the Old Testament regulations regarding tithing.

When God called Israel out of Egypt and gave them the law at Mount Sinai, He basically instituted a three-tithe system. The *first tithe* involved one-tenth of all yearly produce and one-tenth of all the flocks and cattle. This tithe was to be used to support the Levites and priests (Lev. 27:30-34).

The *second tithe* was known as the "festival tithe," which was one-tenth of the nine-tenths that was left. This tithe was to be set apart and taken to Jerusalem. If it was impossible to make the trip with produce and animals, a tenth of their possessions could be sold. The money could be used to make the trip and then to purchase food or animals for offerings in Jerusalem (Deut. 12:5-7; 14:22-27).

The *third tithe*, sometimes identified as the "charity tithe," was given during the third year. It was to be designated for Levites, strangers, the fatherless, and those who were widowed (Deut. 26:12; 14:28-29).[1]

In addition to these tithes, faithful Jews also paid a Temple tax, which is referred to when collectors approached Peter and asked if Jesus paid this tax. Matthew (a former tax collector) identified this amount as "the two drachma" tax (Matt. 17:24). Though we do not know exactly how to translate this amount into buying power at the time of Christ, in A.D. 300 a two drachma piece would normally buy two sheep.[2] This tax was paid annually. Jeremias comments: "The Temple was the most important factor in the commerce of Jerusalem. By means of the Temple treasury, to which every Jew had to pay his annual dues, the whole of world-wide Jewry contributed to the commerce of Jerusalem."[3]

Under the Romans, of course, the Jews also paid various taxes to the Roman government, both within the Empire and in the local areas.[4] It seems logical to assume that when these "God-fearing Jews" became Christians, they were not only loyal to the Roman government, but many continued to take the tithe laws seriously. Numerous trades were practiced by the Jews in the time of Christ.[5] Since the Old Testament laws were based on an agricultural economy where Jews gave a tenth of actual produce and animals, those Jews who now made their income in other vocations figured their three-fold tithe on the basis of currency.

Even in the agricultural society in the Old Testament, God allowed the Jews "freedom in form" in their tithing. Those who lived some distance from Jerusalem could exchange their second tithe in produce and animals for money prior to the trip to Jerusalem, providing they added 20 percent to the value (Lev. 27:31). It seems that the 20 percent was added to maintain the same purchasing power when people left a rural setting to travel to an urban center. As is true even today, it takes more money to live in our cities than it does in farming areas.

In conclusion, when these Jews became Christians, they would have naturally transferred their economic loyalty from Judaism to Christianity. It is no wonder that we see such generous people among these Christians in Jerusalem. They were in the habit of giving regularly and systematically. It was a part of their religious training and commitment. Furthermore, when they understood the grace of God, it appears that they not only calculated tenths, but on occasion generously gave the total profits from the sale of certain properties.

Though the tithe system is never mentioned in the New Testament, it certainly influenced these Jewish Christians. In turn, church history reveals that these Old Testament giving patterns influenced the Gentile community as pagans also became Christians. Though the tithe laws were never perpetuated in Christianity as they were in the Old Testament, they have served as a model to Christians for regular and systematic giving. We cannot ignore this model when we evaluate Paul's instructions to the Corinthians: "On the first day of every week, each one of you should set aside a sum of money in keeping with his income" (1 Cor. 16:1). Today's Christians should consider this Old Testament model when determining their own giving patterns.

GENERAL PRINCIPLES FROM PART 2: THE TEACHINGS OF JESUS CHRIST

THE SEVENTH GENERAL SUPRACULTURAL PRINCIPLE

The truths that Jesus taught about material possessions are normative and supracultural (the gospels).

Some believe that what Jesus Christ taught, particularly in the Sermon on the Mount, is not applicable to the age of the church but, rather, to the messianic kingdom when Jesus will rule on earth. But the principles that emerge from Jesus' teachings are supracultural and verified throughout the rest of the New Testament.

This is not to say that Jesus was not speaking about a future, earthly kingdom for the nation Israel. God *will* fulfill His promises to Israel, which were first stated in the Abrahamic covenant and reaffirmed in the Davidic covenant. At that time, what Jesus taught will indeed be particularly relevant. But these principles were practiced by the New Testament church as well as by the church in the second and third centuries. Therefore, they should be practiced by the church in the twentieth century by believers all over the world.

THE EIGHTH GENERAL SUPRACULTURAL PRINCIPLE

Christians must be careful not to evaluate subjectively what they believe is the Holy Spirit's leading when it comes to giving (John 14:25-26).

This principle does not deny that the Holy Spirit desires to lead every Christian in how he should use his material possessions to further the kingdom of God. However, we must understand and realize that the Spirit's work was special in the apostles' lives. God's plan was first and foremost that these men be led and taught by the Holy Spirit in a supernatural way to reveal to all Christians of all time God's will regarding how to live the Christian life. That revelation is outlined for us in the Holy Scriptures.

It is also true that the Holy Spirit indwells every believer and wishes to lead and guide each of us into the will of God. However, we must not rely on "inner promptings" regarding our use of material blessings without making sure that these perceptions are in harmony with God's revealed truth in the Scriptures. We need to evaluate internal impressions and inner thoughts with the objective principles of the written Word of God.

This is true in all areas of life, but particularly important in the area of giving. Since material things can become so intricately related to "who we are as human beings" as well as to our natural tendencies to be self-oriented, our "inner promptings" may be primarily selfish. It is easy to rationalize in this area of our Christian lives and to deceive ourselves. We need the objective truth of the *Word* of God to evaluate whether or not we are in the *will* of God. This is particularly important in determining *how much* we give, *when* we give, and *where* and *to whom* we give. Most basic, we must evaluate our motives in the light of the Scriptures: the *why* of our giving.

THE NINTH GENERAL SUPRACULTURAL PRINCIPLE

Christian leaders should develop an awareness of the economic structures and practices in every culture in which they are attempting to communicate God's truth in order to utilize these economic experiences to teach people spiritual truths (Jesus' parables).

When we are called upon to teach the Word of God, we can learn a valuable principle of communication from Jesus. Since material needs, worldly possessions, and making a living are so important to all people, we can utilize these concerns and needs as Jesus did in teaching spiritual truth. This was the rationale for the content in more than 25 percent of His parables.

This supracultural principle is particularly applicable to those of us who devote most of our time to the ministry. Since we do not rub shoulders day after day with men and women who live and function in the marketplace, we are often unable to identify with their economic world in practical ways. But, if we do not understand their "language" or their particular set of problems, it is easy to teach the Bible and attempt to make applications in naive and even unrealistic ways.

If these people are going to respect us and listen to our message, we must not only understand their particular world but also be able to touch their world with biblical truth. Furthermore, we must be able to do this with realistic applications, but without compromising the principles of Scripture. Unfortunately, some Christian leaders tend to cater to wealthy people and at the same time avoid the tough ethical issues. At this point, we can learn another valuable lesson from Jesus Christ. He touched the economic world in which He lived without compromise but also without attacking the economic structures that formed the bulwark of His particular society.

THE TENTH GENERAL SUPRACULTURAL PRINCIPLE

Spiritual leaders are responsible to teach believers in the church what God says about material possessions (the apostles' example and personal experience).

Believers must be taught in concrete terms what God says about material possessions. This is not only true of the principles themselves, but Christians must be given specific examples of how to apply these principles. That is why Jesus was so specific in His own teachings. As we continue in our study, we will see that the authors of the New Testament letters also became specific. James included at least eight major "teachings" about material possessions in his letter. The apostle Paul included at least sixteen major teachings on giving in two chapters alone (2 Cor 8-9). These principles must be taught in order for them to be applied.

THE ELEVENTH GENERAL SUPRACULTURAL PRINCIPLE

Economic policies for meeting the physical needs of Christian leaders who devote their full time to ministry must be built upon the totality of God's Word (Mark 6:8-13; Luke 9:1-6).

Some Christians have used the "preaching tour" of the apostles or the seventy-two others who were sent out without provisions as a model for sending out missionaries and Christian workers today. This is unfortunate since these isolated instances were never designed by God to give us specific methodology for supporting Christian workers.

First, as far as we know, Christ only sent these groups out on one occasion without provisions for their material needs. Further, these were not "extended tours." They soon returned to report on what had happened and once again operated under more normal economic conditions.

This observation, however, does not invalidate "the principle of faith" when it comes to trusting God to meet our material needs. It does mean, however, that we must apply the principle of faith in the context of other supracultural principles in the Word of God that relate to meeting material needs. Otherwise, Christian workers who need support can presume upon God and others, and those who are responsible to support Christian leaders can neglect their God-given responsibilities. Both mistakes can lead to incredible hurt, anxiety, insecurity, misunderstanding, and disillusionment.

THE TWELFTH GENERAL SUPRACULTURAL PRINCIPLE

Believers should be motivated to share their material possessions in hopes of receiving present blessings; however, they must realize that the most important perspective in Scripture involves eternal blessings and that their reward may not come in this life (Matt. 19:28-29).

When Jesus told His disciples that it is difficult for wealthy people to "enter the kingdom of heaven"—but not impossible—Peter reminded the Lord that they had "left everything to follow" Him. He then asked, "What then will there be for us?" (Matt. 19:23-27).

Jesus' response to this question is significant. He did not admonish Peter for being concerned about his physical and psychological needs. Rather, He promised Peter and the other apostles that some day ("at the renewal of all things, when the Son of Man sits on his glorious throne"), these men would "sit on twelve thrones, judging the twelve tribes of Israel." Furthermore, Jesus stated that "everyone who has left houses or brothers or sisters or father or mother or children or fields for my sake will receive a hundred times as much and will inherit eternal life" (Matt. 19:28-29).

Though Peter later understood more fully the eternal and spiritual aspects of this promise (1 Pet. 1:3-5), there can be no question that what Jesus said that day became an immediate source of motivation for continuing to serve Christ. Jesus evidently understood that the apostles needed this limited perspective at this moment in their lives. They were just beginning their spiritual journey.

Paul particularly helps us understand more fully the concept of eternal rewards for faithful service. As Christians, we will "all appear before the judgment seat of Christ" (2 Cor. 5:10; see also Rom. 14:10; Eph. 6:8). Paul made clear that when this happens each Christian will "receive what is due him for the things done while in the body, whether good or bad" (2 Cor. 5:10*b*).

The judgment seat of Christ will take place immediately following the coming of Christ for His church (1 Cor. 4:5; 2 Tim. 4:8; Rev. 22:12; cf. Matt. 16:27; Luke 14:14). Paul clearly makes reference to some Christians there whose work will be "burned up" because it is "wood, hay and straw" (1 Cor. 3:12, 15). The work of other Christians will survive because they have built upon the foundation (which is Jesus Christ) with "gold, silver and costly stones" (1 Cor. 3:11, 14).

Though Paul was using figurative language, he was describing a real event. In other words, all true believers will inherit eternal life because of Christ's saving power (1 Cor. 3:15). But some Christians will receive special rewards for being faithful, and other Christians will not receive any rewards because they have not been faithful.

What are these rewards? We are not told specifically, but they are symbolized by crowns. For example, Paul stated in his final letter to Timothy, shortly before he was martyred, "I have fought the good fight, I have finished the race, I have kept the faith. Now there is in store for me the *crown of righteousness*, which the Lord, the righteous Judge, will award to me on that day—and not only to me, but also to all who have longed for his appearing" (2 Tim. 4:7-8). The "crown" Paul was referring to here was not eternal life. That he already had. Rather, it would be a special reward for faithfulness—which is a promise to all believers who are faithful.

Chafer and Walvoord speak to this issue: "The probability is that faithful service on earth will be rewarded by a privileged place of service in heaven. . . . Believers will find their highest fulfillment in loving service for the Savior who loved them and gave Himself for them."[6]

This conclusion introduces us to another important biblical observation. According to the apostle John's revelation, all believers (probably symbolized by the twenty-four elders) will *"lay their crowns before the throne* and say: 'You are worthy, our Lord and God, to receive glory and honor and power, for you created all things, and by your will they were created and have their being'"* (Rev. 4:10-11).

The total biblical perspective, then, is that our basic motivation as Christians in all that we do for Jesus Christ (including how we use our material possessions) should be to accumulate rewards, not to benefit ourselves alone. As we serve Jesus Christ throughout eternity, there will be no mixed motives—as we all have on earth because of our human condition—but our desire will only be to love and honor Jesus Christ for what He has done for us.

In applying the principle stated above—that is, to be motivated to share our material blessings in order to receive blessings in return—we must constantly remind ourselves of this higher and more noble eternal motive. Furthermore, we must be careful not to be enamored with a "prosperity theology" that contradicts this eternal perspective. God has *not* guaranteed that material blessings will come to us in this life if we are faithful givers. If that were true, the apostles would have sat on twelve thrones in Israel before they died. Furthermore, all the believers in Jerusalem would have received one hundred times what they had given up before they passed on to their eternal rewards.

The facts are that those who became Christians in the early years of Christianity were eventually persecuted and driven out of Jerusalem. Some evidently lost what little they had left. And later, those who did have something left were wiped out by a severe famine. Tradition tells us that all but one of the apostles were martyred for the cause of Christ. Only John died a natural death—in exile—but certainly not a wealthy man.

These people *will* be rewarded. It will be a hundredfold for what they have given up for Christ's sake. We too will receive the same rewards in proportion to what we have given up for God's work. However, this promise in all of its fullness will be in God's eternal kingdom, when we inhabit the "new heaven" and the "new earth." And the primary purpose will be to to serve Christ in special ways. It is not wrong to be motivated to be faithful stewards of our material possessions by this wonderful and marvelous eternal reality.

But what about material blessings on this earth? Does God bless His children materially when they are faithful stewards of their material possessions? And what about the many Old Testament promises for material blessings to Israel—*if* they were obedient? Is it wrong for Christians to be motivated by the possibility of material blessings while on this earth?

These questions are important ones and will be explored more in-depth in the chapters to follow. It is particularly important that all Old Testament promises to Israel regarding material prosperity be carefully evaluated by New Testament teachings. The apostle Paul gives us sufficient teaching to make proper judgments and to draw correct conclusions in answering these questions.

THE THIRTEENTH GENERAL SUPRACULTURAL PRINCIPLE

Christians today should apply the principles as taught by Christ and modeled by New Testament Christians, utilizing forms and methods that are relevant in their own particular cultures.

An important factor in biblical Christianity is that God gives us absolutes in the area of principles that are based upon normative "functions" and "teachings" in the Word of God. However, He does not "lock us in" to forms and patterns. This is the genius of Christianity, not only in terms of how the church is structured, but in terms of the way Christians use their material possessions to further God's work. In some instances, Christians may donate actual produce and meat (as the children of God did in the Old Testament) to care for their spiritual leaders, or to meet the needs of others in the church. In other cultures, they may convert these possessions into money, as farmers do in American society. Most American Christians simply give a percentage of their salaries.

God allows even more creativity for those who may be poor. Though Christians must never forget the poor widow who basically put all the money she had in the Temple treasury, the Word of God certainly honors Christians who give their time and skill to further God's kingdom in lieu of actual material possessions. Though this can certainly become a rationalization for Christians who want to keep more of their money for themselves, it is certainly a freedom that God allows for those who are incapable of giving much actual money or possessions. This was certainly true in terms of the apostles, who had already left everything they had to be involved in the work of Christ and were operating without earned income. Though Peter and John had no silver and gold, they gave what they had.

NOTES

1. Jewish authorities differ in their opinion regarding the third tithe. Josephus indicates that it was offered every third year and was in addition to the first and second tithe. Others believe that every third year the second tithe (the festival tithe) was given to the poor and needy in their local communities instead of taking it to Jerusalem.

2. J. D. Douglas, ed., *The New Bible Dictionary* (Grand Rapids: Eerdmans, 1962), p. 840.

3. Joachim Jeremias, *Jerusalem in the Time of Jesus*, trans. F. H. and C. H. Kay (London: SCM, 1969), p. 57.

4. "In Judea direct taxes were collected by imperial officers. A poll tax, or head money, was levied on all persons up to 65 years, women from 12 years, men from 14. Ground tax was one-tenth of all grain, one-fifth of wine and fruit. Custom or tolls on imports and exports and on goods passing through the country were sold to the highest bidders. These men were the hated publicans or tax collectors..., noted for their extortion." Charles F. Pfeiffer, Howard F. Vos, and John Rea, eds., *Wycliffe Bible Encyclopedia* (Chicago: Moody, 1975), 2:1665.

5. There were stone cutters, stone masons, interior craftsmen, maintenance workers, road sweepers, artists, doctors, circumcisers, bath attendants, storekeepers, money changers, and weavers. Some of the more despised trades involved camel drivers, sailors, herdsmen, butchers, dung collectors, copper smelters, tanners, barbers, launderers, and gamblers with dice. See Jeremias, *Jerusalem*, pp. 14-18, 304.

6. Lewis Sperry Chafer and John F. Walvoord, *Major Bible Themes*, rev. ed. (Grand Rapids: Zondervan, 1974), p. 285.

Part 3
Moving Beyond Jerusalem

For approximately five years, the church expanded and grew in Jerusalem. Believers became such a dynamic force that they posed a threat to the Jewish leaders. This led to Stephen's martyrdom and a great outbreak of persecution. From a human perspective, these Christians were practicing their Christianity in incredible ways. Perhaps there has never been a period in Christian history where believers in a particular locality have been such a dynamic witness in the world and have demonstrated such great love and concern for one another as in the church in Jerusalem.

But God's plan for the church was much broader than its influence in Jerusalem. It was to begin there and then to expand to the ends of the earth (Acts 1:7-8). In God's providence, He allowed persecution to become a major factor in causing the church to move beyond Jerusalem in order to carry out the Great Commission. In this section, we will see that process actually taking place. And once again, we will see some singular supracultural principles emerge from these New Testament events that apply to Christians at any moment in history and in every culture of the world.

12. The Church Is Scattered: Acts 8:1-3

13. The Gospel Penetrates Samaria: Acts 8:4-25

14. The Ethiopian Eunuch, Dorcas, and Cornelius: Acts 8:26–11:18

15. The Church in Antioch: Acts 11:19-30

16. Supracultural Principles

12

The Church Is Scattered: Acts 8:1-3

Beginning in Acts 8 Luke records what many Bible interpreters classify as a transitional phase in the history of the church. Stephen's apologetic message before the Sanhedrin and subsequent martyrdom precipitated an all-out attack against the Christians in Jerusalem.

SAUL, THE PERSECUTOR

A young zealous Pharisee named Saul took the lead in organizing and fanning the flames of hatred toward his fellow Jews who acknowledged that Jesus Christ was their personal Savior and Messiah. He stood by when Stephen was stoned, "giving approval to his death" (8:1). Apparently on that very same day "a great persecution broke out against the church in Jerusalem" (8:1b).[1]

Saul's hatred was fanatical. Motivated by his strong personal conviction that Christians were heretics and deserved death according to his view of Old Testament law (see Paul's personal account in Phil. 3:4-6 and Gal. 1:13, 14), he went "from house to house" and "dragged off men and women and put them in prison" (8:3b). During this period of intense persecution, "*all* except the apostles were scattered throughout Judea and Samaria" (8:1c).

There is some question as to how many Jerusalem Christians actually left the city. Luke probably used the word "all" to indicate that *a great number* fled to avoid being thrown in jail. Lange asks, "But did not a single Christian, with the exception of the twelve apostles remain in Jerusalem? It is not probable that such was the fact, particularly when we consider the circumstance that, not long afterwards, chapter 9:26, disciples are found present in Jerusalem, in addition to the apostles, who are themselves not mentioned until the facts stated in v. 27, are introduced."[2]

123

THE GRECIAN JEWS:
"GOD-FEARING JEWS FROM EVERY NATION" (ACTS 2:5; 6:1a)

Several questions arise regarding the great number of Grecian Jews from all over the Roman world who had become believers on the Day of Pentecost and then decided to stay. How long did these people actually remain in Jerusalem? How many were still in Jerusalem when persecution hit full force five years later?

We cannot answer these questions definitively. However, since many of these people had property and vocations in other parts of the world, they probably returned home relatively soon after the Day of Pentecost. After all, Christ did not return to restore the kingdom to Israel as they no doubt had hoped. This would have influenced their thinking greatly since they had to approach this kind of situation pragmatically.

This does *not* mean they became disillusioned with Christianity. Rather, they must have understood more fully that life must go on until Christ *does* return. Consequently, many of these people returned to their native villages and cities and in some instances started churches in their own areas of the world. For example, this is probably how the gospel was first carried back to the city of Rome, resulting in a growing church.[3]

By the time persecution hit Jerusalem, the vast majority of these Jewish (and now Christian) pilgrims had probably returned to their permanent homes. In fact, this likely happened during a relatively short period of time after the beginning of the church in Jerusalem. Those who lived in cities and villages in Judea and even Galilee may have traveled back and forth periodically. This would not be a new experience. As God-fearing Jews they had previously traveled to Jerusalem on a regular basis to worship in the Temple. It would be natural for them to now visit Jerusalem to worship and fellowship with other Jewish Christians, particularly since this is where they first came to understand and believe that Jesus was indeed the Messiah.

THE PERMANENT RESIDENTS IN JERUSALEM:
"THE ARAMAIC-SPEAKING COMMUNITY" (ACTS 6:1b)

The majority of those scattered as a result of the persecution were probably permanent residents of Jerusalem. When the persecution subsided, most of them evidently returned to their homes. This conclusion is substantiated in Luke's record, particularly following his statement in Acts 9:31. After Paul's conversion, "the church throughout Judea, Galilee and Samaria enjoyed a time of peace." Hereafter, there are a number of references to a large and growing contingency of believers in Jerusalem (see Acts 11:1-2; 12:12; 15:22).

Though we cannot be sure of how all of this took place, one thing is clear: we see another part of Christ's earlier statement being fulfilled. Beginning in Acts 8, Christians are forcibly motivated by persecution to leave Jerusalem and "scattered throughout *Judea* and *Samaria.*" And as they traveled beyond Jerusalem, they "preached the word wherever they went" (Acts 8:4).

NOTES

1. The King James Version reads "and at that time. . . . " (8:1*b*). Regarding the time frame involved, Botthard Victor Lechler, *The Acts of the Apostles*, vol. 9 of *Lange's Commentary on the Holy Scriptures*, trans. and ed. Philip Schaff (Grand Rapids: Zondervan, 1968), p. 139, observes,

    The expression [*en ekīnee tee heemera*] is usually understood in the widest sense, as equivalent to: "At that time" (Luther's [and Engl.] version). There is, however, no reason for departing from the literal sense: "On that day." We might rather infer *a priori*, from psychological considerations, as well as from others furnished by the natural sequence of events, that the stoning of Stephen would be immediately followed by an outbreak of fanaticism, of which the Christians generally would be the victims.

2. Lange, *The Acts of the Apostles*, p. 139.

3. Merrill C. Tenney, *New Testament Survey* (Grand Rapids: Eerdmans, 1953), p. 304.

13
The Gospel Penetrates Samaria:
Acts 8:4-25

Though numerous Christians fanned out from Jerusalem and preached the gospel in a number of the cities and locations in Judea, Luke elaborated on what happened in Samaria (see map on p. 128). Philip, one of the seven men appointed to help with the distribution of food to the Grecian widows, "went down to a *city in Samaria*" and proclaimed the message of Jesus Christ (8:5). The city mentioned was probably Samaria itself, a city bearing the same name as the territory.

Samaritans were not true Jews. They were a mixed race, a social situation that had its roots in the dispersion that took place when the Northern Kingdom of Israel was taken captive by the Assyrians in 721 B.C. The Samaritans resulted from Jewish intermarriage with Gentiles. Though they still acknowledged Jehovah God (see 2 Kings 17:24-33), they continued to include aspects of paganism in their worship. Merrill Tenney points out that "the tension between the two peoples was so strong that the Jews who traveled between Judea and Galilee usually avoided Samaria by crossing the Jordan and by using the roads on its Eastern bank."[1]

It was natural for Philip to travel to Samaria. He was a Grecian Jew who lived in Caesarea, a city that bordered the Mediterranean and served as a seaport. It is feasible that Philip often traveled back and forth between Jerusalem and Caesarea, especially after the church was born. Not only was Caesarea inhabited by Samaritans but by pure Gentiles as well. Philip, by living there, had already broken his ties with the Judaism of Judea, and this helps explain why "the Samaritans listened to him, and welcomed his message."[2]

SIMON THE SORCERER'S PROFESSION OF FAITH: ACTS 8:9-25

As a result of Philip's evangelistic preaching and healing ministry, a number of Samaritans responded and believed in Jesus Christ and were

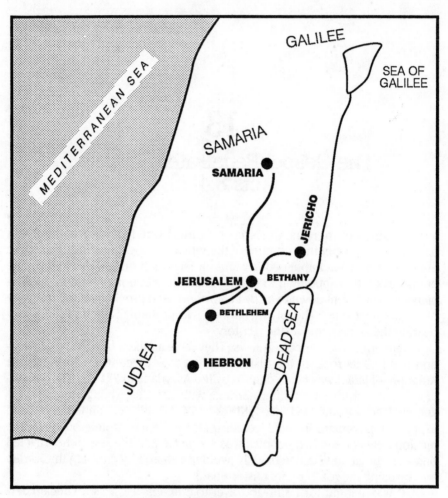

The Scattering of Christians Out of Jerusalem
and Philip's Trip to Samaria

baptized (8:12). Luke then elaborates on a sorcerer named Simon, who had been a popular leader in Samaria before Philip arrived on the scene. A number of his followers shifted their allegiance to Jesus Christ. Intrigued and amazed by the miracles Philip was performing, he too professed belief in Christ and was baptized (8:13).

When the apostles in Jerusalem heard that the people in Samaria had responded to the Word of God, they sent Peter and John to assist Philip. The apostles prayed for these new Christians, and when they "placed their hands on them," these Samaritan believers experienced what had happened on the Day of Pentecost approximately five years earlier (8:15-17): "They received the Holy Spirit" (8:17). We are not told specifically what happened when the Spirit came on them in this special way, but evidently there were—as at Pentecost—some unusual manifestations of power. God was demonstrating that the gospel message was not an exclusive message for "pure Jews." This was necessary because the Jews were so prejudiced against the Samaritans.[3]

Watching these things happen triggered the sorcerer's vain imagination. He wanted the same power as the apostles. Operating from purely selfish motives, he offered Peter and John money for this supernatural ability (8:19). Peter's response was straightforward and uncompromising: "May *your money perish with you*, because you thought you could *buy the gift of God with money*" (8:20).

This problem increasingly penetrated Christianity as the gospel spread throughout the Roman Empire—and beyond—even to this day. Leaders have emerged throughout church history who have used the true message of Jesus Christ to benefit themselves. Wherever they have gone, they have exploited Christians as well as naive people who are sincerely seeking truth. This is probably one reason Luke devoted so much space to explain Simon's actions and Peter's response.

Simon wanted to "cash in" on a good thing. Though people had already identified him as "the great power" (8:10), this kind of *additional* power would give him a position of prominence beyond anything he had ever experienced. His monetary investment—no matter how much Peter demanded—would pay off in terms of more prestige and more income for him personally.

In some respects, Peter's words to Simon remind us of what he said previously to Ananias and Sapphira. The difference is that Ananias and Sapphira were true believers. Simon was not. Perhaps that is why the Holy Spirit did not demand the death sentence for Simon. Peter expressed great concern for this man's spiritual welfare when he told him that his heart was "not right before God." He went on to exhort Simon to "repent of this wickedness and pray to the Lord." If he did, perhaps the Lord would forgive him for having "such a thought" in his heart (8:21-22).

Simon responded by asking Peter to pray for him so that nothing bad would happen to him (8:24). It did not appear to be true repentance. Rather, Simon was basically concerned about himself, not about what he had done to hurt the cause of Jesus Christ. True repentance (a change of heart and mind) leads to godly sorrow for an act of sin. On the other hand, selfish fear is based on what might cause us discomfort and unhappiness.

A Twentieth-century Perspective

In recent times, there have been revelations regarding men in high positions in the Christian world who have been guilty of immorality or misuse of funds. In almost every instance, money, sex, and power have been the basis for their motivations and actions. Rather than expressing godly sorrow for what they have done to the cause of Christ, they have seemingly regretted their actions more so on the basis of how it would inconvenience them and their future rather than because they have hurt Jesus Christ, His ministry, other Christians, and the unbelieving world.

It is not by accident that the first significant story appearing in the book of Acts as the gospel moved outward from Jerusalem involved money, greed, and power. The Holy Spirit wanted all Christians to know that this will be a constant problem within missionary endeavors. There will always be people—both Christians and non-Christians—who will abuse and misuse the true message of Christ to further their own selfish interests.

Notes

1. Merrill C. Tenney, *New Testament Survey* (Grand Rapids: Eerdmans, 1953), p. 242.
2. E. M. Blaiklock, ed., *The Zondervan Pictorial Bible Atlas* (Grand Rapids: Zondervan, 1969), p. 326.
3. Over the years, the religious leaders in Israel developed strong traditions regarding the importance of maintaining a pure race of people in Israel. These beliefs extended to the whole of Israel's life—socially, vocationally, and religiously. The following observations from Jeremias Joachim, *Jerusalem in the Time of Jesus*, trans. F. H. and C. H. Kay (London: SCM, 1969), pp. 297-98, 300-302, helps us understand the extent of this exclusive mentality at the time Jesus Christ was on earth. Jeremias's perspectives also help us comprehend why the apostles were so surprised when Jesus talked with the Samaritan woman. Perhaps more important, what Jeremias observes regarding the Jews' exclusive attitudes toward who can be saved helps us grasp more fully the significance of what happened in Samaria when Peter and John arrived on the scene.

   The value of establishing pure ancestry for a family by means of genealogical traditions and records was not merely theoretical; it assured the family in question of civil rights which full Israelites possessed. The most important privilege was to be known as a family "who [could] marry [their daughters] to priests" (M. Kidd. iv.5; M. Sanh. iv.2; M. Arak. ii.4 *et passim)*. Only women of pure Israelite descent were qualified to bear sons worthy of serving before the altar in Jerusalem. Again we see the intimate connection between social stratification and religion. Only those families who had preserved the divinely ordained purity of the race, which Ezra restored through his reforms, belonged to the true Israel.

But this right of legitimate families to contract marriages with priests was not their only privilege. On the contrary, all the most important honours, positions of trust and public posts were reserved for full Israelites. Proof of pure ancestry was required to become a member of the supreme councils, that is the Sanhedrin and any of the criminal courts of 23 members (M. Sanh. iv.2; cf. b. Sanh. 36b; b. Kidd. 76b) which, according to the Mishnah, had the right of passing capital sentence. A later source (j. Kidd. iv. 5, 65d.49) maintains that this right extended to the clerks and bailiffs of the court too.

Proof of pure ancestry was demanded also for public officers (M. Kidd. iv. 5; J. Kidd, iv. 5, 65d.48)—and here we should think especially of the seven-member local councils of the Jewish communities—and trustworthy men whom the community appointed an almoners (M. Kidd. iv.5; j. Kidd. iv.5, 65b.48f.; b. Pes. 49b Bar.). In every case, genealogies were examined before appointment. . . .

So we see that very important civil privileges were reserved for full Israelites; but we have not yet indicated the most important advantage which these families had. This was in the religious sphere. Thanks to their pure origin, they could share in the merits of their forefathers, which were hereditary and theirs by proxy in two senses. First, the common teaching said that the whole of Israel participated in the merits of the patriarchs, of Abraham in particular. These merits made prayers acceptable, protected from danger, helped in war, were a substitute for each man's lack of merit, expiated sins, appeased the wrath of God and warded off his punishment, saved from *Gehinnom* and assured a share in God's eternal kingdom. But, in addition, each Israelite had a share in the merits and intercession of his own particular ancestors if there were righteous men among them; and conversely if he chose a wife who was not of equal purity of birth, vengeance would come on his children (b. Kidd. 70a). . . .

But even now we have not said the last word. The prophet Elijah was to be the forerunner of the Messiah, to set the community in order, to restore the original purity of Israel, so that the people were ready both inwardly and outwardly for final salvation. The main task in this reestablishment of Israel was "to restore the tribes of Jacob" (Ecclus. 48.10), i.e. according to rabbinic exegesis, to "declare impure," or "pure" to "remove" or "bring nigh" the families who had wrongly been declared legitimate or illegitimate. Only families of pure Israelite descent could be assured of a share in the messianic salvation, for only they were assisted by the "merit of their legitimate ancestry." Here we have the most profound reason for the behaviour of these pure Israelite families—why they watched so carefully over the maintenance of racial purity and examined the genealogies of their future sons- and daughters-in-law before marriage (b. Kidd. 71b). For on this question of racial purity hung not only the social position of their descendants, but indeed their final assurance of salvation, their share in the future redemption of Israel.

14

The Ethiopian Eunuch, Dorcas, and Cornelius: Acts 8:26–11:18

Luke recorded three additional encounters as the gospel spread outward from Jerusalem. The first involved Philip's experience with the Ethiopian eunuch. The next two involved the apostle Peter as he first met Dorcas in Joppa and later traveled to Caesarea to witness the conversion of Cornelius and his household.

Philip's Experience with the Ethiopian Eunuch: Acts 8:26-40

This event is just as significant as Philip's encounter with Simon the sorcerer in Samaria. The Lord had another special assignment for him on a desert road that led from Jerusalem to Gaza. He spoke to Philip quite specifically. He instructed him to leave Samaria and head south toward Gaza (see map on p. 134) to meet the Ethiopian eunuch, who was an "important official in charge of *all the treasury of Candace*, queen of the Ethiopians" (8:27). Several things were significant about this encounter.

First, this man was from an African nation. Philip's missionary tour illustrates graphically his willingness to be a witness "in Jerusalem, and in all Judea and Samaria," but also *"to the ends of the earth"* (Acts 1:8). Second, this man was a *black* Gentile. The message of Christianity knows no boundaries in terms of ethnic background and race.

Third, the Ethiopian was interested in Judaism, for Luke recorded that he "had gone to Jerusalem to worship" (8:27*b*). Fourth, though interested in the Old Testament, he did not understand the gospel of Jesus Christ (8:30-35).

Fifth, when Philip explained who Jesus Christ really was from Isaiah's prophetic statements (8:32-33; cf. Isa. 53:7-8), the man responded in repentance and faith and asked to be baptized (8:36-38). Sixth, and most impor-

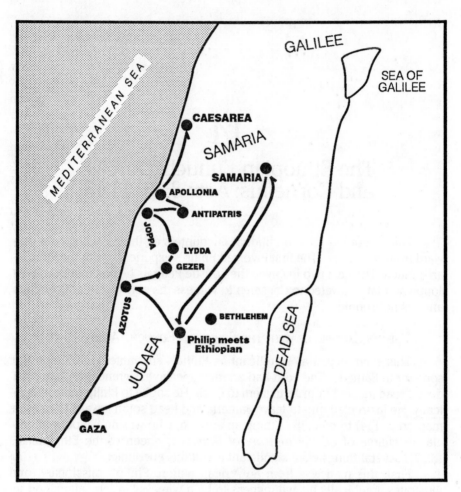

Philip's Missionary Journey

tant for this study, this man was a *prominent* and *wealthy* individual. He was in charge of all the wealth of the queen of Ethiopia.

WHY THIS STORY?

Why did the Holy Spirit inspire Luke to record this event? As we have noted, there are several reasons. But more specifically in terms of this study on material possessions, God wants us to know that wealthy people can and do respond to the gospel. This story adds balance to Christ's encounter with the rich young ruler. When this man—whose wealth was "great"— walked away sorrowfully, Jesus turned to His disciples and said, "How hard it is for a rich man to enter the kingdom of God" (Luke 18:24). When the disciples at that moment asked Jesus, "Who then can be saved?" Jesus made clear that it *was* possible.

Though all people tend to love their material possessions and to put them ahead of God, a rich person *can* respond to the gospel of Jesus Christ (Luke 18:25). The Ethiopian eunuch demonstrates this truth. It is not an accident that Luke, under the inspiration of the Holy Spirit, chose this event to balance the response of the rich young ruler, a story he had earlier recorded in his "former book" (Acts 1:1).

A FOOTNOTE ON PHILIP

Philip does not appear again in the book of Acts until chapter 21. Following his encounter with the Ethiopian eunuch, he "appeared at Azotus," supernaturally transported to this city (see map on p. 134). He then "traveled about, preaching the gospel in all the towns until he reached Caesarea" (8:40)—Philip's own "hometown." Following his evangelistic tour, he may have settled into a more normal schedule, giving attention to his responsibilities as a resident of that city and as a husband and a father to his children. He would have certainly continued to be very active in ministering to the church in Caesarea, as well as making periodic trips to Jerusalem and to other parts of the New Testament world.

When we meet Philip again, years have passed. Paul was on his way to Jerusalem following his major missionary journeys. When he stopped off in Caesarea, he stayed in Philip's home (Acts 22:8). Like other New Testament missionaries, Philip evidently maintained his home in his original place of residence, even though he traveled for significant periods of time. Many of these traveling evangelists took their wives with them on these journeys, as indicated by Paul in his letter to the Corinthians (1 Cor. 9:3-6).

PETER'S EXPERIENCE WITH DORCAS: ACTS 9:32-43

Sometime after Paul's amazing conversion to Christ on the road to Damascus (Acts 9:1-30), the persecution against Christians subsided, and "the church throughout Judea, Galilee and Samaria enjoyed a time of peace." Believers matured spiritually and "grew in numbers, living in the fear of the Lord" (Acts 9:31).

There is no way to pinpoint how long it actually took for this time of intense persecution to end. It probably began to subside rather soon after Paul's conversion. We can say for sure, however, that the "time of peace" (Acts 9:31) must have come within three years. It was during this time period that Paul was in Arabia being prepared by the Lord for his missionary task (see Gal. 1:13-24).

At this point in his narrative, Luke once again focused on the apostle Peter, who continued to travel "about the country" (9:38). While he was visiting the Christians in Lydda, two men came from Joppa, another well-known seaport city located about thirty miles from Jerusalem (see map on p. 138). They urged Peter to come to their city to minister in a special way because of the death of a very prominent Christian woman named Tabitha, which "when translated, is Dorcas" (9:36). Peter responded to their request and was used by God to work a dramatic miracle: he raised Dorcas from the dead (9:40-41).

The name Tabitha is uniquely related to this woman's character. It means gazelle, an animal "distinguished for its slender and beautiful form, its graceful movements and its soft but brilliant eyes." Lange further comments that this name was "frequently introduced by the Hebrews and other oriental nations as an image of female loveliness, and the name was often employed as a proper name, in the case of females."[1]

It is conceivable that Tabitha was given this name after she became a Christian to illustrate that she was a very giving and caring person—which, of course, is a reflection of true beauty (1 Pet. 3:3-4). If her name was changed to conform to her new life-style, her experience would have been similar to Barnabas's, whose name was changed by the apostles to indicate that he was a special encourager (4:36).

WHY THIS STORY?

The Holy Spirit inspired Luke to record this story for a very special purpose. Dorcas was a Christian woman "who was *always doing good* and *helping the poor*" (9:36). Although no evidence indicates that she was wealthy, she used her special talents and what resources she had to make "robes and other clothing" for women who had greater needs than herself (9:39). Evidently the primary recipients of her gifts were poor widows, for when Peter arrived, a number of these women stood around the apostle and showed him the clothes that Dorcas had made for them (9:36b). Note two important things.

First, Dorcas was a deeply loved person in the church in Joppa, so much so that the believers there exerted a great deal of effort to get Peter to come to their city. Obviously this "appreciation" was directly related to Dorcas's incredible example of benevolence and love. She was a very unselfish woman.

Second, Dorcas's ministry to the poor evidently involved not only believers but unbelievers. After Peter had raised Dorcas from the dead, "he called *the believers* and *the widows* and presented them to her alive" (9:41). Here Luke distinguished between those who were Christians and those who were widows. No doubt there were "believing widows" present, but there must have been "unbelieving widows" present as well. If so, Dorcas is a shining example of a woman who carried out Paul's injunction when he later wrote his letter to the Galatians: "Therefore, as we have opportunity, let us do good *to all people*, especially to those who belong to the family of believers" (Gal. 6:10).

To this point in our study, the primary focus for benevolence and giving has been within the local family of believers. But the story of Dorcas demonstrates that our concerns, particularly for the poor, should also include those who do not know Christ but who have legitimate physical needs.

THE ONGOING MIRACLE OF UNSELFISH CARING

Dorcas's miraculous resurrection impacted the whole city of Joppa. Consequently, "many people believed in the Lord," which probably included many of the unconverted widows to whom Dorcas had a special ministry. Obviously the miracle itself became the primary means whereby people were convinced that Jesus was indeed the living Christ, the Savior of the world (John 20:30-31; Heb. 2:2-4).

On the other hand, we cannot deny the impact of the less dramatic miracle that laid the foundation for the greater miracle. Dorcas was a transformed person who demonstrated the love of Jesus Christ to many people by "always doing good and helping the poor" (9:36). Her benevolent and unselfish life-style was, in some respects, a *more important* miracle. People tend to forget the one-time dramatic events—no matter how miraculous. But they cannot forget the ongoing life-style of a loving, caring Christian.

Peter's Experience with Cornelius: Acts 10:1-48

We come now to what may be classified as one of the most significant encounters recorded in the book of Acts. It is also fitting that this event is the last in what we have called a transitional phase in Luke's historic record. In many respects what happened changed the entire focus of world evangelism.

After his experience with Dorcas, Peter stayed on "in Joppa for some time with a tanner named Simon" (9:43). One day about noon, Peter went

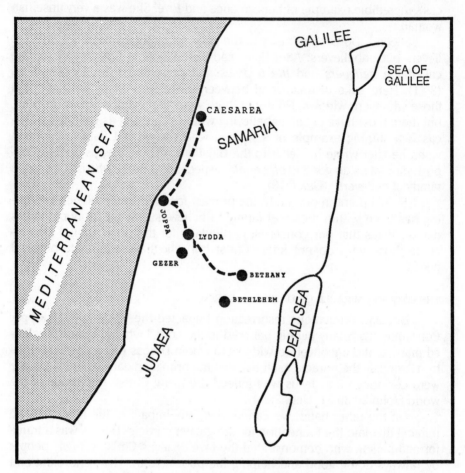

Peter's Journey to Joppa and to Caesarea

up on Simon's housetop to pray. While praying, "he became hungry and wanted something to eat, and while the meal was being prepared, he fell into a trance" (10:10).

This was an unusual experience for Peter. In his vision, he saw a large sheet come down from heaven. In the sheet were all kinds of animals. Without distinguishing between the animals as ceremonially clean or unclean according to Jewish law, a voice called out to Peter telling him to "kill and eat" (10:13).

Peter's response was negative. "'Surely not, Lord! I have never eaten anything impure or unclean'" (10:14).

After offering Peter the opportunity to kill and eat three times, "the sheet" in Peter's vision "was taken back to heaven" (10:16). Needless to say, this was a very troubling experience for Peter. While he was reflecting on what had happened, another event designed by God coincided with Peter's housetop experience.

SOME BACKGROUND ON CORNELIUS

Approximately thirty-five miles away in the city of Caesarea, a Gentile named Cornelius had an unusual experience the day prior to Peter's vision. Cornelius was an official in the Roman army. Though no evidence exists that he and his family were proselytes to Judaism in the full sense,[2] his household was "devout" and "God-fearing" (10:2). Furthermore, Cornelius was very benevolent and also concerned about communion with God. We read that "he *gave generously* to those in need and *prayed to God* regularly" (10:2*b*).

Cornelius, whether he realized it or not, was a fellow-soldier of a centurion in Capernaum who several years before had a direct but unusual encounter with Jesus Christ. This centurion had a servant who was deathly ill. Because the centurion had developed a close relationship with the Jews, having built them a synagogue from his own resources, he persuaded several Jewish elders to ask Jesus to heal his servant. The elders were delighted to approach Jesus for their friend. Luke recorded that "when they came to Jesus, they pleaded earnestly with him, 'This man deserves to have you do this, because he *loves our nation* and has *built our synagogue*'" (Luke 7:4-5).

Both Cornelius in Caesarea and the centurion in Capernaum are examples of men who were not satisfied with the pagan religions prevalent in the Roman Empire. They admired the Jews' religious experience and their commitment to the God of Abraham, Isaac, and Jacob.

In some respects, Gentiles like Cornelius had more rapport with God than His own chosen people. In fact, when Jesus met the friends of the centurion from Capernaum and heard him express, through them, his humble respect and childlike trust, Jesus was "amazed at him." He said, "I tell you, I have not found such great faith even *in Israel*" (Luke 7:9). In a similar fashion, God honored Cornelius's heart attitudes and his desire to please Him. The Lord responded in a special way to this man's prayers and his willingness to share his material possessions with those in need. Consequently, God communicated directly with Cornelius. In a vision, "an angel of God" appeared to him and called him by name.

Amazed, he asked, "What is it, Lord?"

The angel responded and told Cornelius that his *"prayers and gifts to the poor"* had "come up as a memorial offering before God" (10:4). He then instructed Cornelius to send for Peter in Joppa.

THE FIRST GENTILE CHURCH

Cornelius responded immediately to the heavenly messenger's instruction and sent three men to Joppa. When they arrived, God sovereignly arranged for them to meet Peter at the very moment he was descending from Simon's rooftop, still thinking about his own vision and what it meant. When the men explained their mission, God had already prepared Peter's heart to respond. He traveled to Caesarea to meet Cornelius face-to-face.

When Peter arrived, he entered Cornelius's home. He informed Cornelius that he was violating Jewish laws by visiting him. But he also explained his own vision from God, which now had become clearer in meaning (10:28). It should be noted that previously Peter did not seem to have a problem of conscience when he stayed in the house of Simon the tanner, who engaged in one of the despised trades among the Jews. Though it was not considered a dishonorable vocation, it certainly was considered repugnant.

Jeremias comments that dung collectors and tanners worked together "since the former collected the dung needed for fulling and tanning." In fact, these two professions were so repugnant that the religious leaders in Israel designed laws to grant women "legitimate" divorces who were married to these men. According to Jeremias,

> If anyone engaged in one of the three trades in this list [dung-collector, copper smelter, and tanner], his wife had the right to claim divorce before the court, and to be paid the sum of money which had been assured her in the marriage contract in case the marriage was dissolved or her husband died (T. Ket. vii.II, 270). She could even claim a divorce if she knew when she married her husband that he was engaged in one of the three trades in question, and had married him on condition that he could continue in his trade.[3]

Perhaps in this instance Peter was rather smug about what he considered a lack of prejudice. No priest in Israel would have lowered himself in this way. But Peter was totally unaware of how prejudiced he was against Gentiles—even rich men like Cornelius—who was, in some respects, more God-fearing than the Jews themselves. God was in the process of revealing to this great leader that He is no respecter of persons. Jesus died for the sins of the whole world, no matter what their ethnic, social, and economic position in life. Peter was about to learn that lesson.

While Peter was explaining the message of Christ to Cornelius and his household, the Holy Spirit came on those who were listening, just as He had done several years before on the Day of Pentecost. They spoke in various languages and praised God just as the apostles themselves had done as a result of this special baptism of the Spirit (Acts 11:16). This was the third of this kind of event recorded by Luke: the first was when the *Jewish* church was born (Acts 2:1-4); the second was when the *Samaritan* church was born (Acts 8:14-17); the third was when the first *Gentile* church[4] was born (Acts 10:44-46).

Peter faced an immediate challenge. Word soon spread to Jerusalem "that the Gentiles had also received the word of God" (Acts 11:1). Predictably, the "circumcised believers" criticized Peter and accused him of violating Jewish law by entering the home of men who were not circumcised (Acts 11:3). Consequently, Peter explained in full detail what had happened to both him and Cornelius (Acts 11:4-17). When the Christians in Jerusalem heard this explanation, "they had no further objections and praised God saying, 'So then, God has even granted the Gentiles repentance unto life'" (Acts 11:18).

SOME IMPORTANT OBSERVATIONS

Note several things about this remarkable story. First, Cornelius lived in a predominately Gentile city that was occupied by some of the most prominent leaders in the Roman world. Herod the Great built the city and named it after Caesar Augustus. He intended for Caesarea to be the "center of the Roman provincial government in Judea. It served as a showpiece for Roman culture. It contained an enormous amphitheater and a huge temple, dedicated to Caesar and Rome, with huge statues of the emperor."[5]

Pilate, the Roman governor who sentenced Christ to death, also lived in Caesarea. Later, the apostle Paul stood trial before Felix in Caesarea (Acts 23:23-35). It was there that he also made his defense before Porcius Festus and Agrippa (Acts 25:11). Caesarea was no ordinary city in God's scheme of things. It was not by accident that Peter was called to this city to preach the gospel to Cornelius where he once again observed that singular experience identified by Jesus Christ as "the baptism of the Holy Spirit." Seeing Cornelius and his whole household respond to the gospel became a unique bridge that led other New Testament Christians to take another giant step in fulfilling what Christ said they should do in Acts 8:1—to be witnesses "to the ends of the earth."

Second, Cornelius was another rich and influential man. Again, we see the Holy Spirit opening the heart of a very important person to the message of Christ. Men like him, who can build a synagogue with their own private resources (as did the centurion in Capernaum) and who also have the authority to do so in an empire dominated by paganism, were indeed influential. What they could do to help spread the gospel of Christ to the ends of the earth was phenomenal.

Third, God's heart was warmly drawn to Cornelius. He did not know Christ personally, but he prayed and used his material possessions in unselfish ways. Evidently, how a person who is seeking to know God views and uses his material possessions is an important factor in causing God to reach out to him or her. More specifically Cornelius, as a Gentile, was concerned about God's chosen people, the Jews. They were beneficiaries of his benevolence. This is not surprising since God blesses those who bless His people but curses those who mistreat them. This is not only a statement from Scripture but a fact of history (Gen. 12:3).

NOTES

1. John Peter Lange, *The Gospel According to Matthew*, vol. 8 of *Lange's Commentary on the Holy Scriptures*, trans. and ed. Philip Schaff (Grand Rapids: Zondervan, 1969), p. 186.

2. Proselytes or converts to Judaism were of two kinds: "partial adherence" and "full adherence." The essential difference between the two groups was circumcision. Louis Goldberg notes that "Jewish authorities were content not to discriminate against the partial adherent, and the latter was permitted to worship along with the other Jewish people in the synagogue." Charles F. Pfeiffer, Howard F. Vos, and John Rea, eds., *Wycliffe Bible Encyclopedia* (Chicago: Moody, 1975), 2:1418. There are a number of references in the New Testament to both groups of people (Luke 7:2-5; Acts 2:10-11; 8:31; 13:16, 26; 16:14; 17:4, 17; 18:7).

3. Joachim Jeremias, *Jerusalem in the Time of Jesus,* trans. F. H. and C. H. Kay (London: SCM, 1969), p. 308.

4. Some Bible interpreters teach that the church in Antioch was the first Gentile church. In some respects, this is true. However, the concept of the "church" in the New Testament simply involves a group of people who have a special relationship together in Jesus Christ. In that sense, a household that came to Christ—as Cornelius's did—constitutes a church. I frequently refer to a family unit that is Christian as the "church in miniature." I believe this can be substantiated from a careful study of the New Testament; see Gene A. Getz, *The Measure of a Family* (Ventura: Regal, 1976), chap. 1, "The Family—The Church in Miniature."

5. Charles F. Pfeiffer and Howard F. Vos, *The Wycliffe Historical Geography of Bible Lands* (Chicago: Moody, 1968), pp. 103-4.

15

The Church in Antioch: Acts 11:19-30

Following the transitional period beginning in Acts 8:1, Luke picks up the historical story line in 11:19.[1]

> Now those *who had been scattered* by the persecution in connection with Stephen traveled as far as Phoenicia, Cyprus and Antioch, telling the message only to the Jews. Some of them, however, men from Cyprus and Cyrene, *went to Antioch* and began to speak to Greeks also, telling them the good news about the Lord Jesus. (11:19-20)

THE CHURCH IS FOUNDED

Cornelius and his household's conversion set the stage for what happened in Antioch. Peter responded to the Holy Spirit's leading to preach to Gentiles as well as to Jews. And so did a number of Grecian Jews "from Cyprus and Cyrene." We read that "the Lord's hand was with them, and *a great number of people believed* and turned to the Lord" (11:21; see map on p. 144). When the believers in Jerusalem heard about the response to the gospel in Antioch, they chose Barnabas as their "apostolic representative" and sent him to evaluate what was happening.

When Barnabas arrived, there was no question in his mind that what was taking place was the work of the Holy Spirit (11:23). At some point after Barnabas arrived in Antioch, he recognized that he needed help. Knowing that his friend Paul was in Tarsus, he went to look for him and encouraged him to minister with him in the Antiochian church.[2]

Barnabas and Paul ministered together in Antioch "for a whole year." More and more people came to Christ, the church matured, and it was there that "the disciples were first called Christians" (11:26).[3]

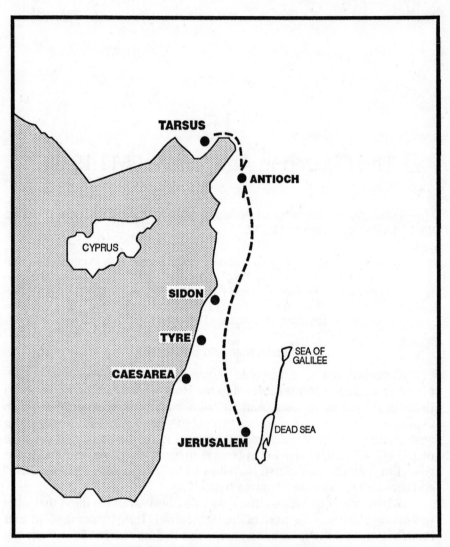

Founding of the Church in Antioch

THE BELIEVERS IN ANTIOCH RESPOND TO HUMAN NEED

The most significant event that took place in the early history of the church in Antioch involves the famine described in the latter part of Acts 11. Agabus, a prophet who came to Antioch from Jerusalem, stood up one day and prophesied "that a severe famine would spread over the entire Roman world." The effects of this famine were going to be particularly felt in Judea. Consequently, Luke recorded that the Christians in Antioch, "each *according to his ability*, decided to provide help" for their fellow believers by gathering together a special gift of money (11:29). Barnabas and Paul were given a special assignment to deliver this gift to the elders in the various churches in Judea.

We are not sure of all the specific details surrounding this famine. However, Harold Hoehner gives some very helpful information that sheds light on Luke's account. Josephus states that "when Helena, the queen of Adiabene, visited Jerusalem she noticed the great famine in Judea." Consequently, "she sent agents to Cyprus to purchase dried figs and to Egypt to buy grain to relieve the Jews of their dilemma."[4] However, this provision did not help the Christians since those Jews who had "defected" to Christianity "were outside the economic commonwealth of Judaism."[5]

The problem, then, was not lack of food, but insufficient money to buy food at inflated prices because of scarcity.[6] This explains why the Christians in Antioch sent money and not food to Judea. As Hoehner states, "It is probable that the Jerusalem Christians used this money to buy food from the Jews who had received help from Helena."[7]

This background information is helpful in understanding Luke's succinct account in the book of Acts. The biblical record simply informs us that the famine happened and that Christians in the church in Antioch responded out of love and concern. This was their opportunity to express in a tangible way, not only their concern for the physical welfare of their fellow Christians, but their appreciation to these believers for having brought the gospel message to Antioch and having sent Barnabas to encourage them in their new faith.

Notice that *each* Christian in Antioch gave to meet this need "according to his ability." As in all the other churches, there were a variety of economic levels. Those who could give a lot, gave a lot. Those who could not give as much, gave what they could. It appears, however, that everyone was involved in some way.

NOTES

1. A definite grammatical connection exists between Luke's statements in Acts 8:1, 4 and in Acts 11:19. Earlier he had reported that the Christians in Jerusalem "*were scattered* throughout Judea and Samaria" (Acts 8:1), and wherever they went, they "preached the word" (Acts 8:4). However, if this transitional section (Acts 8:1–11:18) were omitted in Luke's account, some important content would be omitted as well, such as Paul's and Cornelius's conversions, which must be understood to further understand the rest of Luke's account. The point is that, grammatically and structurally, there is direct and immediate continuity between the scattering of the church "throughout Judea and Samaria" (Acts 8:1, 4) and those who continued to travel even farther from Jerusalem (Acts 11:19) to begin the process of going to "the ends of the earth" (Acts 1:8).

2. Paul was still identified by his Hebrew name *Saul*. However, the name *Paul* will be used throughout this volume for ease in communication even when *Saul* is used in the biblical text.

3. Merrill C. Tenney, *New Testament Survey* (Grand Rapids: Eerdmans, 1953), p. 252, adds the following helpful information regarding the time elements involved regarding the church in Antioch:

    The year of founding the church in Antioch is not stated. Apparently it took place not long after the death of Stephen, probably between A.D. 33 and A.D. 40. Some time would be required for the church to attain sufficient importance in size and in character to bring it to the attention of the church in Jerusalem (11:22). They delegated Barnabas to visit Antioch, where he labored for an indeterminate period, and then went to Tarsus to ask Paul to become his assistant (11:22-26). They labored together for at least a year after that (11:26) before Agabus prophesied the famine which came to pass "in the days of Claudius" (11:28). The implication of the text is that the prophecy was given before the accession of Claudius in A.D. 41, and that the famine came later. Another chronological note is afforded by the reference to Herod Agrippa I (12:1) who died in A.D. 44. Probably the work in Antioch began around A.D. 33 to 35. If the "famine relief" took place about A.D. 44, Barnabas may have begun his connections with Antioch about A.D. 41, which would mean that Paul first came on the scene in A.D. 42.

4. Harold Hoehner, *The Chronology of the Apostolic Age* (diss. presented to the faculty of the graduate school of Dallas Theological Seminary, 1965), p. 46.

5. Ibid., p. 48.

6. Kenneth Gapp, "The Universal Famine Under Claudius," *Harvard Theological Review* 28 (October 1935): 261-62, adds this helpful insight:

    Famine, then, did not consist in an absolute lack of food in the areas afflicted with scarcity. It centered rather in the current price of grain, and was caused by all the factors which raised the price of food. Among these causes primary importance must be given to local failures of the harvest, to the cost of importing grain from other regions, and especially to the speculation in grain and the hoarding which attended the delays in importing additional supplies of food. A universal famine, therefore, need not be explained by a general failure of harvest. It is rather to be found in a general increase in the price of food, and in the universal inability of the poor to purchase food at the current price.

16

Supracultural Principles

The activities of the church in Jerusalem during its first five years have yielded a number of supracultural principles. Just so, when the church was scattered out of Jerusalem, we see more principles emerging, particularly as God was at work in the lives of certain key individuals who came to Christ.

THE FIRST SUPRACULTURAL PRINCIPLE

God sometimes allows difficulties and discomforts to come into Christians' experiences in order to refocus their priorities on eternal values (Acts 8:1-3).

The Christians in Jerusalem constituted a model church in terms of applying the teachings of Jesus Christ regarding the use of material possessions. However, they were also operating with a limited theological perspective that caused them to be satisfied with their present environment and the blessings of God in their lives. Even the apostles themselves lost clear focus on what Jesus taught them—that is, to be His witnesses, *first* "in Jerusalem," *then* "in all Judea and Samaria and to the ends of the earth" (Acts 1:8). Consequently, God allowed persecution to force the Christians out of Jerusalem so they would take the Lord's commission seriously to "make disciples of all nations" (Matt. 28:19).

PAUL'S PERSPECTIVE

This God-ordained process is verified at other moments in New Testament history. Years later, the apostle Paul, who in his unsaved state was the primary persecutor in Jerusalem, viewed his own suffering from this divine perspective. Writing to the Philippians from a Roman prison, he explained: "Now I want you to know, brothers, that what has happened to me has really served *to advance the gospel.* As a result," he continued, "it has become clear throughout the whole palace guard and to everyone else that I am in chains for Christ" (Phil. 1:12-13).

PETER'S PERSPECTIVE

A couple of years later, the apostle Peter wrote to the suffering church "scattered throughout Pontus, Galatia, Cappadocia, Asia and Bithynia" (1 Pet. 1:1). He encouraged them to rejoice, even though they were suffering "grief and all kinds of trials. These have come," Peter explained, "so that your faith—of greater worth than gold which perishes even though refined by fire—may be proved genuine and may result in praise, glory and honor when Jesus Christ is revealed" (1 Peter 1:6-7).

Don't misunderstand. God does not purposely set out to hurt His children. Neither is He to blame for sinful actions such as the behavior of men like Emperor Nero who was probably responsible for Paul's death and perhaps Peter's as well. No one can blame God for this evil man's actions. He operated with his own volition. But the fact remains that God is sovereign, and He can even use evil to achieve good things.

JOSEPH'S PERSPECTIVE

This theological reality was dramatically illustrated when Joseph's brothers sold him mercilessly to a group of Midianite merchants, who, in turn, sold him to Potiphar, one of Pharaoh's officials in Egypt (Gen. 37:25-36). After suffering incredible false accusations, imprisonment, heartache, and persecution for years on end, Joseph eventually became prime minister of Egypt. Much later, he interfaced with his brothers, forgave them, and then arranged to bring his whole family to Egypt so they would survive the famine that threatened their very lives.

After their father Jacob died, Joseph's brothers became extremely frightened of what he might do. They were afraid of retaliation for what they had done years earlier. When Joseph heard about their fears, he responded, "Don't be afraid. Am I in the place of God? *You intended to harm me, but God intended it for good* to accomplish what is now being done, the saving of many lives" (Gen. 50:19-20).

OUR PERSPECTIVE

As human beings, we cannot comprehend God's ways in matters like this. We only know that at times He allows difficulties and discomforts to come into our lives in order to refocus our hearts and minds on eternal values. Sometimes this discomfort involves our material possessions. Though we may not understand what is happening and why, we do "know that *in all things* God works for the good of those who love him, who have been called according to his purpose" (Rom. 8:28).

How true this was among the believers in Jerusalem. As a result of the persecution they experienced, we ourselves have had the opportunity to hear about Jesus Christ and to respond to the gospel message. From a human perspective, had they stayed in Jerusalem, Christianity would have remained a small "sect" and perhaps would have died out altogether. But because the Jerusalem Christians were scattered, the gospel has literally spread around the world.

THE SECOND SUPRACULTURAL PRINCIPLE

Wherever Christianity is active, some people will attempt to use the Christian message to benefit themselves (Acts 8:9-25).

This principle is verified again and again throughout the New Testament. As soon as the church of Jesus Christ was born, it was viewed as "big business" by men and women with selfish intentions. Simon the sorcerer was the first person mentioned who tried to "buy" the power of the Holy Spirit in order to enhance his own political and economic situation.

Whenever God outlines a positive principle such as financially supporting Christian leaders (1 Tim. 5:17), Satan attempts to motivate people to exploit the situation and misuse and abuse that particular principle. For example, when Paul wrote to Titus, whom he left in Crete to establish the churches, he already had to warn this young man against "many rebellious people" who were "ruining whole households by teaching things they ought not to teach—and that *for the sake of dishonest gain*" (Titus 1:11).

This kind of exploitation and abuse is one of the reasons Paul determined at times to preach the gospel free of charge to people who might have misinterpreted his motives. That is why he insisted that any person who was appointed as a spiritual leader in the church should not be "a lover of money" (1 Tim. 3:3) or an individual who was guilty of "pursuing dishonest gain" (1 Tim. 3:8; Titus 1:7). Peter affirmed the same concern when he exhorted the elders in various churches to "be shepherds of God's flock . . . *not greedy for money*, but eager to serve" (1 Pet. 5:2).

Christianity and money are interrelated and inseparable entities. Consequently, wherever Christianity is active, some will attempt to use the Christian message to benefit themselves. But since we know this will happen, believers must be careful not to falsely judge and penalize honest Christian leaders because of those who are dishonest and who take advantage of people. If we apply *all* of the principles God has outlined for us in the area of using our material possessions, we will be able to face these problems and solve them. We will be discerning and, at the same time, be able to avoid either/or reactions.

The Third Supracultural Principle

God is sometimes more patient with uninformed people who are material-istic than He is with people who have more direct exposure to the truth (Acts 8:9-25).

This principle relates to the way God dealt with Simon the sorcerer versus the way He dealt with Ananias and Sapphira. Peter exhorted Simon to repent. However, he pronounced the judgment of death on the Jerusalem couple. Why was God's approach different in these two situations? It would appear that Simon's desire to exploit God's gift of the Spirit with money to further his own prestigious position was as flagrant, if not more so, than Ananias's and Sapphira's desire to gain prestige and prominence by lying about their gift of money for the work of the church. The difference seems to be related to the *amount of knowledge* they had regarding the will of God.[1]

This principle is verified in other situations in Scripture. For example, when God sent Jonah to preach to the pagan Ninevites, they responded in repentance. And, "when God saw what they did and how they turned from their evil ways, he had compassion and did not bring upon them the destruction he had threatened" (Jonah 3:10).

When Jonah saw that God was responding in mercy, he "was greatly displeased and became angry" (Jonah 4:1). God rebuked Jonah's reaction, demonstrating His compassion on those who are ignorant: "But Nineveh has more than a hundred and twenty thousand people *who cannot tell their right hand from their left*, and many cattle as well. Should I not be concerned about that great city?" (Jonah 4:11).

The more we know about God's will, the more accountable we are to live up to the light we have. It should not surprise us if God disciplines us in ways He may not discipline others who do not have the same knowledge. This principle applies to Christians who not only have more knowledge of His will than others but to those who have the *opportunity* to know more about His will yet purposely refuse to take advantage of those opportunities (Heb. 10:25).

This principle is illustrated in one of Jesus' parables. In his absence, a certain master entrusted his servants with a variety of responsibilities. When he returned to his house, he expected them to be busy doing what he had ordered them to do. Jesus applied this to Himself: "From everyone who has been given much, much will be demanded; and from the one who has been entrusted with much, much more will be asked" (Luke 12:48b).

The apostle Paul took this teaching seriously in his own life. Writing to the Corinthians, he said, "Now it is required that those who have been given a trust must prove faithful" (1 Cor. 4:2). As Christians, we have "been given a trust." The challenge we face is that we too "must prove faithful." The more we know, the more responsible we are. The more opportunities we have to learn the will of God, the more we are accountable for the way we use those opportunities. This certainly applies to what the Bible teaches regarding our material possessions.

THE FOURTH SUPRACULTURAL PRINCIPLE

Though it is often difficult for wealthy people to respond to the gospel, it is God's will that we reach these people, for they can influence great segments of humanity with both their social position and their material resources (Acts 8:26-40).

It is not accidental that the Holy Spirit led Luke to record the story of the Ethiopian eunuch, who was "an important official in charge of all the treasury of Candace, queen of the Ethiopians" (Acts 8:27). Think of the influence this man had throughout his country once he responded to the gospel and returned to his homeland. Furthermore, it is not by chance that Luke recorded the story of Cornelius, a man with incredible political power, not only in the city of Caesarea, but throughout Samaria and other countries in the Roman Empire.

As we continue our study, we will observe a number of other prominent people who came to Christ and became extremely influential in helping to spread the gospel. Not only were they able to speak of Christ directly but they were also able to support Christian leaders financially as they carried out the Great Commission.

As with other principles we have discovered regarding how Christians should use their material possessions, this one must be applied carefully and sensitively. But the fact remains that God does want us to reach influential people with the gospel. Many will respond to the message of Christ and, in turn, influence great segments of humanity because of their social position and their material resources. Cornelius's conversion opened the minds of Jewish Christians prejudiced against Gentiles and not only opened a door in his own city, Caesarea, it also opened a door to the great Gentile city of Antioch—which became a missionary center to reach the then known world with the gospel.

THE FIFTH SUPRACULTURAL PRINCIPLE

It is God's will that Christians who have been blessed with material resources use their homes in special ways to offer hospitality to other believers (Acts 10:1-48).

When the church was founded in Jerusalem, Christians had to find new places to be taught the Word of God and to worship. Though they continued to preach the gospel in the Temple courts, they were not long welcomed there. Consequently, they met in homes all over the city.

When the church was scattered and local congregations were planted in other places, neither could they meet in the numerous Jewish synagogues that graced the landscape in various cities throughout the Roman Empire. Consequently, they continued to meet in homes and followed this practice for decades, until they were able to build church buildings sometime in the third century. Since the church was growing rapidly, it was the more affluent Christians who were able to provide homes large enough to house many of these growing churches.

One of the first recorded examples of this involves John Mark's mother. After Peter was miraculously released from prison in Jerusalem, "he went to the house of Mary the mother of John, also called Mark, where many people had gathered [she obviously had a large home] and were praying" (Acts 12:12). He "knocked at the outer entrance" and "a servant girl named Rhoda [only well-to-do people had servants] came to answer the door" (Acts 12:13). Mary was a very wealthy Jewish Christian lady who opened her home to the believers in Jerusalem. We will see that this became a common practice among more well-to-do Christians as the church spread throughout the Roman Empire.

God desires that this principle be applied today in all parts of the world. This does not mean we should not build church buildings, but it does mean that God wants to use people with material possessions who can use their homes in a special way to offer hospitality to other Christians. As we continue our study, we will see how important this principle became when churches continued to be founded and spiritual leaders were appointed to lead these churches. Consequently, we will look at a more specific principle when we study what Paul wrote to Timothy and Titus in his pastoral epistles, particularly as this concept relates to the appointment of elders (see 1 Tim. 3:2 in chap. 34).

THE SIXTH SUPRACULTURAL PRINCIPLE

God desires to use people with material resources who can give great segments of their time to the ministry while still providing for their families (Acts 8:5, 26, 40).

Philip was evidently this kind of man. He had a home and probably a business in Caesarea. However, he spent a great deal of time in missionary work, probably traveling at his own expense.

AQUILA AND PRISCILLA

Aquila and Priscilla stand out as a rare example of a husband/wife team. Paul first met them in Corinth. They had been forced to leave Rome when Emperor Claudius issued an order that all the Jews were to leave the city (Acts 18:1-2). Priscilla and Aquila were tentmakers by trade, a skill Paul had also developed. In the initial days of his ministry in Corinth, he made his living by using this skill, and in some way not described in Scripture, he joined with Priscilla and Aquila in making tents (Acts 18:3).

It appears that Priscilla and Aquila became Christians at this time, probably after listening to their newly discovered business partner explain and interpret the Old Testament prophecies regarding Jesus Christ. When Paul left Corinth, this husband-and-wife team accompanied him until they reached Ephesus (Acts 18:19). They remained in Ephesus and continued the ministry while Paul went on to his home church in Antioch (Acts 18:21-22, 26).

At some point in time, after the ban on Jews living in Rome was lifted, this dedicated couple left Ephesus and went back to their home in the imperial city. For in his letter to the Roman Christians, Paul identified Aquila and Priscilla as his "fellow workers in Christ Jesus." In fact, he stated that "they risked their lives" for him (Rom. 16:3-4). Obviously, they loved Jesus Christ, they loved Paul, and they loved the work of God. When Paul greeted them following their return to Rome, they had once again opened their home as a meeting place for Christians (Rom. 16:5*a*).

It is clear that Priscilla and Aquila were affluent Christians. When they were forced to leave Rome, they probably vacated their home and left it in the hands of servants. They traveled to Corinth, bought or rented another home, and established their business there.

However, after becoming Christians, they left Corinth a year and a half later and traveled on to Ephesus with Paul. Like Philip, they probably utilized their own resources to help finance their ministry. When they arrived in Ephesus, they either rented or bought another house and used that as a meeting place for the church. In fact, when Paul wrote back to the Corinthians from Ephesus, he sent greetings from Aquila and Priscilla who were with him and also from "the church that meets at their house" (1 Cor. 16:19). Wherever they located, they used their home to carry on the ministry.

NEEDED TODAY: MORE AQUILAS AND PRISCILLAS

God needs people who can devote their full time to the ministry and be supported financially by those to whom they minister. But God also wants more men and women like Aquila and Priscilla. Following the model of New Testament Christians, God desires to use people who are willing to utilize their own material resources to support themselves while they give great segments of their time to the ministry. This demonstrates in a concrete way what Jesus had in mind when He told people to store up for themselves "treasures in heaven" rather than "treasures on earth." Aquila and Priscilla are a dynamic example of New Testament Christians whom God allowed to accumulate more than they needed and who, in turn, used their excess in creative ways to further the kingdom of God (Matt. 6:19).

THE SEVENTH SUPRACULTURAL PRINCIPLE

God desires to use Christians who may not have an abundance of material possessions but who unselfishly use what they have, including their skills, to do the work of God (Acts 9:32-43).

This principle must be applied in concert with the two principles we have just looked at. God does not show favoritism toward well-to-do people. He simply desires to use their abundance to carry on His work. But He also wants to use *all* members of the Body of Christ, no matter what their resources. He in no way minimizes their contribution. In fact, as we have seen from the teachings of our Lord, at the judgment seat of Jesus Christ their contribution may be far more significant and far more greatly rewarded than those who have more but who do not give as sacrificially. Dorcas illustrates this principle. Though she evidently was not well-to-do, she was skilled in making clothes, and she used that skill to help others who were in need. Luke made sure he gave her story unusual prominence in the book of Acts (9:36-42).

And so it is today. God wants Christians involved in serving Jesus Christ with the resources they have—though they may not have "much" when they compare themselves with others. God does not want Christians to compare themselves with others in this sense. He wants all of us to be faithful with what we have.

THE EIGHTH SUPRACULTURAL PRINCIPLE

Christians who are unselfish and benevolent become a unique verification to non-Christians that Jesus Christ is indeed the Son of God (Acts 9:32-43).

This principle takes us back to the beginning of our study, to the church in Jerusalem. The very first principle that emerges from this dynamic body of believers is that the way Christians use their material possessions should impact the non-Christian world and encourage people to believe in Jesus Christ (see pp. 51-52).

Dorcas illustrates in a personal way this dynamic process of evangelism. Her love and good deeds were known throughout the city of Joppa. Though it was the miracle of her resurrection that became the specific thing God used to verify the gospel in Joppa, it was the beautiful example of her unselfish life-style that helped open the door for the gospel and added more impact to Peter's miracle.

The world is and always has been filled with selfish people. Because of the principle of sin that is operative in all of us, we naturally tend to look out for ourselves. As a result, Christians like Dorcas, who really care about others, stand out and form a unique verification that Jesus Christ is truly the Son of God and can bring people to life who are dead in their "transgressions and sins" (Eph. 2:1).

We must understand, however, that life-style alone does not bring people to Christ. They must hear the message of the gospel—that Jesus Christ both died and rose again (1 Cor. 15:1-3). However, God never planned for people to hear the gospel out of context and without some kind of evidence that this message is true. Though miracles were performed in the early days of the church, primarily by Jesus Christ and the apostles, to demonstrate God's power (Acts 1:8; Heb. 2:3-4), He designed an ongoing miracle to verify this great salvation message: the love that exists in the Body of Christ (John 13:34-35). And no specific function demonstrates the reality of Christ's love more potently to unbelievers than when Christians share their material possessions to help others in need. More than any other action, this seems to speak the loudest.

We can all testify to the fact that God is doing something special in our lives when this happens. Left *to ourselves*, we would keep everything *for ourselves*. Sharing our material possessions with others in order to further the work of God's kingdom is a specific demonstration of what God did when He gave the world the greatest gift that has ever been given—His only begotten Son (John 3:16). It also demonstrates what He did in changing us from self-centered people to "others-oriented" people. That, indeed, is a powerful witness.

THE NINTH SUPRACULTURAL PRINCIPLE

God's heart responds to non-Christians who are sincerely seeking to please Him and who express their sincerity through being generous with their material possessions (Acts 10:1-48).

This principle is not teaching that people can be saved by good works. All people are saved by grace through faith—not by works of any kind (Eph. 2:8-9). This has always been true, even in Old Testament days. Paul goes to great length in his letters to the Romans and the Galatians to demonstrate that Abraham was made righteous because he *believed* God's promise. He was justified through faith apart from works, just as every person today who finds salvation is justified through faith in Jesus Christ (Rom. 4:18–5:1-2; Gal. 3:6).

However, it is very clear from Cornelius's experience that God was uniquely drawn to this man because "he and all his family were devout and God-fearing." Furthermore, the specific way in which he demonstrated this devotedness to God was that "he gave generously to those in need and prayed to God regularly" (Acts 10:2).

This Roman official was deeply moved by what he observed among the "God-fearing Jews." They too "gave generously to those in need" and "prayed to God regularly." He evidently not only followed the Jewish custom of offering prayers three times a day but of being generous. He had, without doubt, observed "God-fearing Jews" (like those who had come to Jerusalem from all over the world for the Feast of Pentecost—Acts 2:5) faithfully setting aside their three tithes (see p. 112). God responded to Cornelius's desire to know and serve Him.

We see another example of this principle in Philippi on Paul's second missionary journey. Though there were not enough Jewish men in this Gentile city to form a synagogue,[2] as in Caesarea, there was a group of "God-fearing women" that gathered for prayer outside the city gate by a river. On a particular Sabbath day, Paul and the other members of his missionary team also went to this place of prayer "and began to speak to the women who had gathered there" (Acts 16:13).

"Lydia, a dealer in purple cloth from the city of Thyatira" was among them. She too "was a worshiper of God," though she did not know Christ personally. While listening to Paul preach the gospel, the Lord opened her heart, and she responded like Cornelius. "She and the members of her household were baptized" (Acts 16:14-15).

Again we see God sovereignly bringing Christians in touch with unsaved people who are searching for Him and who were demonstrating their sincerity with their acts of worship. Immediately upon becoming a Christian, she unselfishly opened her home to Paul, Silas, Timothy, and Luke. The church that was born that day in Philippi probably continued to meet in her home—indicating once again that God desires people of means to use what they have to serve Him in special ways.

These illustrations do *not* teach salvation by works. This principle simply indicates that God does respond to people who are sincerely seeking to know Him and who are attempting to please Him, such as Cornelius and Lydia, who were following the worship practices modeled by God-fearing Jews.

THE TENTH SUPRACULTURAL PRINCIPLE

When Christians in a particular culture are excluded from social benefits because of their faith in Christ, other believers should set up some type of welfare system to take care of valid human needs (Acts 11:19-30).

This principle is based on what happened to first-century Jews who acknowledged Jesus Christ as their Messiah. They were immediately deprived of gifts of money from the resources set aside by the priests from the third tithe. That is why the Christians in Antioch sent gifts of money to the Christians in Judea during the time of famine.

Another factor to consider is that Rome recognized Judaism as a powerful religious and political system, for it existed long before the Roman Empire itself. Consequently, when Judaism rejected Christianity, it followed that the Romans reflected the same attitudes and actions. We see this reality when Pilate ordered Christ's death at the hands of Roman soldiers because of accusations brought against Him by the Jewish community. This demonstrates the power that Judaism had as an organized religious and political system in the Roman Empire. If Roman leaders could appease the Jews for their own political benefit, they did so. For example, King Herod had James, John's brother, killed, and "when he saw that *this pleased the Jews*, he proceeded to seize Peter also" (Acts 12:3).

In the Western world particularly, welfare systems are set up within the governmental systems to help everyone. Christians benefit since they are part of the system. Consequently, local churches are not faced with this responsibility as were believers in the New Testament world. Nevertheless, what is true in America and other free societies today does not exist in all parts of the world. Consequently, the principle that Christians are responsible to set up welfare systems to take care of valid human needs applies just as it did in New Testament days.

Even though a welfare system may benefit Christians in certain societies, this fact does not exempt the church from helping Christians (and non-Christians) whose total needs are not being met by these systems. But as we will see, careful guidelines must be set up by the church to make certain that people do not take advantage of the generosity of Christians. If people take advantage of societal welfare systems (and they do), it should not surprise us that these people will also take advantage of Christians. In fact, some people target Christians because they know the Word of God teaches how important it is to be benevolent toward people who have human needs. Fortunately, the Scriptures give direction in setting up these guidelines (see Part 6).

THE ELEVENTH SUPRACULTURAL PRINCIPLE

All Christians, according to their ability, should be involved in sharing their material possessions to carry on God's work in the world (Acts 11:19-30).

This principle was first modeled in Jerusalem. The same dynamic can be seen in the church at Antioch. Although we cannot argue conclusively from Luke's statement that *every* Christian participated, it appears they did—at least, each family unit. This also harmonizes with Paul's exhortation to the Corinthians when he said, "On the first day of every week, *each one of you* should set aside a sum of money in keeping with his income" (1 Cor. 16:1-2).

Experience teaches us that some Christians cannot give *anything*—particularly during certain periods in their lives. For example, no one would expect the Christians in Jerusalem who were suffering because of the famine to give to others when they did not even have enough to meet their own needs. However, the time would come when they could reciprocate to meet the needs of other Christians.

Generally speaking all Christians can and should participate in using their material possessions to carry on God's work. Though this may not always be possible during certain crises in our lives, we must remember the example of some New Testament Christians who actually gave out of their poverty (2 Cor. 8:2). Though their gifts may have been similar to that of the poor widow's gift, in God's sight, it represented incredible generosity. Christians, therefore, must not hesitate to give just because they cannot give a lot.

NOTES

1. We must factor into these situations that God does not deal with all people in the same way at any given moment in history. At times He chooses to use certain people as examples to warn others. Since He is God, He has this right. We cannot, as His creatures, dictate to Him what is fair or unfair. Paul made this point clear in his letter to the Romans when explaining God's will in election. Using Pharaoh, the king of Egypt, as an illustration, he wrote, "But who are you, O man, to talk back to God?" (Rom. 9:20).

2. Huber Drumwright, Jr., *The Wycliffe Bible Encyclopedia* (Chicago: Moody, 1975), 2:1640-41, reports the following: "It was required that any community of Jews that contained ten males above 12 years of age support a synagogue (some say ten families, assuming the leadership of a family for each man). It was expected that ten or more men be present for each service. In some communities wealthy men of leisure habitually represented the congregation at the services, supplying regularly the required number." Since Caesarea was a large town, comparatively speaking, there were no doubt a number of synagogues. One report states that there were 480 synagogues in Jerusalem alone, which some believe is an exaggeration. It does indicate, however, that many synagogues existed in large metropolitan areas. This helps explain why Cornelius was a "God-fearing" Gentile. He had been exposed on a regular basis to "God-fearing Jews" worshiping in the synagogues in Caesarea.

Part 4

THE GENTILE CHURCH
AND ITS EXPANDED MISSION

At this point (Acts 13:1) Luke once again picks up the story of the church in Antioch. But in the process, he launches into a new phase in church history: an explosive expansion of the church into the Gentile world. Though Mark initially joined the missionary team, Barnabas and Paul emerged as the primary leaders that God used to launch the first phase of this significant missionary outreach.

It is now that the Holy Spirit introduces us to another singular strategy for communication. New Testament leaders began to write letters to those who had recently been won to Christ. These letters contain both additional and expanded teachings on material possessions. In this unit of study, we will look at what many consider to be the first two New Testament letters. James wrote his epistle as a result of what had happened in Jerusalem and Judea during the early years of the church. If the southern Galatian theory is correct, Paul wrote his first epistle in the interim period between the first missionary journey and the council meeting in Jerusalem.

In addition to the principles that emerge from the *narrative accounts* in the book of Acts, we begin to see an added dimension in the unfolding of God's revelation: *specific teachings* from the New Testament letters that correlate with these narrative accounts. These teachings also yield principles regarding how Christians should view and use their material possessions.

17. Gaining Perspective: The First Missionary Journey

18. James's Letter

19. Paul's Letter to the Galatians

17

Gaining Perspective:
The First Missionary Journey

After Barnabas and Paul left Antioch to deliver a special gift of money to the elders in the various churches in Judea, Luke transports us to Jerusalem ahead of them and records the following events in Acts 12:

- The apostle James's martyrdom at the hands of Herod Agrippa (12:1-2)
- Peter's imprisonment and miraculous deliverance (12:3-19*a*)
- King Herod's unusual death (12:19*b*-23)
- The continued growth of the church (12:24)

When Barnabas and Paul arrived in Antioch (Acts 12:25), John Mark had joined their missionary team. He was Barnabas's cousin (Col. 4:10) and came from a well-to-do Jewish family in Jerusalem. His mother, Mary, is mentioned in conjunction with Peter's deliverance from prison (Acts 12:12).

THE FIRST MISSIONARY JOURNEY: ACTS 13:1–14:28

Though the church of Jesus Christ was launched in Jerusalem, the church in Antioch was destined to become the "missionary center of the Christian world."[1] Receiving direct instructions from the Holy Spirit, several men identified as "prophets and teachers" commissioned Barnabas and Paul and "sent them off" on what has come to be called "Paul's First Mis sionary Journey" (13:1-3). Heading west, these men—accompanied by John Mark—boarded a ship at Seleucia and sailed for Cyprus (13:4). Following is a succinct outline of this first missionary journey (see map on p. 163):

Arrived in *Salamis* on the Island of Cyprus, which was Barnabas's homeland (4:36); preached in the Jewish synagogues (13:5).

Traveled through Cyprus and arrived at *Paphos*, the seat of the Roman government; Sergius Paulus, a man who served as the Roman governor in Cyprus, converted to Christ (13:6-12).

Left Cyprus and sailed to *Perga* in Pamphylia; here John Mark left Barnabas and Paul, and returned to Jerusalem (13:13).

Leaving Perga (at sea level), traveled one hundred miles inland to *Antioch in Pisidia* (an elevation of 3,600 feet); emerging as team leader, Paul delivered lengthy apologetic message in the synagogue; both Jews and Gentiles responded to the gospel, causing intense jealously among the non-responding Jews; hereafter, Luke referred to "Paul and Barnabas" rather than to "Barnabas and Paul" (13:14-52).

Traveled east to *Iconium*; again began preaching in the Jewish synagogue; "spent considerable time there" but were again forced to leave the city because of Jewish opposition (14:1-7).

Traveled to *Lystra*, a totally Gentile and pagan city; Paul and Barnabas worshiped as gods because Paul had healed a crippled man; Paul later stoned because Jews from Antioch and Iconium came and turned the people against the apostles (14:8-20).

Paul miraculously healed from his injuries; went on to *Derbe*; many responded to the gospel (14:21*a*).

Returned to *Lystra*, *Iconium*, and *Antioch* to minister to the new Christians; appointed elders in every church (14:21*b*-23).

Returned to *Perga* to preach (14:24-25*a*).

Traveled to *Attalia* (14:25*b*).

Returned to Antioch in Syria, where they reported on their missionary activities and "stayed there a long time with the disciples" (14:26-28).

THE COUNCIL IN JERUSALEM: ACTS 15:1-35

The next strategic event in the history of the church focused on the council meeting in Jerusalem, which was precipitated by Jewish believers who came to Antioch and began teaching that it was necessary to be circumcised in order to be saved (15:1). Unable to resolve this theological tension, Paul and Barnabas, along with other representatives, were sent by the church in Antioch to consult with the apostles and elders in the church in Jerusalem.

After lengthy reports and discussion, the leaders in Jerusalem decided that salvation was by faith and faith alone. They would not impose Jewish laws on Gentile believers, except to warn them to avoid any form of sexual immorality and any behavior that would cause other Christians to stumble and sin (15:20-21).[2]

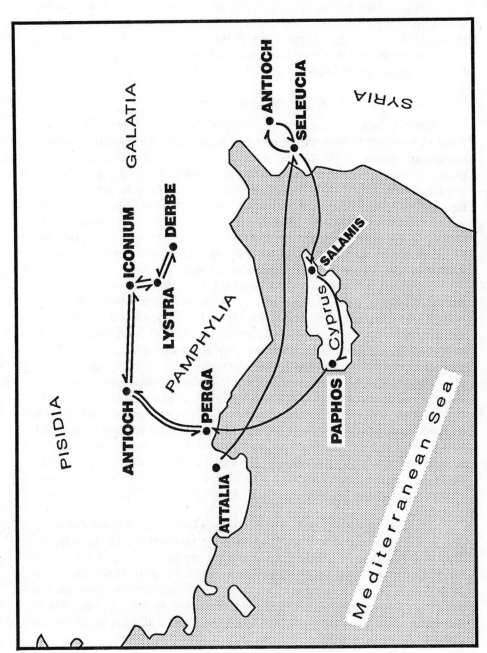

Paul's First Missionary Journey (Acts 13:1–14:28)

To communicate their decisions, the leaders composed a letter, which was also approved by the church. Judas and Silas, two trustworthy men, were sent with Paul and Barnabas back to Antioch to help communicate the message in this "little epistle." When they arrived, "they gathered the church together and delivered the letter. The people read it and were glad for its encouraging message" (15:30-31).

COMPLEMENTARY LETTERS

When Luke wrote his second report to Theophilus (Acts 1:1), he outlined in succinct fashion the events that took place during Paul's various missionary journeys. By design, they are very brief and sketchy church planting reports. These initial and ongoing evangelistic efforts, however, produced new believers who needed instruction on how to live the Christian life. Consequently, Paul and other New Testament leaders began to write letters that contained, among other things, some very important instructions on how Christians should view and use their material possessions. Hereafter, we will look at these epistles as they were written, weaving them into Luke's basic outline in the book of Acts.

There is some question as to the exact dates the various epistles were written. However, most of these letters can be correlated directly and chronologically with the founding of various churches as described by Luke. It is not within the scope of this study to look extensively at the details involved in the writing of each letter. However, we must understand some of the more important historical and cultural factors to help us comprehend more clearly what these New Testament authors said about material possessions.[3]

At this stage of God's unfolding revelation in literary form, two important epistles were written to bring balance to Christian theology, particularly as it relates to how a person is saved and what should subsequently result in the life of that person. The first letter was written by James, who appears to have been the primary leader, or elder and pastor, in the church in Jerusalem. The second was Paul's letter to the Galatians, which may have been written shortly after the first missionary journey.

In our study of the book of Acts, we have looked at all of the *functions* and *activities* recorded in a scriptural unit before attempting to principlize. This was essential in order to develop a proper perspective on what God wants Christians of all time to learn from biblical history. However, as we look at the New Testament epistles, it is more expedient to correlate the principles immediately with the *specific teachings* as they appear. This is the same approach that was used when we looked at what Jesus taught about material possessions.

This change in methodology is also necessary because Luke's literary approach changed. Rather than describing activities in detail that in themselves yield supracultural principles (such as the functions of the church in Jerusalem and the stories of individuals like the Ethiopian eunuch and Cornelius), Luke began to record events much more succinctly and in geographical terms. The epistles were written to enable both spiritual leaders and the average Christian to live in harmony with the will of God. Our observations will focus on what these letters contain regarding material possessions.

NOTES

1. E. M. Blaiklock, ed., *The Zondervan Pictorial Bible Atlas* (Grand Rapids: Zondervan, 1969), p. 329.

2. Relative to the requirements set up in Jerusalem, Merrill C. Tenney, *New Testament Survey* (Grand Rapids: Eerdmans, 1953), pp. 259-60, adds this helpful note:

   James recommended that they be not required to keep all the law, but that they be requested to abstain from certain practices which would be particularly offensive to their Jewish brethren, namely, (1) idolatry, (2) fornication, (3) eating of meat from strangled animals, and (4) eating of blood. These regulations were suggested more as a basis of fellowship than as a platform of ethics, although the first two dealt with moral issues which had to be faced irrespective of Jewish law.
   In some of the manuscript texts of Acts the third phrase, ". . . and from what is strangled," is omitted. Should this reading be correct, the last term, ". . . and from blood," might be interpreted to mean bloodshed or murder. In that case all three requirements would be ethical or moral, and the regulation would mean that these standards would be expected of the Gentiles as essential to moral character.

3. Paul Enns, *The Moody Handbook of Theology* (Chicago: Moody, 1989), pp. 21-22, writes:

   Although it is not the purpose of biblical theology to provide a detailed discussion of introductory matters, some discussion is essential since interpretive solutions are sometimes directly related to introductory studies. Introduction determines issues like authorship, date, addressees, and occasion and purpose for writing. For example, the dating of the book of Hebrews is significant in that it relates to the extent of the suffering of the audience to whom the book is written. Persecution became severe after the burning of Rome in A.D. 64. Even more critical is the issue of the addressees in Hebrews. If the audience is understood to be unbelievers, the book will be studied in one fashion; if the audience is understood to be Hebrew Christians, the book will be understood differently. By way of other examples, the audience of Matthew, Mark, and Luke also determines how these writers are evaluated. For example, Matthew's theological viewpoint ought to be understood from the standpoint of having been written to a Jewish audience. The theological viewpoint of the writer is clearly related to introductory issues.

18

James's Letter

A number of Bible scholars believe that this letter was written by James, Jesus' brother, sometime between A.D. 45 and 50. This was not James the apostle, the brother of John. He was killed by King Herod (Acts 12:1-2) who, in turn, died in A.D. 44. Since the apostle James was martyred *prior* to Herod's death, and since the book of James was written *after* A.D. 44, it is logical to conclude that the James who wrote this letter was the primary leader that Luke referred to when describing the church in Jerusalem (see Acts 12:17; 15:13-21).

James may have written this epistle about the same time the Jerusalem council meeting took place. If so, that would make this letter the first piece of New Testament literature written, other than the little letter that is recorded in Acts 15:23-29. There is one possible exception. Some believe that Matthew could have written his gospel as early as A.D. 50. Others believe it might have been written as late as A.D. 70. The content of James's letter has a distinctive Jewish flavor and sounds like what Jesus taught in the Sermon on the Mount. This adds credence to an early dating of Matthew's gospel.

JAMES 1:9

*The brother in humble circumstances ought
to take pride in his high position.*

EXPOSITION

Many poor people became Christians in the New Testament world. In spite of their constant hope that Jesus would soon return, restore the kingdom to Israel, and reign and rule as their Messiah, people soon discovered rather quickly that following Jesus Christ did not automatically solve their economic problems. Those who became Christians in the midst of "humble circumstances" often remained in "humble circumstances" the rest of their lives. These believers knew nothing of the "prosperity theology" so frequently taught today in the more affluent cultures of the world.

One major thing did change, however. They had a new perspective on life. They had *eternal hope.* Thus, James was writing to encourage anyone in "humble circumstances . . . to take pride in his high position" (1:9).

Here, "humble circumstances" refers to being poor. James was reminding them that in God's sight, what they had materially had nothing to do with their "high position in Christ." They may not have had much by this world's standards, but they were exceedingly "rich" in God's sight. They were "heirs of God and co-heirs with Christ" (Rom. 8:17).

THE FIRST SUPRACULTURAL PRINCIPLE

Christians in the church who do not have a lot of material possessions should not feel inferior to those who have more (James 1:9).

Speaking generally, Paul had to admonish the Corinthians regarding the application of this principle. Certain Christians were looking down on other believers because they thought their spiritual gifts were more important than others. Not so, wrote Paul: "The eye cannot say to the hand, 'I don't need you!' And the head cannot say to the feet, 'I don't need you!' On the contrary," Paul continued, "those parts of the body that seem to be weaker are indispensable, and the parts that we think are less honorable we treat with special honor" (1 Cor. 12:21-23).

This exhortation regarding the way the Lord designed the Body of Christ to function certainly includes the social and economic status of individual Christians. Just because people do not have a lot of material possessions does not mean that they are not important. Poor Christians are just as "rich" as well-to-do Christians in terms of the way God views their position in His church. Consequently, spiritual leaders have a responsibility to encourage these believers not to be intimidated by more well-to-do believers. Neither must Christians with fewer material possessions judge more affluent Christians, criticize them, or question their motives.

JAMES 1:10

*But the one who is rich should take pride in his low
position, because he will pass away like a wild flower.*

EXPOSITION

James directed these words to affluent Christians. As we have already seen, the Scriptures do not teach that having wealth is sinful. But the Bible clearly warns of temptations and difficulties associated with riches. People who are wealthy tend to rely on their material possessions for their security and happiness. They may tend to become materialistic in attitudes and actions, wanting more and more. This can easily lead to arrogance.

James was warning wealthy Christians to boast about their "low position" rather than their money and their ability to make more. In essence, he was saying, "Let people know your riches are not the most important thing in life—not just with words, but with your actions." Let people know that your eternal perspective is far more important than your earthly one. Let people see that you are not putting trust in your wealth, that if you died at any moment (your "low position"), you know that your security is in Christ and in your hope of eternal life. Let people observe that you (to quote Jesus) are storing up "treasures in heaven" rather than "treasures on earth." Let people see that you are not a "double-minded" person (1:8), attempting to serve both "God and money" (Matt. 6:19-21, 24).

James elaborated on his flower analogy and its application to rich people: "For the sun rises with scorching heat and withers the plant; its blossom falls and its beauty is destroyed. In the same way, the rich man will fade away even while he goes about his business" (1:11). All people will someday "fade away." Those without many earthly possessions will enter into their position in Jesus Christ forever. Rich Christians, likewise, even though their material possessions pass away, will also inherit eternal life. At that moment, however, the rich will ask themselves, How does God view the way I have used my material possessions on earth to further the work of His kingdom? What will be the eternal rewards with which I can glorify Jesus Christ forever?

THE SECOND SUPRACULTURAL PRINCIPLE

Christians who have a lot of material possessions should demonstrate humility, realizing that their only true treasures are those they have stored up in heaven (James 1:10).

Christians today need to understand this principle, particularly those of us who live in materialistic and affluent cultures. Without even being aware of it, we can easily convey an attitude of arrogance. Again, a word of caution to Christians who may not have as much as others: people who are insecure or jealous because of their lack can become very critical of affluent Christians and falsely accuse them of pride and materialism.

Those who may not have as much as others must be on guard against projecting on others what might possibly be true of them were they wealthy. It is easy to transfer this attitude to rich individuals who, in reality, do not have a problem with pride. This kind of sinful behavior reflects a judgmental attitude. But Paul exhorted the Roman Christians with these words: "Therefore let us stop passing judgment on one another. Instead, make up your mind not to put any stumbling block or obstacle in your brother's way" (Rom. 14:13).

JAMES 1:27a

Religion that God our Father accepts as pure and faultless is this: to look after orphans and widows in their distress.

EXPOSITION

A person who has accepted Christ as personal Savior and who is conforming his life to Christ's example is living a *religious life* in the true sense of that word. That is what sets those involved in the "Christian religion" apart from those who follow other forms of religious philosophy.

There are many reflections of a person who is deeply religious. But James reminds us that nothing is more basic than how we relate to children without parents and women without husbands, whose needs are not being met. This is not a new concern in God's overall plan. He designed the "third tithe" in Israel for this very purpose (Deut. 14:28-29; 26:12; see p. 112). This continued to be an important focus in the New Testament church, since Jewish widows—once they became Christians—were cut off from the welfare system in Judaism.

As we have already observed, seven highly qualified men were appointed in the Jerusalem church to look after the Grecian widows (Acts 6:1-7). Further, Luke devoted a rather extensive section in his historical record to describe Dorcas and her ministry to widows, both those who were believers and those who were not (Acts 9:32-43). Luke also made sure his readers knew that Cornelius found favor with God even as a non-Christian because "he gave generously to those in need" (Acts 10:2). And, as we will see, Paul gave detailed instructions to Timothy on how widows should be properly cared for by the church (1 Tim. 5:3-16).

THE THIRD SUPRACULTURAL PRINCIPLE

People who are in physical need have a special place in God's heart, and Christians who help meet these needs also have a special place in God's heart (James 1:27a).

James was reinforcing what we have already seen illustrated in our study thus far. God is concerned about the poor, and He notices Christians who share His concern by meeting these human needs. When Christians respond to meet needs with generous and open hearts, God accepts these acts of kindness as being "pure and faultless." God keeps accurate records and will someday reward Christians who have been faithful in this respect.

JAMES 2:1

My brothers, as believers in our glorious
Lord Jesus Christ, don't show favoritism.

EXPOSITION

The focus of the problem among the Christians addressed by James was the way their view of people was based on economic status. They were showing favoritism toward rich people and discriminating against the poor.

Some of these Christians were evidently providing the wealthy with special considerations and at the same time withholding certain considerations from poor people:

> Suppose a man comes into your meeting wearing a gold ring and fine clothes, and a poor man in shabby clothes also comes in. If you show special attention to the man wearing fine clothes and say, "Here's a good seat for you," but say to the poor man, "You stand there," or "Sit on the floor by my feet," have you not discriminated among yourselves and become judges with evil thoughts? (2:2-4)

It is not wrong to give honor to those to whom honor is due—including those who are faithful in serving God with their material possessions. Barnabas and Philemon are classic illustrations of men who were so honored. However, while *honoring* some, these New Testament Christians were *dishonoring* others. They were allocating the poor to a "lower position" because of their economic conditions. This, James stated, is terribly wrong and sinful. It is discriminating and out of harmony with Christian truth.

James elaborated still further. "Listen, my dear brothers," he wrote. "Has not God chosen those who are poor in the eyes of the world to be rich in faith and to inherit the kingdom he promised those who love him?" (2:5). James was teaching that God does not discriminate. Some of those who had the least in the "kingdom of this world" would have all they could want in the "kingdom of God." They may have been poor in material possessions, but they were rich in faith. Since God treats all Christians equally as heirs and joint heirs with Jesus Christ, so should we.

James also pointed out that some of these New Testament Christians—perhaps the leaders in the church—had "insulted the poor" and at the same time had honored those who had exploited and mistreated them (2:6-7). They even gave special honor to people who brought reproach on the name of Jesus Christ. This was the height of prejudice and favoritism—to elevate wealthy unbelievers, who were hostile toward Christ, to positions of prominence in the Christian community while relegating poor believers, who were faithful to Christ, to a place of less prominence. No wonder the poor felt "insulted."

James was trying to squelch the wrong attitudes that had "spilled over" from Judaism into the church. Favoritism ran rampant in Israel, particularly among religious leaders. Social politics permeated the hierarchy.[1] This points out an important concern. When people become Christians, they tend to reflect the mentality that exists in their unbelieving community. Among the wealthy Jews particularly, extravagant living, prejudice and arrogance, and insensitivity were common attitudes and actions. These characteristics were especially rampant in Jerusalem, the center of Jewish religious practice, where many priests accepted Jesus Christ (Acts 6:7).

Since James evidently served as the lead elder or pastor in Jerusalem, he faced these "carryover" attitudes regularly. In most instances, it takes time for changes to take place in people's lives before they begin to reflect the teachings of Jesus Christ. But, if people are truly born again, these changes *will* come, which is the next issue addressed by James. But, first, let us look at the supracultural principle that comes from this passage of Scripture.

THE FOURTH SUPRACULTURAL PRINCIPLE

Christians should never show favoritism toward people who have an abundance of material possessions; conversely, Christians should never be prejudiced against people who have few material possessions (James 2:1).

The sin of prejudice has always been a horrible social disease. Unfortunately, it has often spilled over into the church of Jesus Christ. In New Testament times, this was especially a problem regarding slavery and certain occupations.

The New Testament church was a unique social institution. Since slavery was an acceptable and prominent part of the total Roman society,[2] and since many households came to Christ whole—including the slaves of those households—it created unusual temptations to show favoritism or, by contrast, unusual opportunities to demonstrate Christian love. Paul instructed believing masters to treat their slaves as brothers and sisters in Christ, and he instructed Christian slaves to serve their masters as if they were serving Jesus Christ (Eph. 6:5-9; Col. 3:22–4:1).

Consequently, whole households, including masters, their children, and their slaves, met together to worship Jesus Christ. Though Paul did not attack the evils of slavery per se, he taught a message of love that eventually eliminated this social structure within the Christian community.

In addition to a social ethic that condoned and favored slavery, some unusual problems existed between the upper and lower classes, not only in the Roman Empire generally but also in Jewish society. Those in the upper class actually despised certain trades and would not associate with these people. Jeremias reports that people who practiced certain trades "were, to a greater or lesser degree, exposed to social degradation."[3]

You can imagine what happened when both rich and poor in the Jewish community were converted to Jesus Christ and began to fellowship together in the same place. James was dealing with this kind of "cultural spillover" that always happens when people are thrown together in a new social mix. But the message of Christianity cuts across this kind of sinful behavior and must continue to do so in every culture of the world. However, as stated earlier, it takes time for positive, Christlike changes to take place in attitudes and actions that have been such an integral part of the very fabric of our personalities. James's epistle testifies to this fact.

JAMES 2:17

Faith by itself, if it is not accompanied by action, is dead.

EXPOSITION

Viewed in isolation, this statement appears to be very general. However, in context, James was once again writing about how Christians should view and use their material possessions. Since there are many ways in which we can reflect our faith, it is significant that James chose the subject of material possessions to illustrate good works. To focus the problem, James asked two questions: "What good is it, my brothers, if a man claims to have faith but has no deeds?" (2:14a). "Can such faith save him?" (2:14b).

To make his point, James used the same technique he employed earlier in this chapter to illustrate the sin of showing favoritism (compare 2:2). He posed a hypothetical situation probably based on reality. "Suppose," James wrote, "a brother or sister is without clothes and daily food. If one of you says to him, 'Go, I wish you well; keep warm and well fed,' but does nothing about his physical needs, what good is it? In the same way," James concluded, "faith by itself, if it is not accompanied by action, is dead" (2:15-17).

Jesus also used an illustration to test a person's eternal destiny in Luke 10:25-28. His story was prompted by a question from "an expert" in the law: "Teacher, what must I do to inherit eternal life?"

Knowing this man's knowledge of the Mosaic law, Jesus responded with another question: "What is written in the Law? How do you read it?"

The man answered, "'Love the Lord your God with all your heart and with all your soul and with all your strength and with all your mind'; and, 'Love your neighbor as yourself.'"

Jesus assured the man that if he obeyed the law in these matters, he would have eternal life. But this self-righteous scholar knew that he did not measure up to those two commands. Jesus, of course, was already aware that he did not and that no individual has ever kept the law perfectly. The man responded just as Jesus knew he would—with self-justification and rationalization: "And who is my neighbor?"

Jesus then told the story of the Good Samaritan. After a traveler was robbed, beaten, and left on the road nearly dead, a priest crossed over to the other side and continued on. Likewise, a Levite also passed on the other side. However, a Samaritan—who represented a class of people rejected and avoided by the Jews—helped the man. He cared for his wounds and then took him to an inn where he actually paid for his stay. He also told the innkeeper that when he returned he would pay any additional money that might be needed to cover his tending.

Jesus asked the expert in the law which one of these individuals was a true neighbor to the man who had been victimized. The man could only respond by saying it was "the one who had mercy." Jesus then told the man, who prided himself in being better than Samaritans, to follow the example of the Samaritan.

James helps us understand what Jesus was teaching. This expert in the law claimed to have a personal relationship with God. Yet he had no works to verify his faith. The conclusion is obvious. The man did not have eternal life and would not receive eternal life until he had a true personal relationship with Jesus Christ. When he did, it would affect the way he treated people who were not as economically and socially fortunate as he was.

THE FIFTH SUPRACULTURAL PRINCIPLE

One of the most significant ways saving faith is tested as to its validity and reality is the way in which professing Christians view and use their material possessions (James 2:17).

One of the most important questions being discussed among Christians today relates to how we determine if a person is truly saved. Is it our profession of faith alone? James answered that question with a decided "no." Though only God knows the heart, James did not hesitate to say that "faith by itself, if it is not accompanied by action is dead" (2:17). Personally, I can only interpret this statement in one way. If a person's faith is "dead," that person is still "dead in . . . transgressions and sins" (Eph. 2:1).

When evaluating whether or not a person's relationship with Jesus Christ is real, I have seldom heard anyone attempt to answer this question based upon how a person uses his material possessions. On the other hand, I have heard Christians frequently refer to a person's morality or ethics but never his materialistic and selfish behavior. This is significant since the way we use our material possessions is the very illustration James used to test whether or not a professing Christian is truly saved.

JAMES 4:15

Instead, you ought to say,
"If it is the Lord's will, we will live and do this or that."

EXPOSITION

This exhortation can apply to many aspects of doing the will of God. However, James once again illustrated this truth by referring to the way Christians conduct their affairs economically: "Now listen, you who say, 'Today or tomorrow we will go to this or that city, spend a year there, *carry on business and make money.*' Why," James warned, "you do not even know what will happen tomorrow. What is your life? You are a mist that appears for a little while and then vanishes" (4:14-15). At this juncture James wrote that these Christians ought to consider the Lord's will in all they do. To do otherwise is to "boast and brag," and that, he said, "is evil" (4:13-17).

James was certainly not saying that it is wrong to plan ahead. If he were, he would have been contradicting other statements in Scripture (see p. 87). Furthermore, it certainly is not inappropriate to "go to this city or that city" and conduct business—and even to spend "a year there," if necessary, to complete the transaction. We would be misinterpreting James if we concluded that it is wrong to "make money."

James meant to convey three principles of conduct. First, we must put God at the forefront in all of our planning. That is what Jesus meant when He said that we are to "seek first his kingdom and his righteousness" (Matt. 6:33). Second, we must live our lives on earth realizing that all we are and have come from Him. We have no right to take credit for our own accomplishments. The more God blesses, the more we should praise and thank Him. Third, when our accomplishments involve wealth, we should use it for the glory of God, not simply to build a temporal kingdom for ourselves.

THE SIXTH SUPRACULTURAL PRINCIPLE

All economic and financial planning should be done with an intense desire to be in the will of God in every respect (James 4:15).

We have already noted that the Word of God does not teach against financial planning for the future. For example, Jesus once used an illustration from the building trade: "Suppose one of you wants to build a tower. Will he not first sit down and estimate the cost to see if he has enough money to complete it?" Jesus went on to point out that lack of careful planning could lead to embarrassment: "For if he lays a foundation and is not able to finish it, everyone who sees it will ridicule him, saying, 'This fellow began to build and was not able to finish'" (Luke 14:28-30).

Jesus was not teaching people how to build buildings but to "count the cost" before deciding to be committed disciples. But He was also affirming the importance of careful financial planning. Conversely, however, He used the illustration of the man who planned to build bigger barns and died that very night to demonstrate the fallacy of future planning without considering God's will in all aspects of life (Luke 12:16-20).

This was also James's concern. All of our future planning should be done with one question in mind: Am I living in the will of God? In terms of our economic perspective, whatever business we transact and whatever amount of money we make should all be done for one purpose—to glorify God and to store up "treasures in heaven." It also means we will proceed to do business with a sense of humility, recognizing that it is only because of God's grace that we can do anything (4:17).

Remember, however, that James was not teaching that we cannot proceed with confidence. Christians who are living in the will of God in all respects—including how they use their material possessions—can proceed with great confidence, both in God and in themselves. Christian businessmen and businesswomen should be the most confident people in the world. If we have the right perspective, we can be assured that God is in control of our lives, and no matter what happens, we can trust and praise Him, in the good times *and* in the bad.

JAMES 5:1

Now listen, you rich people, weep and wail
because of the misery that is coming upon you.

EXPOSITION

Now James changes audiences.[4] He *was* speaking to those who were not Christians—though what he says certainly applies to Christians. This shift demonstrates that James expected Jewish people who were not Christians to read this letter. Since he was a prominent Jew before he became a Christian and the primary leader in the Jerusalem church, it is understandable why unbelieving Jews would gain access to this epistle. James anticipated that this would happen and addressed some rather pointed statements to them.

Three teachings. First, James was teaching that *material things do not provide ultimate happiness.* In fact, he warns against misery that will come upon the wealthy (5:1). Second, James was saying that *material things are not enduring.* They "rot." Even our finest clothes deteriorate. James says that even "gold and silver" will corrode or "rust" (5:2-3). Third, James stated that *gold and silver that is hoarded will testify against us* and eat our "flesh like fire" (5:3).

While Jesus was on earth, He told a dramatic story (Luke 16:19-31) that helps us understand what James had in mind with this statement: "There was a rich man, who was dressed in purple and fine linen and lived in luxury every day. At his gate was laid a beggar named Lazarus, covered with sores and longing to eat what fell from the rich man's table."

Eventually, this poor beggar died and joined his father Abraham in heaven. Later, this wealthy man also faced death. However, he did not go to join his father Abraham. Rather, Jesus stated, "In hell, where he was in torment, he looked up and saw Abraham far away, with Lazarus by his side."

The rich man called out to Abraham for pity and asked him to send Lazarus "to dip the tip of his finger in water and cool" the rich man's tongue. "I am in agony in this fire," the rich man said.

Abraham's response to the rich man's request is sobering. "Son, remember that in your lifetime you received your good things," Abraham replied, "while Lazarus received bad things, but now he is comforted here and you are in agony."

Accepting the fact that nothing could be done for himself, the rich man made another request. He asked that Lazarus be sent to warn his five brothers who were living the same life-style he had lived. Again, Abraham's response is sobering: "They have Moses and the Prophets; let them listen to them."

The rich man tried again and begged Abraham to send Lazarus, because if Lazarus came back from the dead, the man was sure his brothers would repent. Once again Abraham responded with bad news: "If they do not listen to Moses and the Prophets, they will not be convinced even if someone rises from the dead."

With this rather detailed story, Jesus illustrated what James was saying in one succinct statement: The rich man's gold and silver and his fine linen clothes were corroded, and that corrosion was testifying against him and eating his "flesh like fire" (5:3).

Three temptations. As James concluded his paragraph, which warned unsaved rich people, he also outlined three temptations that are applicable as well to Christians. First, temptation entices *to accumulate more and more*: "You have hoarded wealth in the last days," James stated (5:3c). The second temptation is *to be unfair and dishonest*. Not only did these rich people accumulate more and more for themselves, they "failed to pay the workmen" they hired to take care of their fields. They were not fair. They were unethical and dishonest. James went on to say that "the cries of the harvesters" who had been cheated had "reached the ears of the Lord Almighty" (5:4). The third temptation is *to be self-indulgent*. James accused these rich people of having "lived on earth in luxury." They had "fattened themselves" for the "day of slaughter." They had prepared themselves for a tragic end.

THE SEVENTH SUPRACULTURAL PRINCIPLE

Non-Christians who put faith in their material possessions and who abuse and misuse other people in order to accumulate wealth must be warned that they will eventually be judged severely by God Himself (James 5:1).

James was assuming that people have the potential to accumulate wealth and live in luxury on earth. This is particularly true in societies that provide people with economic opportunities—such as America. The day is coming, however, when all of that wealth will totally vanish. It has no eternal significance, and people who do not know Christ will not only lose everything they have on earth, they will not have everlasting life either. They will live in lonely isolation, suffering the eternal consequences in hell.

James was also saying something else. Non-Christians who have made their wealth on earth through dishonest means and who have taken advantage of other people in the process will experience greater suffering. There will be degrees of punishment in hell. Thus, James issued a severe warning to every wealthy person on earth who does not know Jesus Christ as personal Savior.

THE EIGHTH SUPRACULTURAL PRINCIPLE

Accumulating wealth brings with it specific temptations for both Christians and non-Christians (James 5:1-3).

Though James was addressing his warning to non-Christians in this section of the letter (5:1-6), certain aspects of his warning also apply to Christians. When we accumulate wealth, we must be on guard against the same temptations all people face. We too will be tempted to be *unfair and dishonest.* How easy it is to rationalize and compromise our ethical conviction when it comes to accumulating material things.

We too will be tempted to be *self-indulgent,* to spend more on ourselves. After all, we conclude, we worked hard to make it, it belongs to us, and we have a right to indulge ourselves.

We too will be tempted to *hoard* what we have—to store up treasures on earth rather than in heaven. After all, the more we have, the more people admire us, look up to us, and hold us in high esteem. Furthermore, there is a great sense of security, power, and status in having lots of material possessions.

The picture is clear. All Christians who have been, or who are, in a position to accumulate wealth must acknowledge that being a Christian does not eliminate these temptations. In fact, Satan may make a special attack on wealthy Christians, just as he did on Jesus Christ. He offered Jesus the kingdoms of the world in all their splendor if He would only bow down and worship him. Jesus' response is a divine model for all Christians who are tempted to abuse their wealth. We must say, "Away from me, Satan! For it is written: 'Worship the Lord your God, and serve him only'" (Matt. 4:10).

The apostle Paul recognized that these temptations would come to people who acquire wealth. Therefore, he wrote to Timothy and encouraged him to warn these believers: "People who want to get rich fall into temptation and a trap and into many foolish and harmful desires that plunge men into ruin and destruction" (1 Tim. 6:9-10).

NOTES

1. Joachim Jeremias, *Jerusalem in the Time of Jesus*, trans. by F. H. and C. H. Kay (London: SCM, 1969), p. 196, has written

   that the influence of the new aristocracy depended on their power politics, exercised sometimes ruthlessly ("lances," "fist") sometimes by intrigue ("whisperings," "reed pens"), and that by this means they were able to control the most important offices in the Temple as well as the taxes and money: this meant all the permanent chief-priestly offices at Jerusalem, such as that of captain of the Temple—we see . . . that this was usually filled by a near relative of the high-priest—and the Temple overseer immediately below him, as well as the office of Temple treasurer. Thus the text shows that they took care to choose all the chief priests from among the sons and sons-in-law of the high priests and former high priests.

2. Slavery within the Roman Empire was quite different from slavery as we have come to know it in Western culture prior to the Emancipation Proclamation. Relative to the social situation in the New Testament world, Merrill C. Tenney, *New Testament Survey* (Grand Rapids: Eerdmans, 1953), pp. 49-50, explains:

   Slaves made up a large proportion of the population of the Roman empire. No exact figures are obtainable, but probably less than half of the inhabitants of the Roman world were free men, and only relatively few of them were citizens with full rights. War, debt, and birth recruited the ranks of the slave population at a rapid rate. Not all of them were ignorant. Many, in fact, were physicians, accountants, teachers, and skilled artisans of every kind. Epictetus, the renowned Stoic philosopher, was one of them. They performed most of the work in the great agricultural estates, they acted as household servants and as clerks in business houses, and publishers employed them as copyists. Where modern enterprises operate by machinery, the ancients used cheap labor.

   The effect of slavery was debasing. The ownership of slaves made the masters dependent upon the labor and skill of their servitors to the extent that they lost their own ingenuity and ambition. Morality and self-respect were impossible among those whose only law was the will of an arbitrary master. Trickery, flattery, fraud, and fawning obedience were the slave's best tool to obtain what he wanted from his superiors. In many households the children were entrusted to the care of these menials who taught them all of the vices and sly tricks that they knew. Thus the corruption that prevailed among the oppressed classes spread to their overlords.

3. Jeremias, *Jerusalem*, p. 303.

4. In the preceding paragraph (4:13-17), James was dealing with a similar subject: material wealth. However, he was speaking to believers. His main point was that God should always be at the center of their business activities. However, beginning in chapter 5, he directs his exhortations to non-Christians. Note that when he makes this transition, he no longer identifies those he is writing to as "brothers." A careful analysis of 5:1-6 in context reveals that James does not address his thoughts to Christians again until he reaches v. 7.

19

Paul's Letter to the Galatians

Paul probably wrote his letter to the Galatians from Antioch shortly after he and Barnabas returned from the first missionary tour through southern Galatia (Acts 13:1–14:28) and sometime prior to the Jerusalem council described in Acts 15.[1] The fact that Paul said nothing in his letter about the conclusions reached at the Jerusalem council (which relate so directly to his teachings regarding "law and grace") seems to indicate that this historic meeting had not yet taken place.

Paul's concerns in his letter to the Galatians were totally different from those in James's epistle. James was writing from the viewpoint of a Jewish Christian who was deeply concerned with the fact that true believers should demonstrate their new life in Christ through their works—particularly in terms of how they view and use their material possessions. Paul, on the other hand, was emphasizing the freedom we have in Christ, both as Jews and Gentiles (5:1). He devoted most of this letter to defending justification by faith and faith alone.

It should not surprise us, then, that Paul had very little to say about how a Christian should view and use his material possessions in this letter. That was not his primary concern. However, as he concluded this letter, he did have two important things to say about this matter.

GALATIANS 6:6

Anyone who receives instruction in the word
must share all good things with his instructor.

EXPOSITION

Paul was not concerned about himself when he wrote this statement. Rather, he was concerned that elders and pastors who devote themselves to the ministry of the Word of God should be cared for financially. Assuming an early dating for this letter, Paul and Barnabas would have just returned from the first missionary journey, during which they "appointed elders" in several of the churches they had founded (Acts 14:23). Paul was concerned that these new believers understand their financial responsibilities to those who minister to them spiritually. This, of course, correlates with what Paul wrote to Timothy in a later letter: "The elders who direct the affairs of the church well are worthy of double honor [remuneration], especially those whose work is preaching and teaching" (1 Tim. 5:17).

THE NINTH SUPRACULTURAL PRINCIPLE

Local church leaders whose primary ministry is teaching the Word of God should be given priority consideration in receiving financial support (Gal. 6:6).

The principle of caring for the economic needs of people who serve Jesus Christ vocationally appears frequently throughout the Scriptures. However, in Galatians, Paul added a more specific element to the general principle stated earlier in this study: recipients of spiritual nourishment should "share all good things with his instructor" (6:6).

Perhaps what lies behind this biblical principle is the fact that teaching the Word of God brings with it greater accountability, not only in the presence of men and women, but in the sight of God Himself: "Not many of you should presume to be teachers, my brothers, because you know that we who teach will be judged more strictly" (James 3:1). Putting it in more down-to-earth terms, James was telling us that teaching the Word of God is "risky business." To lead people in the wrong direction and out of the will of God will bring with it some very serious consequences.

Paul may have also had another pragmatic reason in mind when he instructed the Galatians to support their spiritual leaders. He referred to the accountability that goes with this responsibility when he wrote to Timothy: *"Do your best* to present yourself to God as one approved, a workman who does not need to be ashamed and who *correctly handles the word of truth"* (2 Tim. 2:15). To teach the Word of God effectively takes a great deal of time and effort, especially if it is done in a manner that is well-pleasing to God. In that sense, Paul was simply saying—as Jesus did—"The worker deserves his wages" (1 Tim. 5:18; Luke 10:7).

GALATIANS 6:10

Therefore, as we have opportunity, let us do good to all people, especially to those who belong to the family of believers.

EXPOSITION

Dorcas serves as a special illustration of what Paul had in mind: she "was always doing good and helping the poor" (Acts 9:36). More specifically, she assisted believing and unbelieving widows by providing clothing she had made.

Since Paul included "all people" in this injunction to the Galatians, he was probably referring specifically to the way we can use our material possessions to assist both Christians and non-Christians. He made clear, however, that our priority should be the needs of "the family of believers"—that is, those in the church. Christians are to "do good to all people" when they "have opportunity." Paul seems to be saying that Christians should utilize their opportunities *now* and not be caught off guard when a need presents itself.

Some believe that Paul's statement to the Corinthians about the Galatian churches adds clarity to this exhortation: "And now about the collection for God's people: Do what I told the Galatian churches to do. On the first day of every week, each one of you should set aside a sum of money in keeping with his income, saving it up, so that when I come no collections will have to be made" (1 Cor. 16:1-2). Evidently, the Galatian Christians took Paul's exhortations seriously to plan ahead so they could minister economically to both Christians and non-Christians—so much so that Paul used them as an example for the Corinthians.

THE TENTH SUPRACULTURAL PRINCIPLE

Christians should plan ahead so they can be prepared to minister economically, first and foremost, to their fellow Christians who are in need but without neglecting non-Christians (Gal. 6:10).

Practically speaking, Christians should not only set aside money regularly to support their spiritual leaders; they should also save money to help with emergency needs. Opportunities always come our way to support worthy causes. If we do not have money in escrow for God's work, it will not be possible to experience the joy that comes from giving when those unforeseen opportunities present themselves.

SUPRACULTURAL PRINCIPLES IN PERSPECTIVE, PART 4

JAMES

1. Christians in the church who do not have a lot of material possessions should not feel inferior to those who have more (James 1:9).

2. Christians who have a lot of material possessions should demonstrate humility, realizing that their only true treasures are those they have stored up in heaven (James 1:10).

3. People who are in physical need have a special place in God's heart, and Christians who help meet these needs also have a special place in God's heart (James 1:27a).

4. Christians should never show favoritism toward people who have an abundance of material possessions; conversely, Christians should never be prejudiced against people who have few material possessions (James 2:1).

5. One of the most significant ways saving faith is tested as to its validity and reality is the way in which professing Christians view and use their material possessions (James 2:17).

6. All economic and financial planning should be done with an intense desire to be in the will of God in every respect (James 4:15).

7. Non-Christians who put faith in their material possessions and who abuse and misuse other people in order to accumulate wealth must be warned that they will eventually be judged severely by God Himself (James 5:1-3).

8. Accumulating wealth brings with it specific temptations for both Christians and non-Christians (James 5:1).

GALATIANS

9. Local church leaders whose primary ministry is teaching the Word of God should be given priority consideration in receiving financial support (Gal. 6:6).

10. Christians should plan ahead so they can be prepared to minister economically, first and foremost, to their fellow Christians who are in need but without neglecting non-Christians (Gal. 6:10).

NOTE

1. Well-known scholars disagree as to *when* Galatians was written and *to whom*. For example, J. B. Lightfoot, *St. Paul's Epistle to the Galatians*, 10th ed. (London: Macmillan and Co., 1890), pp. 18-35, believes the letter was written after Paul's second missionary journey through northern Galatia. On the other hand, Sir William Ramsay, *An Historical Commentary on St. Paul's Epistle to the Galatians* (New York: G. P. Putnam's Sons, 1900), pp. ii, 478, has contended that "the churches of Galatia" were those of Antioch, of Pisidia, Iconium, Derbe, and Lystra, which Paul established on his first missionary journey through southern Galatia. Merrill Tenney, *New Testament Survey* (Grand Rapids: Eerdmans, 1953), pp. 266-67, points out that "the importance of the difference of interpretation is that the southern Galatian theory allows for an earlier dating of Galatians and for a better explanation of its historical setting."

Part 5

PAUL'S MISSION: THE SECOND JOURNEY

In the previous section, we began a new phase in our study. In addition to using the activities and functions described by Luke in the book of Acts as our main source for deriving principles to guide twentieth-century Christians in the use of their material possessions, we began to look at the literature written by various New Testament leaders.

In the epistles of James and Galatians, we noted how the unique theological circumstances and cultural issues at that moment in the history of the church affected what both James and Paul stated regarding material possessions. This helps clarify the importance of biblical theology in determining God's will in all aspects of Christian doctrine and living. God's unfolding revelation gives unusual insight and an enlarged perspective on God's plan for believers of all time, no matter what their cultural or ethnic background.

The observations and conclusions in this section take us a step further into the world of the New Testament as we follow Paul on his second missionary journey. In writing letters to the Thessalonian and Corinthian churches, he has given us biblical material that confronts every twentieth-century Christian with some of the most specific supracultural principles on how to use material possessions in the whole New Testament.

20. Gaining Perspective: The Second Missionary Journey

21. Paul's First Letter to the Thessalonians

22. Paul's Second Letter to the Thessalonians

23. Paul's First Letter to the Corinthians

24. Paul's Second Letter to the Corinthians, 8:1-24

25. Paul's Second Letter to the Corinthians, 9:1-15

26. Moving from Specific to General Principles

20
Gaining Perspective:
The Second Missionary Journey

After Paul and Barnabas returned from the Jerusalem council meeting, they spent a period of time teaching and preaching in Antioch. Then "some time later Paul said to Barnabas, 'Let us go back and visit the brothers in all the towns where we preached the word of the Lord and see how they are doing'" (Acts 15:36). Following the meeting in Jerusalem, Paul quickly emerged as the primary leader of this missionary team, a transition that began to take place on the first journey when Barnabas began to take on a supporting role.

Just prior to this second journey, Paul and Barnabas had their well-known controversy. Barnabas wanted John Mark to accompany them. However, Paul disagreed, since Mark "had deserted them in Pamphylia" on the first journey. These two giants in the faith "had such a sharp disagreement that they parted company. Barnabas took Mark and sailed for Cyprus, but Paul chose Silas and left, commended by the brothers to the grace of the Lord" (Acts 15:37-40).

It is not within the scope of this study to discuss who may have been right and who may have been wrong. Suffice it to say that Luke's historical account from this point forward focused on the apostle Paul and his various companions in the ministry. As Peter was destined to be "an apostle to the Jews," Paul was destined to be "an apostle to the Gentiles" (Gal. 2:8). Though many Jews continued to respond to the gospel through the ministry of Paul, he put his time and effort into reaching Gentiles—particularly as he moved farther out from Palestine and into the other countries that made up the Roman Empire.

THE SECOND MISSIONARY JOURNEY:
ACTS 15:36–18:22

Following is a brief summary of Paul's second tour (see map, p. 189):

Paul and Silas traveled northward, reversing former route he and Barnabas took on first missionary journey; arrived once again in *Derbe* (15:41–16:1*a*).

Traveled on to *Lystra*; Timothy joined missionary team "as they traveled from town to town" and "delivered the decisions reached by the apostles and elders in Jerusalem" (16:1-5).

Traveled on "throughout the region of Phrygia and Galatia"; went on down to *Troas*, where Paul received Macedonian call (16:6-10).

Luke joined the missionary team; they boarded a ship and sailed to *Neapolis* (16:11).

Traveled on to *Philippi*, a Roman colony in the leading city of that district of Macedonia; Luke recorded three significant events: first, Lydia and her household converted to Christ; second, Paul cast a demon out of a young slave girl, resulting in persecution from her owners (consequently, Paul and Silas put in prison, but miraculously delivered); third, Philippian jailer and his household converted to Christ (16:11-40).

Luke probably stayed in Philippi[1] while Paul, Silas, and Timothy "traveled through *Amphipolis* and *Apollonia* and came to *Thessalonica*"; won some Jews to Christ and a number of God-fearing Greeks, but Jewish jealousy resulted in persecution (17:1-9).

Traveled on to *Berea*; once again, ministered in synagogue as in Thessalonica; however, more openness to the gospel in Berea; many Jews believed, as well as a number of prominent Gentiles; again, persecution; Paul eventually left Berea, but Silas and Timothy stayed (17:10-15).

Paul traveled on to *Athens* and "reasoned in the synagogue with the Jews and God-fearing Greeks"; also taught from day-to-day in the marketplace as he had opportunity; spiritual results limited (17:16-34).

Paul traveled on to *Corinth*; met Aquila and Priscilla; once again, joined by Silas and Timothy; many Corinthians believed and were baptized; *Paul composed the two letters to the Thessalonian Christians* (18:1-18).

Paul "left the brothers" (evidently Silas and Timothy); "sailed for *Syria*, accompanied by Priscilla and Aquila" (18:18).

Arrived at *Ephesus* where Paul left Priscilla and Aquila (18:19-21); wrote 1 Corinthians when he revisited this city on third missionary journey (19:1-41).

Traveled from Ephesus to *Caesarea*; probably visited church in Jerusalem, then "went down to *Antioch*"[2] (18:22).

THE THESSALONIAN AND CORINTHIAN LETTERS

The founding of the Thessalonian and Corinthian churches soon gave birth to four important New Testament letters. While Paul was establishing the church in Corinth on this second journey, he wrote two letters to the

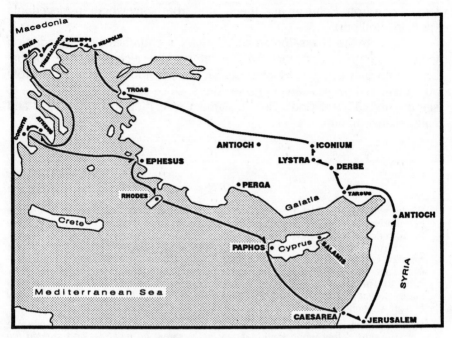

Paul's Second Missionary Journey (Acts 15:36–18:22)

Thessalonian Christians. Later, on his third journey, he wrote the Corinthian letters, one from Ephesus and the second from somewhere in Macedonia (perhaps Philippi).

Because the Thessalonian and Corinthian churches were founded on the second journey, and since the four letters to these churches were probably written between A.D. 51 and A.D. 57, we will look at what Paul wrote about material possessions in these letters. Once again, we will be able to see the unfolding of God's New Testament revelation in its historical and cultural environment.

NOTES

1. While recording the historical account in the book of Acts, Luke began to use the plural pronoun in 16:10: "After Paul had seen the vision, *we* got ready at once to leave for Macedonia" (16:10*a*).

   From this point forward, until they left Philippi, Luke presented himself as a traveling companion with Paul, Silas, and Timothy. When these men left Philippi, however, Luke wrote, "When *they* had passed through Amphipolis and Apollonia, they came to Thessalonica, where there was a Jewish synagogue" (17:1). We can conclude, therefore, that Luke probably stayed on in Philippi to help establish this new and growing church.

2. Luke's account is not clear as to where Paul went once he arrived in Caesarea. He simply reported that when Paul "landed in Caesarea, *he went up and greeted the church* and *then went down to Antioch*" (18:22). Does this mean that he "went up" to *Jerusalem* and then "went down" to Antioch? Most Bible interpreters believe it does. (See Luke's phraseology in 15:2 and 11:27.) Or does Luke mean that Paul simply "came up" from the point where his ship arrived in Caesarea and visited the church in that city? This is also a possible interpretation, but it does not have as much contextual support.

21
Paul's First Letter to the Thessalonians

After being forced to leave Thessalonica, Paul was deeply concerned about the spiritual welfare of the believers he had left behind. When he arrived in Athens, he was so exercised in his heart that he sent Timothy back to see how they were doing (3:1-5). When Timothy returned, he brought good news to Paul, who had moved on to Corinth. Evidently, Paul immediately penned a letter to these believers (3:6-8). It is clear that the theological and sociological climate in Thessalonica affected what Paul wrote to these Christians about how they were to view and use their material possessions.

The content of this letter focused, first, on his thankfulness for the Thessalonians' love and faith in Christ (1:2-3). Second, Paul encouraged them to continue living in a pure and upright manner (3:11–4:12). Third, he clarified certain doctrinal teachings—particularly regarding the second coming of Jesus Christ (4:13–5:11). However, Paul also dealt with two important concepts related to material possessions.

1 THESSALONIANS 2:9

Surely you remember, brothers, our toil and hardship;
we worked night and day in order not to be a burden
to anyone while we preached the gospel of God to you.

EXPOSITION

This statement comes from the autobiographical section of this letter. Beginning in chapter 2, Paul reflects on his experience when he and his missionary companions (Silas and Timothy) first arrived in Thessalonica. They had come from Philippi where he and Silas suffered severe physical abuse and imprisonment (Acts 16:22-24). When they arrived in Thessalonica, they were still experiencing the physical and emotional trauma of having been incarcerated and severely beaten (2:2).

By sharing this personal experience, Paul was emphasizing a principle that consistently governed his life and ministry. Had they been men who were motivated by "impure motives" (2:3), they would never have subjected themselves to the persecution they encountered in Philippi, nor would they have taken the same risks in Thessalonica. "We are not trying to please men," Paul wrote. "You know we never used flattery, nor did we put on a mask to cover up greed" (2:4-5).

Having disclosed to the Thessalonians their true motives, Paul reminded them that they were "apostles of Christ"[1] (2:7). Because of this divine appointment and divine mission, they had a right to ask the Thessalonians to care for their physical needs. But while in Thessalonica, Paul and his companions did not use this apostolic privilege. Rather, they "worked night and day" so they would not burden the Thessalonians with this responsibility. They did not want these new believers to misinterpret their motives. They were not trying to please anyone but God (2:4).

Note, however, that while these men were ministering in Thessalonica, they willingly received material gifts from the Christians they left behind in Philippi (Phil. 4:15-16). The issue under consideration, therefore, is not whether Christian workers should or should not receive financial assistance for serving Christ. Paul later clarified this matter in his letter to the Corinthians: "The Lord has commanded that those who preach the gospel should receive their living from the gospel" (1 Cor. 9:14; see context in 1 Cor. 9:7-18 and exposition on 1 Cor. 9:14-15a in chap. 23).

On occasions when Paul did not have sufficient funds, he did not use this right or privilege. Rather, he helped provide for his physical needs through some other kind of effort, such as making tents (1 Cor. 9:1-3). He did not want the people he was reaching for Christ to falsely accuse him of being in the ministry to benefit himself. Most important, Paul was concerned that these people clearly understand that salvation is a free gift and not something that can be earned or bought (1 Cor. 9:18). Conversely, once believers understood that salvation was purely by grace, once they had come to know Paul well enough to understand his true motives, and once he had taught them their obligation to give, he never hesitated to receive gifts of money to care for his and others' daily needs.

Though Paul spent his initial days in Corinth making tents with Priscilla and Aquila, it did not keep him from ministry. We read that "every Sabbath he reasoned in the synagogue, trying to persuade Jews and Greeks" (Acts 18:4). However, "when Silas and Timothy came from Macedonia" and joined Paul in Corinth, he "devoted himself exclusively to preaching" (Acts 18:5). In other words, Silas and Timothy brought a gift of money from the Macedonian churches that enabled Paul to once again relinquish his tent-making vocation and spend his full time in ministry.

THE FIRST SUPRACULTURAL PRINCIPLE

Christian leaders should look to fellow Christians for financial support, not to the unbelievers they are attempting to reach with the gospel (1 Thess. 2:9).

The apostle Paul stands out as a clear model when it comes to applying this principle. Not only do we see it illustrated in his ministry at Thessalonica (2:9), we see it throughout his life. In some instances, Paul applied this principle in his ministry to new Christians as well. Though the Thessalonians eventually joined the other Macedonian churches in becoming some of his most ardent financial supporters, Paul was very cautious in receiving money from these new believers until they were sufficiently taught the true meaning of the gospel and understood his own heart motives (2:9-10).

Paul did not hesitate to teach new Christians their responsibility to give. This can be deduced from the fact that, while Paul was establishing the church in Thessalonica, the Philippians were already supporting his ministry (Phil. 4:16). This principle has at least three important points of application in twentieth-century churches.

First, people who desire to have a vocational Christian ministry should look to believers for financial support. Second, those who are spiritual leaders in local churches should make sure they teach Christians their God-given responsibility. If people are not taught, it is very difficult for Christians who feel called to vocational ministry to generate the support they need. Third, Christians who seek support for their ministry should look primarily to Christians they have ministered to spiritually. They should establish their reputation in some substantial way so that they are indeed workers who "deserve their wages" (1 Tim. 5:18).

1 THESSALONIANS 4:11-12

*Make it your ambition to lead a quiet life,
to mind your own business and to work with your hands,
just as we told you so that your daily life may win the respect
of outsiders and so that you will not be dependent on anybody.*

EXPOSITION

This exhortation provides a helpful balance to what happened in the early years of the church. There has probably never been a moment in the history of God's people where Christ's love was demonstrated so dramatically as among the Christians in Jerusalem when they shared their possessions with one another.

Part of their motivation, however, was God's promise that Christ would return to restore the kingdom to Israel (Acts 1:6). In view of this expectation, it is more understandable why their material possessions did not have as strong a grip on their minds and hearts as among many Christians today.

When Christ did not return immediately, as these Christians had anticipated, it certainly did not affect the validity of the doctrine of the second coming of Christ. Nor did it affect the aspect of the doctrine we call *immanency*—that is, that Christ could return at any moment. Paul taught this doctrine and believed it with all his heart. It appears that it was not until he wrote his last letter that he fully realized that he was probably going to die before Christ returned (2 Tim. 4:6-8).

When Jesus told the apostles on Ascension Day that it was not for them "to know the times or dates the Father has set by his own authority" (Acts 1:7), He established a guideline for Christians of all times. Paul lived his life as if Christ could come at any moment, and he taught this doctrine of hope to those he led to Christ. However, he continued with great diligence to be about his Father's business right up to the time he died. Even though God used Paul to write Scripture, he was limited in knowledge, as we are.[2]

The Thessalonians' response. When Paul and his associates came to Thessalonica, he taught these people about Christ's overall redemptive plan. They responded with such commitment and dedication that their faith was spoken about all over Macedonia and Achaia (1:8). Everywhere people were discussing the way in which these people had "turned to God from idols to serve the living and true God, and *to wait for his Son from heaven*" (1:9b-10a). For Christians to take the doctrine of the second coming seriously—and especially that Christ could return at any moment—can have both a positive and a negative effect.

On the positive side, it should affect the way we live. God's grace in saving us, as well as the expectancy of His coming, should encourage us to be people that are "eager to do what is good" (Titus 2:11-14). As mentioned earlier, this should involve the way we view and use our material possessions.

On the negative side, Christians have misinterpreted this doctrine and have allowed their misunderstanding to affect their daily lives in nonbiblical ways. They have sometimes used the promise of Christ's return as a rationalization to be lazy and unconcerned about meeting their daily needs. This was evidently the problem in Thessalonica. Perhaps these Christians had heard about the Jerusalem Christians and how they cared for each other. Perhaps in their own poverty they had received gifts from benevolent Christians and had used this as an opportunity to take advantage of others' unselfishness. Or perhaps they were just so excited about the prospect of being delivered from their earthly circumstances that they were spending all of their time talking about it and not working to earn a living. Whatever the circumstances, Paul had to admonish some of them.

Paul's admonitions. First, Paul wrote, "Make it your ambition to lead a quiet life, to mind your own business and to work with your hands" (4:11*a*). Evidently, some of these believers who had inappropriately interpreted the doctrine of the second coming of Christ were using their spare time—which they had a lot of—to get into trouble. Second, Paul reminded them that he had already instructed them to work and not to use their Christian experience as an excuse for laziness (4:11*b*). Third, Paul told them that lazy Christians who do not work to make an adequate living are bad examples to non-Christians—particularly when they take advantage of others. Paul exhorted them not to "be dependent upon anybody" (1 Thess. 4:12).

This final observation is particularly important in evaluating the way the Thessalonians were living compared with the Jerusalem Christians. The believers' behavior in Jerusalem won the respect of unbelievers and served as a means to help bring people to faith in Christ. By contrast, the Thessalonians' behavior brought disrespect. This is a criterion by which we may evaluate many aspects of the way we interpret and apply various Christian truths.

It is true that Jesus warned the apostles that they would be hated because people hated Him. However, He was referring primarily to religious leaders. The primary reason the scribes and Pharisees hated our Lord was because He was so popular with the masses. And as Jesus predicted, the apostles were also hated by the religious leaders, particularly in Jerusalem, because many of their Jewish followers became disciples of Jesus Christ. Understandably, this threatened these religious leaders.

Generally speaking, then, when Christians live for Christ as they should, they will be respected by the majority of non-Christians even though these people may not respond in faith. And as in New Testament days, non-Christian religious leaders who lose their followers will feel threatened and respond negatively.

THE SECOND SUPRACULTURAL PRINCIPLE

Christians should work hard to provide for their economic needs so that they are not criticized by unbelievers for being lazy and irresponsible (1 Thess. 4:11-12).

Paul modeled this principle at a *personal* level, and the Jerusalem Christians stand out as an unusual *corporate* model. Though many non-Christians were attracted to Christ, they were not drawn into this community because the believers were lazy. Rather, they were impressed with their love and concern for one another.

And so it should be today in every church no matter what the cultural conditions. There should always be a considered balance between caring for those who have needs, while at the same time working hard as a group of Christians to earn a living that will not only meet personal needs but have something left over to share with others (Eph. 4:28).

God's "unfolding revelation" gives us balance in determining how Christians should view and use material possessions. Though we are to be unselfish and generous with what we have, we should not allow our Christian love to encourage irresponsibility in others. Neither should other Christians take advantage of Christian generosity. We are all to be diligent, seeing the opportunity to make a living as a wonderful gift from God. As we do, we will also impact non-Christians.

NOTES

1. The Greek word *apostolos* means literally a delegate, a messenger or one sent forth with orders. In the New Testament, however, the term *apostle*, almost without exception, is used in a distinct sense. It refers primarily to the men Jesus Christ selected out of the larger group of disciples and "named as apostles" (Luke 6:13; Matt. 10:1-4). When Judas betrayed the Lord, he was eventually replaced by Matthias, who was "numbered with the eleven apostles" (Acts 1:26).

    Paul also classified himself as an "untimely born" apostle. He described himself as called to be an apostle but "not fit to be called an apostle" because he "persecuted the church of God" (1 Cor. 15:8-9). Though he did not feel worthy to be an apostle, Luke's record in the book of Acts verifies Paul's claim and testimony. He was an apostle in the primary sense.

    There is a secondary sense, however, in which the word "apostle" is used in the New Testament. Luke called Barnabas an apostle (Acts 14:4-14). And as we have seen in the Thessalonian letter, Paul classified Silas and Timothy as fellow apostles (2:6-7). He may have used this same description of Andronicus and Junias (Rom. 16:7). But these descriptions are not used in the primary sense. On the one hand, these fellow missionaries were messengers and delegates sent forth by Jesus Christ as any missionary or Christian leader. But in a primary sense, apostles were those men who were eyewitnesses of Jesus Christ and who were taught by Him personally and specially selected for an initial ministry in bringing into being the Body of Christ, His church. See George W. Peters, *A Theology of Church Growth* (Grand Rapids: Zondervan, 1981), p. 17; Gene A. Getz, *Sharpening the Focus of the Church* (Wheaton, Ill.: Victor, 1984), pp. 123-26.

2. In some miraculous way, the Holy Spirit guided Paul in recording the inspired Word of God but, at the same time, withheld from him certain specific details regarding the second coming of Jesus Christ. The fact that Paul was able to write inspired statements without knowing all there was to know about the future bears witness to the divine nature of Scripture. This should not surprise us since the Old Testament prophets were able to accomplish this divine feat consistently. They oftentimes did not understand the distinctions between the first coming of Christ and His second coming. Yet they were writing and proclaiming the very words of God. As we study the unfolding of God's revelation as recorded by these men in Holy Scripture, we can appreciate the marvelous miracle that took place when God inspired them over a process of time to give us the Holy Scriptures.

22

Paul's Second Letter to the Thessalonians

Paul wrote a follow-up letter to the Thessalonians just a couple of months after his first letter. He clarified yet further some issues regarding the second coming of Christ and once again addressed the problem of "idleness" that existed in the church (1 Thess. 4:11-12). As has been true in every church throughout the centuries, some in Thessalonica did not respond to the will of God. Consequently, Paul had to take more extreme measures. He issued two more basic exhortations regarding how to handle those believers who were deliberately disobedient.

2 THESSALONIANS 3:6

In the name of the Lord Jesus Christ, we command you,
brothers, to keep away from every brother who is idle
and does not live according to the teaching you received from us.

EXPOSITION

Paul's words certainly reflect seriousness and apostolic authority. The Greek word for *command* was often used to describe a general in the army who was giving orders to his troops. The word *ataktous* (translated "idle" or "unruly") was used to describe soldiers who were not maintaining rank.[1]

The "word picture" is clear. Paul was deeply disturbed. He and his missionary companions had modeled diligence when they ministered among them. Accordingly, he once again reminded them of this: "you yourselves know how you ought to follow our example. *We were not idle* when we were with you, nor did we eat anyone's food without paying for it. On the contrary, we worked night and day, laboring and toiling so that we would not be a burden to any of you" (3:7-9).

Paul reiterated their apostolic right to receive monetary help. But, he reminded them, they had not used this right so that they might be a "model" for these believers "to follow" (3:9). Not only were some of these Christians ignoring their example, they were also ignoring Paul's previous instructions.

Initially Paul had exhorted them regarding this matter while he was with them (3:10). Then he had reminded them of their model (1 Thess. 2:7-9). He also repeated in writing the exhortation he had given them face-to-face (1 Thess. 4:11). Finally he had ended his first letter by asking all the Christians in Thessalonica to also "warn those who are idle" (1 Thess. 5:14). The Greek word translated "idle" is a strong one. In this context, it means to be guilty of lazy behavior. As Morris points out, "it denotes culpable idleness or loafing."[2]

Paul's disturbance is understandable. Some of these believers had persistently and blatantly ignored the will of God. They were without excuse. It was time to take action. Paul issued an order to the Christians in Thessalonica to disassociate themselves from every believer who continued to live such an irresponsible life. They were not to tolerate this kind of behavior in the Christian community any longer.

THE THIRD SUPRACULTURAL PRINCIPLE

Christians should separate themselves from other Christians who are persistently irresponsible in not providing for their own economic needs (2 Thess. 3:6).

This principle demonstrates dramatically how displeased God is when Christians do not work hard to earn a living and, in the process, take advantage of others. In a sense, Paul grouped "lazy Christians" into the same category as "immoral Christians." When writing to the Corinthians, he had to deal with a man who was engaging in immorality with his "father's wife," a sin that did not "occur even among pagans" (1 Cor. 5:1b). Paul himself was astounded. "And you are proud!" he wrote. "Shouldn't you rather have been filled with grief and have *put out of your fellowship* the man who did this?" (1 Cor. 5:2).

Christians are not to fellowship with believers who, after being warned, continue to live in flagrant sin of *any* kind. Paul considered laziness and taking material advantage of other Christians as a "flagrant sin." Church discipline is for two basic reasons. First, we need to maintain purity in the church. We are not to continue to allow flagrant and open sin to continue to be practiced among believers. Not only does it hurt the testimony of a local body of believers, but it will tend to corrupt the church. Others will begin to take similar liberties.

The second purpose for church discipline is to bring about godly sorrow in the one who has been disciplined. Though Paul was very direct in his dealings with the sinful man in Corinth (he exhorted them to "expel the wicked man"; 1 Cor. 5:12b), yet he was quick to encourage these believers to restore him and "reaffirm" their "love for him" once he had turned from his sin (2 Cor. 2:8). Paul also underscored this purpose for discipline when he wrote to the Galatians: "Brothers, if someone is caught in a sin, you who are spiritual should restore him gently. But watch yourself, or you also could be tempted" (Gal. 6:1-2).

Though church discipline should be administered with a great deal of sensitivity and humility, it must be done if we intend to obey God. Since some of the Thessalonian Christians had been repeatedly taught what was proper and right regarding work habits, and since they refused to respond, they were to be excluded from the fellowship of believers. To restate the principle, Christians should separate themselves from other believers who are persistently irresponsible in not providing for their own economic needs (3:6).[3]

Paul's exhortation, of course, does not apply to believers who *want* to work but cannot but, rather, to those who *can* work but will not. Hopefully, when this principle is applied in love, those disciplined will respond by beginning to live in the will of God. And when they do, they should be totally forgiven and quickly restored.

2 THESSALONIANS 3:10*b*

If a man will not work, he shall not eat.

EXPOSITION

When Paul ministered among these Christians face-to-face, he had already warned them that believers who will not work should not be given food (3:10*a*). To keep providing them with the necessities of life would only encourage their irresponsibility.

Paul's words, taken out of context, may appear to be harsh and insensitive. However, these people *needed* "tough love." They were not responding whatsoever to Paul's gracious and repetitious exhortations. Furthermore, Paul's intention was not to "kick these people out." Rather, he was attempting to "get their attention" and to bring needed changes in their lives. Thus, Paul concluded by saying, "Do not associate with him [that is, any brother or sister who is idle] *in order that he [or she] may feel ashamed*" (3:14).

To make sure the Thessalonian Christians really understood his motives, Paul clarified that they should not regard this person "as an enemy," but "as a brother" (3:15). In other words, they were to approach this individual as a member of the family of God, dealing with each person lovingly but firmly. Paul had already modeled this "parental approach." He and his fellow missionaries, Silas and Timothy, had ministered among these believers just "*as a father deals with his own children*, encouraging, comforting and urging" them to "live lives worthy of God" (1 Thess. 2:11-12). Paul was simply asking the more mature Christians in Thessalonica to continue this nurturing process with those who needed discipline.

On the more personal and pragmatic side, there is another reason Paul might have been disturbed. He and his fellow missionaries had voluntarily given up the right to financial support and had diligently and sacrificially earned their own living in order to be a model to these people. When some of these Christians did not respond, either to their example or their exhortations, Paul had to feel a certain amount of disappointment. He was human and had to feel "used." Even so, Paul's overriding concern was that these people were willfully walking out of the will of God after having been reminded again and again.

THE FOURTH SUPRACULTURAL PRINCIPLE

Christians who can, but do not, work for a living should not be given economic assistance (2 Thess. 3:10b).

As illustrated by Paul, this principle is to be practiced only after Christians have been thoroughly taught that they are out of the will of God and after they persistently refuse to respond. But it must be applied, and the reason is simply explained. Lazy people who are given economic assistance will continue to take advantage of others' generosity. This is affirmed again and again in culture generally. People think of all kinds of ways to misuse and abuse a welfare system. Unfortunately, Christians are not exempt from this kind of behavior.

Probably no biblical principle is more difficult to apply. Manipulative Christians can easily make other Christians feel guilty. It is difficult to resist a person who cries out, "How can you do this to me and call yourself a Christian?" However, a "hungry stomach" will do wonders for lazy Christians. As in other aspects of Christian living where believers are not practicing the will of God, it sometimes takes a traumatic experience to enable these people to break out of their sinful habits.

This principle is also difficult to apply when more than one person is involved. Paul was certainly not teaching that we should be insensitive to innocent family members who become victims because of a lazy father or mother. But here again, we must develop an approach to discipline that will deal with the offender without making innocent people suffer.

Paul's exhortations regarding laziness and church discipline have a number of applications. The more general principle is that Christian leaders have a responsibility to deal with people who persistently violate the will of God in all aspects of their lives. We are not to ignore sin in the Body of Christ and "look the other way." Neither are we to allow people to continue in sin after repeated modeling and warnings. Christian leaders are to "take special note" (3:14a) of any individual who is ignoring God's will in this way and administer church discipline in a sensitive, loving, humble, and protective way (Gal. 6:1-2). In its extreme form, this means disassociation and exclusion from fellowship in the local Body of Christ.

A BROADER PERSPECTIVE ON A BIBLICAL WORK ETHIC

All of these instructions in the Thessalonian letters having to do with being diligent in economic matters are reinforced in other places in Scripture. The book of Proverbs particularly underscores what Paul was saying and provides Christians with divine wisdom in being diligent in our work habits:

> How long will you lie there, you sluggard? When will you get up from your sleep? (6:9)

> Lazy hands make a man poor, but diligent hands bring wealth. (10:4)

> The sluggard craves and gets nothing, but the desires of the diligent are fully satisfied. (13:4)

> The laborer's appetite works for him; his hunger drives him on. (16:26)

> Laziness brings on deep sleep, and the shiftless man goes hungry. (19:15)

> Do not love sleep or you will grow poor; stay awake and you will have food to spare. (20:13)

> I went past the field of the sluggard, past the vineyard of the man who lacks judgment; thorns had come up everywhere, the ground was covered with weeds, and the stone wall was in ruins. I applied my heart to what I observed and learned a lesson from what I saw: A little sleep, a little slumber, a little folding of the hands to rest—and poverty will come on you like a bandit and scarcity like an armed man. (24:30-34)

NOTES

1. Leon Morris, *The Epistles of Paul to the Thessalonians: An Introduction and Commentary*, vol. 13 of *The Tyndale New Testament Commentaries* (Grand Rapids: Eerdmans, 1956), pp. 100, 144.

2. Morris adds another helpful explanation regarding Paul's exhortation to the Corinthians to separate themselves from the immoral brother (1 Cor. 5:9-11) and his command to the Thessalonians to separate themselves from the lazy Christians (2 Thess. 3:6, 14-15):

   The treatment of such a man is to withdraw from close fellowship with him. *Sunanamignusthai* is a double compound with "the first preposition *sun* denoting 'combination,' the second *ana* 'interchange'" (Lightfoot). It literally means "Don't mix yourselves up with him." This very expressive word gives the idea of familiar intercourse which is thus prohibited in the case of the erring brother. This is not as stringent a course as that advocated in 1 Cor. v. 9-11 (the only other passage in the New Testament where this verb is used), for there it is added that one is not to eat with the offender in question. Here it is only the exercise of familiar intercourse that is restrained. Paul is insisting that the erring one be regarded as a brother and treated in such a way as to bring him to his senses. So he adds *that he may be ashamed.* (Ibid., p. 149)

Though Morris points out that Paul seemed to insist on a more stringent approach with the sexually immoral, the facts are that Christians were not to fellowship with either the "immoral believers" in Corinth or with the "idle believers" in Thesssalonica. In both cases, church discipline was involved. Though Morris points out that Paul exhorted the Corinthians "that one is not to eat with the offender in question," it is difficult to understand how Christians can separate themselves from erring Christians who are lazy and disobedient and yet fellowship with them over a meal. Nevertheless, Morris's point is well made and needs to be considered when applying church discipline in this kind of situation.

3. In recent years lawsuits have been brought against churches because certain individuals have been disciplined and excluded from fellowship. A careful study of these situations often reveals that methods of excommunication have, at times, been used that are out of harmony with biblical teachings and principles. For example, certain sins have been made public before the "whole church" when it has not been necessary or appropriate. When a person is approached personally and privately about sin and refuses to repent of that sin but voluntarily and quietly withdraws from the church, it is not biblical to "announce" that sin to the whole church. The only justification for doing so is when that individual continues to make slanderous statements about the church that create misunderstanding and divisions. Even then, all communication should be done sensitively and cautiously, though openly and honestly. It should never be vindictive.

A careful study of all passages on church discipline reveals that methods of church discipline should always be used in an effort to restore a person who has sinned. This means selecting and using approaches that protect the person involved, even though that person may choose to continue to violate the will of God. Carefully practicing Paul's injunctions in Galatians 6:1-2 is the key to avoiding misunderstandings and retaliation on the part of a Christian who refuses to respond with repentance and godly sorrow.

On the other hand, some people are so hardened in their sin that they will sometimes do all they can to bring reproach on the cause of Christ and attempt to benefit themselves financially through a lawsuit. To avoid this possibility, church leaders should carefully document in writing every step taken in church discipline. These documents, however, should not be distributed to the person involved—only read in his presence so that he knows what these statements are and that they will be placed in a confidential file.

Furthermore, every encounter and confrontation should involve more than one church leader so that verbal comments and exchanges can be verified by two or three witnesses. That is why the plural pronoun in Galatians 6:1-2 is so important: "Brothers, if someone is caught in a sin, you [plural] who are spiritual should restore him gently."

Christians have also misapplied Jesus' teachings in Matthew 18:15-17, which has led to some legal problems of late. Here Jesus was referring to an offense by one Christian against another, not a sin against the whole body of Christ. The problem of laziness in Thessalonica and the immorality in Corinth were sins against the whole church and needed to be dealt with by more than one spiritual leader as outlined by Paul in Galatians 6:1-2. In these instances, a solitary leader should not be involved, even in the initial confrontation.

In Matthew 18, Jesus was teaching that personal offenses should be handled initially one on one. If the problem cannot be resolved, the person sinned against should take one or two other Christians along who can help in the communication process. Then, if the problem is still not resolved, it should be taken to a larger assembly. The mistake made at this point is to interpret Jesus' reference to "the church" as the "whole church body." This may also refer to an assembly of leaders in the church, who then can decide the extent to which the problem should be made public if it cannot be resolved.

We must be careful not to superimpose upon Jesus' teachings, or any teachings of Scripture, a methodology or pattern that grows out of our own cultural understanding rather than out of the true spirit and meaning that the biblical writers had in mind. When we carefully apply biblical principles and use methods that are in harmony with the purpose of these principles, we can avoid many of the negative problems that result. On the other hand, we must never fail to apply biblical principles or compromise scriptural teachings because of cultural situations. On the other hand, we must not misapply scriptural principles and use methods that are out of harmony with those principles.

23

Paul's First Letter to the Corinthians

To understand the setting of Paul's first letter to the Corinthians, we need to recreate some events that are only alluded to and not spelled out in the biblical record. Evidently, Paul wrote a letter to the Corinthians that is no longer in existence. He refers to that letter in 1 Corinthians 5: "I have written you in *my letter* [commonly called the "lost letter"] not to associate with sexually immoral people" (v. 9). Evidently, what he had shared in that "first letter" was misunderstood and Paul felt it necessary to clarify what he actually meant—which he does in 1 Corinthians 5:10 and following.

When Paul wrote this lost letter, he was probably in Ephesus, the same city in which he composed 1 Corinthians, while he was ministering there during the third missionary journey (16:8). Evidently, three men from Corinth—Stephanas, Fortunatus, and Achaicus (16:17)—came to Ephesus and delivered a written response to Paul's lost letter. Paul made reference to their response in 1 Corinthians 7: "Now for the matters you *wrote* about. . ." (v. 1).

When Stephanas, Fortunatus, and Achaicus arrived in Ephesus, they also reported some of their own concerns. In addition, they brought a gift of money to help meet Paul's physical needs (16:17-18). Since the Corinthians as a church had been remiss in using their material possessions to further the gospel of Christ, these three men evidently took on themselves the responsibility to assist Paul.

Paul spoke to a number of concerns when he wrote 1 Corinthians: divisions in the church, immorality, lawsuits, marriage problems, food sacrificed to idols, abuse of the Lord's Supper, misuse of spiritual gifts, lack of order in church services, and false teaching about the resurrection of Christ. His writing style was informal. In some instances, he was probably answering questions they had asked, both in the letter they had sent him and as verbalized by Stephanas, Fortunatus, and Achaicus. However, he was also speaking to issues and concerns that had been passed on to him by others, such as some people from "Chloe's household" (1:11).[1]

In Paul's second letter to the Corinthians, we find the most comprehensive section of teaching in the whole Bible regarding how Christians should use their material possessions. But first we need to look at three important statements in this prior letter, which in turn will help us understand more fully what Paul wrote in 2 Corinthians.

1 CORINTHIANS 9:14-15*a*

In the same way, the Lord has commanded that those who preach the gospel should receive their living from the gospel. But I have not used any of those rights.

EXPOSITION

In chapter 8 Paul exhorts the Corinthians to give up certain rights in order to keep weaker Christians from stumbling and sinning. The case in point involved eating food that had been sacrificed to idols. Paul gave his own perspective on this: "Therefore, if what I eat causes my brother to fall into sin, I will never eat meat again, so that I will not cause him to fall" (8:13).

Paul, then, expanded on his own personal philosophy on individual rights. The example he used at length involved his rights as an apostle to receive financial support. To demonstrate that he indeed had this right, he asked three questions (9:7):

> Who serves as a soldier at his own expense?
>
> Who plants a vineyard and does not eat of its grapes?
>
> Who tends a flock and does not drink of the milk?

Very few, if any, of the Corinthians would have disagreed with Paul in this matter. However, he built his case further when he quoted from the law of Moses: "Do not muzzle an ox while it is treading out the grain" (9:9). Paul then became specific in relationship to his ministry among the Corinthians: "If we have sown *spiritual seed* among you," he asked, "is it too much if we reap a *material harvest* from you? If others have this right of support from you, shouldn't we have it all the more?" (9:11-12).

Again, the Corinthians would have to conclude that it was both biblical and logical that Paul had this right. However, he went on to remind them that he had not insisted on financial support—even though in Judaism those "who work in the temple get their food from the temple and those who serve at the altar share in what is offered on the altar. In the same way," he concluded, "the Lord has commanded that *those who preach the gospel should receive their living from the gospel"* (9:13-14).

WHY SUCH A LENGTHY EXAMPLE

Paul was establishing another principle with this personal illustration. If he gave up *this right* (to financial support), was it too much to ask those Corinthians who were not bothered in their consciences by eating meat offered to idols to give up *that right* so that weaker Christians would not stumble and fall into sin? This passage emphasizes several important spiritual truths. The first we have come across frequently in our study: those who minister in the Word of God should be supported by the people they minister to. However, here this principle was secondary in Paul's mind. He was actually concerned that Christians be willing at times to give up certain rights in order to serve others.

On the other hand, the secondary message in this passage also speaks volumes regarding how Paul viewed material possessions. A lesser person in Paul's circumstances would have a very difficult time turning down gifts of money. This is a temptation all people face, including ministers of the gospel. Paul's example demonstrates the importance of maintaining pure motives, unselfish attitudes, and nonmaterialistic goals—no matter what our vocation. To give up rights in the realm of time and in the area of convenience is one thing. But it is still another to give up rights to material possessions. Few Christians have ever been able to measure up to Paul's sterling character in this area of life.

THE FIFTH SUPRACULTURAL PRINCIPLE

Even though God has commanded that spiritual leaders be cared for financially by those they minister to, there are times when it is the part of wisdom for spiritual leaders to give up that right (1 Cor. 9:14-15a).

When Paul applied this principle to his own life and ministry, he was not suggesting that other spiritual leaders were out of the will of God if they did not give up this right. He was saying, however, that no action on the part of a Christian leader demonstrates more dramatically purity of motive and concern for God's reputation than giving up money that belongs to you by divine decree. May God give us more spiritual leaders who are willing to practice this principle in order to avoid actions that might become a stumbling block to both unbelievers and immature Christians.

Conversely, this principle should in no way encourage Christians to take financial advantage of spiritual leaders. To do so is to violate the will of God. Perhaps this is one of the primary reasons Paul, before sharing his personal experience, strongly emphasized God's plan for caring for spiritual leaders' physical needs. He did not want his own approach to this matter to create hardships for other Christian leaders.

1 CORINTHIANS 16:2

On the first day of every week, each one of you should
set aside a sum of money in keeping with his income, saving it up,
so that when I come no collections will have to be made.

EXPOSITION

Paul was speaking here of a collection of money that he was taking for the poor Christians in Jerusalem. He may have had two basic motives for wanting this project to be successful. First, he was deeply concerned about the needs of these people. But for years some of the Jewish Christians in Jerusalem had been suspicious of his ministry to the Gentiles. Perhaps he hoped that a generous gift would demonstrate to these Jewish believers the validity of his mission to the Gentiles (see 2 Cor. 9:13-14).

Sometime earlier Paul had shared this special need with the Corinthians. Their initial response was positive and even enthusiastic (2 Cor. 8:10-11). However, they had not followed through on their commitment. They had failed to set aside money on a regular and systematic basis in order to be prepared when Paul would eventually come to Corinth to take their gift to Jerusalem. What should be their response? How should they follow through? What did Paul expect? Evidently, these were some of the questions reported to Paul.

Consequently, he responded with a very direct and specific plan. Following the tradition that quickly evolved in the first century, the Corinthian Christians were meeting on the first day of the week. This was distinct from the Jewish sabbath and was set aside for Christian worship to remember the resurrection of Christ. Therefore, Paul exhorted every Christian in Corinth to "set aside a sum of money" on this day for this special offering. He did not specify the amount. However, he stated that all were to participate, and what they gave was to be "in keeping with each individual Christian's income" (16:2a).

Paul was also specific in terms of methodology. It was not only to be set aside every week but it was to be saved up so that when Paul arrived, they would not have to take special offerings to try to reach a particular goal (16:2b). For a Jew like Paul, systematic giving had been a part of his religious heritage. As a zealous Pharisee, he had probably practiced the three-tithe system most of his life. In his unconverted days he may even have been one of those radical religious leaders who even tithed on "mint, dill and cummin" (Matt. 23:23).

But these Gentile Christians would have had very little teaching about giving and certainly fewer models. Though there was a Jewish synagogue in Corinth, paganism ran rampant in the city. There would have been very little exposure to "God-fearing Jews" who were good examples in this aspect of their lives.

Though Paul did not mention a percentage of their income in this passage, he was definitely speaking in terms of percentages. Each Christian was to determine that percentage in the light of how God had prospered him. Furthermore, that percentage was to be predetermined. They were not to simply give from what they "had left over" or what they felt like giving from week to week. It is clear from this passage that it was to be a carefully designed program of stewardship.

Paul was not absolutizing here in terms of "methodology." Rather, he was giving these Christians specific guidance that would fit their cultural situation. However, his directive yields an important principle that is substantiated elsewhere in the New Testament: saving up and giving to God's work should be systematic and regular.

THE SIXTH SUPRACULTURAL PRINCIPLE

Christians should set aside a certain percentage of their income on just as regular a basis as they are paid in order to be able to systematically give to God's work (1 Cor. 16:2).

The Word of God, from beginning to end, teaches that giving should be systematic and regular. We are to be consistent in this area just as in other areas of Christian living. For example, we are to consistently live lives free from immorality (Eph. 4:17-25), dishonesty, and inappropriate anger (Eph. 4:25-28). We are to consistently avoid "unwholesome" talk and anything that is destructive to others (Eph. 4:29-32). Stating it positively, all believers are to "be imitators of God" and to "live a life of love, just as Christ loved us and gave himself up for us as a fragrant offering and sacrifice to God" (Eph. 5:1-2).

Just so, Christians are to *consistently* share their material possessions in order to carry out the work of God in this world. And we should be *systematic* and *regular* in our giving. If our work is regular, our income will be regular. Our giving should also be regular.

Just as physical needs are regular among all Christians, causing us to have to work and earn a living from day to day, the needs for carrying on God's work are consistent and regular. Christian leaders who earn their living serving Christ and the body of Christ have regular physical needs just as those who earn a living in other vocations.

This focuses a very important question. What percentage should a Christian set aside on a consistent basis from his regular income? The children of Israel were to give 10 percent of their resources to support their spiritual leaders. They were to set aside another 10 percent to be able to worship God as a family. And every third year, they were to set aside 10 percent to meet the needs of others. However, the Holy Spirit did not lead New Testament writers to specify amounts and percentages.

OLD TESTAMENT INFLUENCE ON THE EARLY CHURCH

Those who first came to Christ in Jerusalem were "God-fearing Jews"—men and women who would no doubt have been faithful in giving at least three tithes. No one who understands habit patterns in a religious system would deny that the three-tithe plan in Israel became an influential factor in helping these Jewish Christians determine their giving patterns in the church of Jesus Christ. If this is what God expected under law, they would tend to at least use this as a basis for evaluating how much they should give in view of God's saving grace. In fact, at times, these New Testament Christians gave beyond the amounts designated in the three-tithe system—particularly in the early days of the church as it functioned in Jerusalem.

Does this mean that Christians are obligated to follow the three-tithe system? The answer must be "no" since God does not reiterate this system as an absolute form or method for Christians. However, what the Israelites practiced at God's command provides believers with a strong pragmatic model for evaluating their own giving patterns.

First, if we are going to give systematically and regularly, we must predetermine the percentage or amount. Second, if we are going to give "according to our ability" (as the Christians in Antioch did) and if we are going to give "proportionately" (as Paul exhorted the Corinthians to do), we must carefully and honestly determine how much that will be. Third, if we are going to make sure God's work gets done in God's way, we must also look at the pragmatic factors. Why did God specify certain amounts to carry on His work in the Old Testament? Is there something unique about the 10 percent amount as it relates to supporting those who carry out the Great Commission on a full-time basis? Is there something unique about the 10 percent amount to make sure family members worship God and learn His will as they should? Is there something unique about the 10 percent amount specified to help meet the needs of others who are not as fortunate as we are?

These are questions we must carefully consider when we determine how much we should give on a regular and systematic basis. From a pragmatic point of view, one thing is crystal clear. If all Christians gave the same regular amounts to the church as the Jews gave to maintain their religious system, there would never be unmet economic needs in the ministry today. Furthermore, if all Christians gave proportionately as God has blessed them—which God says we should—some would be giving much more than three tithes to God's work.

1 CORINTHIANS 16:3-4

Then, when I arrive, I will give letters of introduction
to the men you approve and send them with your gift to Jerusalem.
If it seems advisable for me to go also, they will accompany me.

EXPOSITION

Though Paul was doing the planning regarding this collection, he did not handle the money personally. He exhorted the Corinthians to raise the funds, to store it up, and to keep it until he arrived. Then they were to choose people they personally trusted to transport the gift. True to form, Paul wanted to be above reproach in all respects so that no one could accuse him of raising this money to benefit himself. Paul indicated that he had hoped to go to Jerusalem himself if it worked into his schedule and the individuals chosen by the Corinthians could actually accompany him. However, Paul wanted this gift to be taken to Jerusalem whether or not he was able to go along.

We have already observed that Paul was extremely cautious as to how and when he received monies for his own personal ministry. He was just as cautious as to how he handled monies that were given to meet the needs of others. He did not want to give anyone an opportunity to question his motives or to accuse him of misappropriating funds. Once again, we see Paul's exceptional character. Not only would he never take what did not belong to him, but he would never engage in any kind of activity that could be misinterpreted either by Christians or non-Christians. What a powerful lesson for all Christian leaders today.

THE SEVENTH SUPRACULTURAL PRINCIPLE

Those who handle and distribute monies that are given to God's work should be above reproach in all respects and should be held accountable (1 Cor. 16:3-4).

What an important principle in today's world when some prominent "Christian" leaders have been guilty of violating God's will in this matter. In applying this principle, we would do well to follow Paul's model.

First, Christian leaders who receive money directly to meet their own needs should set up a plan whereby they do not have to handle the money personally without a careful reporting and accountability system. Furthermore, they should never make decisions on their own regarding the amounts they personally receive.

Second, there should be more than one person selected to handle money for God's work. These people should be approved by those who know them to be people of integrity. God established this principle very quickly in the history of Israel when leaders were appointed to assist Moses. They were to "select capable men from all the people—men who fear God, trustworthy men who hate dishonest gain" (Ex. 18:21; Deut. 1:13). And it is certainly not by accident that those who were selected to be deacons in the church (men and women in serving roles) were to be individuals who did not, and would not, pursue "dishonest gain" (1 Tim. 3:8*b*). They were to be "trustworthy in everything" (1 Tim. 3:11*b*).

NOTE

1. We are not told who Chloe actually was. But R. V. G. Tasker, *The Gospel According to St. Matthew: An Introduction and Commentary*, vol. 1 of *The Tyndale New Testament Commentaries* (Grand Rapids: Eerdmans, 1961), p. 39, gives this helpful information: "As her name is mentioned, it is perhaps more likely that she was an Ephesian than a Corinthian. But we do not know. Nor do we know whether she was a Christian, though this may be judged probable. At any rate, members of her household had *declared* the situation to Paul. The word means 'made clear.'"

24

Paul's Second Letter
to the Corinthians, 8:1-24

Paul wrote his second letter to the Corinthians from somewhere in Macedonia (perhaps Philippi).[1] It was prompted by Titus's return from Corinth and his report that these believers had responded quite positively to the straightforward exhortations in his first letter. Consequently, when Paul wrote his second letter, he expressed joy at their favorable response (7:5-16). However, he was still concerned about the way they were handling their finances. Apparently Titus indicated that some of the Corinthians were still confused and frustrated about Paul's exhortations regarding this aspect of their lives. We can reconstruct what evidently happened.

The Corinthians had been the first church to respond to Paul's request to raise money for the needy Christians in Jerusalem (8:9). In fact, their enthusiastic response had motivated the churches in Macedonia to also participate in this project (8:1-2; 9:1-2). But, since the Corinthians had not followed through on their financial commitments, Paul exhorted each of them to immediately "set aside a sum of money" each week, based upon their personal incomes (1 Cor. 16:1-2; 2 Cor. 8:6).

Predictably, this exhortation created some negative reactions. Like many twentieth-century Christians, they had not put God first in their financial planning, and they felt the financial crunch. When Titus reported these reactions to Paul, he penned his second letter. After commending them for their positive response in other areas of their Christian lives, he elaborated on what he had told them to do in his initial communication.

2 Corinthians 8:1-2

And now, brothers, we want you to know about
the grace that God has given the Macedonian churches.

> *Out of the most severe trial, their overflowing joy and*
> *their extreme poverty welled up in rich generosity.*

EXPOSITION

Since some of the Corinthians reacted negatively to Paul's instructions to give regularly, systematically, and proportionately (1 Cor. 16:1-2), this is no doubt why Paul began this section on giving by calling their attention to the Macedonian churches (probably the Philippians, the Thessalonians, and possibly the Bereans). He reminded the Corinthians that the believers in these churches had given generously in the midst of a very difficult situation. In fact, Paul used the phrase "extreme poverty" to identify their economic circumstances.

The Macedonians "gave as much as they were able, and even *beyond their ability*" (8:3). Philip Hughes helps us understand their situation more clearly when he comments: "So far from enjoying conditions of material wealth and prosperity which would have enabled them to subscribe without discomfort, they gave in circumstances of the severe testing of affliction and rock-bottom poverty."[2]

This kind of giving is *not* something God *expects* from His children. He is aware that we have basic needs, and nowhere in Scripture are Christians commanded to give away what is necessary for their own existence. Furthermore, God wants us to use wisdom in preparing for circumstances beyond our control. A number of Proverbs emphasize the importance of future planning (see p. 87). But the believers in Macedonia seemed to ignore these factors, both as related to their present circumstances and to future emergencies. They gave beyond what may be considered as "common sense."

The Macedonian Christians were not responding to coercion. Paul may have even warned them against this kind of sacrificial giving. But "entirely on their own" (8:3b), they responded by "urgently pleading" with Paul and his fellow missionaries to be able to do something for other Christians in need (8:4).

The way in which the Macedonian church responded took Paul off guard. We are not told exactly what happened. We only know that he was pleasantly surprised. And he affirmed that what the Macedonians had done in first giving themselves to the Lord was "in keeping with *God's will*" (8:5b; Rom. 12:2).

The larger context in which Christians are to use their material possessions involves, first of all, presenting to the Lord their "bodies as living sacrifices" (Rom. 12:1). Once they take this step, it follows naturally that they view everything they have as belonging to God. And it is this perspective that makes material gifts "a fragrant offering, an acceptable sacrifice, pleasing to God" (Phil. 4:18). The Macedonian believers are a beautiful illustration of this important principle. They "gave themselves first to the Lord" (8:5).

THE EIGHTH SUPRACULTURAL PRINCIPLE

Every local body of believers needs real-life examples of other churches that are positive models in the area of giving (2 Cor. 8:1-2).

Modeling is an important principle in helping Christians learn how they should use their material possessions. The apostles, both as individuals and as a group, demonstrated unusual commitment in this area. They left houses, lands, and their businesses to follow Christ. As local churches were planted throughout the New Testament world, this divine plan continued to unfold.

Paul was certainly utilizing this approach in his second letter to the Corinthians. Initially these believers seemed to think they were doing rather well in this area of their corporate life. After all, their eager response to the financial needs of the poor Christians in Jerusalem had motivated the Macedonians to participate (9:2). However, they had not matched their "talk" with their "walk." In an ironic reversal, Paul used the Macedonians as a positive model for the Corinthians (8:1-5, 8).

We need to give this principle special attention in affluent areas of the world. Many of us in the Western church have no concept of sacrificial giving. And yet there are groups of Christians in Third World countries that are "Macedonian" in nature. *They* are giving out of *poverty*,[3] and the American church is not even giving out of *plenty.* American Christians need to know about these believers. It will help activate many to greater commitment.

2 CORINTHIANS 8:6

So we urged Titus, since he had earlier made a beginning, to bring also to completion this act of grace on your part.

EXPOSITION

This special project had been in progress for some time, having been initiated by Paul even before he wrote his first letter to the Corinthians. On Titus's first return visit, he helped the Corinthians get started. On his second visit, he was following Paul's instructions to bring this project "to completion." This is probably what brought some negative reactions from the Corinthians.

THE NINTH SUPRACULTURAL PRINCIPLE

Christians need to be held accountable when they make financial commitments to God's work (2 Cor. 8:6, 10-11; 9:3).

When it comes to giving, many Christians have good intentions. Like the Corinthians, they may respond enthusiastically when they hear about special needs. However, also like the Corinthians, it is easy to forget commitments. Notice how many steps Paul took to make sure the Corinthians followed through on their financial commitments:

First, he sent Titus to help them complete the project (8:6).

Second, he wrote them a personal letter, encouraging them to "finish the work" (8:10-11).

Third, he sent a group of "brothers" ahead of time to make sure they had collected the money before he himself arrived (9:3).

Fourth, he alerted them to his personal plans to arrive with some Macedonian Christians so that they would be prepared and not be embarrassed (9:4).

Paul's plan illustrates accountability. It also demonstrates how easy it is for all of us to conveniently forget what we have set out to do, especially when our own "desires" overshadow the "needs" of others. Consequently, we too need constant reminders.

2 CORINTHIANS 8:7

But just as you excel in everything—in faith, in speech,
in knowledge, in complete earnestness and in your love
for us—see that you also excel in this grace of giving.

EXPOSITION

When the Corinthians were converted to Christ, they were given an abundance of spiritual gifts, or "grace gifts" (1 Cor. 1:5, 7). Paul returned to this subject in his second letter and reminded these believers that they did "excel in everything" (8:7a). However, as Paul enumerated the ways in which this grace was manifested—"in faith, in speech, in knowledge"—he broadened the concept beyond spiritual gifts. He referred to "complete earnestness" and "love" (1 Cor. 8:7)—qualities that are much more comprehensive than spiritual gifts in that they reflect spiritual maturity.

Consequently, when Paul encouraged the Corinthians to "also excel in this grace of giving," he was referring to more than a special spiritual gift. Just as the Corinthians were to utilize their gifts in the context of a growing manifestation of love, so they were *all* (not just some of them) to continue being involved in sharing their material possessions.

Paul was not simply referring to the spiritual gift of giving bestowed on certain individuals in the Corinthian church (see also Rom. 12:6-8). He was dealing with a *spiritual quality* that all believers should and must develop if they are going to be in the will of God. Paul was once again reminding the

Corinthians that they had not responded as he had hoped. If they were as "spiritual" as they seemed to think they were (which, of course, they were not), then they should take a careful look at their lives.

THE TENTH SUPRACULTURAL PRINCIPLE

It is God's will that all Christians excel in the grace of giving (2 Cor. 8:7).

It is true that some believers have a greater desire to give than others. Is this a special gift of the Holy Spirit? Some believe it is. But my own personal opinion is that in most instances this is simply reflective of Christians who have learned the joy of giving. They have matured in this area. They have been obedient, and they are now experiencing the blessing of being unselfish and benevolent.

Whatever our position on spiritual gifts, Christians should never rationalize away their responsibility to give because they do not have a desire to do so and then conclude that God has not "gifted" them in this area of their lives. We have seen that this is something God wants all of us to be involved in, just as He wants all of us to first give ourselves to the Lord (Rom. 12:1-2). Indeed, giving regularly, systematically, and proportionately is the will of God for every Christian. This was the message Paul was sending to the Corinthians. Though different Christians in Corinth would give different amounts, everyone was to be involved. And to be in the will of God, each of us must also be involved in our own local churches.

2 CORINTHIANS 8:8

I am not commanding you, but I want to test the sincerity of your love by comparing it with the earnestness of others.

EXPOSITION

Paul did not "command" the Roman Christians to "offer their bodies as living sacrifices to God"; rather, he "urged" or "beseeched" them. He made clear that they certainly *owed* this response "in view of God's mercy" (Rom. 12:1). But Paul knew that God wanted their response to be one that was based upon their own willingness to do so. Again we see the correlation between giving our material possessions and presenting our bodies to God. Though we certainly owe it to the Lord to be generous people because of His generosity to us, yet He wants our gifts to come from willing hearts.

The Macedonian model. However, Paul had another point in mind. He was open with the Corinthians in stating that he wanted "to test the sincerity of" their "love by comparing it with the earnestness of others" (8:8). This is why he began this section of his letter by illustrating what the Macedonian churches had done. How sincere were the Corinthians? Perhaps Paul had gotten word that they were defending themselves; that is, they may have concluded that they had been as responsive and generous as they could be.

Paul responded by reminding them of the Macedonians—a model that would enable them to evaluate the *extent* to which they were generous. Perhaps the Corinthians had also talked about what they wanted to do, but had not yet done it. By contrast, the Macedonian Christians had not only talked about it, they had actually followed through. But, whatever the dynamics, Paul did not hesitate to let the Corinthians know that they needed to follow through with their good intentions.

The example of Jesus Christ. Just in case the Corinthians were not moved as they should have been by what the Macedonians had done, Paul added a model that they could in no way ignore—nor can we. It is the example of Jesus Christ Himself: "For you know the grace of our Lord Jesus Christ, that though he was rich, yet for your sakes he became poor, so that you through his poverty might become rich" (2 Cor. 8:9). Jesus demonstrated the greatest act of grace ever performed. Paul explained this dynamic in his letter to the Philippians when he wrote about the great *kenosis*—Christ's self-emptying when He gave up the glories of heaven to identify with us in our humanity (Phil. 2:5-8).

In essence, Paul was communicating to the Corinthians (and to us) that when we truly understand what Christ has done for each of us, it should not be necessary to have a "command" in terms of our response to God's love. By implication, Paul was also teaching that Christians who do not give regularly, systematically, proportionately, and joyfully do not have a proper perspective on Christ's incarnation. Neither do they have a proper appreciation of "God's mercies" in providing their redemption. When we have this total perspective, what appears to be a moral duty and responsibility becomes a wonderful and joyous privilege.

THE ELEVENTH SUPRACULTURAL PRINCIPLE

God does not want Christians to respond to a command to share their material possessions but, rather, to respond out of hearts of love that reflect sincere appreciation for His gift of salvation (2 Cor. 8:8-9).

There is no question but that God wants believers to walk in His will in all respects. As Paul wrote to Titus, it is "the grace of God that brings salvation," that "teaches us" to live this kind of life in the will of God (Titus 1:11-12). However, just as God wants us to respond to His grace and love as a motivating factor in offering our "bodies a living sacrifice," He also wants us to respond to the same love and grace as a motivating factor in offering our material possessions to Him.

When Paul reminded the Corinthians that he did not want them to respond to a "command" to share their material possessions, he at the same time reminded them of Jesus Christ, who willingly "became poor" so that they (and all believers) "might become rich" (8:9). Jesus Christ is our example in every respect. And what He, "who being in very nature God," did for the world in giving His very life as a humble servant, even unto death, should constantly motivate Christians to joyfully give their material possessions in a generous way.

2 CORINTHIANS 8:12

For if the willingness is there,
the gift is acceptable according to what one has,
not according to what he does not have.

EXPOSITION

Graciously and sensitively, Paul reminded the Corinthians that the year previous (probably sometime in A.D. 56) they had taken the lead in this project. Now, it seems, they had stopped giving to the project altogether because they did not feel they had the resources to do so. Paul did not accept this rationale as valid. Therefore, he encouraged them to "finish the work, so that your eager willingness to do it may be matched by your completion of it," but only if it is "according to your means" (8:11).

Paul was dealing with a sensitive subject. He did not want to issue a command, putting them under pressure and needlessly raising their guilt level. On the other hand, he believed that they had not responded as they should. Paul was convinced that they were able to complete the project, even if they could not respond as they had originally hoped.

We may also see in this passage something about Paul's personality. He was a strong, goal-oriented individual. When he set his mind to something, he always attempted to complete it. Furthermore, he had on previous occasions demonstrated impatience with people who did not follow through on commitments. This was dramatically illustrated in the disagreement with his friend Barnabas. But Paul was not here responding to the Corinthians in an identical way. Paul was holding the goal out in front of the Corinthians that they themselves had established, and he was pointedly but gently exhorting them to finish the work they had begun.

The Corinthians were having difficulty raising the amount of money they had originally hoped to give to the needy Christians in Jerusalem. Perhaps initially they were overly enthusiastic and unrealistic as to what they could do. Or they may have become victims of certain circumstances that made it difficult for them to follow through. However, they had also been negligent in setting aside the monies on a week-to-week basis, which in turn meant that they had not been carrying out this project regularly and systematically. Consequently, they were not able to reach their goal because they had already spent the money for their own needs and desires.

Paul recognized this problem. He knew that they would not be able to collect money they had already spent. He also recognized that because of this negligence on their part, they would not be able to give what they had hoped and originally planned to give. Therefore, he reminded them that what they set aside was "acceptable according to what they had" at that point in time. It would not, and should not, be evaluated on the basis of *what they did not have.*

The facts seem to be that if they now tried to give as they had originally intended, it would put them under unusual pressure. Money spent is money spent. Therefore, Paul encouraged them to begin where they were at that moment in their lives and to collect the money week by week on the basis of what they could do. God would then recognize and honor their "willingness."

THE TWELFTH SUPRACULTURAL PRINCIPLE

God accepts and honors believers' gifts once they begin to give regularly and systematically, even though they may not be able to give as proportionately as they eventually will be able to once they have their economic lives in order (2 Cor. 8:10-12).

God wants all Christians to begin immediately to organize their financial affairs so they can put God first in the use of their material possessions. Though they may not be able to give in a proportional way until they get their financial house in order, they should make a start. God will then honor them based on their willingness, rather than on what they do not have to give at that moment in their lives. However, as we will see, once believers take this step, God often makes it possible for them to begin to give proportionately and in a generous way.

2 CORINTHIANS 8:13

Our desire is not that others might be relieved while you are hard pressed, but that there might be equality.

EXPOSITION

The clues begin to mount as we read through this letter. It seems that Paul was speaking to concerns that the Corinthians themselves had voiced. As stated earlier, his instructions in his first letter to give regularly and systematically (1 Cor. 16:1-2) evidently brought a negative reaction. There were those in Corinth who felt this would put them under pressure. In reality, it was their own negligence that had caused this problem. But it is also understandable why they would not be fond of sharing their own material possessions to meet others' needs when they themselves would have to sacrifice.

At this juncture, Paul attempted to defend his own motives. He did not want to make life difficult for them while they were helping others. Rather, he was simply attempting to help people who were in greater need than the Corinthians. Paul was in no way advocating a socialist system where all share and share alike. He was dealing with a specific situation in which Christians were experiencing unusual trials and were in deep economic need. As a result, he approached those he knew had *more* in order to help those who had *less.* "Equality" here simply refers to mutual sharing in the midst of a crisis.

Paul went on to explain why he had asked the Corinthians to share with the Christians in Jerusalem. "At the present time," he explained, "your plenty will supply what they need, so that in turn their plenty will supply what you need. Then there will be equality" (8:14). The Corinthians were probably not as bad off as they thought. He addressed them as having "plenty" at this point in their lives—at least, "plenty" in terms of what it would take to meet their own needs and still have some left to share with others who had a need greater than they.

Paul also reminded the Corinthians that there might come a time when they had a need and the Jerusalem Christians would be able to respond the way he was asking them to respond. To make his point, he referred to the Old Testament experience in the wilderness when God provided the children of Israel with manna and quail. When the Israelites did what God had commanded them—gathering only as much as they needed each day—everything worked out as God had intended. Moses testified, "He that gathered much did not have too much, and he that gathered little did not have too little" (8:15; Ex. 16:13-18).

Paul's reference to the Old Testament without explaining the context points to the possibility that he or Apollos or perhaps Peter (1 Cor. 1:12) had already instructed the Corinthians regarding the way God led Israel in the Old Testament. Paul had also reviewed for them the law of Moses, comparing what God has presently done for all of us with His grace and love in Jesus Christ. Though Paul did not impose the giving patterns of the Old Testament on the Corinthians, or on any group of New Testament Christians, it can be safely assumed that most Christians understood God's requirements in Israel.

Everywhere Christ was preached, the Old Testament was taught as foundational for understanding the grace of God. The challenge facing every Christian is not to take advantage of the grace of God simply because he is not under the Mosaic law. Because the law no longer condemns us, our temptation is the same as that of the Roman Christians who had to be admonished not to "go on sinning so that grace may increase" (Rom. 6:1).

This is the essence of Paul's letter to the Galatians and also to the Romans. What Paul eventually wrote in these letters regarding justification by faith, he had probably taught believers face-to-face in various geographical settings. In addition to New Testament doctrine, imagine the amount of Old Testament truth, including the purpose of the law, he must have taught during his year and a half in Corinth and his three-year stay in Ephesus. Luke recorded that he taught daily in the "lecture hall of Tyrannus" for two years (Acts 19:9).

THE THIRTEENTH SUPRACULTURAL PRINCIPLE

It is not the will of God that some Christians cannot meet their physical needs while other Christians with abundance could help them in their time of need (2 Cor. 8:13-14).

The Bible does not teach that it is wrong to have an "abundance" of material possessions. Neither does it teach that Christians should give away everything they have to help others in crisis, putting *themselves* in a state of need. Rather, Scripture simply teaches that God wants Christians who have sufficient material possessions to be willing to share with other Christians who do not.

What Paul was teaching the Corinthians was also a temporary solution. From all that he taught the Thessalonians and Corinthians, we can see that he wanted all Christians to be free from having to rely on others to meet their needs. On the other hand, Paul recognized that some needs would be ongoing—such as people who had no family to help them and who were unable to work because of age or illness. But the totality of Scripture teaches that in the majority of situations, God's people will be able to work and earn their own living and "not be dependent on anybody" (1 Thess. 4:11-12).

2 CORINTHIANS 8:16-24

I thank God, who put into the heart of Titus the same concern I have for you. For Titus not only welcomed our appeal, but he is coming to you with much enthusiasm and on his own initiative. And we are sending along with [Titus] the brother who is praised by all the churches for his service to the gospel. What is more, he was chosen by the churches to accompany us as we carry the offering. . . . In addition, we are sending with them our brother who has often proved to us in many ways that he is zealous, and now even more so because of his great confidence in you. As for Titus, he is my partner and fellow worker among you; as for our brothers, they are representatives of the churches and an honor to Christ. Therefore show these men the proof of your love and the reason for our pride in you, so that the churches can see it.

EXPOSITION

Verses 16-17. Paul let the Corinthians know how encouraged he was that Titus, his missionary companion, shared the same concern that he had. This concern was for the Corinthians—that is, that they might respond in the way Paul had just described. In spite of the questions and reactions from these Christians, Titus was willing "with much enthusiasm and on his own initiative"—to once again come to Corinth in order to receive their special offering.

If we read between the lines, we can understand Paul's thanksgiving to God regarding this young man. While dealing with a sensitive subject, it was of immense encouragement to Paul to have another missionary share the same burden and to take the responsibility for collecting the Corinthian gifts.

Verses 18-19a. We are not sure who Paul was referring to when he made reference to "the brother."[4] We do know, however, that this man had a good reputation among the various churches that were involved in providing money for the poverty-stricken Christians in Jerusalem. These churches had actually chosen this man of integrity to accompany Paul, Titus, and the others who were asked to "carry the offering."

Verse 22. Here Paul made reference to a second "brother" who also is anonymous. This man could have been any of those mentioned in endnote 4. As was true of the "first brother," this man was also a very committed Christian. He had proved his zealousness "in many ways." Furthermore, Paul let the Corinthians know that this brother also had "great confidence" in them—just as Titus did. In other words, both unidentified brothers who were accompanying Titus shared the same concerns as did Paul and Titus. Both also shared the same confidence in the Corinthians—that they indeed would respond as God intended.

Verses 23-24. Paul's final words in chapter 8 indicate that he was concerned that not everyone in the Corinthian church would know who Titus and these two brothers were. Even though Titus had been there before, Paul did not take for granted that the group in Corinth was the same. Indeed, any church body is dynamic and constantly changing. Consequently, Paul identified Titus as his "partner and fellow worker" among the Corinthians. If anyone in the church criticized these men, Paul was appealing to the other Christians in Corinth who knew Titus to defend his character. Regarding the two unidentified brothers, Paul affirmed their role as "representatives of the churches and an honor to Christ." If any of the Corinthians had questions about their qualifications for this task, they could check this matter out with the other churches involved in offering this gift.

Paul concluded by appealing to the Corinthians to demonstrate their love when these men arrived. He wanted to make sure that they responded properly in order to prove to these men as well as the other churches that Paul was, indeed, correct in his confidence in the Corinthian Christians. Needless to say, Paul worked hard to be sensitive and yet to deal with all of the issues involved in "financial communication." He had learned from experience how important it is to make sure that everyone understands both motives and actions. And, of course, Paul was very much aware of how important it is to be doubly conscientious when it comes to the subject of money.

On the other hand, potential misunderstandings and negative reactions in no way deterred Paul from dealing with the subject directly. He knew that *money* and *ministry* are a hand-in-glove necessity. Furthermore, he also knew that the way Christians use their material possessions is a strong reflection of where they are in their spiritual growth. As Charles Ryrie points out, "How we use our money demonstrates the reality of our love for God. In some ways, it proves our love more conclusively than depth of knowledge, length of prayers or prominence of service. These things can be feigned, but the use of our possessions shows us up for what we really are."[5]

THE FOURTEENTH SUPRACULTURAL PRINCIPLE

It is the will of God that no one particular Christian leader have to handle the financial needs of the Christian community alone (2 Cor. 8:16-19, 22-24; 9:3-4).

Handling money in God's work is a heavy responsibility. One reason for this is the emotional risks involved. There will be rejection and criticism from those who are either carnal or selfish. There will be criticism even from those who simply do not understand—or who do not want to understand. And there will always be potential accusations of dishonesty or selfishness from both Christians and non-Christians.

Paul faced all these painful problems, even though his motives were always pure. He faced emotional reactions from Christians simply because he was teaching an aspect of the will of God that always makes people feel guilty and uncomfortable when they are, at that moment of their lives, living out of the will of God. Every Christian leader who is both faithful in trying to care for the economic needs in doing God's work, and who at the same time teaches what God has to say about faithful stewardship, will face the same problems. No Christian leader should have to bear this burden alone.

NOTES

1. Regarding the origin of this letter, R. V. G. Tasker, *Second Epistle of Paul to the Corinthians*, vol. 8 of *The Tyndale New Testament Commentaries* (Grand Rapids: Eerdmans, 1958), p. 15, gives this helpful comment: "The Second Epistle to the Corinthians was almost certainly written in the late autumn of A.D. 56 from a town in Macedonia, after Paul had met Titus who had brought back reassuring news of the condition of the Corinthian church. The provenance of the Epistle can clearly be deduced from vii. 5, 7; and Macedonia or more specifically Philippi, as mentioned as the place of origin in some mss, though that information may be no more than an inference from the Epistle itself."

2. Philip E. Hughes, *The New International Commentary on the New Testament: Paul's Second Epistle to the Corinthians* (Grand Rapids: Eerdmans, 1962), p. 288. On pp. 289-90 Hughes points out further that vv. 3-5 "constitute one continuous sentence in the original, as follows: 'For in accordance with their ability, I testify, indeed, contrary to their ability, of their own accord, with much entreaty beseeching of us the favour, namely, fellowship in the ministry to the saints, and not just as we had expected, but they gave their own selves first to the Lord and to us by the will of God.'"

3. For an excellent illustration of this kind of giving in a Third World country, see "The Church That Learned to Give," by Lyle Eggleston, *Moody Monthly* 88, no. 11 (July/August 1988), pp. 31-32.

4. For an interesting study on the potential identity of "the brother" mentioned in 2 Cor. 8:18, see Hughes, *Second Epistle to the Corinthians*, pp. 312-16. He lists a number of possibilities: Luke, Barnabas, Timothy, Aristarchus, Sopater, Secundus, John Mark, Tychicus, Trophimus, and Souter. My personal speculation is that it was Luke. If it was, however, why would Paul not mention his name? This is especially mysterious since Paul often mentioned people by name, both those who were his friends and those who were not (e.g., see Rom. 16:1-24; 2 Tim. 4:9-21).

5. Charles C. Ryrie, *Balancing the Christian Life* (Chicago: Moody, 1969), p. 84.

25

Paul's Second Letter
to the Corinthians, 9:1-15

In some respects, it is unfortunate that the translators inserted a chapter division at this point. The first five verses[1] of chapter 9 belong with most of what Paul wrote in chapter 8. On the other hand, this breaking point provides us with a natural division between two truth-filled sections of Scripture and an opportunity to review and develop continuity before we look at a chapter that contains more supracultural principles regarding material possessions than any other in the Bible.

2 CORINTHIANS 9:1-2

There is no need for me to write to you about
this service to the saints. For I know your eagerness to help,
and I have been boasting about it to the Macedonians,
telling them that since last year you in Achaia were ready to give;
and your enthusiasm has stirred most of them to action.

EXPOSITION

Paul lived among the Corinthians for at least a year and a half (Acts 18:11). He was convinced that they really wanted to be generous people, in spite of their worldly attitudes and behavior (1 Cor. 3:1-4). Otherwise, he would not have "boasted" to the Macedonians about their "eagerness to help" others. When the need was presented, they responded enthusiastically. However, they had not followed through on their good intentions. The "willingness" was there, but they had not completed the project. In this sense, there *was* a need for Paul to write to them "about this service to the saints."

Was Paul naive? Is this a contradiction with his disclaimer in verse 1? Some might ask, Was Paul attempting to manipulate the Corinthians with "smooth talk"? If we were to answer "yes" to these questions, we would be accusing Paul of contradicting everything he stood for in terms of integrity and honesty (see 1 Thess. 2:3-6).

Paul was being both optimistic and realistic. He knew that generally the Corinthians were willing. At the same time, he knew that some were reacting and some were uninformed. Therefore, he wanted to put his thoughts in writing so that there would be no misunderstandings.

This is not an unusual communication technique. Effective leaders often follow-up telephone conversations with letters summarizing their thoughts and conclusions. Why? Memories fade. People get busy doing other things and sometimes fail to follow through. Furthermore, it helps assure that both parties have really understood what has been said or agreed to.

More important, we must also realize that Paul was not merely acting at a human level. He was writing under the inspiration of the Holy Spirit, who knew that Christians throughout the centuries would need the "Corinthian example." Their enthusiasm and initial willingness had, indeed, motivated the Macedonian Christians to respond. And this provides us with another enduring principle.

THE FIFTEENTH SUPRACULTURAL PRINCIPLE

Christians who are generous will motivate other Christians to also be generous (2 Cor. 9:2).

This principle was modeled in a dramatic way in the church in Jerusalem. Ironically, we now see it verified by the way the Corinthians initially responded to help meet the needs of those Christians in Jerusalem who were now in desperate need themselves. Paul let the Corinthians know that it was their example that had motivated the Macedonians to get involved in this project.

And so it is today. Christians who have not been taught to give, or who have been taught and yet are unresponsive, need to see other Christians enthusiastically using their material possessions to further the work of God's kingdom. They need to observe joyful giving so that they might respond with the same enthusiasm.

2 CORINTHIANS 9:3-4

*But I am sending the brothers in order that our
boasting about you in this matter should not prove hollow,
but that you may be ready, as I said you would be. For
if any Macedonians come with me and find you unprepared,
we—not to say anything about you—would be
ashamed of having been so confident.*

EXPOSITION

Paul was somewhere in Macedonia when he wrote 2 Corinthians, probably waiting for the Macedonians themselves to complete their own collection. He was also anticipating that some of these Christians would accompany him to Corinth. Since Paul had been bragging about the way in which the Corinthians had initially responded, he wanted to make sure they were prepared so that they would not embarrass him or themselves. Plummer offers a perspective helpful in understanding Paul's purpose for writing these verses: "He is not afraid that they will refuse to give, but he is afraid that they would be dilatory for want of organization. It will produce a bad impression if the money is not ready when it is wanted. He carefully limits his anxiety to this 'particular.'"[2]

THE SIXTEENTH SUPRACULTURAL PRINCIPLE

Christians who make commitments financially should be on guard against embarrassing their spiritual leaders, as well as themselves, by being negligent in following through on their commitments (2 Cor. 9:3-4).

This is a pragmatic principle. In giving us the example from which we derive this principle, Paul was honest about his own feelings. If the Corinthians were unprepared, it would cause embarrassment. That is why Paul worked hard to make sure they had all the facts and did *something* about it.

Christians today must be aware that their leaders are human beings and are subject to uncomfortable feelings and even embarrassment when commitments have been made without follow-through. Understandably, there will be circumstances that make it impossible for Christians to give as they had hoped. However, Paul was not referring to this kind of situation. The Corinthians' lack of response was caused primarily by their own negligence and poor financial planning. This kind of behavior among Christians today makes life difficult for Christian leaders—even embarrassing. It should not happen among those who claim to follow Jesus Christ.

2 CORINTHIANS 9:5a

So I thought it necessary to urge the brothers to
visit you in advance and finish the arrangements
for the generous gift you had promised.

EXPOSITION

The Corinthians made a *promise* based on projected future earnings. They were not presuming on God's grace. Otherwise, Paul would have admonished them for making a promise they could not fulfill. Conversely, he boasted to others about what they had promised to do. The Corinthian problem was not their *promise*, but their *failure to follow through* on their commitment by setting aside money week by week from their earnings.

THE SEVENTEENTH SUPRACULTURAL PRINCIPLE

God wants Christians to take a step of faith and trust Him to enable them to be able to give certain amounts of money based upon future earnings (2 Cor. 9:5a).

If Christians only gave from what they had already accumulated, much of God's work would go undone. Paul knew it would take a lot of money to meet the needs of the poor Christians in Jerusalem. He also knew that the amount needed could not be generated with a "one-time" offering. Consequently, he presented the need to the various churches, asking people to make a long-range commitment to this project and then to begin to lay aside monies every week to fulfill their faith promise.

There are, of course, some common-sense rules that must be applied in this kind of financial planning. First, we must project what we believe we can give based upon our potential performance, which must be evaluated realistically by both our past and present income. Most of us use this practical guideline regularly in terms of making purchases, planning business ventures, and working out budgets that cover many areas of our personal and vocational lives. Unfortunately, some Christians do not do this well and get themselves into serious financial difficulties.

The second guideline relates to the principle of faith. God wants His children to trust Him for the future. He certainly does not want us to be unrealistic and foolish in our projections. But neither does He want us to be so reserved and hesitant that we do not trust Him to provide beyond what may be a human possibility. It takes wisdom, advice, and prayer to maintain a proper balance between proper planning and trusting God to provide.

In essence, the Corinthians made a "faith promise." They were not able to follow through, not because they were unrealistic, but because they were negligent. If there had been circumstances beyond their control, Paul would have certainly put them totally at ease. Rather, Paul corrected their thinking with proper instruction and then challenged them to follow through to the best of their ability.

2 CORINTHIANS 9:5*b*

Then it will be ready as a generous gift,
not as one grudgingly given.

EXPOSITION

Paul became more specific as to why he was sending Titus and the two brothers ahead of time. He was not being purposely redundant. Rather, he was introducing them to another concern. They had promised to give a "generous gift." If Paul arrived in Corinth and the money had not been collected as they had promised, then it would create greater pressure since it would be much more difficult to accumulate the money. What the Corinthians would try to gather together after Paul and his traveling companions arrived would be given in a "grudging" manner. This Paul wanted to avoid at all costs.

THE EIGHTEENTH SUPRACULTURAL PRINCIPLE

Christians should organize and plan their giving in a systematic way so that they can give generously and not respond in a grudging fashion (2 Cor. 9:5b).

When money is available because we have planned our giving, it becomes a joyful experience to share that money with others. We have not only prepared our hearts for "that moment," but we have prepared our hearts "ahead of time" since we have arranged our giving in relationship to our overall financial plans. (In American society we call this a "budget.")

Conversely, when Christians do not plan their giving, they usually do not have money to give. All of us tend to allow our standard of living to rise to the present level of income. Then, when we are asked to give, either regularly to meet the ongoing needs of the ministry or to make special gifts for special needs, we respond grudgingly. This is understandable since we have already spent our excess on our own needs and desires, or we have laid the excess aside for ourselves.

Under these circumstances, negative emotions are predictable. Oftentimes we not only have no excess to give to God's work, but we are also worried that we will not even have enough money to meet what we believe are our own needs. As the Corinthians demonstrate, this problem is often not God's problem. It is *our* problem for not becoming systematic planners and givers.

2 CORINTHIANS 9:6

*Remember this: whoever sows sparingly
will also reap sparingly, and whoever sows
generously will also reap generously.*

EXPOSITION

Any farmer knows that if he sows seeds sparingly, he will reap a small harvest. Conversely, if he sows seeds generously, he will reap an abundant harvest. Paul used this agricultural experience to illustrate Christian giving. The analogy must be carefully interpreted and applied, however, since Paul was not referring to *quantity* but *quality*. When it comes to giving, God does not measure the seed by *how much* is actually sown. Rather, He measures how much is sown by what is *available* to sow. Paul was teaching what Christ taught when He referred to the widow in the Temple who gave more than those who gave much because she gave sacrificially rather than out of plenty.

Some have interpreted Paul's teaching on "sowing generously" and "reaping generously" to be a "prosperity theology." Nowhere in Scripture are Christians taught to *give* in order to *gain* earthly abundance.[3] Rather, giving is to be motivated by an unselfish heart that is willing to share unconditionally with those in need, regardless of the monetary return.

THE NINETEENTH SUPRACULTURAL PRINCIPLE

Christians who are generous in their giving will receive generous blessings; conversely, Christians who are not generous in their giving will not receive generous blessings (2 Cor. 9:6).

Biblical generosity involves *proportional* giving and especially *sacrificial* giving. That is why the Macedonians were very generous. They gave out of their poverty, which was very little in terms of quantity. However, in God's sight, it was indeed generous giving.

Furthermore, God's generous blessings in response to generous giving includes more than material possessions. It involves, for example, seeing others respond generously because we have been a model. There is always joy and satisfaction in knowing we have helped someone else draw closer to God and walk in His will more faithfully.

The greatest blessing we will receive, however, will come in eternity when we hear our Savior say, "Well done, good and faithful servant!" (Matt. 25:21). When we are able to take our crowns and rewards we have received for our faithfulness and place them at the feet of Jesus—reflecting our love for God all over again—we, of all people, will be rewarded beyond anything we can ever anticipate or comprehend while on earth.

2 CORINTHIANS 9:7

Each man should give what he has decided in his heart to give, not reluctantly or under compulsion, for God loves a cheerful giver.

EXPOSITION

Paul wanted to make sure the Corinthians prepared their *hearts* as well as their *gifts*. All that Paul had given them by way of instruction was intended to help them to not only gather the money together in a systematic fashion but to do so with willingness. When the time came for them to present the gift publicly to Paul and his co-workers, they would be able to give cheerfully because the money was in hand.

Though it is clear from Scripture that God wants Christians to be *generous*, He also wants us to give *cheerfully*. He does not want us to give "reluctantly or under compulsion." In fact, if we do not give out of hearts of love, God is not pleased with our gifts.

THE TWENTIETH SUPRACULTURAL PRINCIPLE

Every Christian is ultimately responsible to give to God on the basis of his own heart decision (2 Cor. 9:7).

Does this mean that Christians should not give if they cannot give cheerfully? If this were true, Paul would not have encouraged the Corinthians to give when they had negative attitudes. His hope, of course, was that careful planning would correct their hearts.

The primary point Paul was making to the Corinthians and to all of us is that we must give careful attention to planning our giving. Lack of preparation and organization will always lead to resentment and resistance. Therefore, all of us are responsible to make sure we order our lives accordingly—which, in turn, will lead to joy and blessings in giving.

2 CORINTHIANS 9:8

And God is able to make all grace abound to you,
so that in all things at all times, having all that
you need, you will abound in every good work.

EXPOSITION

Heretofore we have noted that most of God's promises for being faithful with material possessions relate to eternity and not to this earth. However, here Paul was talking about temporal blessings. Paul reminded the Corinthians that if they were faithful and generous in helping others, God would take care of them. They would have all that they needed "in all things and at all times." And with what God provided, they would be able to "abound in every good work" (9:8).

THE TWENTY-FIRST SUPRACULTURAL PRINCIPLE

When Christians are faithful in their giving, God has promised to meet their needs (2 Cor. 9:8).

God has never promised to give us everything that we want or desire. However, He *has* promised to meet our needs. The apostle Paul knew what this meant by personal experience. This is why he wrote to the Philippians

—who sacrificed significantly to help him—reassuring them that God would meet all of their needs "according to his glorious riches in Christ Jesus" (Phil. 4:19).

We must note, however, that part of God's grace may be the strength to endure difficult economic times and to learn "the secret of being content in any and every situation" (Phil. 4:12). Paul's personal testimony was that he had learned that secret. And Christians can claim the same promise today. If we are faithful, God will be faithful.

2 CORINTHIANS 9:11a

You will be made rich in every way
so that you can be generous on every occasion.

EXPOSITION

Probably no verse has been misinterpreted and misused more than this statement, particularly by high-powered evangelists and so-called "prosperity theologians." If you want to accumulate material possessions, they say, then "sow your seed" and it will grow and multiply one hundredfold.[4]

What did Paul mean? Some believe that he was not speaking of *material* possessions at all but rather of *spiritual* riches. But perhaps Paul had both in mind. If he were not speaking of material possessions, how could he then say that these Corinthians would be able to "be generous on every occasion"? Furthermore, his agricultural analogy in verse 10 also implies that Paul was talking about material blessings as a result of being generous with their material gifts (9:10).

It seems, then, that Paul *was* teaching that if the Corinthians were generous, based upon their own resources, God would provide them with material blessings so they could continue to invest in the kingdom of God and see people come to Christ and grow in Christ. In this sense, they would be "enlarging the harvest of their righteousness." The focus here is not on what they would *receive* but what they could *give* in order to do God's work in the world.

Paul may have also been speaking here of being rich in *grace*, meaning that, because of God's gift of grace, they would be able to be "generous on every occasion" no matter what their economic situation. In this sense, they would be able to respond like the Macedonians who actually gave out of poverty, which in God's sight was a "generous gift."

Earlier Paul made clear that "the *grace* that God had given the Macedonian churches" enabled them to give, and "out of the most severe trial, their overflowing joy and their extreme poverty welled up in *rich generosity*" (8:1-2). This explanation, however, does not contradict the interpretation that Paul was speaking of material blessings as well as spiritual blessings (the gift of grace). This leads us to another principle.

THE TWENTY-SECOND SUPRACULTURAL PRINCIPLE

When Christians are generous, God has promised to enable them to continue to be generous (2 Cor. 9:11).

Whatever our interpretation of Paul's promises to the Corinthians, it is clear that he was not promising them that they would become rich in the sense of having an *abundance* of material possessions. However, he seems to definitely be referring to having *sufficient* material possessions to be able to share with others. We can conclude, then, that one of the promises God gives Christians is that, when they are faithful in helping others, they will have their own needs met and will be able to continue to help others. The emphasis in Scripture is not on the *amount* we give or on the *amount* we receive but simply on *giving* from what we *do* have—whether little or much.

2 CORINTHIANS 9:11b-13

> *And through us your generosity will result in*
> *thanksgiving to God. This service that you perform*
> *is not only supplying the needs of God's people but is also*
> *overflowing in many expressions of thanks to God.*
> *Because of the service by which you have proved yourselves,*
> *men will praise God for the obedience that accompanies*
> *your confession of the gospel of Christ, and for your*
> *generosity in sharing with them and with everyone else.*

EXPOSITION

Paul reminded the Corinthians that not only would their generous gift meet the "needs of God's people," it would also cause many people to praise God. People would thank God for these material blessings. They would also thank God for the Corinthians and the Macedonians and all of the other Christians who contributed to meet their needs. And they would thank and praise God for who He is.

Hughes captured in a very graphic way what the apostle Paul had done to this point:

> Thus the Apostle enthusiastically but tenderly leads the Corinthians on until, with him, they have risen to that spiritual height from which they are able to see Christian giving in the splendid sweep of its true perspective—not as a burden which cramps life and engenders regret, but as a privilege of grace that enlarges and enriches the soul of the giver, relieves the wants of others, and in its outworking causes many to return praise to God.[5]

One of Paul's major concerns was the way the Christians in Jerusalem still tended to view Gentile believers. James taught that "faith by itself, if it is not accompanied by action, is dead" (James 2:17). Furthermore, his example of Christian works was the way in which people share their material possessions with those who are in serious need (James 2:14-16).

Paul was definitely desirous of demonstrating to the Jerusalem believers in a tangible way that the Corinthians, as well as other Gentile Christians, were truly born again. Thus, he wrote that these Christians in Jerusalem would "praise God for the obedience that accompanies your confession of the gospel of Christ." In other words, here was proof that their faith was real. The Corinthians would become in a authentic way Paul's "letter, written on our hearts, known and read by everybody. You show," Paul continued, "that you are a letter from Christ, the result of our ministry, written not with ink but with the Spirit of the living God, not on tablets of stone but on tablets of human hearts" (2 Cor. 3:2-3). This was the visual message Paul was excited about communicating to the Jerusalem Christians through the Corinthians' generosity.

THE TWENTY-THIRD SUPRACULTURAL PRINCIPLE

Generous Christians cause others to praise and worship God (2 Cor. 9:11-13).

Nothing brings a more positive response among Christians than to see other Christians being faithful stewards of their material possessions. Though it may create appropriate guilt in the lives of those who are not obeying God as they should, it will still bring a response of thanksgiving and praise in the hearts of those who want to respond to God's Spirit in all things.

True, there will always be those who will be critical and negative because of their own carnality and worldliness. But for the most part, these people are simply unhappy with other people who give because it reveals their own lack of response to God. In spite of these isolated instances, the principle is true: generous Christians do cause others to praise and worship God. This is especially true among those who benefit from this generosity.

2 CORINTHIANS 9:14

*And in their prayers for you their hearts will go out
to you, because of the surpassing grace God has given you.*

EXPOSITION

Not only would the Christians in Jerusalem know beyond a shadow of a doubt that the Corinthian Christians (and their fellow believers in Macedonia) were true believers, they would also develop a closer relationship with them—even though they may never meet on this earth. They would be drawn together as they prayed for one another. No longer would "the dividing wall of hostility" that often separated Jewish believers from Gentile Christians exist. Rather, they would see in a new and vital way that the barrier was destroyed once and for all by Jesus Christ (Eph. 2:14). Paul looked forward to seeing this happen between the Christians in Jerusalem and the Gentile believers, not only theologically, but as those who received these gifts responded with hearts of love, compassion, and thanksgiving.

THE TWENTY-FOURTH SUPRACULTURAL PRINCIPLE

People respect and love Christians who are unselfish and generous (2 Cor. 9:14).

It has often been said that people cannot hate people who truly love. So it can also be said that people cannot ultimately resent Christians who are unselfish and generous with their material possessions. Just as Paul was confident that the generosity among Gentile Christians in the first-century world would break down the theological and cultural barriers that existed because of Jewish prejudice, just so, Christians who are unselfish and generous will also break down the social and cultural barriers that exist among Christians in the twentieth-century world. Generally speaking, people do respect and love Christians who are unselfish and generous.

Thanks be to God for His indescribable gift! (9:15). No one can improve upon Paul's final declaration to this extensive section on Christian giving. Jesus Christ is the "indescribable gift." God the Father is the "giver." It was He who "so loved the world that he gave his only Son, that whoever believes in him shall not perish but have eternal life" (John 3:16). And it is because of this "indescribable gift" that all Christians can respond to each other and share what they have materially in order to further the work of God's eternal kingdom!

NOTES

1. Some Bible interpreters of a more liberal persuasion have theorized that the first five verses of chapter 9 are not a genuine part of the original letter. They view it as a fragment from some other letter that either by accident or by design found its way into Paul's second letter to the Corinthians. However, as Philip E. Hughes, *The New International Commentary on the New Testament: Paul's Second Epistle to the Corinthians* (Grand Rapids: Eerdmans, 1962), points out, this theory has little external evidence or the support of tradition:

    The very close connection in thought between the closing section of chapter 8 and the opening section of chapter 9 has been recognized by many excellent commentators. Plummer, for instance, says not only that the conjunction "for" is "very intelligible," but also that "if the division between the chapters had not been so misplaced, no one would have proposed to separate ix. 1-5 from viii. 6-14.". . . Regarding the mention of Achaia rather than Corinth in verse 2, it is sufficient to turn back to the opening salutation of this epistle, which shows that it was addressed not merely to "the church of God which is at Corinth," but also in fact to "all the saints which are in the whole of Achaia" (1:1), so that there is quite certainly nothing incongruous about the mention here of Achaia, which is the inclusive term (pp. 321-22).

2. Hughes, *Second Epistle to the Corinthians*, p. 325.

3. See Bruce Barron, *The Health and Wealth Gospel: A Fresh Look at Healing, Prosperity & Positive Confession* (Downers Grove, Ill.: InterVarsity, 1987).

4. See Michael Horton, ed., *The Agony of Deceit: What Some TV Preachers Are Really Teaching* (Chicago: Moody, 1990).

5. Hughes, *Second Epistle to the Corinthians*, p. 338.

26

Moving from Specific to General Principles

No section of the Word of God provides believers with more comprehensive guidance regarding their material possessions than Paul's two letters to the Thessalonians and his two letters to the Corinthians. Following are the twenty-four specific principles formulated from the previous chapters of Part 5.

SPECIFIC PRINCIPLES IN PERSPECTIVE FROM PART 5

1 THESSALONIANS

1. Christian leaders should look to fellow Christians for financial support, not to the unbelievers they are attempting to reach with the gospel (1 Thess. 2:9).

2. Christians should work hard to provide for their economic needs so that they are not criticized by unbelievers for being lazy and irresponsible (1 Thess. 4:11-12).

2 THESSALONIANS

3. Christians should separate themselves from other Christians who are persistently irresponsible in not providing for their own economic needs (2 Thess. 3:6).

4. Christians who can, but do not, work for a living should not be given economic assistance (2 Thess. 3:10b).

1 CORINTHIANS

5. Even though God has commanded that spiritual leaders be cared for financially by those they minister to, there are times when it is the part of wisdom for spiritual leaders to give up that right (1 Cor. 9:14-15a).

6. Christians should set aside a certain percentage of their income on just as regular a basis as they are paid in order to be able to systematically give to God's work (1 Cor. 16:2).

7. Those who handle and distribute monies that are given to God's work should be above reproach in all respects and should be held accountable (1 Cor. 16:3-4).

2 CORINTHIANS

8. Every local body of believers needs real-life examples of other churches that are positive models in the area of giving (2 Cor. 8:1-2).

9. Christians need to be held accountable when they make financial commitments to God's work (2 Cor. 8:6, 10-11; 9:3).

10. It is God's will that all Christians excel in the grace of giving (2 Cor. 8:7).

11. God does not want Christians to respond to a command to share their material possessions but, rather, to respond out of hearts of love that reflect sincere appreciation for His gift of salvation (2 Cor. 8:8-9).

12. God accepts and honors believers' gifts once they begin to give regularly and systematically, even though they may not be able to give as proportionately as they eventually will be able to once they have their economic lives in order (2 Cor. 8:10-12).

13. It is not the will of God that some Christians cannot meet their physical needs while other Christians with abundance could help them in their time of need (2 Cor. 8:13-14).

14. It is the will of God that no one particular Christian leader have to handle the financial needs of the Christian community alone (2 Cor. 8:16-19, 22-24; 9:3-4).

15. Christians who are generous will motivate other Christians to also be generous (2 Cor. 9:2).

16. Christians who make commitments financially should be on guard against embarrassing their spiritual leaders, as well as themselves, by being negligent in following through on their commitments (2 Cor. 9:3-4).

17. God wants Christians to take a step of faith and trust Him to enable them to be able to give certain amounts of money based upon future earnings (2 Cor. 9:5a).

18. Christians should organize and plan their giving in a systematic way so that they can give generously and not respond in a grudging fashion (2 Cor. 9:5b).

19. Christians who are generous in their giving will receive generous blessings; conversely, Christians who are not generous in their giving will not receive generous blessings (2 Cor. 9:6).

20. Every Christian is ultimately responsible to give to God on the basis of his own heart decision (2 Cor. 9:7).

21. When Christians are faithful in their giving, God has promised to meet their needs (2 Cor. 9:8).

22. When Christians are generous, God has promised to enable them to continue to be generous (2 Cor. 9:11).

23. Generous Christians cause others to praise and worship God (2 Cor. 9:11-13).

24. People respect and love Christians who are unselfish and generous (2 Cor. 9:14).

GENERAL PRINCIPLES FROM PART 5

As we look carefully at the specific principles from the Thessalonian and Corinthian letters, we will see at least two important principles of a more general nature that need to be stated and explained. These two principles are supported and reinforced by the numerous principles outlined in the study as a whole.

THE FIRST GENERAL SUPRACULTURAL PRINCIPLE

The local church is God's primary context for maintaining accountability in the area of material possessions.

It is important to correlate this overarching principle with another that became clear in our study of the church in Jerusalem. (See the Second General Supracultural Principle in chap. 11.) This principle is stated as follows:

It is by divine design that local churches provide the primary context for determining how Christians use their material possessions to further the work of God's kingdom.

Every true believer is a part of the *universal* church (1 Cor. 12:13; Eph. 4:11-16). However, when we study the New Testament, we cannot bypass the concept of the *local* church. In fact, approximately 95 percent of all references to the *ekklesia* are references to local, visible, and organized expressions of the universal church.[1] Jesus Christ came to build His church (Matt. 16:18), and as we have seen, Luke's historical record in the book of Acts is an account of the founding of local churches. Moving out from Jerusalem, assemblies of believers were established throughout the Roman world.

We cannot bypass the concept of the *local church* when it comes to determining how Christians should use their material possessions. This principle becomes especially relevant as we attempt to practice the principle of *accountability*. Paul affirmed and expanded on these two interrelated principles in his second letter to the Corinthians:

First, he was writing to the *local* church at Corinth (2 Cor. 8:10).

Second, he began his discourse on giving by using the Macedonian *churches* as a model (2 Cor. 8:1).

Third, when he informed the Corinthians that he was going to be sending along another "brother," he not only made sure they knew that this man was "praised by all the *churches*" but that he was also "chosen by the *churches*" to accompany him and Titus as they transported the offering to Jerusalem (2 Cor. 8:18-19). This is why Paul could say a little later in the letter that these men were "representatives of the *churches*" (2 Cor. 8:23).

Parachurch ministries and the problem of accountability. Practically speaking, it is very difficult to hold Christian leaders accountable outside local church structures unless these leaders themselves determine that they are going to be accountable to the Christian public at large by means of a careful and thorough system of reports and by setting up a responsible board of directors. Even then, it is a simple matter for Christian leaders in parachurch organizations to still be able to waste money, misuse funds, and misappropriate gifts that are given in response to requests for specific needs. In recent years, we have seen this illustrated dramatically and particularly by televangelists.

Does the Bible teach that Christians should give only to their local churches in order to practice the principle of accountability? The answer to that question is a decided "no." But the Scriptures give us direct guidance as to how to determine where we should give. God allows "freedom in form" when it comes to doing His work in the world (see p. 23). Consequently, this freedom has brought into existence a number of ministries that are involved in carrying out the Great Commission. In this sense, many of these parachurch organizations are performing a number of functions God designed for local churches.

It is not wrong for these organizations to exist. Neither is it inappropriate for Christians to support these ministries. In fact, many of these organizations are able to reach biblical goals in our society that are virtually impossible for local churches to achieve. The tasks are too enormous and the opportunities too numerous for even "groups" of local churches (denominations) to do all that needs to be done.

It is important, however, for Christians to evaluate their giving patterns to organizations outside their own local churches by considering other important guidelines that God gives us in Scripture. The following questions will assist believers in deciding whether or not to support a particular ministry outside their local church and, if so, how much they should give.

To what extent are we supporting those who are ministering to us and to our families?

A very important and foundational guideline in determining whether or not to support a parachurch ministry or an individual involved with another Christian organization is the extent to which we are meeting our financial obligations in our own local body of believers. The Scriptures make clear that believers have a responsibility to first and foremost take care of and encourage those Christians in *material* ways who have ministered to them in *spiritual* ways (Rom. 15:27).

This principle surfaces again and again throughout our study (see pp. 95-96; 181-82; 206-8; 258-60; 319-20). The principles of Scripture that guide us in our giving certainly make clear that if we give to other Christian organizations and neglect the spiritual leaders in our local churches, we are not operating within the will of God.

What percentage of our income should we give to our local churches before we consider supporting other Christian ministries?

Though certainly not an absolute guideline, a good rule of thumb is for Christians to give at least 10 percent of their income to their local churches before they support additional ministries. God's plan in the Old Testament required the children of Israel to give 10 percent to support their spiritual leaders (see p. 112). If we use this approach as a pragmatic example, it will guarantee that local church leaders will never be neglected by the very people they are ministering to. If all Christians were committed to giving at least a tithe to their local church, and then to give proportionally beyond a tithe to other ministries, there would be few financial problems in local churches or parachurch ministries.

What kind of accountability system does the parachurch organization promote and practice?

A Christian should never give to any Christian organization that does not make special efforts to be totally accountable to its donors and to the Christian public at large. Furthermore, we must not allow ourselves to make decisions to give based primarily on emotional stories and financial appeals followed by statements that the particular ministry will not be able to survive without our financial support. This is often a psychological strategy that is used again and again to manipulate God's people to give. In some instances, these appeals are not based on all the facts, misrepresent the truth, or communicate outright untruths.

Does this mean it is wrong for parachurch organizations to make appeals for funds? Not at all. And success stories are certainly appropriate. God's people need to know what is happening as a result of their giving. These reports, however, must be truthful in all respects. The major problem Christians face is to be able to determine if these appeals are factual and if those in the organization are using the funds in a responsible way. One thing is sure. If there are no regular reports, we can be sure the organization is not acting responsibly toward the public it supposedly serves.

In recent years, Christian leaders involved in parachurch ministries have been concerned about their responsibility to practice the principle of accountability. Consequently, they have formed The Evangelical Council for Financial Accountability.[2] Though there are other ways to maintain and communicate accountability to the Christian public, any organization that is a member of this council is certainly attempting to demonstrate that it is a credible organization and worthy of financial support.

What kind of reputation do the organization and its leaders have, both in their Christian community and in the world at large?

Christians should have a very broad base of information before they support Christian organizations outside their local churches. One important factor to consider is the established reputation of an organization and its leaders. This reputation should be "above reproach" both in the Christian community and in the secular world. Furthermore, this reputation should have been established and maintained for a lengthy period of time. If the organization is new, it is doubly important to consider the already established reputation of its founders and leaders.

Christians can also feel comfortable supporting individual missionaries and Christian workers who, like the apostle Paul, have established their own personal reputation. These individuals, however, should be involved with Christian organizations that have also established reputable credentials in carrying out the Great Commission. Obviously, these organizations should be sound doctrinally and should be well-known for holding their employees accountable for the way in which they use their time and resources in furthering the work of the kingdom of God.

Local churches and accountability. Local churches must also be diligent in holding their *spiritual leaders* accountable. In fact, spiritual leaders in the church should take the primary responsibility to make sure this actually happens—just as Paul did. He is an outstanding model in wanting to be above reproach in terms of receiving and distributing monies and other material goods: "We want to avoid any criticism of the way we administer this liberal gift. For we are taking pains to do what is right, not only in the eyes of the Lord but also in the eyes of men" (2 Cor. 8:20-21).

Practically speaking, there is no feasible way for *individual Christians* to be held accountable when they are not participating members of a local body of believers. God designed churches to be this kind of accountability system in all areas of our Christian lives—including the way we give. Christians who purposely avoid being accountable to other believers and to their spiritual leaders are just as guilty of being unsubmissive to the will of God as are Christian leaders who refuse to make themselves accountable to other members of the Body of Christ.

THE SECOND GENERAL SUPRACULTURAL PRINCIPLE

It is important that Christian leaders maintain a high level of communication in order to enable Christians to be obedient to God's will in the way they use their material possessions.

THE PAULINE MODEL

Paul demonstrated this principle in an unusual way. Note the steps he took before he exhorted the Thessalonians to discipline those who were lazy and who were not providing for their own physical needs:

- He modeled this principle with his own life (Acts 18:3; 2 Thess. 3:7-9).

- He taught these believers their responsibility face-to-face after he led them to Christ (2 Thess. 3:10).

- He wrote them a letter and reminded them of the way he and his missionary companions had modeled this principle (1 Thess. 2:7-9).

- He taught them a second time in his letter that they should be responsible in this area of their lives (1 Thess. 4:11-12).

- He ended his first letter by exhorting all believers in Thessalonica to admonish those who were not diligent (1 Thess. 5:14).

We see the same level of communication when Paul dealt with the Corinthians regarding their failure to follow through in their giving as they had promised they would:

- He gave them specific instructions as he closed his first letter (1 Cor. 16:2).

- He followed up these instructions by sending Titus to meet with them personally in order to reinforce what he had written (2 Cor. 8:6).

- He wrote a second letter, responding to their questions and reactions by sharing with them the Macedonian model (2 Cor. 8:1-5).

- He elaborated extensively as to why they should finish this project (2 Cor. 8:7-15).

- He also told them he was going to send Titus back again, accompanied by two additional men, in order to help them follow through (2 Cor. 8:16-24; 2 Cor. 9:5).

- Paul sensitively reminded the Corinthians that it was they who had motivated the Macedonians to give in the first place (2 Cor. 9:1-4).

- To avoid any embarrassment, he informed the Corinthians that some of the Macedonians would probably be with him when they came to receive the gift they promised to give (2 Cor. 9:4).

IMPLEMENTING PAUL'S MODEL

It is clear that Paul maintained a high level of communication when it came to informing Christians regarding their financial responsibilities. To some the steps may appear redundant, but the Holy Spirit knew that Christian leaders down through the centuries needed these examples of communication. He also knew that Christians need to understand why this kind of communication is essential.

God has ordained this process because He is aware, first of all, that most Christians find it easy to be negligent in doing the will of God in this area. Second, God also knows His children often do not hear what He says without extensive repetition. That is why He has given us a Book that contains "many books"—both in the Old and New Testaments—that are filled with repetition.

Paul worked hard to "over communicate" without being harsh. He did so with grace and love. But he did not hesitate to become very direct when Christians consistently ignored God's will. Though Paul communicated extensively, he was always honest. He never overstated the needs, nor did he resort to methods that were out of harmony with divine principles.

When Paul wrote to the Corinthians in his first letter, he said, "Follow my example, as I follow the example of Christ" (1 Cor. 11:1). Though he was referring to his Christian example generally, what he wrote certainly applies to his communication style regarding how Christians should view and use their material possessions. We too need to directly but sensitively and honestly communicate this aspect of the will of God to all Christians. And all Christians need to know that this kind of communication is God-ordained.

Unfortunately, the way in which some Christian leaders in recent years have violated scriptural principles in communicating in the area of finances has made it very difficult for those who want to communicate in a biblical fashion. Because of high-powered and dishonest tactics, many Christians automatically respond negatively to any reference to money. This is unfortunate and is in itself an unbiblical reaction. Consequently, Christians need to evaluate why they are responding in inappropriate ways. They should not penalize their own spiritual leaders who are sincerely attempting to do the will of God.

Christians, however, must realize that there is a natural tendency for all of us to react negatively to God's demands on our lives, particularly in the area of finances. The Corinthians certainly illustrate this reality. Paul's message touched the very fabric of their inner being—and it touches ours. This is why there is so much biblical instruction on this subject. God knows we need it. Jesus was right when He said, "Where your treasure is, there your heart will be also" (Matt. 6:21).

NOTES

1. Robert L. Saucy, *The Church in God's Program* (Chicago: Moody, 1972), pp. 16-17, gives the following helpful information on the way the word *church* is used in the New Testament:

   A Greek concordance reveals that there are 114 occurrences of *ekklesia* in the New Testament. . . .
   1. The local church. Predominately, *ekklesia* applies to a local assembly of all those who profess faith and allegiance to Christ. In this sense the singular *ekklesia* refers to a specific church, as that at Thessalonica (1 Th. 1:1) or any nonspecified individual assembly ("every church," 1 Co. 4:17). The plural *ekklesiai* also designates a group of churches or assemblies in a particular region ("churches of Judea," Gal. 1:22); or a nonspecified number of churches ("other churches," 2 Co. 11:8); or for all the churches together ("all churches," 1 Co. 7:17).
   2. The universal church. *Ekklesia* also designates the universal church. In this usage the concept of a physical assembly gives way to the spiritual unity of all believers in Christ. *Ekklesia* in this sense is not the assembly itself but rather those constituting it; they are the church whether actually assembled or not. This is clearly evident in the early persecution of the church at Jerusalem. Even when believers are scattered abroad and in their homes, they are "in church" (Ac. 8:1-3). The application of traits of personality, such as edification and fear, to the church also shows that it was a term descriptive not only of the Christian assembly but of Christians themselves (Ac. 9:31). The *ekklesia* was therefore all those spiritually united in Christ, the Head of the church. There is no concept of a literal assembly in this sense of *ekklesia*, nor does the New Testament, as will be seen later, have any organizational structure for the church universal. The unity is that of the Spirit in the body of Christ (Eph. 4:4).

2. The Evangelical Council for Financial Accountability (ECFA), P.O. Box 17456, Washington, D.C. 20041.

Part 6
PAUL'S MISSION:
THE THIRD JOURNEY AND IMPRISONMENT

This unit of study follows Paul on his third missionary journey and then on to Jerusalem where at one time, as an unsaved Jew, he had persecuted Christians. Ironically, he was almost killed as a Christian in the very city where he approved of Stephen's death. In the providence of God, his life was spared and he was transported to Caesarea for trial.

Because Paul had appealed to Caesar after arriving in Caesarea, King Agrippa eventually sent him on to Rome, even though he found him not guilty. When Paul eventually arrived in the imperial city, he was allowed to stay in his own rented quarters while under Roman guard.

This period in Paul's life generated some rich New Testament literature. His epistle to the Romans was written on his third missionary journey shortly before he left for Jerusalem. And when he arrived in Rome, he penned his four prison epistles—Philemon, Ephesians, Colossians, and Philippians. All of these letters provide us with additional supracultural principles that expand our understanding regarding the way God wants Christians to view and use their material possessions. Paul's letter to the Romans also introduces us, at least indirectly, to the subject of borrowing and debt. Consequently, a chapter is devoted to gaining perspective on this subject from the Old Testament Scriptures.

27. Gaining Perspective: The Third Missionary Journey

28. Paul's Letter to the Romans

29. A Biblical Perspective on Borrowing and Debt

30. Paul's Trip to Jerusalem and Rome

31. Paul's Letter to Philemon

32. Paul's Letters to the Ephesians and Colossians

33. Paul's Letter to the Philippians

27

Gaining Perspective:
The Third Missionary Journey

Following his second missionary journey, Paul once again spent some time at his home base church of Antioch. Then he decided to retrace most of his steps in order to strengthen "all the disciples" (Acts 18:23) who became believers on his second journey. Though Luke does not specify who accompanied Paul on this trip, it appears from a later reference that both Timothy and Erastus became his traveling companions (Acts 19:22).

PAUL'S TRIP IN PERSPECTIVE: ACTS 18:23–21:16

Here is a brief outline of Paul's third missionary journey (see map on p. 252):

> Once again traveled through southern *Galatia*; entered the region of Phrygia; descended the valley of the Meander to Ephesus (Acts 18:23–19:1).

> Ministered in *Ephesus* for two years; had a number of encounters with both Jews and Gentiles; serious riot occurred because of threat to pagan economy; wrote his first letter to the Corinthians in A.D. 56; eventually left for Macedonia (Acts 19:2–20:1).

> Ministered throughout *Achaia* and *Macedonia*; sailed from Philippi to *Troas*; some time during stay in Macedonia wrote second letter to the Corinthians in A.D. 57 (Acts 20:2-6).

> Spoke to the believers in Troas and left the next day, traveling by foot to *Assos* (Acts 20:7-14).

> Sailed to *Samos* and on to *Miletus*; sent for Ephesian elders (Acts 20:15-38).

> Sailed to *Tyre* in Syria where the believers urged Paul not to go to Jerusalem (Acts 21:1-6).

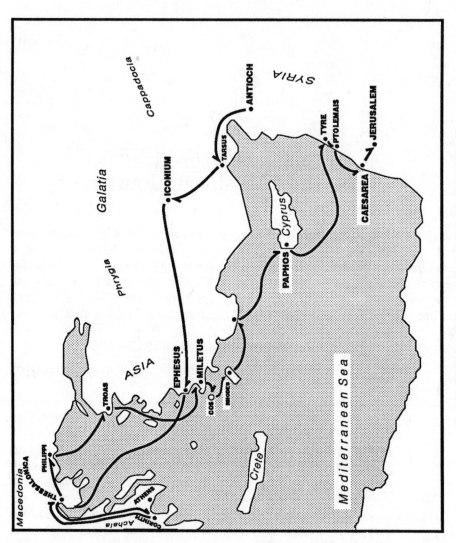

Paul's Third Missionary Journey (Acts 18:23–21:16)

Continued voyage from Tyre to *Ptolemais* and spent a day with the believers there (Acts 21:7).

Traveled to *Caesarea* and stayed a number of days with Philip the evangelist; while there, Agabus came from Judea and prophesied what would happen to Paul in Jerusalem; again, Paul "would not be dissuaded" (Acts 21:8-14).

Went on to *Jerusalem* accompanied by some disciples from Caesarea; stayed in the home of Mnason (Acts 21:15-16).

PAUL'S LETTER TO THE ROMANS

Paul had never been to Rome before he wrote to this church. He penned this letter on this third trip in A.D. 58, either in Corinth or in Philippi just before he sailed on to Troas. In the closing chapters of Romans, Paul indicated that he had preached as far as Illyricum (15:19). Furthermore, he had in hand the offering the churches of Macedonia and Achaia had gathered for the poor Christians in Jerusalem (15:26). At that time, he already anticipated that he would not be received very hospitably by some of his Jewish brethren in Jerusalem. He hoped, however, to leave Jerusalem after a short stay to visit Rome and then to go on to Spain (15:24, 28, 32). As we will see in chapter 28 these hopes did not materialize. He made the trip to Rome, but not as a free man.

The first eleven chapters of Romans deal with the great doctrines relating to sin, salvation, justification, sanctification, predestination, and election. Chapters 12-16 contain practical teachings regarding how to live in the will of God once we have personally experienced these great doctrinal truths in our lives.

The first two verses in Romans 12 capsulate Paul's structure and content in the entire letter. He begins by saying, "Therefore, I urge you, brothers, in view of God's mercy . . ." (12:1*a*). In referring to "God's mercy," Paul was succinctly summarizing everything he had written in the first eleven chapters. Since God has mercifully and graciously provided a marvelous escape from sin's death penalty, he was appealing to these believers "to offer" their "bodies as living sacrifices, holy and pleasing to God" (12:1*b*). They were not to "conform any longer to the pattern of this world, but be transformed." This transformation would take place as they renewed their minds, with the end result being that they would "be able to test and approve what God's will is—his good, pleasing and perfect will" (12:2).

The remaining chapters show believers how to conform their lives to the will of God. Though Paul outlined a number of propositions that describe how this should be done, three important statements explain how Christians should carry out God's will in their lives in relationship to their material possessions. In the next chapter, we will look specifically at these statements and at the three supracultural principles that emerge from these exhortations. Significantly, we have not encountered these principles heretofore in our study.

28

Paul's Letter to the Romans

Though Paul has a great deal to say in Romans 12-16 regarding how to live in the perfect will of God, he touches on a specific subject in chapter 13 that relates to material possessions. Paul was concerned that the believers in Rome show respect to government leaders, particularly by paying taxes and revenues. What Paul taught them was especially pertinent since they were living in the very city where all major governmental decisions were made regarding the whole Roman Empire. In fact, some of these Christians probably lived a stone's throw away from the emperor's palace. Romans 13:7 contains an important exhortation introducing us to the subject of a Christian's financial responsibility to government.

Romans 13:7

Give everyone what you owe him:
if you owe taxes, pay taxes; if revenue, then revenue;
if respect, then respect; if honor, then honor.

EXPOSITION

Paul outlined two basic areas of obligation. The first is *financial* and the second is *attitudinal.* In the financial area, Paul was probably referring to the tax that was levied on persons and property, a tax similar to federal, state, and local taxes in the U.S. This was the tax the Pharisees and Herodians were referring to when they approached Jesus and asked Him if it was right to pay taxes to Caesar. Jesus responded by telling them to "give to Caesar what is Caesar's, and to God what is God's" (Matt. 22:21).

Ironically, this was one of the issues raised when Jesus was taken into custody and was falsely accused before Pilate: "We have found this man subverting our nation," the religious leaders charged. "He opposes payment to Caesar and claims to be Christ, a king" (Luke 23:2). In addition to taxes, Paul made reference to paying "revenue." This money probably referred to the tax that was levied on goods. It would correspond in part to state sales tax in certain parts of the U.S.

Paul also dealt with an *attitudinal* obligation. Not only are Christians to pay taxes, they are to do so with a proper spirit. If we owe "respect"— which we do—then we are to give respect. If we owe "honor"—which we do—then we are to give honor. This poses a problem for some Christians. How can we respect those who may not deserve it because of their behavior? How can we honor government leaders if they disqualify themselves from receiving honor?

Jesus Christ certainly sets the example in this matter. He disagreed with Herod Antipas, the ruler in Galilee, and Tiberius Caesar, the ruler of the Roman Empire. In many respects, their values were in total opposition to His. But Christ still respected these men because of their God-ordained positions. And one way He demonstrated that respect was by paying taxes.

THE FIRST SUPRACULTURAL PRINCIPLE

Christians should always be responsible and honest citizens in their own societies by paying all governmental taxes and revenues (Rom. 13:6-7).

A Christian's most important citizenship exists in relationship to Christ's Body, His church (Eph. 2:19-22). And from an eternal perspective, our true citizenship is in heaven (Eph. 2:6). In reality, we are "foreigners and aliens" on this earth. However, the Word of God teaches that we are also citizens of our earthly society. Consequently, we have a responsibility to help maintain law and order by providing money to support people in leadership and various governmental programs.

The greatest problem among Christians in today's society is not an inaccurate theology regarding our responsibility to pay taxes. Rather, the challenge all of us face is to be totally honest. There are many ways to cheat the government without being detected. Unfortunately, some Christians fall prey to this kind of behavior in direct violation of the will of God. Rather than taking advantage of the government, we are to pray "for kings and all those in authority, that we may live peaceful and quiet lives in all *godliness* and *holiness*" (1 Tim. 2:2). The KJV* reads that our lives are to be characterized by "godliness and honesty."

The Word of God allows no room for rationalization in this matter. Either we are honest or dishonest. Our honesty should not be dependent upon the ethics of our government leaders. Any form of dishonesty on their part does not make it right for Christians to engage in the same kind of sinful behavior.

*King James Version.

ROMANS 13:8

Let no debt remain outstanding,
except the continuing debt to love one another,
for he who loves his fellowman has fulfilled the law.

EXPOSITION

A casual reading of this exhortation may give the impression that Paul was teaching that it is always wrong to borrow money. Most serious commentators disagree with such an understanding of Paul's teaching. Several perspectives exist on this verse of Scripture,[1] but John Murray is representative when he says, "This cannot be taken to mean that we may never issue financial obligations, that we may not borrow from others in case of need."[2]

It may be unwise and even out of God's will in certain circumstances to borrow money, but this is not what Paul was referring to in this verse. He was simply saying that if we owe money, we should pay it. In context, this includes taxes and every kind of revenue that is required by the government (13:7).

The Scriptures broaden this concept to include *any kind of debt*. In the New Testament world, it involved wages. This is why James wrote, "Look! The wages you failed to pay the workmen who mowed your fields are crying out against you. The cries of the harvesters have reached the ears of the Lord Almighty" (James 5:4). It is utterly sinful to hire people to perform tasks with no intention of paying them.

This command also certainly involved the repayment of any money that was borrowed. And it goes without saying, there should be repayment of anything that was ever stolen. Paul was so conscientious about this kind of obligation that after he led Onesimus to Christ, he personally offered to repay Philemon (Onesimus's owner) anything this slave had stolen (Philem. 17).

THE SECOND SUPRACULTURAL PRINCIPLE

Christians who owe people money or goods should always pay what they owe (Rom. 13:8).

It is indeed unfortunate that some who claim to be followers of Jesus Christ violate this principle with every degree of regularity. Some Christians simply borrow money and do not repay it. Or if they do make payments, they are always late or woefully behind.

This kind of behavior is even more deplorable when it characterizes pastors and other Christian leaders. I have heard tragic stories of ministers who have transferred to churches in other cities, leaving behind a string of unpaid debts. Fortunately, these situations seem to be the exception rather than the rule. But one instance among those who claim to be spiritual leaders is one too many.

Some Christians do not intentionally set out to violate this principle. Little by little they allow themselves to get into debt beyond their ability to return the money on a predetermined and agreed to repayment schedule. They are guilty of poor planning or impulsive buying. For these people, easy credit is a curse rather than a blessing. Either they need to utilize credit cards cautiously and only as a convenience for not carrying cash or writing checks, or they need to destroy them. If they cannot use them within their budgeted guidelines, they need to avoid credit buying altogether.

There are, of course, economic crises that affect all people, including Christians. We may have entered into financial agreements with every potential to make our loan payments on time. Everyone involved in the agreement is satisfied that the arrangement is a proper risk. But circumstances arise beyond everyone's control.

What should a Christian do when this happens? There are some important guidelines in the next chapter, but at this juncture, it is important to emphasize that all Christians need wise financial counsel as to the best approach in faithfully applying this principle from Romans 13:8. However, people who are caught in this kind of situation should be the first to communicate with their creditors to indicate their desire to meet all financial obligations and to work out an acceptable plan to do so. This may mean liquidating certain assets to generate instant cash to pay debts.

What Paul said here in Romans raises some additional questions. What guidelines are there in Scripture regarding borrowing money and going into debt? When is it wrong? When is it unwise? When is it appropriate? We will speak to these questions in the next chapter.

ROMANS 15:27

They were pleased to do it, and indeed they owe it to them.
For if the Gentiles have shared in the Jews' spiritual blessings,
they owe it to the Jews to share with them their material blessings.

EXPOSITION

When Paul wrote to the Romans, he was preparing to leave for Jerusalem with a group of men to deliver the gift of money for use among needy Christians. In fact, he reported that he was already on his way (15:25), which means he was probably ready to leave for Jerusalem the moment he finished his dictation. The money was in hand, which, as seen in Part 5, had been collected over a period of time by the churches in Macedonia and Achaia (1 Cor. 16:1-5).

As Paul began to conclude this letter, he explained the spirit and motivation that caused these Macedonian and Achaian Christians to gather this money. First, "they were *pleased* to do it" (15:27*a*). In spite of the problem that had occurred in Corinth, Paul could now share the concern and compassion these Christians demonstrated toward the Jewish Christians in Jerusalem who were suffering from economic deprivation. Evidently the Corinthians had responded maturely to Paul's exhortations in his second letter (2 Cor. 8-9).

Paul went on to state *why* a Christian should share his material possessions with others. Though the churches in Macedonia and Achaia responded out of concern, Paul made clear that they also had an *obligation* to help these needy Christians in Jerusalem. "They owe it to them," he wrote and then explained why (15:27).

The message of Christianity first came to the Jews. Jesus Christ Himself was a Jew. The apostles were all Jews. The first converts to Christianity were Jews. And it was the Jewish Christians in Jerusalem who first brought the message of Jesus Christ to the Gentiles, primarily because of persecution (Acts 8:1, 4; Acts 11:19-21).

This persecution and scattering, as we have seen, led to some serious economic problems among many of these believers. When they eventually returned to Jerusalem, some may have lost all they had. And since many of these Jews who initially responded to the message of Christ were already among the lower classes, it is understandable why many Christians in Jerusalem were in financial need.

Frederick Lewis Godet wrote, "The indigence of those first believers must have been increased day by day by the violent hatred of the Jewish authorities and of the upper classes; comp. Jas. 2:4-6. What easier for rich and powerful families than to deprive poor artisans, who had become the objects of their reprobation, of their means of subsistence!" Godet further points out that this is not an unusual phenomenon among Christians: "This is an event which is reproduced everywhere when there is a transition from one religious form to another; so in Catholic countries where Protestantism is preached; among the Jews, among the heathen of India or China, etc., when one of their own becomes a Christian."[3] Gentile Christians had a definite obligation to care for those who sacrificed and made it possible for them to hear the gospel of Jesus Christ and to respond in faith. Thus, "they owe it to the Jews to share with them their material blessings" (15:27*b*).

THE THIRD SUPRACULTURAL PRINCIPLE

All Christians have an obligation to support God's work in material ways (Rom. 15:27).

Earlier we noted two important corollary principles from Paul's second letter to the Corinthians. First, God does not want Christians to respond to a command to share their material possessions but, rather, to respond out of hearts of love that reflect sincere appreciation for His gift of salvation in Christ (2 Cor. 8:8-9; see p. 218). Second, every Christian is ultimately responsible to give to God on the basis of his own heart decision (2 Cor. 9:7; see p. 233). It may appear that this third principle from Romans, which focuses on *obligation*, contradicts these two principles from 2 Corinthians. In reality, all three of these principles are complementary, not contradictory.

To understand this apparent tension more fully, we need to consider a larger perspective on Christian commitment. The Scriptures make clear that we are *all obligated* to present ourselves to God because of His gift of eternal salvation in Christ. To *not* understand that this action on our part is obligatory is to be totally ignorant of what God has done for us through His sovereign and elective grace. At the same time, however, we should present our bodies to God *freely* in response to His mercy, love, and grace.

Just so, we have an obligation to give to God's work. However, it should at the same time be given freely and voluntarily from hearts of love. In Christ, it is possible to blend these two concepts. Once we understand God's grace, it becomes a "blessed obligation" to give, not an oppressive burden. Conversely, if we do not have this perspective, either we do not understand God's grace, or we understand it but do not appreciate it. If this is the case, we are living self-centered and carnal lives.

This seeming paradox can be illustrated with the concept of being a slave to Christ and yet experiencing freedom. How can this be? There is only one way to be truly free in our hearts and lives and that is to live in harmony with God's will. Then and only then can we experience the reality of this antinomy. This principle also applies to the way we use our material possessions. True *freedom* to give comes once we truly understand how *indebted* we are to Jesus Christ for His gift of eternal life.

NOTES

1. Charles Hodge, *Commentary on the Epistle to the Romans* (Grand Rapids: Eerdmans, 1950), p. 409, affirms this same concept:

   The idea which a cursory reader might be disposed to attach to these words, in considering them as a direction not to contract pecuniary debts, is not properly expressed by them; although the prohibition, in its spirit, includes the incurring of such obligations, when we have not the certain prospect of discharging them. The command, however, is "Acquit yourselves of all obligations, tribute, custom, fear, honour, or whatever else you may owe, but remember the debt of love is still unpaid, and always must remain so; for love includes all duty, since he that loves another fulfills the law."

   W. H. Griffith Thomas, *St. Paul's Epistle to the Romans* (Grand Rapids: Eerdmans, 1946), pp. 355-56, adds this helpful interpretation:

   The Christian is not to incur anything which he is unable to pay, and knows that he is unable when it is incurred. He ought to be able to render back what is rightfully claimed from him. If he should have to borrow anything and the repayment is required, he ought to be able to meet his liability. How simple, and yet how searching is this requirement. Men judge Christians by their promptness in fulfilling obligations and in paying their bills, and it is a fine, natural, and legitimate test. A spirituality that is not ethical carries its own condemnation and is certain to elicit the disgust and opposition of all practical, honest people.

2. John Murray, *The New International Commentary on the New Testament: The Epistle to the Romans*, 2 vols. (Grand Rapids: Eerdmans, 1965), p. 158.

3. Frederick Lewis Godet, *Commentary on Romans* (Grand Rapids: Kregel, 1977), p. 484.

29

A Biblical Perspective
on Borrowing and Debt

In recent years, the subject of debt has become somewhat controversial among a number of well-meaning Christians. The most extreme position is that the Scriptures teach that no debt whatsoever is allowed within God's ideal plan for our lives.

THE BIBLICAL PERSPECTIVES

Dealing with this subject is in some respects a departure from the flow of God's unfolding revelation in the New Testament. However, if we do not explore what the Word of God says about this issue now, there will be no opportunity to do so. In actuality, the New Testament writers did not address this subject, at least not in a direct fashion.

Why, then, deal with the issue? The answer is twofold. First, the most extreme position on the subject is often based on Paul's statement "Let no debt remain outstanding" (Rom. 13:8), or "Owe no man anything" (KJV). Some view this understanding of Romans as axiomatic, then use Old Testament passages to support the interpretation that no Christian at any moment in history or in any culture of the world is to ever go into debt.

The second reason this subject must be addressed is that New Testament principles dealing with material possessions certainly relate to the subject of debt. In fact, going into debt may violate several of these principles. Furthermore, even though there are no direct teachings on this subject in the New Testament, statements about it abound in the Old Testament. It is important that we understand these teachings and integrate them with New Testament principles.

PAUL'S PERSPECTIVE

Well-known Bible scholars agree that Paul was not teaching that all debt is a violation of the will of God (see p. 257). The most basic and logical interpretation of Romans 13:8 is that Paul was simply teaching that when a Christian owes anything—whether taxes, revenues, respect, or honor—he is to pay it. Furthermore, a Christian must realize there is a debt we can never fully repay—the debt to love others (Rom. 13:7-8).

Though Paul probably did not have borrowing and debt in mind, at least as we envision it today, what he stated certainly applies to these economic circumstances. When money is due, it should be paid. Otherwise, we do owe others what is rightfully theirs. To default on any agreed to loan payments would certainly be classified as a violation of Paul's intent when he wrote that as Christians we are to "let no debt remain outstanding."

JESUS' PERSPECTIVE

It is not necessary to review all that Jesus had to say about this subject, except to state that He never addressed the issue as being right or wrong. Rather, He acknowledged the practice of borrowing and loaning money in the Roman Empire without making value judgments. Furthermore, He often used these economic settings as illustrative material to teach spiritual truths. As in all free enterprise systems, the economy of the Roman Empire was highly integrated with financial approaches that involved indebtedness. Consequently, Jesus accepted this reality but, at the same time, taught people how to live an upright and spiritual life in that kind of society (see p. 67).

AN OLD TESTAMENT PERSPECTIVE

Before we look at the Old Testament teachings, it is important to understand the cultural, economic, and spiritual differences that existed in Israel prior to the time they went into captivity and before they eventually became a part of the Roman Empire.

The cultural and economic setting. A. E. Willingale gives us some helpful insights when speaking of the time that Israel occupied their own land and determined their own economic destiny as a self-contained nation:

> Loans in Israel were not commercial but charitable, granted not to enable a trader to set up or expand a business but to tide a peasant farmer over a period of poverty. Since the economy remained predominately agricultural up to the end of the monarchy, there developed no counterpart to the commercial loan system already existing in Babylonia in 2000 BC. Hence the legislation contains not mercantile regulations but exhortations to neighbourliness.[1]

We must understand this unique agricultural setting to be able to interpret correctly what God had in mind for Israel. There was no need for these people to purchase property since they had received it at no cost from God Himself: "large, flourishing cities you did not build, houses filled with all kinds of good things you did not provide, wells you did not dig, and vineyards and olive groves you did not plant" (Deut. 6:10*b*-11).

Because of God's material provisions for the children of Israel, there was no need to establish businesses based upon a free enterprise system. Rather, they were able to make a living from the land they had received free from indebtedness. Initially, at least, they did not even need to build houses and plant the fields. Consequently, business loans of any kind were unnecessary.

The spiritual setting. God had also promised His people that He would provide unusual blessings if they obeyed Him: "The Lord will open the heavens, the storehouse of his bounty, to send rain on your land in season and to bless all the work of your hands. *You will lend to many nations but will borrow from none*" (Deut. 28:12).

The whole of Deuteronomy 28 is devoted to "blessings for obedience" (vv. 1-14) and "curses for disobedience" (vv. 15-68). God assured Israel that if they obeyed all His laws, He would make them "the head, not the tail" (Deut. 28:13). But the opposite would be true if they disobeyed Him. Rather than being free from bondage to others, "the aliens" who lived among them "would rise above" them "higher and higher." By contrast, Israel would "sink lower and lower. He [the alien] will lend to you, but you will not lend to him," God warned. "He will be the head, but you will be the tail" (Deut. 28:43, 45).

If Israel obeyed God in all respects, they would be a self-contained nation, totally free from any need for economic assistance from other nations. They would be able to lend money to other nations in distress, which would be a dynamic witness to their pagan neighbors. The ungodly Canaanites would be able to see how God was providing for Israel's economic needs in a miraculous way because of their faithfulness to Him. By contrast, if the children of Israel disobeyed God, they would deteriorate economically. Not only would they be unable to meet their own needs, they would have to borrow from their pagan neighbors in order to survive (Deut. 28:47-48).

Willingale reminds us that this unique economic setting in Israel "changes in the New Testament." Israel now existed in a totally different situation culturally and economically. The Jews had to adapt their laws to a commercial economy. In some instances, they circumvented some of these laws for purely selfish reasons. But it is also true that they could not practice some of these laws and survive in the Roman culture. Jesus recognized this reality as well.

Interpretation and application today. The challenge twentieth-century Christians face is to interpret these Old Testament teachings without transplanting Old Testament laws into another cultural setting in a legalistic, literal fashion. At the same time, we must not bypass the spirit of these laws. Though designed for Israel, they yield timeless principles that are supracultural, for, as we will see, they are affirmed by New Testament teachings. With this challenge in mind, consider the following Old Testament statements.

EXODUS 22:25

If you lend money to any of my people among you who is needy,
do not be like a moneylender; charge him no interest.

EXPOSITION

This Old Testament law and others like it must be interpreted in its cultural setting. When the children of Israel came into the land, God was going to give them everything, with the promise that, if they obeyed Him, He would give them even more. Yet the Lord recognized there would "always be poor people" (Deut. 15:11). Thus, He prefaced this law on lending money in Exodus 22:25 by warning the Israelites to never "take advantage of a widow or an orphan. If you do," God said, "and they cry out to me, I will certainly hear their cry. My anger will be aroused, and I will kill you with a sword; your wives will become widows and your children fatherless" (Ex. 22:22-24).

The picture is clear. How could they who had received everything as a free gift from God turn around and take advantage of the poor and needy? How could they even consider loaning money and charging interest to their fellow Israelites who were already in a desperate financial situation? To do so would be an ultimate act of selfishness and sin. God forbade it.

Moses' statement following Exodus 22:25 gives an even greater perspective on God's concern. It was not a violation of God's law to loan a fellow Israelite money, and even to take some kind of pledge in lieu of interest. However, if that pledge was his "neighbor's cloak," he was to "return it to him by sunset, because his cloak is the only covering he has for his body" (Ex. 22:26-27). As Lange points out, God was interceding for those in extreme poverty: "The lender may require a pledge of the creditor, but his covering (outer garment) he must return to him before sunset, lest he suffer from the nocturnal cold."[3]

Moses elaborated on these laws in Leviticus and Deuteronomy. He made clear that God was very concerned about anyone in Israel who, for some reason or another, "becomes poor and is unable to support himself" (Lev. 25:35). In those cases, Moses restated the same law he had outlined in Exodus: "*Do not take interest of any kind* from him, but fear your God, so that your countryman may continue to live among you. *You must not lend him money at interest* or sell him food at a profit. I am the Lord your God, who brought you out of Egypt to give you the land of Canaan and to be your God" (Lev. 25:36-38).

God had given them everything. How could they, in turn, take advantage of those less fortunate and actually force them into a position where they could no longer live in the land that God had given them? This also explains why no Israelite was to require his neighbor to give anything as a pledge for a loan that was necessary to provide for a living. Thus, the Lord became specific: "Do not take a pair of millstones—not even the upper one—as security for a debt, because that would be taking a man's livelihood as security" (Deut. 24:6). Even though no interest was charged on a loan, the lender under these conditions would put the borrower in an impossible situation. Not only would he be unable to pay back the loan, but he would not even be able to provide for his basic needs. In that case, the "lender" would be making the "borrower's" problem even worse (see also Deut. 24:10-15, 17-18).

THE FOURTH SUPRACULTURAL PRINCIPLE

Christians must never take economic advantage of poor people, whether Christians or non-Christians (Ex. 22:25).

We cannot establish a universal principle from these Old Testament laws that it is *always* wrong to lend money to fellow Christians and even to charge interest. However, if a Christian ever takes advantage of another Christian—especially poor people—there is no question but that it is sinful behavior. It is an affront to God, who has freely given us the gift of salvation. Furthermore, it is an ultimate act of selfishness on our part.

The New Testament contains illustration after illustration demonstrating that believers should take care of those in need and not take advantage of them. Whether it was the widows (Acts 6:1-7) or the poor Jewish Christians in Jerusalem (Acts 11:19-30), believers responded with generosity. The Macedonian believers gave out of their poverty in order to help others who were in worse poverty (2 Cor. 8:1-2).

Jesus affirmed the importance of caring for needy parents (Matt. 15:4-6), and Paul underscored this principle by classifying any Christian who does not care for a needy family member as one who has "denied the faith" and is "worse than an unbeliever" (1 Tim. 5:8). James succinctly reinforced this principle: "Religion that God our Father accepts as pure and faultless is this: to look after orphans and widows in their distress" (James 1:27a).

PSALM 37:21

The wicked borrow and do not repay,
but the righteous give generously.

EXPOSITION

Following the flow of God's unfolding revelation in the Old Testament, it is logical to look next at this proverb in Psalm 37. In concise fashion, David interpreted and explained the promises given to Israel relative to the Promised Land. If Israel obeyed the Lord, it would never be necessary for her to borrow money from her pagan neighbors. She would always have sufficient for herself and plenty left over to give to others. Conversely, wicked people—those who do not obey the laws of God—will find themselves in a state of desperation. They will have to borrow money to survive and never have enough resources to pay it back.

Carl B. Moll has given a very helpful commentary on this verse: "The wicked, through God's curse resting upon him, is reduced to poverty, so that he is compelled to borrow, and cannot pay; whereas the righteous hath even abundance not only for his own wants, but for the wants of others." In essence, Moll is stating that what David wrote in Psalm 37:21 is a *proverb* that was derived from the *promise* in Deuteronomy: "For the Lord your God will bless you as he has promised, and you will lend to many nations but will borrow from none" (Deut. 15:6).[4]

THE FIFTH SUPRACULTURAL PRINCIPLE

Christians who obey God's Word will be able not only to meet their own economic needs but to help others who are in need (Ps. 37:21).

Inherent in David's parable is a profound principle affirmed in the New Testament, particularly in 2 Corinthians. Paul taught that when Christians are faithful in their giving, God has promised to meet their needs (2 Cor. 9:8; see also Phil. 4:19). Furthermore, he taught that when we are generous, God has promised to enable us to continue to be generous (2 Cor. 9:11).

Paul was not teaching prosperity theology (see pp. 234-35). Nor was he saying we would always have excess resources. Rather, he was teaching that God will care for us when we are faithful in sharing what we have with others and He will always give us the grace to continue to share with others, even if we find ourselves in a difficult financial situation. For some Christians who are in a state of poverty, just being able to give someone "a cup of cold water" is being generous.

Will faithful and generous Christians ever need to borrow money to meet their needs? The Bible does not speak to this question directly. Part of God's provision in our culture may be an opportunity to be involved in responsible borrowing to meet *special* needs—such as helping a son or daughter through college, or in buying a car or a house. But when there are basic and immediate human needs that are not being met—such as a need for food, clothing, and temporary shelter—the Word of God teaches that if all Christians are generous as God says they should be, there will never be a need for poor Christians to dig themselves in deeper by borrowing money. As Paul wrote to the Corinthians, "Our desire is not that others might be relieved while you are hard pressed, but that there might be equality. At the present time your plenty will supply what they need, so that in turn their plenty will supply what you need. Then there will be equality" (2 Cor. 8:13-14).

DEUTERONOMY 15:1-3

At the end of every seven years you must cancel debts.
This is how it is to be done: Every creditor shall
cancel the loan he has made to his fellow Israelite.
He shall not require payment from his fellow Israelite
or brother, because the Lord's time for canceling debts has
been proclaimed. You may require payment from a foreigner,
but you must cancel any debt your brother owes you.

EXPOSITION

These commands to cancel debts have puzzled a lot of people. However, what God was requiring here is consistent regarding Israel's unique economic position once they arrived in Canaan. Two important factors need to be considered in explaining what God had in mind.

First, note the context of this statement. Moses had just reminded Israel of their responsibility to "the aliens, the fatherless and the widows" who lived among them. "At the end of *every three years*," they were to "bring all the tithes of that year's produce and store it in" the various towns. Then, those in need could "come and eat and be satisfied" (Deut. 14:28-29). Moses went on to state their responsibility "at the end of *every seven years*" (Deut. 15:1) toward poor people who had borrowed money in order to survive. Moses was still outlining laws that governed relationships to people who were in a desperate economic situation.

Second, note what Moses was actually saying in a still larger context. In the book of Exodus, God had commanded that the children of Israel were to sow their fields and harvest crops for six years. However, "during the seventh year," they were to "let the land lie unplowed and unused. Then," God continued, "the poor among your people may get food from it, and the wild animals may eat what they leave. Do the same with your vineyard and your olive grove" (Ex. 23:11).

The command to cancel debts refers to this seven year period of time (Deut. 15:1-3). God was expressing concern through Moses for those who had borrowed money from their fellow Israelites. They too were not allowed to cultivate their fields during the seventh year. Keil and Delitzsch explain:

"If no harvest was gathered in, and even such produce as had grown without sowing was to be left to the poor and the beasts of the field, the landowner could have no income from which to pay his debts."[5]

Consequently, Moses outlined a plan for handling these debts. Those who had loaned money to poor people (which was to be loaned without interest; Ex. 22:25), were not to put pressure on these people to pay back what they owed during this seventh year. Keil and Delitzsch translate verse 2 as follows: "This is the manner of the release. Every owner of a loan of his hand shall release (leave) what he has lent to his neighbour; he shall not press his neighbour, and indeed his brother; for they have proclaimed release for Jehovah."[6] Moses was not issuing a command to cancel debts once and for all. Rather, the debt payment was simply to be postponed. Lenders were not to put pressure on these poor people during this seventh year.

Wilhelm J. Schroeder agrees with Keil and Delitzsch:

> The clear reference to the land-rest or release, which was for the year, and the force of the Hebrew word rendered exact, more correctly urge or press, and the whole spirit of the Mosaic Law, which was not to destroy obligations of this kind, but to guard the poor and unfortunate against undue severity or oppression, are all in favor of the interpretation which regards the release as for the year. This interpretation is now almost universally accepted.

Schroeder adds this comment: "It seems further clear that the release had reference only to loans, and to loans lent because of poverty, not to debts contracted in the purchase of goods."[7]

This interpretation also explains the exception that the children of Israel "may require payment from a foreigner" (Deut. 15:3). Foreigners were not obligated to allow their land to lie uncultivated during the seventh year, putting them in the same predicament as the poor in Israel. In other words, Israel not only had the right to charge interest for loans to foreigners, but they could also insist that those loans be paid off even during this seventh year.

The specific economic conditions and requirements described in this Old Testament passage cannot and should not be duplicated in other cultural situations. However, it contains an important principle that captures the spirit of God's intent and should be applied universally.

THE SIXTH SUPRACULTURAL PRINCIPLE

Christians must set the example of being gracious to people who have borrowed money with good intentions and then have faced crises beyond their control that has made it difficult for them to make their loan payments on time (Deut. 15:1-3).

There will always be times when people borrow money and have difficulty repaying it. As Christians, what should we do?

Personal loans. If we have made a personal loan, we naturally have more control over the circumstances. First of all, personal loans to fellow Christians should be made with full awareness that those we are attempting to help may not be able to repay. In that sense, we should be willing to make it a gift if necessary or postpone payments indefinitely. This decision should be made in one's heart and mind before a personal loan is ever made.

Is it right for a Christian to ever make a loan to a fellow Christian and charge interest? The Scriptures do not give a definitive answer to this question. As demonstrated, this aspect of the Old Testament law does not apply to other cultural and spiritual situations. However, the *spirit* of those laws does apply. To loan money to poor people with the intent of making money violates both Old and New Testament teachings.

Business loans. If a loan has been secured through a recognized loan organization, Christian loan officers have the responsibility to function within the guidelines of that agency. If the business is not operated within proper ethical guidelines, a Christian should look elsewhere for a job. If Christians own the business, they should set up guidelines that reflect the spirit and principles of Christianity.

The principle involving grace and forgiveness, however, in no way allows a Christian to take advantage of either an individual or an organization. Borrowed money should always be paid back. Though certain laws in our own society protect the rights of individuals and organizations during times of crises, these laws should never be used by Christians to justify serious risk in borrowing or to avoid paying back borrowed money on a reasonable and feasible payment schedule.

PROVERBS 22:7

The rich rule over the poor,
and the borrower is servant to the lender.

EXPOSITION

Here is another Old Testament proverb that must be interpreted in the light of Old Testament laws and in view of what was actually happening in Israel's history. What we have studied thus far gives a helpful perspective on the proverb under consideration.

Note first that Solomon was drawing a contrast between the "rich" and the "poor." In this sense, he was referring to the prohibition in the laws of Moses that those who have a lot must never take advantage of those who have little. When people are in such a state of poverty that they do not have enough to meet their needs for food and shelter, they will often borrow—if they can—out of desperation. And when they do, they become "servants to the lender."

Unfortunately, this happened in Israel again and again, and people became slaves in a literal sense. Because there was no way to pay back what they borrowed, they lost everything they had. This is why the prophets cried out so vehemently against this unfair treatment of poor people.

One of the most dramatic illustrations of the way in which Israel violated God's laws regarding lending and borrowing took place after a number of Israelites returned to the Promised Land, first, under the leadership of Zerubbabel (536 B.C.) and then under Ezra (458 B.C.). Several years later when Nehemiah arrived to help rebuild the walls of Jerusalem, he found an incredible situation. Because of a famine, many of the poor people in Israel had already *mortgaged their fields, their vineyards, and their homes* in order to buy grain (Neh. 5:3). Still others, in order to keep their property, had borrowed money from their Jewish brothers to pay taxes to King Artaxerxes (Neh. 5:4). The problem was compounded by the fact that these fellow Jews charged these poor people interest—which, of course, was a direct violation of the laws of Moses. To make matters worse, they charged *exorbitant* interest rates.

Those who borrowed money to survive faced another problem when their crops failed. Because of the famine, their Jewish brothers and sisters took away their property and sold their children into slavery. Thus, the people cried out to Nehemiah, "Although we are of the same flesh and blood as our countrymen and though our sons are as good as theirs, yet we have to subject our sons and daughters to *slavery.* Some of our daughters have already been enslaved, but we are powerless, because our fields and our vineyards belong to others" (Neh. 5:5). Solomon's proverb is literally illustrated in this situation: "The rich rule over the poor, and the borrower is servant to the lender" (Prov. 22:7).

Nehemiah confronted the situation directly. He rebuked the nobles and officials among the Jews: "I told them, 'You are exacting usury [interest] from your own countrymen!'" (Neh. 5:7b). Nehemiah was so disturbed he called a large meeting to deal with the problem. "What you are doing is not right," he proclaimed. "Shouldn't you walk in the fear of our God to avoid the reproach of our Gentile enemies? I and my brothers and my men are also lending the people money and grain. But let the exacting of usury [interest] stop! Give back to them immediately their fields, vineyards, olive groves and houses, and also the usury you are charging them—the hundredth part of the money, grain, new wine and oil" (Neh. 5:9-11).

Fortunately, the Israelites responded to Nehemiah's exhortations. Had they not done so, God's judgment would have fallen on them, as it had before, because of their selfish and greedy behavior.

Solomon in all of his wisdom understood this kind of social disease and sin. His words were directed more specifically to the rich than to the poor, for it was they who had the power to "rule over the poor." It is the rich who force "the borrower" to be "servant to the lender." It is they who exploit these innocent people at will, particularly in times of economic deprivation.

Is there general wisdom in Solomon's proverb for those of us who live in a twentieth-century culture where lending and borrowing is such an integral part of our economic social structures? The answer is a decided "yes," even though the literal aspects of this proverb may not apply (such as being sold into slavery). It is possible for people in any culture to find themselves "in bondage" to those from whom they have borrowed money.

THE SEVENTH SUPRACULTURAL PRINCIPLE

Before Christians borrow money for any purpose, they should consider all of the circumstances and seek wisdom from others who can help them evaluate all aspects of the decision, including the risks involved (Prov. 22:7).

Any form of borrowing brings with it a certain amount of bondage. As Otto Zockler states, "Indebtedness always destroys freedom, even though no sale into slavery of him who is unable to pay should ever take place."[8]

Certain financial decisions, however, can be made that do not involve high risk. The lower the risk, the less the sense of bondage. The amount of money borrowed when weighed against liquid assets, of course, is a very important factor in the total equation. What will we actually lose if we cannot repay the loan? For example, could we possibly be obligated the rest of our lives? That is a terrible price to pay in order to attempt to achieve an economic goal. In that sense, Solomon's statement is applicable.

PROVERBS 22:26-27

*Do not be a man who strikes hands in pledge or
puts up security for debts; if you lack the means to pay,
your very bed will be snatched from under you.*

EXPOSITION

When the Lord warns against something once, it is important. When He warns against it several times, it is paramount. Note the following additional warnings from Proverbs:

He who puts up security for another will surely suffer, but whoever refuses to strike hands in pledge is safe (11:15).

A man lacking in judgment strikes hands in pledge and puts up security for his neighbor (17:18).

My son, if you have put up security for your neighbor, if you have struck hands in pledge for another . . . free yourself, like a gazelle from the hand of the hunter, like a bird from the snare of the fowler (6:1, 5).

Once again Solomon was dealing with a significant problem in Israel when he warned against taking on an obligation for someone else's indebtedness. Zockler helps us understand the seriousness of the situation: "The frequent warnings which our book [Proverbs] contains against giving security for others are to be explained doubtless by the severe treatment, which, in accordance with the old Hebrew jurisprudence, was awarded to sureties; for their goods might be distrained or they even sold as slaves, just as in the case of insolvent debtors."[9]

Solomon's exhortations are not in themselves making judgments on those who are lenders. Rather, he was warning those who might become victims of others—probably poor people—by putting themselves in a position of bondage to moneylenders. Evidently those who often put up surety were also poor, for if they were not, they could have easily covered the debt involved.

The Scriptures teach that this is a foolish decision and one that a person should attempt to reverse as quickly as possible. This is why Solomon made the issue so urgent. "Go and humble yourself," he said. "Press your plea with your neighbor! Allow no sleep to your eyes, no slumber to your eyelids" (Prov. 6:3b-4). In other words, do everything you possibly can to free yourself from this kind of financial bondage.

Does this mean that a Christian today should never "put up security" for someone? A. R. Fausset responds to this question: "This precept does not forbid suretiship in cases where charity and brotherly kindness dictate it." Rather, he believes that Solomon's teaching "only forbids such suretiship as is without a due regard to one's self, to him for whom you are surety, and to the other party to whom you make yourself bound."[10] In other words, any Christian who decides to help someone in this way should be willing and able to cover the complete debt in case of default.

THE EIGHTH SUPRACULTURAL PRINCIPLE

Christians who guarantee another person's loan based upon their own assets should make sure they are able to repay the loan without placing themselves in a position where they cannot meet other financial obliga-tions, including their indebtedness to the Lord (Prov. 22:26-27).

There are times when a Christian may co-sign a note for another individual without violating the will of God. In fact, it may be a gracious and generous act of love. However, any person who guarantees a loan in this way should be prepared to assume the entire loan without serious consequences. But in our culture today it is wise to heed the Old Testament warnings against this practice and to encourage others who need help to wait until they are in a financial position so as not to need this kind of economic assistance. Though there are exceptions to this rule, they should be made rarely and cautiously, considering all of the scriptural principles that relate to how a Christian should view and use his material possessions.

WHEN IS BORROWING WRONG?

If the Scriptures do not teach against borrowing per se, then when does going into debt become an irresponsible decision that leads us directly out of the will of God and into sinful attitudes and actions? The following biblical principles will help us answer this question.

THE NINTH SUPRACULTURAL PRINCIPLE

Christians are out of God's will when they knowingly borrow money that they cannot pay back according to a predetermined agreement (Rom. 13:8).

As stated earlier, all borrowing involves a certain amount of risk. But when we make foolish decisions based upon ignorance, we are acting irresponsibly and can very quickly find ourselves in violation of God's will. Following are several guidelines that will help us avoid irresponsible decisions that may lead us to sin against God:

- We are out of God's will when we borrow money to buy things to glorify ourselves and not God (Matt. 6:3-4).

- We are out of God's will when we borrow because we are in bondage to materialism (Matt. 6:24)—when our treasures are on earth rather than in heaven.

- We are out of God's will when any form of dishonesty is involved in borrowing money (1 Tim. 6:10).

- We are out of God's will when we use borrowed money to achieve any goals that are out of the will of God (Rom. 12:1-2).

Christians are out of God's will when they cannot give God the "firstfruits" of their income because they have obligated themselves to pay off debts (Prov. 3:9; 1 Cor. 16:2).

Solomon wrote, "Honor the Lord with your wealth, with the *first fruits* of all your crops" (Prov. 3:9). Years later Paul exhorted the Corinthians: "On the first day of every week, each of you should set aside a sum of money in keeping with his income" (1 Cor. 16:2).

It is clear from both Old and New Testaments that when we cannot set aside money on a regular, systematic, and proportional basis for God's work because we have obligated ourselves financially, we have ceased putting God first in our lives. That is not true if this happens because of economic reversals beyond our control. In most instances, however, it is caused when we have materialistic goals that in turn lead us to make irresponsible decisions. Put another way, God's will is no longer a priority. We should never make decisions to borrow money that make it impossible, even temporarily, to give to God's work regularly, systematically, and proportionately.

CORRECTIVE STEPS

First, if we are in violation of any of these biblical principles, we should confess our sins to God and accept His forgiveness (1 John 1:9). We must acknowledge that violating scriptural principles inevitably leads to sinful attitudes and actions. Indeed, in most instances, violating these principles is in itself sin.

Second, we must take steps as quickly as possible to bring our lives into harmony with God's will. If we owe money we cannot pay, we need to immediately draw up a plan to correct the situation. We then need to communicate with every creditor in order to let each one know the specific steps we plan to take.

Third, we must include in this plan a way to give regularly and systematically to God's work. Paul's words to the Corinthians are certainly applicable in these difficult economic circumstances (see chap. 23). Because of poor financial planning, these New Testament Christians were in violation of the will of God in not being able to give as they should.

Paul's exhortations to the Corinthians pose another question. Should Christians give regularly and systematically to the Lord's work when they have debt payments that are overdue? This is a difficult question to answer since the Scriptures do not speak directly to this issue. However, we must remember that we are also in debt to God for His gracious provision of salvation. Should we stop giving to His work because we are in financial difficulty with our creditors?

Larry Burkett believes that "the first portion of everything we receive belongs to God. It doesn't belong to anybody else, even a creditor." Furthermore, he points out that Christians who make the commitment to give regularly to God are "always better money handlers, and as a result of their commitment to God, they will honor their commitment to their creditors." It has also been his experience that "rarely does a creditor object to this arrangement once he understands this kind of commitment."[11]

Burkett is advocating that Christians who are behind in debt payments should contact their creditors with a plan of action, spelling out how they are going to care for these debts on a regular and systematic basis. They should also include in the plan their intentions to give a certain amount of their income regularly and systematically to their church.

What Burkett has experienced is that most creditors feel comfortable with this kind of planning since it indicates honesty and moral integrity. People who have these kinds of values can normally be trusted to pay off their debts over a period of time. Certainly Christians who establish these priorities will be honored and blessed by God in economic ways that will eventually enable them to not only meet their financial obligations to their creditors but also be able to begin to give *proportionately* to the work of God.

BORROWING AND CHURCH DEBT

Some teach that it is always out of God's perfect will for a church body to go into debt. The most obvious case in point involves church-building projects. This is another issue never directly addressed in Scripture. We have no illustrations of buildings ever being constructed in the New Testament. This does not mean it would have been wrong. These believers found it difficult to do so because of the political and economic conditions that existed both within the Jewish culture as well as in the Roman Empire as a whole. In the meantime, Christians met in homes, particularly those owned by more well-to-do believers.

In the Old Testament, the children of Israel built the Tabernacle in the wilderness and, later, the Temple in Jerusalem (Ex. 25:1-9; 1 Chron. 29:1-9). In these instances, the people financed the projects with their own freewill offerings and gifts. They did not borrow money or any other form of material substance, first of all because there were enough resources in Israel. The sheer number of family units involved made this possible.

A second reason they did not borrow money is that they did not have a commercial loan system set up in Israel. This was not necessary, as we have seen, since they operated on an entirely different economic plan. Furthermore, it was not necessary to go outside their own social system to borrow money; they had sufficient resources within their own nation to complete these projects.

PRAGMATIC CONSIDERATIONS

No one would deny that it is ideal for a church body to never go into debt, just as it would be ideal for a Christian family to never go into debt in building a home. However, there are several pragmatic considerations that make it virtually impossible for some churches to build without borrowing, just as it is usually impossible to buy a home in our culture without incurring a certain amount of debt.

The first consideration relates to available resources. Small, independent churches face this problem regularly. They have no large denominational structures to look to for assistance. In order to have a permanent facility, it is almost essential to borrow.

The second pragmatic factor is psychological. In American culture, particularly, it is very difficult to attract people to a meeting place that does not reflect permanence. Generally speaking, people do not take a ministry seriously without a church building. There is a direct correlation between their sense of security and their commitment, which reflects our cultural mentality. Try as we might, we cannot ignore this factor when it comes to a meeting place for the church.

This factor alone puts Christian leaders in a difficult position. On the one hand, you cannot build without a sufficient number of family units. On the other hand, it is difficult to attract people to a facility that is not permanent. To insist that those who are committed construct the building debt-free only adds to the problem and puts the ministry in a more difficult position. The work may never grow large enough to make it possible to ever have a permanent facility.

SOME PRACTICAL GUIDELINES

The following guidelines, presented in the form of reflective questions, are based upon practical considerations as well as on biblical principles:

1. Is it possible to use a semi-permanent facility until there are enough family units to construct a permanent building? For example, some churches lease office or warehouse space that gives a feeling of permanency.

2. Is the projected building project designed in phases, making it possible to increase the number of family units while at the same time increasing the size of the facility?

3. Is there a general sense of unity among the people regarding the projected plans to build? The greater the unity, the easier it will be to fund the project.

4. Are the people involved committed financially? Christians who give regularly, systematically, and proportionately will be amazed at how much money they can generate for this kind of project while, at the same time, maintaining the ministry as God intended.

5. To what extent is the debt mentality in our culture restricting people in their willingness to give for the purpose of minimizing church debt? This kind of thinking is based upon a philosophy of materialism rather than biblical principles.

6. Is it possible to build debt-free? If so, it should be set as a goal, even if it means postponing the project for a period of time. This goal must be realistic, however, or people will become discouraged.

7. Is it possible to secure a church loan and to guarantee that loan without personal signatures? Scripture does not teach that it is absolutely wrong to take this approach. However, it warns against obligations that could create economic hardships in case of foreclosure. People who are willing to guarantee a loan should be financially willing and able to pay off the debt if there is an unforeseen crisis. Generally speaking, it is wise to avoid this approach if at all possible.

NOTES

1. A. E. Willingale, *The New Bible Dictionary* (Grand Rapids: Eerdmans, 1962), p. 304.

2. Ibid.

3. John Peter Lange, *Exodus*, vol. 1 of *Lange's Commentary on the Holy Scriptures*, trans. and ed. Philip Schaff (Grand Rapids: Zondervan, 1969), p. 94.

4. Carl B. Moll, *The Psalms*, vol. 5 of *Lange's Commentary on the Holy Scriptures*, p. 256.

5. C. F. Keil and F. Delitzsch, *The Pentateuch*, vol. 1 of *Commentary on the Old Testament*, trans. James Martin (Grand Rapids: Eerdmans, 1973), p. 369.

6. Ibid., p. 370.

7. Wilhelm J. Schroeder, *Deuteronomy*, vol. 2 of *Lange's Commentary on the Holy Scriptures*, p. 136.

8. Otto Zockler, *The Proverbs of Solomon*, vol. 5 of *Lange's Commentary on the Holy Scriptures*, p. 192.

9. Ibid., p. 83.

10. A. R. Fausset, *A Commentary: Critical, Experimental and Practical on the Old and New Testaments* (Grand Rapids: Eerdmans, 1948), 3:429.

11. Larry Burkett, *Answers to Your Family's Financial Questions* (Pomona, Calif.: Focus on the Family, 1987), pp. 112-13.

30

Paul's Trip to Jerusalem and Rome

When Paul returned from his third missionary journey, he stayed in Caesarea for a while in the home of Philip, one of the seven men appointed years earlier to be in charge of distributing food to the Grecian widows (Acts 21:8-9). From Caesarea, Paul traveled to Jerusalem and stayed in the home of Mnason, a Christian we know only by name.

PAUL'S EXPERIENCE IN JERUSALEM (ACTS 21:1–23:35)

Following is a succinct outline of the events that transpired while Paul was in Jerusalem:

Paul received warmly by leaders of the Jerusalem church (21:17-19).

Paul warned regarding the thousands of Jews who had believed in Christ but who were still "zealous for the law" (21:20-26).

Paul accused by some Asian Jews of teaching against the law and having brought Gentiles into the sanctuary of the Temple (21:27-29).

Riot erupted; a number of people tried to kill Paul, but he was taken into custody by a Roman commander (21:30-36).

Paul requested permission to address the crowd; gave detailed description of background, conversion, and supernatural call to preach gospel to the Gentiles (21:37–22:21).

Crowd erupted when Paul mentioned his ministry to the Gentiles; commander took Paul aside and interrogated him; discovering he was Roman citizen, commander fearful of having put him in chains (22:22-29).

Commander released Paul to appear before Sanhedrin; another riot erupted but Paul once again taken into custody by the Romans (22:30–23:10).

Lord appeared to Paul and encouraged him, telling him that he would have opportunity to testify for Christ in Rome (22:11).

More than forty men plotted to kill Paul by asking commander to have him brought before Sanhedrin once again with the pretense of wanting more information; Paul's nephew overheard plot and informed Roman commander, who had Paul transferred to Caesarea to appear before Governor Felix (23:12-35).

PAUL'S STAY IN CAESAREA (ACTS 24:1–26:32)

Following is a brief summary of the events that transpired in Caesarea:

Paul accused before Felix by a delegation of Jewish leaders from Jerusalem (24:1-9).

Paul defended himself (24:10-21).

Felix adjourned session, kept Paul under guard, gave him limited freedom (24:22-23).

Felix called for Paul and listened to him explain about Christ but really hoped for bribe (24:24-26).

To please the Jews, Felix left Paul in prison for two years, at which time he was succeeded by Porcius Festus (24:27).

Paul accused before Festus by another Jewish delegation from Jerusalem (25:1-7).

Paul once again defended himself and appeals to Caesar (25:8-12).

Festus consulted King Agrippa (25:13-22).

Paul appeared before King Agrippa and gave his personal testimony; Agrippa found Paul not guilty but had no choice but to recommend he be sent to Rome since Paul appealed to Caesar (25:23–26:32).

PAUL'S TRIP TO ROME (ACTS 27:1–28:31)

Following is a chronology of Paul's trip to Rome (see map on p. 283):

Under charge of a centurion, Paul and fellow prisoners sailed from Caesarea aboard a ship bound for cities in the province of Asia (27:1-2).

Following day stopped at Sidon, then sailed around Cyprus to Myra (27:3-5).

At Myra, centurion transferred passengers to large Alexandrian ship sailing directly to Italy; after difficult trip, ship made port at Fair Havens (27:6-8).

Against Paul's advice, ship left Fair Havens; driven out to sea by furious northeast storm; eventually suffered shipwreck but all able to get ashore on the island of Malta (27:9-44).

Crew spent three months on Malta, warmly received by the Phoenician people (28:1-10).

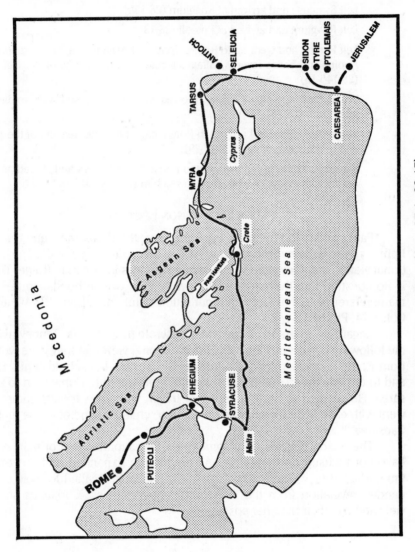

Paul's Journey to Rome (Acts 27:1–28:15)

Left Malta and arrived at Syracuse (28:11-12).

Left Syracuse and arrived at Rhegium (28:13a).

Left Rhegium and arrived at Puteoli (28:13b).

Left Puteoli and went on to Rome; Roman Christians met Paul at market of Appius and Three Taverns, villages located south of Rome on Appian Way (28:14b-15).

When Paul arrived in Rome, allowed to live by himself with soldier to guard him (28:16).

Three days after Paul arrived in Rome, called together leaders of the Jews and told his experience (28:17-29).

Stayed in Rome in his own rented house for two years and shared gospel boldly with everyone who came to see him (28:30-31).

PAUL'S FOUR PRISON EPISTLES

Paul's letters to Philemon, the Ephesians, the Colossians, and the Philippians were written during the period A.D. 56 or 57–A.D. 60 or 61. The traditional view is that they were written while Paul was in prison in Rome. There is no question that they were written while Paul was in bonds, since Paul made reference to that fact in all four letters (Philem. 1; Eph. 3:1; 4:1; 6:20; Col. 1:24; Phil. 1:12-13).

Regarding where Paul was when he wrote these letters, Tenney makes the following comment: "Probably the traditional view that they were written from Rome is correct, for the allusions to Caesar's household (Phil. 4:22) and to the Praetorian guard (1:13) would apply better to Rome than to Caesarea. He seemed to be in a center of travel, where his friends came and went with ease, which would be much more characteristic of Rome than of Caesarea."[1]

The prison epistles yield some important supracultural principles we have not focused on heretofore. As the church expanded and grew over time, it faced new challenges. These new challenges called for new or expanded revelation from the Holy Spirit regarding how Christians should view and use their material possessions.

NOTE

1. Merrill C. Tenney, *New Testament Survey* (Grand Rapids: Eerdmans, 1953), p. 314.

31

Paul's Letter to Philemon

Philemon was a wealthy Christian businessman who lived in Colossae and who became a believer as a result of Paul's missionary efforts (v. 19). Since the apostle evidently did not have a direct ministry of evangelism in Colossae, Philemon may have become a Christian on one of his business trips to Ephesus, where he probably heard Paul teach in the lecture hall of Tyrannus (Acts 19:9).

Paul identified Philemon in his personal letter as "a dear friend and fellow worker" (v. 2). Since they evidently had not traveled together in evangelistic work, Philemon may have supported Paul financially and, like the believers in Philippi, became a fellow worker by developing a partnership in the gospel (Phil. 1:5; 4:15-16). Philemon's economic status can be deduced from several factors in this brief but enlightening letter.

First, the church in Colossae met in his home (v. 2). We cannot reconstruct the exact size of his dwelling, but structures have been discovered in the New Testament world that could comfortably seat up to five hundred people in the garden room alone. These homes were built, not to house four or five people, as in our culture today, but to provide living quarters for an extended family—including married children and servants. Philemon's home seems to fit this picture.

Second, Philemon was a man given to hospitality. Paul wrote, "Your love has given me great joy and encouragement, because you, brother, *have refreshed the hearts of the saints*" (v. 7). Paul was probably referring to the way Philemon opened his home to his fellow believers in Colossae, as well as to traveling evangelists and teachers. Evidently, Philemon had on occasion made this provision for Paul. Whatever the facts, Paul felt free to ask Philemon for a place to stay (v. 22).

A third factor points to Philemon's wealth. Only well-to-do men in the New Testament world had servants. A young man named Onesimus, and a major subject in this letter, was one of those servants. When Philemon became a Christian, he took Paul's instructions seriously to treat his slaves as fellow believers, as brothers and sisters in Jesus Christ (see Eph. 6:5-9; Col. 3:22–4:1). But Onesimus was initially a rebellious and irresponsible young man and did not respond to the gospel of Christ. He took advantage of his new freedom and new relationship with his master and escaped from Philemon's household, evidently stealing certain items.

PHILEMON 18

If he has done you any wrong
or owes you anything, charge it to me.

EXPOSITION

In the providence of God, Onesimus ended up in Rome and came in contact with Paul while he was in prison. There the apostle led him to a personal relationship with Jesus Christ and taught him the Word of God. Onesimus responded to Paul's loving exhortations, and a deep friendship developed between this old apostle and the young slave.

Onesimus became a great source of encouragement as he ministered to Paul's personal needs. Though the apostle wanted Onesimus to stay with him in Rome, he reminded his friend of his responsibility to his real master. Consequently, Paul wrote this letter to Philemon in order to rebuild a relationship between Onesimus and Philemon: "I appeal to you, for my son Onesimus, who became my son while I was in chains. Formerly he was useless to you, but now he has become useful both to you and to me" (vv. 10-11). Philemon's attempt to do God's will in his relationship with his slaves points to another supracultural principle.

THE ELEVENTH SUPRACULTURAL PRINCIPLE

Christians who put God first in their lives may open the door for people to take material advantage of them (Philem. 18).

If Christians are given to hospitality as God says we should be, there will always be people who will abuse our generosity. This should not surprise us. There are always risks in obeying Christ. This does not mean that we should allow people to take advantage of us. But some people will, no matter how hard we try to avoid it.

Being a follower of Christ at times means suffering with Christ—including the way people "took what they could get from Jesus" and then "walked away." This is what happened when He fed the multitudes (John 6:1-15). They were initially elated and followed Him because their needs were met (John 6:26). But when Jesus tested their true motives, "many of his disciples turned back and no longer followed him" (John 6:66). We must never allow this kind of fickleness and manipulation to keep us from loving people and using our material possessions to help others. God wants us to use discretion but to *always* be generous.

PHILEMON 14, 18-19

But I did not want to do anything without your consent,
so that any favor you do will be spontaneous and not forced. . . .
If he has done you any wrong or owes you anything, charge it
to me. I, Paul, am writing this with my own hand. I will pay
it back—not to mention that you owe me your very self.

EXPOSITION

Onesimus had wronged Philemon. He owed him the money or goods he had stolen. Consequently, Paul informed his friend that he would pay it back for Onesimus. But in the same breath, he reminded Philemon that he owed his very conversion to their previous interaction about the gospel of Christ. In fact, the apostle implied that Onesimus's debt to Philemon should be more than canceled in view of what Philemon owed Paul for his new life in Christ.

Though this may look like manipulation, it was Paul's gentle but straightforward way of being honest. If Philemon felt any sense of guilt at this moment, Paul would not consider that to be his problem but Philemon's. This man did owe Paul a debt that he could never repay with his material possessions.

What Paul wrote also reflected the deep friendship and love that existed between Paul and Philemon. Perhaps Philemon even recognized in Paul's words a bit of "tongue-in-cheek" communication. Whatever we read between the lines, Paul's message was clear. On the one hand, he sincerely offered to pay Philemon what Onesimus owed him. On the other hand, he reminded Philemon that he owed his friend and mentor a huge debt as well.

THE TWELFTH SUPRACULTURAL PRINCIPLE

Christian leaders should utilize methods of communication that create both a sense of obligation and a spirit of spontaneity and freedom (Philem. 14, 18-19).

Paul demonstrated this unique balance on other occasions. He let the believers in Corinth know that he knew how eager they were to help the poor Christians in Jerusalem. In fact, he even told them that he did not feel it necessary to write to them about it. But, just in case they did not understand, he did write. In addition, he sent "the brothers in order that" his boasting about them would not prove to be untrue. He wanted them to be ready with the gift so that he would not be embarrassed and neither would they.

Paul used the same basic approach with his good friend Philemon, who, unlike the Corinthians, was a mature Christian. All of us, then, need a certain amount of "God-designed pressure" in order to be faithful and obedient to God. True, we may feel a certain amount of guilt. However, when we are out of the will of God, we *should* feel guilt. If we do not, we may have already allowed our consciences to become hardened to the Word of God and the Holy Spirit (1 Tim. 4:2).

It is a difficult task for Christian leaders to maintain this kind of balance in their communication. On the one hand, most leaders do not want to be rejected by those who resent the will of God. Consequently, they tend to avoid issues that create guilt. On the other hand, some leaders become insensitive and uncompassionate, and put people under undue pressure. Others are masters at manipulating people with guilt—an approach that certainly violates biblical principles.

Paul's communication model reflects balance. He illustrated with his own life that we should not manipulate people. But, at the same time, he did not hesitate to let people know that they had an obligation to be generous and benevolent, even if it did create a certain amount of emotional discomfort.

PHILEMON 20-22

*I do wish, brother, that I may have some benefit from you
in the Lord; refresh my heart in Christ. Confident of your
obedience, I write to you, knowing that you will do even more
than I ask. And one thing more: Prepare a guest room for me,
for I hope to be restored to you in answer to your prayers.*

EXPOSITION

Here Paul illustrated another important factor in his communication with people regarding the way they should use their material possessions. He expected the best, particularly from those he knew truly loved Jesus Christ. He was "confident" that his friend would respond. In fact, he told Philemon that he knew that he would do "even more" than he had asked.

What is Paul hinting at? Some believe he was suggesting that Philemon give Onesimus his complete freedom. Paul did not condone slavery, but he never attacked it head-on as being wrong. He approached this social problem by telling masters to love their slaves as Christ loved them and by instructing slaves to serve their masters as if they were serving Jesus Christ. Legalities did not make much difference if people were practicing principles of love. Philemon and Onesimus were brothers in Christ and in this sense equals, both experiencing liberty and freedom in Christian fellowship. If I had to speculate on what took place, I would guess that Philemon did give Onesimus his freedom.

The final request in verse 22 indicates again the degree of friendship that existed between these men. Normally Paul did not ask favors for himself. But in this instance, he did not hesitate to ask Philemon to "prepare a guest room" for him. He knew his request would not be misinterpreted. Paul felt very secure in this relationship, for if he sensed he had offended Philemon with his previous comments, he certainly would have hesitated to make this final request.

THE THIRTEENTH SUPRACULTURAL PRINCIPLE

Christian leaders should not hesitate to ask for help when there is a need, both for others and for themselves (Philem. 20-22).

In some respects Paul was out of character when he asked Philemon for personal help. On the other hand, he illustrates that Christians do have a right to make their needs known. Though he was certainly cautious and sensitive, he was also specific.

This personal request correlates with another principle Paul practiced consistently. He looked to those he had ministered to in a special way for his financial support. This factor is dominant in his letter to Philemon, and this explains why Paul took a freedom that he usually did not.

In today's world, a number of Christians violate biblical principles by going to two extremes. Some are very open in asking for help from people they have never ministered to and with whom they have had no personal relationship. Conversely, others are so timid and reserved they never make their needs known to anyone. Both approaches violate biblical principles.

32

Paul's Letters to the Ephesians and Colossians

When Paul wrote to Philemon, it also gave him an opportunity to send two additional letters—one to the Ephesians (a general letter to be read to the various churches in the area),[1] and one to the Colossians. Tychicus probably delivered these letters, accompanied by Philemon's slave Onesimus (Eph. 6:21; Col. 4:7-9).

Ephesus was a large center for idolatrous worship in the Asian world. As always, idolatry and materialism go hand-in-hand, and this was dramatically illustrated when Paul spent two years preaching and teaching in the lecture hall of Tyrannus. Paul's ministry was so effective, it began to cut into the profits of the idol business. Luke recorded that "a silversmith named Demetrius, who made silver shrines of Artemis" became so angry that he called a meeting of all of those who were involved in businesses that were related to idolatrous practices.

"Men, you know we receive a good income from this business," Demetrius declared.

> And you see and hear how this fellow Paul has convinced and led astray large numbers of people here in Ephesus and in practically the whole province of Asia. He says that man-made gods are no gods at all. There is danger not only that our trade will lose its good name, but also that the temple of the great goddess Artemis will be discredited. (Acts 19:26-27a)

Though Demetrius disguised his motives somewhat by referring to his pagan religious convictions, his main concern was his "pocketbook." As a result of this meeting with the business people in Ephesus, there was a serious riot, and if the city clerk had not stepped in to calm the crowd, Paul could have been killed (Acts 19:35-41).

291

AN OLD TESTAMENT PERSPECTIVE

Paul faced this kind of persecution because he did not compromise God's message. This was not a new phenomenon. The prophets in the Old Testament were often rejected by the people of Israel when they addressed the issues of idolatry and materialism. At times, they were persecuted and even killed. Though their negative responses were related to a number of issues in their lives that were out of the will of God, it is not surprising that one of the areas that brought the most negative reaction was when they dealt with the way in which the Israelites had violated the will of God with their material possessions.

The prophet Amos was called by God to preach at Bethel. Though this was the residence of Jeroboam II who ruled Israel at the time, it had become a center of idol worship. On one occasion, Amos cried out against their mistreatment of the poor by taking bribes and then depriving "the poor of justice in the courts" (Amos 5:11-12; see also 2:6-7). Amos faced so much opposition because of his preaching that he had to leave Bethel and return to Judah, where he then put his message in writing.

THE PROPHETS

Isaiah was also called by God to confront the tribe of Judah. "Woe to those who make unjust laws," he proclaimed, "to those who issue oppressive decrees . . . making widows their prey and robbing the fatherless" (Isa. 10:1-2; see also 1:23-25; 33:15-16). Because Isaiah delivered God's message, he was scoffed at and criticized. In fact, tradition states that he was eventually martyred by being sawed in two (Heb. 11:37).

Jeremiah has often been identified as the "weeping prophet" (Jer. 9:1; 13:17). God called him to pronounce judgment on Judah, which he did faithfully for more than forty years. One of his messages condemned these people for dishonesty and for failing to pay wages to workers (Jer. 22:13; see also 7:1; 8:13; 9:23-24; 15:13). During this time, Jeremiah faced incredible opposition that resulted in beatings and even imprisonment (Jer. 11:18-23; 12:6; 18:18; 20:1-3; 26:1-24; 37:11–38:28). Along with a number of other prophets of God, he paid a difficult price for delivering God's message to these sinful people.

Against this backdrop, it is more understandable why the prophets faced such rejection and abuse. They were dealing with the very heart of the Israelites' problem—idolatry, which was reflected in their materialistic approach to life.

As we move into the New Testament arena, we see that human nature has not changed. This is why there are similar reactions to pointed messages dealing with sins that relate to materialism. Much of Jesus' rejection related to what He said about the materialistic attitudes of the religious leaders in Israel (Matt. 26:3-4; cf. Matt. 25). And Paul's most intense rejection came from those whose income was threatened by the message of Christianity. His experience in Ephesus illustrates this.

THE FOURTEENTH SUPRACULTURAL PRINCIPLE

Christians may face criticism or even retaliation when their commitment to do God's will conflicts with others' materialistic value systems (Acts 19:23-41).

People have not changed in their hearts. Anytime the message of Christianity cuts across the sinful practices of non-Christians and threatens their profits, Christians can expect to be ridiculed, criticized, and even ostracized. Some believers actually lose their jobs because they refuse to participate in dishonest business practices that oftentimes require outright lying in order to survive economically. In some instances, there is unusual pressure on Christians from non-Christian business associates because an honest, conscientious, and industrious person in the organization makes everyone else "look bad."

Unfortunately, even Christians are guilty of being critical of other Christians who are committed to doing the will of God. This is more often true when it comes to money matters since our material possessions naturally tend to become an intricate part of our lives. Since, as Jesus reminded us, our earthly treasures very quickly become "matters of the heart," we tend to become more emotionally involved. It is easy to become defensive.

When Christians join in this kind of behavior, even to a slight degree, it is unfortunate. Believers have only one recourse if they want to be in the will of God. They must respond positively and in a supportive manner to God's message regarding how they should view and use their material possessions. And when they do, they are revealing that they are not threatened by this message. Rather, they will be the first to proclaim that message to others and, in the process, be willing to risk potential rejection and even retaliation.

THE EPHESIAN CORRESPONDENCE

The letter to the Ephesians contains a great deal of Bible doctrine (chaps. 1-3) and numerous instructions regarding how to live out Christian truth in our day-to-day Christian walk (chaps. 4-6). As in Paul's epistle to the Romans, he provides a larger context for helping Christians gain a biblical perspective on their material possessions. When he exhorted the Romans to offer their bodies "as living sacrifices, holy and pleasing to God," and not to "conform any longer to the pattern of this world," he was establishing a frame of reference for Christian living that would impact all that these believers did. Needless to say, taking this step in the Christian life is basic to being able to keep from conforming our lives to the "pattern of this world" in terms of greed and the desire for material things.

Paul established the same frame of reference for the Ephesians. Following is a significant statement related to how a Christian should view and use his material possessions. Note also how this exhortation correlates with the concern Paul addressed in his letter to Philemon. Onesimus, who probably accompanied Tychicus when he delivered this letter, was a dynamic example of what should happen to a person who is truly converted to Jesus Christ. Perhaps Onesimus was seated by Paul's side when he wrote this letter. And when he dictated the following exhortation, I can imagine Paul glancing at Onesimus with an affirming grin. This young slave was living proof that Christ changes people.

EPHESIANS 4:28

He who has been stealing must steal no longer,
but must work, doing something useful with his own hands,
that he may have something to share with those in need.

EXPOSITION

Stealing was a prominent activity in the Roman Empire. It was a particular temptation for slaves whose masters had become Christians. We have just seen this illustrated rather dramatically in Paul's letter to Philemon.

Since stealing was such a common practice, it was not uncommon for these bad habits to carry over into the lives of those who professed Christ. As in other areas of morality and ethics, it took time for these people to, first of all, know what God expected and, second, to respond obediently to the will of God.

When giving this exhortation not to steal, Paul did not stop with a "thou shalt not." He went on to instruct them to actually work harder in order to have money left over so that they could share with other people (Eph. 4:28). What an incredible testimony it must have been to see people reverse their field so dramatically. Rather than continuing to be unethical *takers*, they actually became Christlike *givers*.

THE FIFTEENTH SUPRACULTURAL PRINCIPLE

Christians should work hard to make an honest living, not only to take care of their own needs, but to help others in need (Eph. 4:28).

It is no secret that many people in today's world have been taught to do everything they can to get something for nothing. If they do not steal money outright from their employers, they steal time, which is a form of money. Paul stated that a Christian should never steal; rather, he should be engaged in useful work, not only to take care of his own needs, but to help meet the needs of others.

How many Christians begin the day on the job with the objective in mind to work hard in order to make money to give away? If this were our attitude, our "work" would definitely take on new meaning. Furthermore, we would have a number of employers who would be overwhelmed with our productivity. Think also of the doors that this would open for a direct Christian witness. This is no doubt one of the things Peter had in mind when he wrote, "Live such good lives among the pagans that, though they accuse you of doing wrong, they may see your good deeds and glorify God on the day he visits us" (1 Pet. 2:12).

THE COLOSSIAN CORRESPONDENCE

The letters to the Ephesians and Colossians can be considered twin epistles. They are very similar. But Paul had particular concerns he wanted to share with the Colossians that he did not share in his circular letter to the Ephesians and to the other churches in Asia.

Though we have conjectured that Philemon, who lived in Colosse, probably came to Christ under Paul's ministry while visiting Ephesus, Tenney speculates that the *majority* of these people "must have been evangelized . . . perhaps by Timothy and Epaphras (Col. 1:7) who itinerated while Paul preached in Ephesus."[2] However, even though Paul did not start the church in Colosse, he may have visited the city. Yet he wrote that there were some in Colosse he had never met (Col. 2:1). Perhaps this is because he spent some private time in Philemon's home without engaging in an extensive ministry to the whole church.

As in his letter to the Ephesians, Paul established a broad frame of reference for Christian living. Then, he made some specific statements that are related to our study.

COLOSSIANS 3:23-24

Whatever you do, work at it with all your heart,
as working for the Lord, not for men, since you know that
you will receive an inheritance from the Lord as a reward.
It is the Lord Christ you are serving.

EXPOSITION

The context for this exhortation related to slaves and the way in which they were to do their work. As stated earlier, Paul did not condone slavery. However, neither did he attack this social problem directly. To do so would have created serious problems for Christians in the Roman Empire.

Here we see his approach to the problem. He exhorted slaves to obey their earthly masters, not only when they were watching in order to "win their favor," but to do so "with sincerity of heart and reverence for the Lord" (Col. 3:22). In other words, they were not to be faithful to their masters simply to benefit themselves, just as we are not to serve the Lord to benefit ourselves. Rather, they were to serve *both* the Lord and their masters with the same heart motives that reflected sincerity and reverence.

Paul went a step farther. He actually reminded these slaves that in reality they were serving the Lord Christ when they served their earthly masters (Col. 3:24). Consequently, if they did their work as if they were "working for the Lord" and not men, they would receive their ultimate reward from the Lord Himself.

Peter stated that there are also some practical benefits to this approach: "Who is going to harm you if you are eager to do good?" (1 Peter 3:13). He acknowledged that serving others with respect may not always bring positive response, but it usually does.

THE SIXTEENTH SUPRACULTURAL PRINCIPLE

Christian employees should work hard to serve their employers (both Christians and non-Christians) as if they are actually serving the Lord (Col. 3:23-24).

Though the illustrations in the Word of God frequently focus on slave/master interaction, the principle involved applies to any kind of employee/employer relationship. When we faithfully serve those who employ us, God views our effort as *actually serving Jesus Christ*—no matter what our employers' spiritual status. This perspective alone could dramatically change the Christian work force. The sad part is that many Christians do serve their employers as they serve Jesus Christ—halfheartedly. Paul made clear that this should not be.

COLOSSIANS 4:1

Masters, provide your slaves with what is right and fair,
because you know that you also have a master in heaven.

EXPOSITION

Paul approached masters in the same way he approached slaves. He commanded them to treat these people as brothers and sisters in Christ. Writing to the Galatians, he made this point very clear: "There is neither Jew nor Greek, *slave nor free*, male nor female, for you are all one in Christ Jesus" (3:28). Paul also exhorted masters to provide their slaves with what was "right and fair," which certainly included proper provisions or wages. Since these *earthly* masters were now servants of their *heavenly* Master, they should be able to understand how a servant should be treated. Paul was telling them to treat their slaves in the same way that they wanted to be treated by God.

If Christian masters took Paul seriously, as Philemon did, it is understandable why slavery eventually disappeared in the Christian community. When people obeyed the Word of God, it was impossible to maintain this kind of social structure indefinitely.

THE SEVENTEENTH SUPRACULTURAL PRINCIPLE

Christian employers should always treat their employees fairly in every respect (Col. 4:1).

Christian employees should work hard to serve their employers (both Christians and non-Christians) as if they are actually serving the Lord (Col. 3:23-24). Conversely, Christian employers should always treat their employees fairly—just the way they want God to treat them.

Again, this fairness should be equally applied to both Christians and non-Christians. There should be no prejudice. Furthermore, they should do everything they possibly can to encourage their employees. This certainly involves paying a living wage. And when employees work hard and faithfully to increase profits, employers should do whatever they can to share those profits equitably with those who made it possible.

NOTES

1. Francis Foulkes, *The Epistle of Paul to the Ephesians: An Introduction and Commentary*, vol. 10 of *The Tyndale New Testament Commentaries* (Grand Rapids: Eerdmans, 1963), p. 19, makes the following comments regarding the circular nature of the Ephesian letter:

   It was sent to a number of churches in a particular area, probably the Roman province of Asia. Internal and external evidence provide much to support this view. There are two forms of the suggestion. One copy of the letter, it is supposed, was taken round to the different churches, and a gap was left for the bearer to fill in the name as he went. Against this it has been argued that such an expedient cannot be paralleled in ancient letter-writing, but the answer can be given that "so simple and common sense a plan does not require to be justified by precedence." Alternatively, it is suggested that there were a number of copies of the letter each bearing a different place-name. The copy addressed to Ephesus then became the letter accepted, because Ephesus was the most important church.

2. Merrill C. Tenney, *New Testament Survey* (Grand Rapids: Eerdmans, 1953), p. 321.

33

Paul's Letter to the Philippians

Paul's letter to the Philippians is very personal. While writing to his close friends in Philippi, he used the personal pronoun at least one hundred times. There were a number of reasons that Paul felt so close to the Philippians. However, this letter focuses on an important and predominant factor. These believers had cared for his physical needs on a continuing basis. That is immediately obvious as he begins the letter.

PHILIPPIANS 1:3-5

I thank my God every time I remember you. In all my prayers for all of you, I always pray with joy because of your partnership in the gospel from the first day until now.

EXPOSITION

From the moment Paul succeeded in winning someone to Jesus Christ in Philippi, he experienced an eager and cooperative spirit (Acts 16:13-15). Lydia, a saleslady of purple garments and a proselyte to Judaism, responded first to the gospel. Then her whole household became Christians.

But perhaps the most memorable event in Paul's relationship with Lydia was when she insisted that he and his fellow missionaries (Silas, Timothy, and Luke) stay in her home—using it as a base for their ministry (Acts 16:15). It is also probable that her home became the first permanent meeting place for the new believers in Philippi.

Paul remembered this event and was possibly referring to it when he wrote that he prayed "with joy" because of their "partnership in the gospel from the first day" (1:5). From the very moment Lydia and her household believed in Christ, they began to fellowship together in her home (Acts 16:15). This "partnership in the gospel" was "from the first day until *now.*" Their fellowship that began in Lydia's home in the early days of the Philippian church was an *ongoing* experience. Again and again, after Paul had left

Philippi to start new churches, these Christians sent gifts to meet Paul's material needs (4:15-16). And now, once again, they had sent a gift to him while he was in prison in Rome. Epaphroditus, perhaps an elder and pastor in the church at Philippi, had delivered the gift, almost losing his life in the process (2:29-30). Epaphroditus returned to Philippi carrying Paul's letter of of deep joy and thanksgiving.

THE EIGHTEENTH SUPRACULTURAL PRINCIPLE

Christians who faithfully support God's servants in material ways create unusual joy in the hearts of those who receive their gifts (Phil. 1:3-5).

Anyone in the ministry whose physical needs are faithfully met by fellow Christians can identify with Paul's experience when he wrote to the Philippians. He joyfully thanked God every time he remembered them. Christians who support others financially should give with this in mind. Not only do we cause God's heart to rejoice but we bring joy and happiness to those we support. This is why Paul closed his letter to the Philippians by saying, "I *rejoice greatly* in the Lord that at last you have renewed your concern for me" (4:10*a*).

THE NINETEENTH SUPRACULTURAL PRINCIPLE

Christians who faithfully support God's servants in material ways enrich those servants' prayer lives by making prayer a joyful experience (Phil. 1:3-5).

This principle is closely related to the preceding one and grows out of the same scriptural passage. However, the focus here is on *joy in prayer.* This is how the Philippians' gifts affected Paul. He always prayed "with joy" because of their faithful participation in his ministry. Every time he received a gift, his prayer life was enriched.

Only Christian workers who receive financial support from those they minister to can really identify with this reality. But it is true. As one who has been financially supported in Christian ministry for many years, I am well aware of how faithful givers have brought joy to my prayer life. This is not only because of the way my own needs have been met but because of the way Christians have helped me meet the economic needs of others. Understanding this principle ought to bring added joy as well to those who give to support others.

PHILIPPIANS 2:29-30

Welcome him in the Lord with great joy, and honor men
like him, because he almost died for the work of Christ,
risking his life to make up for the help you could not give me.

EXPOSITION

When Epaphroditus arrived in Rome, he delivered the Philippians' gift of money to Paul. But when he did, he found a man who needed more than money. Paul needed encouragement and continual economic assistance. Rather than return to Philippi immediately, Epaphroditus decided to stay by his friend's side. He felt such a keen sense of responsibility to Paul that he nearly died in fulfilling that duty. We do not know exactly what Epaphroditus did that endangered his life to meet Paul's needs. But there are several clues.

First, it was probably a physical illness, for Epaphroditus "almost died" (2:27). Though the Greek word for "ill" could refer to either psychological or physical illness, few "die" from psychological problems, unless the stress is so great that it results in a heart attack or serious ulcers. In those days this could have easily resulted in death.

A second clue is that whatever caused Epaphroditus's problem, it involved "risking his life to make up for the help" the Philippians could not give him (2:30). He could have worked so hard to make additional money that he overextended his body and mind, leading to some kind of physical and psychological deterioration. Whatever happened, Epaphroditus demonstrated unusual commitment to both Paul and the Philippians.

In Paul's final words about Epaphroditus, he made clear that this man should be given due recognition for his sacrificial service: "Welcome him in the Lord with great joy, and honor men like him" (2:29). It almost appears that Paul was afraid that the Philippians might not understand why Epaphroditus was gone so long. Or conversely, Paul may have been concerned that they might question his Christian commitment for returning to Philippi because of homesickness (2:26). The latter concern is more likely, since Paul clarified that it was his idea for Epaphroditus to return, and he wanted him to be welcomed joyfully and with full awareness of this man's sacrificial service for Jesus Christ.

THE TWENTIETH SUPRACULTURAL PRINCIPLE

Christians who make special sacrifices to help meet the material needs of God's servants should be honored in special ways by others in the Body of Christ (Phil. 2:29-30).

This principle is similar to the one that emerges from the way in which the apostles showed their appreciation to Barnabas when he demonstrated unusual generosity in the Jerusalem church (Acts 4:36). They evidently changed his name to conform to his generous spirit. There can be no greater honor, for a name that means "son of encouragement" would be a constant reminder to others of the way in which Barnabas reflected the unselfishness of Jesus Christ (see pp. 45-46).

If Barnabas represents Christian leaders in general, Epaphroditus represents spiritual leaders in the local church. He went beyond the call of duty, sacrificing his own needs and desires to help Paul in his time of need, and he did it for those Christians who composed the church he served as pastor.

Many pastors devote most of their lives to helping others, often neglecting their own families to minister to the larger family of God. They often serve long hours. They are always on call. Their lives are not their own, with little privacy. They often work seven days a week, and in many instances, are not paid commensurate with their education, experience, and dedication as are many of their fellow Christians in the business world. And the majority of pastors I rub shoulders with do all this without complaining or feeling sorry for themselves. They have voluntarily chosen to be servants of Jesus Christ and others.

And yet, these leaders are often the last to be shown special appreciation and honor. They are often taken for granted. Unfortunately, they are even misunderstood, misinterpreted, and criticized when they attempt to take some time off. And if they dare ask for a raise in salary, they are accused of being materialistic and self-serving. Sadly, Christians are too quick to point to those few spiritual leaders who have abused their sacred role and have taken advantage of others. Against the backdrop of a few unfaithful shepherds, they judge their own pastors.

There are exceptions, of course. Some churches practice this principle very well. But often it is woefully neglected. In these cases, the church should take a careful look at what Paul said about Epaphroditus and how the Philippians were to honor his sacrificial efforts.

PHILIPPIANS 4:10-11

*I rejoice greatly in the Lord that at last you
have renewed your concern for me. Indeed, you have
been concerned, but you had no opportunity to show it.
I am not saying this because I am in need, for I have
learned to be content whatever the circumstances.*

EXPOSITION

Paul seldom talked about his own needs, but when he had one, he admitted it. There was no subtle pride in his personality that was injured because of his lack of "things." He did not go around trying to be something he was not. He lived within his means, and when he lacked, he was not too proud to accept help.

As he wrote to the Philippians, thanking them for their gifts, he reflected this humility. He was rejoicing that they had once more helped him in a time of need. He had missed their help for a period of time, but he quickly and sensitively communicated that he knew they had never stopped being concerned. Rather, he said, "You had no opportunity to show it."

It is possible only to speculate as to why the Philippians had temporarily stopped supporting Paul materially. Perhaps they did not know about his needs in Rome. Maybe they themselves were so poverty stricken they could not help. Whatever the reason, Paul wanted them to know he understood but was excited about their renewed help.

After letting the Philippians know how happy he was about the gift they had sent, he hurried to tell them he was not playing on their sympathy. This is total honesty. Paul was highly concerned that his motives never be misinterpreted. On some occasions, as we have seen, he actually refused what was coming to him as an apostle of Christ to avoid being a stumbling block to non-Christians or to new babes in Christ (1 Cor. 9:1-18; 1 Thess. 2:9).

THE TWENTY-FIRST SUPRACULTURAL PRINCIPLE

God's servants should be open and honest about their material needs, but they should avoid any form of dishonesty and manipulation by playing on others' sympathy (Phil. 4:11).

Some Christians methodically work at giving the impression that they are always in need. Christian leaders who make their living doing religious work can also be tempted to take advantage of members of Christ's Body. This should never be. Unfortunately, there are some who do, which makes it very difficult for those who do not.

Again Paul was a marvelous example in this respect. He let the Philippians know about his needs, but at the same time he made sure he was not playing on their sympathy. May God give us more Christians with this kind of integrity.

PHILIPPIANS 4:12

I know what it is to be in need, and I know what it is to have plenty. I have learned the secret of being content in any and every situation, whether well fed or hungry, whether living in plenty or in want.

EXPOSITION

Paul had an unusual capacity to adapt to various situations and circumstances, and still reflect contentment (2 Cor. 11:23–12:10). The "situations" he wrote about in his letter involved his material needs—being "well fed or hungry," and "living in plenty or in want."

THE TWENTY-SECOND SUPRACULTURAL PRINCIPLE

All Christians should learn to be content in the difficult times as well as in the prosperous times (Phil. 4:12).

It is true that God has promised to meet our needs. However, this does not mean that we will always have everything we need to make life *comfortable*. It is one thing to be happy and content when we have food on our table, clothes on our back, shelter over our heads, and some money in the bank. But what if all these things were missing? How content would we be? How would we adapt? Paul could say, "I have learned to be content *whatever* the circumstances" (4:11*b*).

PHILIPPIANS 4:14-17

Yet it was good of you to share in my troubles.
Moreover, as you Philippians know, in the early days of your
acquaintance with the gospel, when I set out from Macedonia,
not one church shared with me in the matter of giving
and receiving, except you only; for even when I was in
Thessalonica, you sent me aid again and again when
I was in need. Not that I am looking for a gift, but
I am looking for what may be credited to your account.

EXPOSITION

Paul was a great believer in maintaining a ministry of encouragement. As he concluded this letter to the Philippians, he commended them for their *exceptional commitment* as compared with other churches, for the *abundant gifts* they had sent him, and for their *sacrificial spirit*—their willingness to give even when their own material needs were not being met.

According to R. P. Martin, Paul uses an analogy in verse 17 to communicate how he felt about the gifts the Philippians had sent him. He referred to a "fruitful investment" that "gained interest." In fact, the key words he used in this statement were used by people involved in lending institutions in Paul's day. Martin explains: "What the Philippians gave as their gift was like an investment which would pay rich dividends in the service of the kingdom, as accumulating interest (*karpos*) stands to the credit (*logos*) of the depositor. At the last day, such generous and unstinted service which expressed itself in practical monetary support would not go unrecognized or unrewarded."[1]

Christian leaders who make their living in the ministry should serve Jesus Christ with the view that they are storing up treasures in heaven for those who support them financially (Phil. 4:14-17).

Those who support Christian leaders in the ministry are accumulating special rewards in heaven based on the fruit that results. But the lesson we learn from Paul in his letter to the Philippians is that those who are supported by others should serve the Lord with this in mind. Part of their motivation should be to accumulate eternal rewards for their donors. Paul was more excited about what was being credited to the Philippians' account in heaven than he was about the gift he had received (4:17).

As one who is supported by others in the ministry, this truth has given me a new perspective. As I do my work for God, I realize that I am not only serving the Lord, I am serving those who support me. It is exciting to know that whatever spiritual results come from my earthly ministry will be shared in eternity with those who have made my efforts possible.

PHILIPPIANS 4:18-19

I have received full payment and even more; I am amply supplied, now that I have received from Epaphroditus the gifts you sent. They are a fragrant offering, an acceptable sacrifice, pleasing to God, and my God will meet all your needs according to His glorious riches in Christ Jesus.

EXPOSITION

Paul made a similar statement to the Corinthians: "And God is able to make all grace abound to you, so that in all things at all times, having all that you need, you will abound in every good work" (2 Cor. 9:8). When Christians are faithful in their giving, God has promised to meet their needs (see pp. 233-34).

When interpreting this text in Paul's letter to the Corinthians, we looked at how God meets the *personal* needs of *every* Christian when each is faithful. However, there is a broader meaning, both in His promise to the Corinthians and in the restatement of His promise to the Philippians. God also promises to take care of *groups* of Christians when together they are faithful as a body of believers.

THE TWENTY-FOURTH SUPRACULTURAL PRINCIPLE

God's promise to meet needs applies to the church as well as to individual believers in that church (Phil. 4:19).

As Christians who live in the Western world, we are so used to thinking in terms of *individualism* that we lose sight of the corporate nature of Christianity. Consequently, we tend to *personalize* all promises in the Bible and fail to realize that many promises are *collective* in nature. This is true in the area of giving. When Paul wrote to the Philippians, thanking them for their generous gifts, he said, "And my God will meet all your needs according to his glorious riches in Christ Jesus" (4:19). He was confident that not only would God meet the needs of the individual members of the church in Philippi, but He would meet their needs as a corporate body. And in meeting their needs as a corporate body, He would also be meeting personal needs.

To be more specific, when a church is faithful in giving, God may choose to bless certain individuals in the church who, in turn, can help others in the church who are giving more sacrificially. In this sense, Paul's statement to the Corinthians applies to Christians within specific local churches as well as to churches helping other churches: "Our desire is not that others might be relieved while you are hard pressed, but that there might be equality" (2 Cor. 8:13).

SPECIFIC PRINCIPLES IN PERSPECTIVE

ROMANS

1. Christians should always be responsible and honest citizens in their own societies by paying all governmental taxes and revenues (Rom. 13:6-7).

2. Christians who owe people money or goods should always pay what they owe (Rom. 13:8).

3. All Christians have an obligation to support God's work in material ways (Rom. 15:27).

THE OLD TESTAMENT

4. Christians must never take economic advantage of poor people, whether Christians or non-Christians (Ex. 22:25).

5. Christians who obey God's Word will be able not only to meet their own economic needs but also to help others who are in need (Ps. 37:21).

6. Christians must set the example of being gracious to people who have borrowed money with good intentions and then have faced crises beyond their control that has made it difficult for them to make their loan payments on time (Deut. 15:1-3).

7. Before Christians borrow money for any purpose, they should consider all of the circumstances and seek wisdom from others who can help

them evaluate all aspects of the decision, including the risks involved (Prov. 22:7).

8. Christians who guarantee another person's loan based upon their own assets should make sure they are able to repay the loan without placing themselves in a position where they cannot meet other financial obligations, including their indebtedness to the Lord (Prov. 22:26-27).

9. Christians are out of God's will when they knowingly borrow money that they cannot pay back according to a predetermined agreement (Rom. 13:8).

10. Christians are out of God's will when they cannot give God the "first-fruits" of their income because they have obligated themselves to pay off debts (1 Cor. 16:2).

PHILEMON

11. Christians who put God first in their lives may open the door for people to take material advantage of them (Philem. 18).

12. Christian leaders should utilize methods of communication that create both a sense of obligation and a spirit of spontaneity and freedom (Philem. 14, 18-19).

13. Christian leaders should not hesitate to ask for help when there is a need, both for others and for themselves (Philem. 20-22).

EPHESIANS

14. Christians may face criticism or even retaliation when their commitment to do God's will conflicts with others' materialistic value systems (Acts 19:23-41).

15. Christians should work hard to make an honest living, not only to take care of their own needs, but to help others in need (Eph. 4:28).

COLOSSIANS

16. Christian employees should work hard and serve their employers (both Christians and non-Christians) as if they are actually serving the Lord (Col. 3:23-24).

17. Christian employers should always treat their employees fairly in every respect (Col. 4:1).

PHILIPPIANS

18. Christians who faithfully support God's servants in material ways create unusual joy in the hearts of those who receive their gifts (Phil. 1:3-5).

19. Christians who faithfully support God's servants in material ways enrich those servants' prayer lives by making it a joyful experience (Phil. 1:3-5).

20. Christians who make special sacrifices to help meet the material needs of God's servants should be honored in special ways by others in the Body of Christ (Phil. 2:29-30).

21. God's servants should be open and honest about their material needs, but they should avoid any form of dishonesty and manipulation by playing on others' sympathy (Phil. 4:11).

22. All Christians should learn to be content in the difficult times as well as in the prosperous times (Phil. 4:12).

23. Christian leaders who make their living in the ministry should serve Jesus Christ with the view that they are storing up treasures in heaven for those who support them financially (Phil. 4:14-17).

24. God's promise to meet needs applies to the church as well as to individual believers in that church (Phil. 4:19).

NOTE

1. Ralph P. Martin, *The Epistle of Paul to the Philippians: An Introduction and Commentary*, vol. 11 of *The Tyndale New Testament Commentaries* (Grand Rapids: Eerdmans, 1959), p. 181.

Part 7

THE FINAL YEARS
OF THE NEW TESTAMENT ERA

As we have looked at the New Testament letters in the basic chrono-logical order in which they were written, we have seen a clear relationship between what was happening in the Christian culture generally and what was taught regarding material possessions. As we look at the letters that were written during the final years of the New Testament era, we will see the same correlation. However, we will notice a more significant relationship between what was happening, not only in the Christian community but in the Roman culture at large.

34. Paul's Pastoral Letters: 1 Timothy

35. Paul's Pastoral Letters: Titus, 2 Timothy

36. 1 Peter, Hebrews

37. 2 Peter, Jude, and 1, 2, 3 John

38. Revelation

34
Paul's Pastoral Letters: 1 Timothy

It is possible to distinguish some unique changes in Paul's personality and perspective following his first imprisonment in Rome. He was still a highly motivated man (Phil. 3:13b-14). But he now knew he might face death through martyrdom rather than old age. He was well aware of Nero's unpredictable nature. Earlier, he had hoped to be alive when Christ returned, but even his eschatological perspectives had changed (1 Cor. 15:51-57; 1 Thess. 4:15-18).

Knowing his time might be short, he began to look more and more to the younger men who had served with him to continue the ministry they had begun together. This is one of Paul's purposes in writing the pastoral epistles: two letters to Timothy, and one to Titus. All three of these letters were written as Paul approached this final stage in his life.

The biographical data in these epistles reveals that Paul must have been set free to continue his missionary activity for a period of time following his first imprisonment in Rome.[1] The activities he alluded to do not correlate with the events recorded by Luke in the book of Acts. With this background in mind, note the specific statements and principles in the pastoral epistles that relate directly to how Christians should view and use their material possessions. Once again we will see the unique process involved in God's unfolding revelation.

If Paul was acquitted after appearing before the Roman emperor, it must have been in A.D. 60 or 61. His letter to Timothy demonstrates that he had some concerns about the state of the church at this moment in history. As any organization expands and ages, it faces new challenges. This was certainly true in the New Testament churches. Not surprisingly, several of Paul's specific concerns related to material possessions. Though he dealt with several of these issues in previous letters, he now became more specific.

1 TIMOTHY 3:2

Now the overseer must be above reproach, the husband of but one wife, temperate, self-controlled, respectable, hospitable.

EXPOSITION

All Christians should be given to *hospitality* (see Rom. 12:9-13; Heb. 13:1-2; 1 Peter 4:8-9). However, in Paul's first letter to Timothy, as well as in his letter to Titus (1:6, 8), he relates this quality in a special way to those who are to be appointed as spiritual leaders in the church. This was particularly important in the New Testament world since Christians had no choice but to meet in homes. And it follows naturally that it was only those men who had homes large enough who were often the men who were selected to be elders in the New Testament churches.

"Eldership" and "hospitality" are corollary concepts. Selfishness and being a Christian leader are incompatible, both from a divine and a human perspective. Unfortunately, there were men in the New Testament world who aspired to be spiritual leaders but who wanted only the position, not the responsibility to serve others. The apostle Paul had to speak directly to this issue when he wrote to Timothy and Titus.

THE FIRST SUPRACULTURAL PRINCIPLE

Spiritual leaders in the church should be generous Christians who are willing to use their material possessions to serve those they shepherd and lead (1 Tim. 3:2; Titus 1:6, 8).

This principle does not imply that spiritual leaders must be affluent. They must be willing, however, to share what they have—little or much—to minister to others in the church. The size of their homes is not the important issue, nor is it the amount of money they can give. Rather, it involves the degree to which they are willing to sacrifice and share with others what is theirs. If that desire and willingness is not there, they should not seek or accept this appointment.

This does not mean leaders should neglect their own families to serve the church. This would violate another qualification for leadership—to be able to "manage his own family well" (3:4). When we neglect our own family members in order to help others, we are in danger of creating resentment and negative attitudes in their hearts toward the work of God—and even toward God Himself.

If we desire to be spiritual leaders in the church, we should evaluate this principle carefully and what it means in our particular cultural situations. Is it possible to apply this principle without creating undue anxiety and stress in our lives personally and in the lives of those closest to us? Is it possible to apply it and not be intimidated by those who are more affluent and have larger homes?

It is important to understand that people who have less materially are often more susceptible to intimidation. Usually, this is not true because affluent leaders set out to intimidate those who are not as affluent as they are. Spiritually mature "Philemons" and "Corneliuses" do not purposely make others feel uncomfortable. It often happens naturally because of the way people with fewer material possessions perceive people with more. They often feel insecure but without justifiable reason.

All people, then, who desire to be spiritual leaders must evaluate whether or not they can serve with others who may have more material possessions than they without being intimidated, judgmental, or jealous. If they cannot overcome these attitudes, they must conclude they are not mature enough to handle this kind of responsibility in the church.

1 TIMOTHY 3:2-3, 8

Now the overseer must be . . . not given to drunkenness, not violent, but gentle, not quarrelsome, not a lover of money. . . . Deacons, likewise, are to be men worthy of respect, sincere, not indulging in much wine, and not pursuing dishonest gain.

EXPOSITION

The Bible does not say that a Christian should be "free from money" but rather, "free from the *love* of money." It is a human tendency, however, for all people to love money. When Paul wrote to Timothy and Titus (Titus 1:7), he was particularly concerned about spiritual leaders. He recognized that this would be a normal temptation for those who were appointed to be elders in the church. The apostle Peter showed the same concern when he exhorted the elders in various churches to not be *"greedy for money,* but eager to serve" (1 Peter 5:2).

The New Testament world was filled with individuals who had false motives. Paul called them "rebellious people, mere talkers and deceivers" (Titus 1:10). They were prominent personalities who were "teaching things they ought not to teach—and that for the sake of *dishonest* gain" (Titus 1:11). As the church expanded and grew, problems of this nature multiplied. Therefore, as Paul faced the closing days of his own ministry, he wanted to make sure that only those individuals were appointed to be elders in the church who were, first of all, seeking God's "kingdom and his righteousness" (Matt. 6:33).

Again, Paul did not believe it was an incompatible situation for people who are wealthy to serve as spiritual leaders in the church. Philemon certainly illustrates this point. He was a man who had a lot of money but who did not love it. Paul paid him a great tribute: "Your love has given me great joy and encouragement, because you, brother, have refreshed the hearts of the saints" (Philem. 7).

What Paul wrote regarding those who were to be elders, he also wrote regarding men and women who would serve as deacons. Elders had the primary responsibility to give overall management to the churches. In this sense, they were shepherds. One of their primary responsibilities was to teach the Word of God (1 Tim. 5:17).

Deacons and deaconesses were to serve the church in a more cultural way, helping to take care of the material needs of people. This was illustrated in the church in Jerusalem when seven men were appointed to take care of the widows who were neglected in the daily distribution of food (Acts 6:1-7).

The Word of God teaches that all spiritual leaders must be characterized by unselfishness when it comes to their material possessions. First, they must be "hospitable." Second, no individual in this position should be "a lover of money." Third, they should be totally and absolutely honest—"not pursuing dishonest gain."

THE SECOND SUPRACULTURAL PRINCIPLE

Christians who occupy leadership roles in the church should be totally trustworthy when it comes to financial matters (1 Tim. 3:2-3, 8; Titus 1:7-8).

As the church grew and expanded throughout the New Testament world, so did the number of people who wanted to get into leadership roles in the church out of purely selfish motives. Though an age-old problem (as we have seen with Simon the sorcerer in Samaria), more and more people wanted to "cash in" on this unique opportunity. Because of their very commitment and character, Christians were vulnerable to being led astray by self-serving leaders.

And so it is today—even more so. With the advent of modern media (print, radio, television, video), Christian hucksters have come "out of the woodwork." They are experts in taking advantage of naive and caring Christians. And one of their points of strategy is what has come to be called "prosperity theology." Not only do they appeal to our God-given desire to obey God, but they blend this desire with our natural tendency to want to be blessed materially. Consequently, they have developed a "self-centered" approach to giving that has become an incredible heresy in the twentieth-century world. Unfortunately, it has worked among many of God's people, and in the process, has padded the pockets of a number of "so-called" spiritual leaders.[2]

This is another reason Christians ought to focus their giving in their local churches, where spiritual leaders can be approved and appointed by those who know their true character. Furthermore, these spiritual leaders can more easily be held accountable, although operating at a local church level in itself is not a guarantee against dishonesty and greed. However, this kind of inappropriate behavior is less likely to occur if a local church is functioning according to the biblical principles that are so clearly outlined in the Word of God.

Having stated these warnings, it must be quickly added that this in no way gives Christians in local churches the right to make it difficult for their spiritual leaders. Just because there are some today who have abused their spiritual leadership role does not mean that this is true of the majority.

1 TIMOTHY 5:3

Give proper recognition to those widows who are really in need.

EXPOSITION

This directive introduces us to one of the most lengthy sections in the New Testament having to do with material possessions. Though Paul was addressing a unique cultural situation in the Roman Empire, what he wrote yields some relevant and helpful guidelines for Christians in every culture of the world.

The problem. When Jews became Christians, they were automatically cut off from the welfare system in Israel. Furthermore, since there was no official provision in the Roman Empire for these people, caring for needy Christians became the sole responsibility of local churches. As Christianity spread and grew in numbers, more and more people emerged who had special needs.

Predictably, more and more people also began to take advantage of the generous spirit that existed among believers. In actuality, it was a two-sided problem. Not only did older people tend to look to the church to meet their needs, but family members who had older parents and relatives who were in need also began to look to the church rather than considering their own responsibility to care for these people.

The solution. Paul addressed the issue because it was a serious problem in Ephesus. He quickly expressed his concern for those people who were not having their needs met. But he also emphasized that only those who were "really in need" should receive consistent support. The particular group of people in the New Testament world who frequently fell into the category of those in need were widows.

Paul made clear that the children or grandchildren of widows had the primary responsibility to take care of these needy people: "If a widow has children or grandchildren, they should learn first of all to put their religion into practice by caring for their own family and so repaying their parents and grandparents, for this is pleasing to God" (5:4). To make sure they understood what he was saying, Paul spelled out how serious it was for any family member to neglect his relatives when they were in physical need: "If anyone does not provide for his relatives, and especially for his immediate family, he has denied the faith and is worse than an unbeliever" (5:8).

Qualifications for assistance. Paul next set up some specific requirements for allowing widows to be consistently supported by the church. If no family member was available to take care of these people, then the church should consider supporting them. However, Paul declared that no widow might be put on the list of widows unless

- she was more than sixty

- has been faithful to her husband

- and was well-known for her good deeds, such as bringing up children, showing hospitality, washing the feet of the saints, helping those in trouble, and devoting herself to all kinds of good deeds (5:9-10).

Dealing with younger widows. Paul next addressed the issue that may have precipitated the problem in the first place. He instructed Timothy not to allow "younger widows" to be supported by the church. This must have been a problem in the Christian world because so many men lost their lives serving in the Roman wars. Since these young Christian wives were left without the normal means of financial support, it became a temptation to look to the church for help.

Paul instructed these young women to marry again and to establish homes. If young women were allowed to be supported by the church, they would be put in a position of being tempted to be immoral. They would "get into the habit of being idle and going from house to house. And not only do they become idlers," Paul continued, "but also gossips and busybodies saying things they ought not to" (5:13).

It may appear that Paul was being harsh and insensitive. In actuality, he was dealing with a very real problem. He was not addressing something that *might* take place, but rather, it was something that had *already* taken place. Paul was speaking from a posture of realism.

Older widows with an inheritance. Paul finally instructed Timothy to apply the same standard to "any woman who is a believer" who "has widows in her family" (5:16). To understand what Paul meant, we must understand the cultural situation. Not only were there young women whose husbands had been killed in the Roman wars, there were also older, wealthy women who had lost their husbands. These women were left with large extended families, involving grown children, and some of the young daughters or daughters-in-law who had also lost their husbands. Paul was simply stating that in these cases, women who have been left with an inheritance from their husbands should not look to the church for help. Rather, they should use this money to take care of their daughters or daughters-in-law who have been left in a similar situation.

In conclusion, Paul was not proposing a system that would neglect people with true needs. This would be in contradiction to everything we have seen thus far in our study. It simply indicates that anytime Christians begin to practice principles of generosity, there will be those who will take advantage of that generosity. In the New Testament world, those who were most tempted to do so were young widows. Furthermore, it was not only the young widows themselves who were tempted but family members who wanted to burden the church with the responsibility of caring for these young women rather than facing the financial responsibility themselves.

THE THIRD SUPRACULTURAL PRINCIPLE

The selection of people who receive consistent help from the church should be based upon specific scriptural guidelines (1 Tim. 5:3-16).

The church should certainly be a caring community of believers. People in need should be helped. However, just as the church in the first-century world needed guidelines, so the twentieth-century church needs guidelines.

Biblical guidelines for today. Though the cultural dynamics are different in many societies in today's world, the specific guidelines outlined by Paul still apply when considering financial support for needy people—particularly on a *consistent* basis.

First, the church should make sure there are no other sources of support—including assistance from various governmental agencies. If people in need have access to welfare systems, they should use those resources to the full. This was not possible for widows in the first-century world, but fortunately, it *is* possible in many countries today.

The second guideline is that people in need should look first to their own families for assistance. Specifically, Paul placed this responsibility on children and grandchildren. The tragedy in our society is that family members who should be taking the lead in assisting their parents often neglect this responsibility and force an additional burden on the needy one—the burden of looking for help elsewhere. This is unfair, insensitive, and selfish.

No wonder Paul became so direct. It was also happening in the first-century world—even among those who claimed to be Christians.

The third guideline relates to the *qualifications* for those who receive financial support from the church when there is no other source of help—either from welfare systems or from the extended family. Since Paul's criteria relate specifically to widows, they cannot be transferred directly to all people in need in every different culture of the world. However, inherent in this criteria are some supracultural qualifications.

Biblical qualifications for today. A person who receives consistent support from the church should be a *believer.* As we have seen in Paul's letter to the Galatians, this in no way means that the church should not help unbelievers (Gal. 6:10). But *consistent* and *long-range* support should involve only believers.

A person who receives consistent support from the church should be an *older believer.* A widow who received this kind of support in the New Testament church had to be more than sixty years old. The reason for this is that younger widows had opportunities to care for themselves financially in ways that older people did not. Furthermore, younger people should be encouraged to become financially independent. In fact, Paul encouraged all Christians to become financially independent and to even have enough left over to share with others (Eph. 4:28; cf. 1 Tim. 6:18).

Does this mean that a person has to be at least sixty years old in every cultural situation to receive this kind of help from the church? Not necessarily. This specific guideline, however, indicates that a person should be up in years and not able to care for himself.

A person who receives consistent support from the church should be a *mature believer.* Paul's standard was extremely high. A person worthy of this kind of support should have lived a Christian life characterized by sexual purity (1 Tim. 5:9*b*). Furthermore, that person should have an excellent reputation built over a lengthy period of time (5:10). Though all the ways in which a widow developed her reputation may not apply everywhere, Paul gave us enough information to discern how a good reputation is built (5:10):

- The way we relate to our own children and grandchildren

- The way we have demonstrated hospitality and concern for other people when they have faced crisis periods in their lives

- The way we have served other people in the church

- The way we have helped others who have faced troubling times

APPLYING THIS PRINCIPLE TODAY

Fortunately, the American church does not face these problems as often as churches in other cultures. The need is not as great because of our welfare systems and our affluent society. However, there are still people who are truly in need. But some people will try to take advantage of the church, particularly when the church begins to function according to New Testament principles and begins to care for those in need as God intended. The more we practice these biblical principles, the more we must set up criteria to make sure we do not violate these principles in other ways.

Paul demonstrated once again that wherever there is a positive, Satan can turn it into a negative. But this in no way should stand in the way of doing everything God wants us to do; it in no way gives Christians an excuse for neglecting our God-given responsibility to meet the needs of those who are truly in need.

1 TIMOTHY 5:17

The elders who direct the affairs of the church well
are worthy of double honor, especially those
whose work is preaching and teaching.

EXPOSITION

Elders who do an exceptional job in leading the church "are worthy of double honor." The Greek word *timē* (translated "honor") refers to remuneration or honoraria. The word for "double" makes reference to generous or ample financial support.[3] The *amount* should be contingent on *how well* a spiritual leader carries out his duties. Again, Paul's focus was on those who devote a great deal of time to "preaching and teaching" the Word of God, which correlates with the directive in his letter to the Galatians (see Gal. 6:6). Here Paul amplified on this and made clear that certain elders should be rewarded financially for faithful and productive work in God's kingdom.

Paul was bringing balance to his earlier statements regarding the qualifications for elders. He had warned Timothy not to appoint leaders in the church who love money (3:3) and who in any way, shape, or form were dishonest (3:8). He also had cautioned against supporting people in the church who did not measure up to very high standards (5:3-16). To make sure that the believers in Ephesus did not overreact to these exhortations, Paul immediately clarified that he did not want faithful elders or pastors to be penalized financially because of his earlier statements.

THE FOURTH SUPRACULTURAL PRINCIPLE

Pastors and teachers who are hardworking, efficient, and productive in the ministry should be rewarded financially (1 Tim. 5:17).

This principle indicates that God has not eliminated from human nature the need for earthly rewards and recognition. Interestingly, one of the most motivating rewards, even for Christian workers, is financial remuneration that reflects appreciation for a job well done. The Scriptures themselves promote "merit pay." As Paul stated, "the hardworking farmer should be the first to receive a share of the crops" (2 Tim. 2:6).

Unfortunately, churches and other Christian organizations are often negligent in applying this principle. In fact, there seems to be normal expectations that those who serve Jesus Christ vocationally should be paid less than people in the business world who occupy similar positions in terms of qualifications and time demands. This approach to caring for spiritual leaders is not in harmony with the teachings from the Word of God.

On the other hand, this principle must be applied carefully. It can be abused by spiritual leaders themselves. It can be used selfishly and manipulatively to justify materialistic motives and actions. That is why it is important to apply any particular principle from Scripture in the context of other teachings and principles that bring biblical balance to all we do as believers.

1 TIMOTHY 6:10

For the love of money is the root of all kinds of evil.
Some people, eager for money, have wandered from the faith
and pierced themselves with many griefs.

EXPOSITION

Paul concluded his letter to Timothy with a series of warnings against the negative effects of materialism and how these influences cause Christians to depart from God's perfect will. Much of what Paul says is an echo of what Jesus taught and what James later wrote in his epistle.

Unfortunately, all of us—both Christians and non-Christians—are tempted to love material things. But we need not submit to this kind of temptation. It is possible to maintain a proper balance. God has provided a way of escape if we will only trust Him to help us find it and then act on what we know to be His will (1 Cor. 10:13).

The following teachings are clear-cut and self-explanatory, especially in view of other scriptural exhortations and illustrations we have already read and interacted with in this study:

But godliness with contentment is great gain. For we brought nothing into the world, and we can take nothing out of it. But if we have food and clothing, we will be content with that. (6:6-8)

People who want to get rich fall into temptation and a trap and into many foolish and harmful desires that plunge men into ruin and destruction. (6:9)

Command those who are rich in this present world not to be arrogant nor to put their hope in wealth, which is so uncertain, but to put their hope in God, who richly provides us with everything for our enjoyment. (6:17)

Command them [the rich] to do good, to be rich in good deeds, and to be generous and willing to share. In this way they will lay up treasure for themselves as a firm foundation for the coming age, so that they may take hold of the life that is truly life. (6:18-19)

THE FIFTH SUPRACULTURAL PRINCIPLE

A Christian's first priority should be to focus on godliness and contentment rather than on riches, which often brings discontentment (1 Tim. 6:6-10; 17-19).

Paul was not teaching that poor people are "content" and that wealthy people are "discontent." This would contradict Scripture and reality. A number of Proverbs help us understand this principle. On the one hand, Scripture recognizes that poverty brings with it a lot of difficulties.

A poor man is shunned by all his relatives—how much more do his friends avoid him! Though he pursues them with pleading, they are nowhere to be found. (19:7)

The poor are shunned even by their neighbors, but the rich have many friends. (14:20)

Wealth brings many friends, but a poor man's friend deserts him. (19:4)

Having little of this world's goods can be a painful existence, and that is why there are so many exhortations in Scripture not to mistreat these people. But many proverbs also warn against the problems that can come with wealth. In fact, there are far more exhortations of this nature than those that deal with the plight of the poor.

A good name is more desirable than great riches; to be esteemed is better than silver or gold. (22:1)

For riches do not endure forever, and a crown is not secure for all generations. (27:24)

Do not wear yourself out to get rich; have the wisdom to show restraint. (23:4)

> Cast but a glance at riches, and they are gone, for they will surely sprout wings and fly off to the sky like an eagle. (23:5)

The more we study the Word of God, the more we understand that it teaches balance. Certainly this is what the proverb means, "Keep falsehood and lies far from me; *give me neither poverty nor riches*, but give me only my daily bread. Otherwise, I may have too much and disown you and say, 'Who is the Lord?' or I may become poor and steal, and so dishonor the name of my God" (30:8-9).

When Christians set their goals to become rich rather than to become godly, they are headed for serious trouble. Ultimately, they will not find contentment. And if their focus is wealth, they will not be able to resist the temptations that invariably come their way. They will eventually find themselves in "a trap." They will be controlled by many "foolish and harmful desires that plunge men into ruin and destruction" (1 Tim. 6:9). It is in this context that Paul states that "the love of money is the root of all kinds of evil" (1 Tim. 6:10).

All Christians, then, should set their foremost goal to be godly people—to "seek first his kingdom and his righteousness" (Matt. 6:33a). If they do, everything else will come into focus. As Jesus said, "all these things will be given to you as well" (Matt. 6:33b). If God brings wealth and prosperity, Christians will be able to handle the temptations that come with these blessings—if they use what God gives them to not only meet their own basic needs but to also use their excess in creative ways to invest in God's eternal kingdom. That is why Paul also told Timothy to "command" the rich "to do good, to be rich in good deeds, and to be generous and willing to share" (6:18).

NOTES

1. Merrill C. Tenney, *New Testament Survey* (Grand Rapids: Eerdmans, 1953), pp. 332-33, gives the following helpful internal evidence to demonstrate that the three pastoral epistles must have been written after Paul was released from prison and was traveling again:

> The chronological relations of the Pastorals to the Prison Epistles seem clear from their reference to Paul's companions. Many of these are identical with those of the Prison Epistles, but are located in places which show that they had left Paul's immediate vicinity. Timothy had been left at Ephesus while Paul was en route to Macedonia (I Tim. 1:3), whereas on the last trip that Timothy took with Paul the order of procedures was from Macedonia to Asia (Acts 20:4-6), and Timothy did not remain in Ephesus. Demas had deserted Paul (II Tim. 4:10), whereas the Prison Epistles included him among the group at Rome (Philem. 24). Titus was left in Crete (Titus 1:5), and then went to Dalmatia (II Tim. 4:10), but on none of the journeys in Acts did Paul go to Crete, nor did he have Titus with him when he finally did go there during the voyage to Rome. Mark was in Asia (4:11) where Paul had recommended him in one of the Asian letters (Col. 4:10). Luke was still with him (II Tim. 4:11). Tychicus had gone on his errand to Ephesus (4:12).

Paul himself had visited Ephesus (I Tim. 1:3), Crete (Titus 1:5), Nicopolis (3:12), Corinth (II Tim. 4:20), Miletus (4:20), and Troas (4:13), and was presently located in Rome (1:17). He was in prison (1:16) and was quite sure that the end of his life was not far away (4:6, 7). Altogether the situation was very different from that described by the Prison Epistles.

2. See Michael Horton, ed., *The Agony of Deceit: What Some TV Preachers Are Really Teaching* (Chicago: Moody, 1990); Bruce Barron, *The Health and Wealth Gospel: A Fresh Look at Healing, Prosperity & Positive Confession* (Downers Grove, Ill.: InterVarsity, 1987).

3. See Donald Guthrie, *The Pastoral Epistles: An Introduction and Commentary*, vol. 14 of *The Tyndale New Testament Commentaries* (Grand Rapids: Eerdmans, 1957), p. 105.

35

Paul's Pastoral Letters: Titus, 2 Timothy

Paul had left Titus in Crete so that he "might straighten out what was left unfinished and appoint elders in every town" (Titus 1:5). Overall, he had fewer things to say about material possessions in this letter than he did in his first letter to Timothy. For one reason, the churches in Crete were relatively new and just getting organized, whereas the churches in Ephesus and the surrounding area had been in existence for several years and the Christians there were facing the normal concerns that go with age and growth. Nevertheless, Paul shared some of the same basic concerns that he shared with Timothy, especially when appointing those who would lead the church (see Titus 1:6-7 compared with 1 Timothy 3:2-3).

What Paul wrote to Titus, however, adds some additional perspectives on the problems faced by Christians in the first-century church and how Paul wanted those problems resolved. One of the primary tasks facing Titus was to appoint spiritual leaders who would not only lead the church as godly models but who would *counteract* the influence of leaders who had already emerged and were leading the church astray. Furthermore, their motives were purely self-oriented and materialistic.

TITUS 1:10-11

For there are many rebellious people, mere talkers
and deceivers, especially those of the circumcision group.
They must be silenced, because they are ruining whole
households by teaching things they ought not to teach—
and that for the sake of dishonest gain.

EXPOSITION

One of Paul's primary solutions in silencing false teachers was to have Titus appoint men who were the opposite in terms of what they believed and how they lived. Not only would they need to model Christlikeness and nonmaterialistic motives, they must also confront these individuals. They were to "hold firmly to the trustworthy message as it has been taught." In so doing, they would be able to "encourage others by sound doctrine and refute those who oppose it" (Titus 1:9).

THE SIXTH SUPRACULTURAL PRINCIPLE

So-called Christian leaders who are teaching false doctrine and manipulating people in order to pursue dishonest gain should be silenced (Titus 1:10-11).

Why it is difficult to practice this principle. First, we do not have the same revelatory insight and direct authority as Paul and certain other apostolic leaders. For example, when Paul was on the island of Cyprus, he looked directly at Elymas the sorcerer and, with direct insight from the Holy Spirit, revealed the thoughts and intents of this evil man's mind and heart: "Will you never stop perverting the right ways of the Lord?" He then pronounced blindness on Elymas (Acts 13:4-12).

Second, many leaders who are guilty of this kind of behavior are outside of our realm of responsibility and accountability. This is particularly true of those who have developed a "ministry at large" by means of radio and television. Even some who are associated with a local church are difficult to control and hold accountable.

Third, some of our legal systems have become so complex that even our government finds it difficult to prosecute and silence these people. Consider, for example, the scandals surrounding the televangelists in the late 1980s.

What Christians can do to practice this principle. First, all local churches should have a system of checks and balances that make it virtually impossible for a Christian leader to practice this kind of behavior.

Second, if lack of accountability occurs—which it can in spite of numerous precautions—and if nothing is done to correct the situation, Christians should not continue to support that church with contributions or attendance. They should seek out a church that practices biblical principles of accountability.

Third, Christians should not support any Christian organization where its leaders are violating the basic principles outlined in Scripture regarding material possessions. If all Christians practiced these principles, we would be able to take giant steps in silencing leaders who are "ruining whole households by teaching things they ought not to teach—and that for the sake of dishonest gain" (Titus 1:11).

Fourth, Christian leaders who have the authority to do so should not avoid confronting and exposing people who are violating the principles of the Word of God. This must be done, however, in a biblical fashion, following the guidelines outlined in Scripture (see Matt. 18:15-17; Gal. 6:1-2; Titus 3:9-10).

Fifth, Christians should pray that God will protect Christian leaders from falling into Satan's trap. Furthermore, they should do all they can to support Christian leaders who are committed to practicing the principles of Scripture.

2 TIMOTHY 3:1-2a, 4b-5

Paul wrote his second letter to Timothy shortly before he was sentenced to death, probably by Nero. It contains his final words to the Christian world before he entered heaven's glory to receive his eternal rewards (2 Tim. 4:7-8). Still believing that the Lord's return was imminent, he issued a strong warning to believers.

> *But mark this: There will be terrible times in the last days.*
> *People will be lovers of themselves, lovers of money . . .*
> *lovers of pleasure rather than lovers of God—having a form of*
> *godliness but denying its power. Have nothing to do with them.*

EXPOSITION

Somewhere at some point in time, Paul was suddenly taken into custody and once again imprisoned in Rome. Some speculate that his place of arrest may have been Troas or Nicopolis.[1] Paul's final chapter in this letter gives us some clues as to where he was traveling and what may have happened.

We know he stopped in Corinth, where Erastus chose to stay (2 Tim. 4:20a). He stopped in Miletus, where he "left Trophimus sick" (2 Tim. 4:20b). Paul also made reference to his stop at Troas, where he left his cloak and some scrolls (2 Tim. 4:13). We have no way, of course, of determining a specific order in these geographical references. Evidently, he also bypassed Ephesus because he stated that he "sent Tychicus there" (2 Tim. 4:12).

Before he died, Paul made a powerful and prophetic declaration in this passage (2 Timothy 3:1-5) regarding what would happen shortly before the return of Christ. The supracultural principle to follow is obvious.

THE SEVENTH SUPRACULTURAL PRINCIPLE

As the Day of Christ draws nearer, Christians should avoid the increasing tendency to intensify love for self, money, and pleasure (2 Tim. 3:1-2a, 4b-5).

Paul made clear in his final letter that Christians are to disassociate themselves from people who are self-centered, materialistic, and hedonistic. "Have nothing to do with them," Paul warned (2 Tim. 3:5). We can quickly establish two facts in our culture today. First, we are nearer to the second coming of Christ than ever before. If the time was near when Paul wrote his second letter to Timothy, what can be said about two thousand years later? Second, the world in general reflects the trends outlined by Paul. This is certainly true in American culture. Many people are "lovers of themselves, lovers of money" and "lovers of pleasure rather than lovers of God" (2 Tim. 3:2, 4). We are manifesting these characteristics more every day.

The challenge that faces all of us as Christians is that we not allow ourselves to "love the *world* or anything in the world" (1 John 2:15). This is why Paul exhorted the Roman Christians to avoid allowing their lives to "conform any longer to the pattern of *this world*" (Rom. 12:2).

There is only one basic solution to this problem. We must be continually "transformed by the renewing" of our minds. It is only then that we will "be able to test and approve what God's will is—his good, pleasing and perfect will" (Rom. 12:2). What Paul tells the Roman Christians as he begins chapter 12 is foundational to everything we do—including the way in which we view and use our material possessions.

As the Day of Christ draws near, believers should intensify their efforts to practice the principles of the Word of God. We should give increased attention to being "strong in the Lord and in his mighty power." We should take seriously Paul's exhortation to the Ephesians to "put on the whole armor of God so that" we "can take" our "stand against the devil's schemes" (Eph. 6:10-18).

We must take seriously Paul's words in guarding against fellowship with people who will pull us down to their level. In some instances, we should not even associate with people whatsoever who have given themselves over to materialism and sensuality. If we do, we will become like them.

The Word of God does not teach isolation from the world; otherwise it would be impossible to live (1 Cor. 5:9-11). What the writers of Scripture are speaking to is that if we associate closely (more literally, have fellowship) with people who are not walking with God, we will soon begin to reflect the same traits. This is particularly true when it comes to associating with people who are materialistic. Many Christians have succumbed to temptation and have developed the same mind-set, in some cases without realizing it. When this happens, they have allowed themselves to be "conformed to the pattern of this world."

NOTE

1. For some helpful information and speculation as to where, why, and how Paul was arrested and taken to Rome a second time, see Merrill C. Tenney, *New Testament Survey* (Grand Rapids: Eerdmans, 1953), p. 339.

36
1 Peter, Hebrews

The remaining letters written during the closing years of the New Testament era were by Peter, John, Jude, and an unknown author who wrote Hebrews. Again, let us look at these letters as they were written chronologically.

A LETTER TO THE "SUFFERING CHURCH": 1 PETER

The greatest tension the church faced in its early years was with Judaism. The doctrines of Christianity were in direct conflict with the traditions of Israel. Conflict with the Roman government was minimal, primarily because Christianity was a spiritual movement, not a political one. Jesus set the tone for this approach when He responded to Pilate's question, "What is it you have done?" Jesus responded, "My kingdom is not of this world" (John 18:35b-36a).

The second reason the Christian movement did not conflict significantly with the Roman Empire is that Christianity itself grew out of Judaism, a religion that was permitted, and actually protected, by the state. It was Rome's policy that various religious movements that did not conflict with the state would be tolerated. Consequently, as long as Christians did not create problems, they were allowed to operate rather freely. Their penetration of society with the Christian message was basically a peaceful experience.

Things began to change as Christianity became an entity in itself and stood out as a movement separate from Judaism. It became more threatening, particularly to men like Nero. Paul's death actually marks the transition from peaceful coexistence with Rome to a time of persecution in various parts of the Empire.

LIVING FOR CHRIST IN A MATERIAL WORLD

The apostle Peter wrote his letter to encourage Christians facing persecution. These believers were primarily Jewish but also included Gentiles. He addressed his first letter "to God's elect, strangers in the world, scattered throughout Pontus, Galatia, Cappadocia, Asia and Bithynia" (see map on p. 348). His comments regarding living for Christ in a material world fit the political conditions that existed at that time:

> These [trials] have come so that your faith—of greater worth than gold, which perishes even though refined by fire—may be proved genuine and may result in praise, glory and honor when Jesus Christ is revealed. (1:7)

> For you know that it was not with perishable things such as silver or gold that you were redeemed from the empty way of life handed down to you from your forefathers, but with the precious blood of Christ, a lamb without blemish or defect. (1:18-19)

> For you have been born again, not of perishable seed, but of imperishable, through the living and enduring word of God. For, "All men are like grass, and all their glory is like the flowers of the field; the grass withers and the flowers fall, but the word of the Lord stands forever." (1:23-25a)

> Dear friends, I urge you, as aliens and strangers in the world, to abstain from sinful desires, which war against your soul. Live such good lives among the pagans that, though they accuse you of doing wrong, they may see your good deeds and glorify God on the day he visits us. (2:11-12)

> Offer hospitality to one another without grumbling. (4:9)

> Be shepherds of God's flock that is under your care, serving as overseers—not because you must, but because you are willing, as God wants you to be; not greedy for money, but eager to serve. (5:2)

EXPOSITION

Peter's message is clear. These believers were being persecuted. The apostle encouraged them to focus on spiritual and eternal values—not on the things that were being taken away from them—in some instances, their earthly existence. Peter encouraged them to see as one of God's primary purposes in allowing trials the strengthening of their faith (1:7).

That would enable them to understand more fully that their redemption was based upon the blood of Jesus Christ, not upon "perishable things such as silver or gold" (1:18-19). They would be able to perceive more clearly the enduring nature of the Word of God, and the eternal life it gives, as compared with the decaying material world—including our bodies. Apart from Christ, men and women will wither and perish just "like grass" and "the flowers of the field" (1:23-25a). These believers would also experience more realistically—because of their persecution—that their real citizenship is in heaven, not on earth. Furthermore, they were having an opportunity to be purified from the world's system and at tne same time, to stand out as Christlike examples (2:11-12).

Peter also encouraged these believers to not lose sight of their responsibility to care for each other and to share what they had, even though much of their world's goods were in jeopardy (4:9). Finally Peter warned spiritual leaders to check their motives and not to succumb to the temptation to take advantage of their flocks during this time of persecution (5:2).

THE EIGHTH SUPRACULTURAL PRINCIPLE

God allows periodic persecution to help Christians put more emphasis on the spiritual and eternal dimensions of life rather than on the material and temporal (1 Pet. 1:7, 18-19, 23-25a; 2:5, 11-12; 4:9; 5:2).

In essence, this is the same principle we discussed when the church faced persecution in Jerusalem (see pp. 147-49). It is repeated here to emphasize another dimension—that of "periodic persecution." Though it is the will of God generally that Christians not suffer on this earth and that we be able to "live peaceful and quiet lives in all godliness and holiness," history demonstrates that Christians need periodic awakenings in order to refocus their values from the "things of this world" to the "things of heaven." When life is persistently free from difficulties, and when we are able to accumulate more and more of this world's goods, we tend toward a materialistic mindset, just as our pagan counterparts. Like them, we begin to exchange "the truth of God for a lie" and begin to worship and serve "created things rather than the Creator" (Rom. 1:25). When we do, we are conforming to the pattern of this world (Rom. 12:2).

What does this principle say to those of us who are living in America? Is it possible for Christians to refocus priorities before God allows external pressure to cause it to happen? Yes, if we will listen to the Word of God and if we will learn lessons from history. Time will tell if American Christians will refocus now—when it is relatively easy—or later when it may be a painful experience.

Interestingly, I have noticed some readjustments in my own present circumstances where I pastor in the Dallas Metroplex. We have been through a difficult recession that was precipitated by the oil crisis. Few of us have been unaffected by the domino effect. In the process, I have seen Christians refocus their priorities. I have noticed that Christians are more attentive to the Word of God and are making more intensive effort to be open to doing the will of God.

Will this renewal last? Will it endure as our economic situation improves? Unfortunately, many will forget quickly—just as Christians have done for centuries. Will something more painful happen in our society to once again bring us to our knees, to force us to rely upon eternal and enduring qualities of life rather than on the perishable aspects of this world—such as silver and gold? Only time will tell. Meanwhile, let us heed the words of the apostle Paul when he spoke of the failures of the children of Israel: "These things happened to them as examples and were written down as warnings for us, on whom the fulfillment of the ages has come. So, if you think you are standing firm, be careful that you don't fall!" (1 Cor. 10:11-12).

A Separation from Judaism: Hebrews

As the church grew and spread, a number of Jews professed faith in Christ but continued to be ardent in their adherence to the Old Testament law. This was particularly true in Jerusalem. Eventually a break had to come. Professing Christians could not continue indefinitely to be a part of Judaism as a "religious system" and Israel "as a nation," and still be a part of the church and the kingdom of God.

The book of Hebrews was written by an unknown author to help Jewish Christians understand and appreciate their heritage but, at the same time, establish a new identity in Jesus Christ. They were now a part of the church. Their focus was to be on a spiritual kingdom—not on an earthly one. Though the promises to Israel were still intact in the heart and mind of God, this was not to be the focus of Christian believers, either Jew or Gentile.

There are at least three exhortations in this letter regarding how these Christians were to view and use their material possessions. What is said adds additional light and perspective on this subject, although we have looked at similar directives in previous epistles.

Hebrews 13:2

Do not forget to entertain strangers [that is,
to show hospitality to strangers], for by so doing
some people have entertained angels without knowing it.

We have encountered the directive to "show hospitality" to fellow believers several times before. Both Paul and Peter exhorted believers generally and Christian leaders specifically to demonstrate this practice in the use of material possessions (Rom. 12:13; 1 Tim. 3:2; Titus 1:8; 1 Pet. 4:9; 5:2). But here in the letter to the Hebrews, Christians were encouraged "to show hospitality to *strangers*"—that is, to those believers they did not know personally. This is the first time Christians were so directed in the New Testament literature.

THE NEED FOR A LARGER PERSPECTIVE

The need for this broader perspective on showing hospitality may be related to the fact that those receiving this letter were Hebrew Christians, some of whom were deeply influenced by a very legalistic approach to caring for others. For example, some orthodox Jewish sects, such as the Essenes, actually "refused to eat with anyone whose carefulness in dietary, tithing and piety rules was not proven by being a member of his own sect."[1] When these people became Christians, they often carried their legalistic rules into their Christian practices and actually refused to allow traveling Christians to enter their homes unless they kept the same "rules" as they did. Since these people were "strangers" and they had no way of knowing how these people actually conducted their lives, they refused to show them hospitality.

This exhortation, then, would be a corrective to a very cautious and community-centered approach to helping fellow Christians. Not only were they to care for the needs of believers who were involved in their own local churches, they were to be open to helping all Christians, no matter where they lived. Accordingly, F. F. Bruce gives this helpful comment: "Christians travelling from one place to another on business would be specially glad of hospitality from fellow Christians. Inns throughout the Roman Empire were places of doubtful repute . . . and would provide very uncongenial company for Christians."[2]

ENTERTAINING GOD'S MESSENGERS

Immediately following the exhortation "to entertain strangers," the author of Hebrews went on to record that "some people have entertained angels without knowing it" (Heb. 13:2). Many Bible commentators agree that this was probably a reference to Abraham's experience when he entertained three men "near the great trees of Mamre while he was sitting at the entrance of his tent." One of these men turned out to be the Lord Himself accompanied by two angelic beings (Gen. 18:1-33).

Though the reference to angels in Hebrews no doubt refers to angelic beings in a primary sense, it does not follow that the author is "necessarily encouraging his readers to expect that those whom they entertain will turn out to be supernatural beings traveling incognito."[3] Rather, the term *angels* can also refer to *messengers* who are serving Jesus Christ as apostles, prophets, evangelists, and pastors and teachers. These are "angel/messengers" who have been assigned to these missionary responsibilities by Jesus Christ in order to equip and build up the universal Body of Christ (Eph. 4:11-13). In other words, among these strangers who knocked on the doors of Christian dwellings may be true servants of God who are called in a special way to carry out the Great Commission.

CHRIST'S PARABLE OF THE SHEEP AND THE GOATS

Christ made clear in this parable that, in the day of judgment, He (the King) will reward those who cared for Him when He was hungry and thirsty.

"I was a stranger," He said, "and you invited me in, I needed clothes and you clothed me, I was sick and you looked after me, I was in prison and you came to visit me" (Matt. 25:35b-36).

Those who will be recipients of God's blessings, even in that day, will be puzzled. They will ask the Lord when they had done these things for Him (Matt. 25:37-38). "The King will reply," Jesus said, speaking of Himself, "'I tell you the truth, whatever you did for one of the least of these brothers of mine, you did for me'" (Matt. 25:40). Jesus' reference to his "brothers" was a reference to those who were serving with Him.

Here again, the Word of God was making reference to the importance of caring for people who devote their time to ministry. In essence, the author of Hebrews was warning these believers that they might pass up the unique opportunity to do so if they did not show hospitality to strangers.

HEBREWS 13:5, 16

Keep your lives free from the love of money and
be content with what you have, because God has said,
"Never will I leave you; never will I forsake you." . . .
And do not forget to do good and to share with others,
for with such sacrifices God is pleased.

EXPOSITION

In conjunction with this exhortation, Thomas Hewitt comments:

> The Christian's habits of thought and life in connection with money are a touchstone of his character. Such habits must be free from covetousness and avarice, for the love of money can be as detrimental to a man's spiritual life as sensuality. The way of victory over this evil is to be content with such things as you have.[4]

Paul's words to Timothy in his first letter serve as an excellent biblical commentary on this rather concise statement (1Tim. 5:6-10, 17-18). His reassuring words to the Philippians (4:11-13) also elaborate on this exhortation. He affirmed that he could do everything through Christ who gave him strength (Phil. 4:13). This adds meaning to the quoted portion in the above Hebrews passage: "God has said, 'Never will I leave you; never will I forsake you'" (Heb. 13:5b).

In the Old Testament era, the children of Israel repeatedly offered *animal sacrifices* to atone for sins. In the New Testament era, Jesus Christ became the ultimate and *final sacrifice* (Heb. 10:11-18). Once believers experience the wonderful gift of salvation, they are then to offer their bodies as *living sacrifices*—not to atone for their sins—but to offer worship, praise, thanksgiving, and appreciation to God for His mercy (Rom. 12:1-2). As we have seen before—especially in Paul's letter to the Philippians—one of the specific ways that believers can offer these spiritual sacrifices to God is by the way they use their material possessions to help others (Phil. 4:18).

The author of Hebrews underscores the same truth: Christians are to show hospitality, even to brothers and sisters in Christ that they do not know personally. By so doing, they demonstrate that they are "free from the love of money" and are relying on Jesus Christ to meet their needs—even though they may share during times when they are rather needy themselves—just as the Macedonians did, when they gave out of what they did not have (2 Cor. 8:1-2).

In a fitting conclusion, the author of this letter reminded them that God is very pleased when we share what we have with others. It is a sacrifice that is especially acceptable to Him and brings joy to His heart. And once again, we are reminded that God will never forget the way we use our resources to help others in need.

THE NINTH SUPRACULTURAL PRINCIPLE

All Christians are to show hospitality, not only to those believers in a specific local Christian community, but to those whom they may not know personally (Heb. 13:2, 5, 16).

The Scriptures do not teach that believers are to have an "open hands policy" for every stranger who passes by and claims to be a Christian in need. We will see this more specifically when we look at the epistles of Jude and John. We must be discerning, even as our fellow believers had to be in New Testament days.

The Scriptures do teach, however, that our generosity must extend beyond our own local churches. Though we may never be able to fellowship together face-to-face, all believers belong to the family of God. Speaking of the universal church, Paul wrote, "There is one body and one Spirit—just as you were called to one hope when you were called—one Lord, one faith, one baptism; one God and Father of all, who is over all and through all and in all" (Eph. 4:4-6).

Some people will take advantage of this principle of Christian hospitality. They know Christians are to be generous—even toward strangers—and they will purposely use this as a means to play on people's sympathy and their desire to do the will of God in all things. However, there are some biblical guidelines for dealing with "fraudulent Christians." We will look at these guidelines in the next chapter.

NOTES

1. George Wesley Buchanan, *To the Hebrews: Translation, Comment and Conclusions*, 2d ed. (Garden City, N.Y.: Doubleday, 1976), p. 230.

2. F. F. Bruce, *Commentary on the Epistle to the Hebrews* (Grand Rapids: Eerdmans, 1964), p. 390.

3. Ibid., p. 391.

4. Thomas Hewitt, *The Epistle to the Hebrews: An Introduction and Commentary*, vol. 15 of *The Tyndale New Testament Commentaries* (Grand Rapids: Tyndale, 1960), pp. 206-7.

5. Bruce, *Epistle to the Hebrews*, p. 390, gives this helpful comment regarding those in the New Testament world who might exploit Christian generosity:

> The opportunity of free board and lodging might tempt some unscrupulous characters to masquerade as Christians. Proteus Peregrinus in Lucian's satire comes to mind [Lucian, *The Death of Peregrinus*, 11ff.]; and the necessity of some rough-and-ready rule of thumb for detecting impostors is implied in the *Didache*: "Let every apostle who comes to you be received as the Lord, but he must not stay more than one day, or two if it is absolutely necessary; if he stays three days, he is a false prophet. And when an apostle leaves you, let him take nothing but a loaf, until he reaches further lodging for the night; if he asks for money, he is a false prophet" [*Didache* 11:4-6]. Some Christians who had been deceived by such impostors might be chary of offering hospitality too readily next time they were asked for it, but here they are encouraged with the remark that some who have given hospitality to passing strangers found that they were entertaining "angels unawares." Those who are given to hospitality find that such happy experiences far outweigh the unhappy ones.

37

2 Peter, Jude, and 1, 2, 3 John

Peter and Jude addressed the issue of false teachers whose primary motives were selfish and materialistic. John addressed a specific heresy known as gnosticism. This false teaching affected particularly the doctrine of Christ and His divine-human state. The persecution phase that Peter wrote about in his first epistle had subsided, and the church was now facing a new problem—false teaching. Peter proceeded to address this issue in his second letter.

2 PETER 2:3a

*In their greed these [false] teachers will
exploit you with stories they have made up.*

EXPOSITION

It is true that the greed or covetousness referred to here includes more than a lust for money. It certainly includes power and pleasure—especially sexual gratification. But this simply reminds us that these three selfish and insidious motives (money, power, and sex) have revealed themselves from the very early years of the church. Furthermore, these false motives are based on dishonesty, which combine to form a subtle means to exploit Christians with fabricated stories.

Christians have always been vulnerable to false stories. After all, we believe in a supernatural Christ who brought us a supernatural message. Furthermore, Jesus Christ passed this message on to others who, in turn, were instructed to share these marvelous truths with the whole world. In order to demonstrate the validity of this divine message, God instituted a plan, which He outlined in Hebrews: "This salvation, which was first announced by the Lord, was confirmed to us by those who heard him. *God also testified to it* [this message of salvation] by signs, wonders and various miracles, and gifts of the Holy Spirit distributed according to his will" (Heb. 2:3*b*-4).

Unfortunately, Christians, even in the first century, were not always careful to make sure that what they were hearing was true. Furthermore, they were not always cautious in evaluating the true nature of "signs, wonders and various miracles" that God gave to confirm the truth of His message. Oftentimes, they did not determine if people were truly using a gift of the Holy Spirit to make the message clear. That is why Paul told the Thessalonians, "Do not put out the Spirit's fire; do not treat prophecies with contempt." But, Paul quickly warned them to "test everything," and to "hold on to the good." They were to "avoid every kind of evil" (1 Thess. 5:19-22).

False teachers quickly learned they could exploit innocent and sincere believers. They saw it, not only as an opportunity to fulfill their sexual desires, but to accumulate money. Mixing truth with error and good with evil, they became "experts in greed" (2 Pet. 2:14*b*). Peter had little patience with these individuals: "But these men blaspheme in matters they do not understand. They are like brute beasts, creatures of instinct, born only to be caught and destroyed, and like beasts they too will perish. They will be paid back with harm for the harm they have done" (2 Pet. 12-13*a*).

JUDE 12*a*

These men are blemishes at your love feasts,
eating with you without the slightest qualm—
shepherds who feed only themselves.

EXPOSITION

Needless to say, these false teachers were not concerned whatsoever for those they were exploiting. They had no consciences, since they would even partake of the Lord's Supper, desecrating the very institution God established to remember the broken body and shed blood of Christ. Their focus was only on themselves. Thus Jude wrote, "They are clouds without rain, blown along by the wind; autumn trees, without fruit and uprooted— twice dead. They are wild waves of the sea, foaming up their shame; wandering stars, for whom blackest darkness has been reserved forever" (Jude 12*b*-13).

THE TENTH SUPRACULTURAL PRINCIPLE

Christians should be on guard against false teachers who are motivated by selfishness and greed and who exploit people with fabricated stories (2 Pet. 2:3*a*, 14*b*; Jude 12*a*).

In today's society, Christians should be on guard against the very same tactics. I have read enough "fund-raising" letters while being privy to the facts to know that these letters have been written by "experts in greed." Some of these letters contain "fabricated stories" designed to move people emotionally—stories that are exaggerated and, in some instances, cannot be verified. Though some of these stories contain "half truths," they are fabricated nevertheless.

Does this mean it is wrong to tell stories to motivate people to give and share their material possessions? Not at all. We need to know what the needs are, and there is no better way to communicate a need than to tell a real-life story. However, the story must be true in all respects.

Fund-raising letters are not wrong. Unfortunately, however, "experts in the field" have discovered that people do not respond to the simple facts. Most people have to be exposed to a crisis or something very dramatic before they will respond financially. Thus, the experts have learned how to get people to "open their pocketbooks." If there is no real crisis, part of their strategy is to create one. Or they will fabricate a breathtaking story, emphasizing particularly the dramatic aspects of conversion to Christ.

A lesson for Christians today is never to respond to fund-raising letters or any form of fund-raising appeal without knowing a great deal about the circumstances surrounding the appeal. This includes having a good awareness of the reputation of those who are involved. If Christians violate these cautions, they will respond to needs that do not exist and give money to organizations that are not accountable for the way in which they spend the money. Conversely, Christians who respond to these appeals are often neglecting their responsibility to support people who are truly in need and who will not resort to these kinds of tactics. This is perhaps the greater tragedy— and very discouraging to Christian leaders who are attempting to abide by the principles of Scripture.

JOHN'S THREE EPISTLES

The apostle John probably wrote his three epistles about the same time that he wrote his gospel. They were written for the churches in Asia sometime in the last third of the first century. Tension that existed between the Jews and Christians was virtually over. Theological arguments over justification by faith versus works had pretty much subsided.

The church faced a new problem. With a great number of Gentiles believing in Christ, Christians were faced with an heretical doctrine called gnosticism. Gnostics taught that "spirit is good" but "matter is evil." Consequently, this affected their view of Jesus Christ—how He, who was very God, could inhabit a material body. John wrote to help clarify the fact that Jesus Christ was in every sense the God-man, and anyone who denied that Jesus Christ had come in the flesh, could not be of God (1 John 2:22).

Regarding material possessions, John made a general statement in his first letter about the world and the things in the world. It is all-inclusive and certainly is a foundational passage for Christians to formulate their own biblical philosophy as to how they should view and use their material possessions.

1 JOHN 2:15-16

Do not love the world or anything in the world.
If anyone loves the world, the love of the Father
is not in him. For everything in the world—
the cravings of sinful man, the lust of his eyes
and the boasting of what he has and does—
comes not from the Father but from the world.

EXPOSITION

The world and the things of this world are normally not evil in themselves, including our material possessions. What God originally created "was very good" (Gen. 1:31). However, the entrance of sin into the world's system changed everything (Rom. 8:20-21). One of the results of sin has been for us to love what God has created rather than God Himself (Rom. 1:25). And when we do, we are on a toboggan slide of sinful behavior, motivated by the cravings of our sinful hearts, the lusts of our eyes, and the boasting of what we have and do.

Our material possessions, of course, are an intricate part of the world. And again, they are not sinful in themselves. That is why Paul made clear to Timothy that "the *love* of money is a root of all kinds of evil"—not money itself (1 Tim. 6:10).

Matter itself then is not evil—as the Gnostics taught. This is why Jesus Christ could become a man and inhabit a human body. Just so, Christians—who also live in bodies of flesh—can also live lives worthy of God, so long as they present their bodies to Him as a living sacrifice (Rom. 12:1). Furthermore, Christians can also possess material things and still use them for the glory of God.

We will be tempted, of course, to love what we have, so we must be on guard against the sinful cravings and lusts that are a part of our sinful nature, which has not been eradicated through conversion to Jesus Christ. This is also why Paul exhorted Timothy to "command those who are rich in this present world not to be arrogant nor to put their hope in wealth, which is so uncertain, but to put their hope in God, who richly provides us with everything for our enjoyment" (1 Tim. 6:17).

THE ELEVENTH SUPRACULTURAL PRINCIPLE

Christians must be on guard against establishing false distinctions between what is "material" and what is "spiritual" (1 John 2:15-16).

It should not surprise us that as believers we have difficulty harmonizing what belongs to us and what belongs to God. On the one hand, it is easy to *say* that everything we have is the Lord's (it eases our consciences) and then proceed to keep most of it for ourselves.

The "grace givers." This can easily happen to people who put a strong emphasis on the grace of God. For example, many of these people resist, and even resent, any kind of approach to giving that suggests percentages and particular amounts. They are quick to point out that we are under grace in the New Testament—not under law as in the Old Testament. They make clear that they do not believe that the Old Testament tithe system any longer applies.

However, many times when what these people actually give is recorded, measured, and evaluated, it does not come close to any form of regular or proportional giving. Unfortunately, some of these people actually use "grace" as an excuse for "license" and their tendency to "love money."

The "defensive givers." This false distinction is also manifested in the way some people react to messages on money. As long as their spiritual leaders concentrate on moral issues, they affirm what is being taught. But the moment they are exposed to what the Bible says about material possessions, they become defensive, uncomfortable, and sometimes critical. It should not surprise us that many of these people are the ones who have set up this false dichotomy in their spiritual lives and also represent those who are not regular and systematic givers. They have not integrated material possessions into their definition of spirituality.

The "secret givers." Another manifestation of this false dichotomy is the way in which Christians react against any form of openness regarding how they use their material possessions. They insist that this part of their life must be totally private and secret. Unfortunately, many people who take this approach are manifesting a guilty conscience, coming up with scriptural reasons to cover up their lack of faithfulness. A true perspective and interpretation as to what Scripture teaches regarding material possessions leads to *openness* rather than privacy (see pp. 83-85).

In conclusion, Christians who have a proper view of their material possessions and who are giving regularly, systematically, and proportionately are not defensive regarding the subject of money. In fact, they are just as excited about what the Bible teaches in this area as they are about the other great truths of Scripture. On the one hand, they enjoy the "things of this world" that have been given to them for their benefit and enjoyment. On the other hand, they do not love these things more than they love God. They do not allow their sinful cravings and the lust of their eyes to lead them to be materialists. Neither do they allow their tendency toward pride to lead to arrogance. They have properly integrated the *material* with the *spiritual*. They are seeking first the kingdom of God (Matt. 6:33).

2 JOHN 10-11

If anyone comes to you and does not bring this teaching
[that Jesus Christ has come in the flesh], do not take him
into your house or welcome him. Anyone who
welcomes him shares in his wicked work.

EXPOSITION

In Hebrews, Christians are encouraged to "entertain strangers" (Heb. 13:2). But the apostle John made very clear that "entertaining strangers" does not apply to those who deny the true nature of Jesus Christ. Here John was speaking directly to the form of gnosticism that began to penetrate Christian thought in the latter part of the first century. Since Gnostics were philosophical thinkers who taught that matter is evil and spirit is good, it follows naturally that they would deny that God as infinite pure spirit could inhabit a physical body. Consequently, they denied that Jesus Christ was perfect God and perfect man.

John's exhortation to not even allow this kind of person to enter one's house or his warning not even to greet such a one may seem contradictory to his repetitive emphasis on demonstrating love and acceptance to others. We must understand, however, that John was directing these concerns toward false teachers who were leading Christians astray and using these opportunities to take financial advantage of them. In that sense, they were like the "mere talkers and deceivers" Paul described in his letter to Titus. They were "ruining whole households by teaching things they ought not to teach —and that for the sake of sordid gain." Thus, Paul wrote, "they must be silenced" (Titus 1:10-11).

We must also understand that John was not addressing the issue of private hospitality per se. Rather, he was addressing participants in a *house church*: the "you" in "if anyone comes to you" is plural. In other words, these Christians were not to officially welcome this person to address the church body. To do so would be to expose these believers to what John earlier identified as a "deceiver" and an "anti-Christ" (2 John 7).

THE TWELFTH SUPRACULTURAL PRINCIPLE

Christians should not support religious teachers and leaders who claim to be Christians but who deny that Jesus Christ came as God in the flesh (2 John 10-11).

This principle provides a balance to the principle that Christians are to show hospitality, even to those we do not know personally. The Word of God also teaches that we are not to provide economic assistance for those who deliberately teach doctrines that contradict the teachings of Scripture.

And this principle applies in a specific way to those who do not have a correct view of Christ's deity and the incarnation.

Does this mean that a Christian should never invite a person inside his home who does not believe that Jesus Christ is God? Not at all. What John was teaching is that we should not open our home (and particularly our church) to show hospitality to false teachers. This, of course, is a different expression of love than to simply invite a person in to discuss the Scriptures.

Applied more specifically to the twentieth-century world, this principle means that Christians should not be in association with leaders who do not teach the truth regarding Jesus Christ. For example, Christians should not associate with a church where the leaders do not teach the deity of Christ. And by all means, they certainly should not give their money to support teachers and leaders in a church or organization that claims to be Christian but denies that Jesus Christ is God.

This, of course, provides another guideline for our giving. Not only must people and organizations be above reproach in the kind of life-style they promote in order to be worthy of financial support, but they must also be sound in doctrine.

3 John 5, 8

Dear friend, you are faithful in what you are doing
for the brothers, even though they are strangers to you. . . .
We ought therefore to show hospitality to such men
so that we may work together for the truth.

EXPOSITION

In this third letter, the Holy Spirit once again provides a balance that is so characteristic of Scripture. As we just noted, John warned against false teachers in his second letter and forbade these believers to show hospitality to the traveling so-called "Christian" missionaries who had a false view of Christ. But in his third letter, he commended Gaius for practicing hospitality toward *true* Christian workers.

Furthermore, John publicly exposed another church leader named Diotrephes who violated the principle of showing hospitality to God's servants. He actually refused to welcome the apostle John as well as other Christian leaders. He even excommunicated Christians from the church who attempted to practice the principle of hospitality (3 John 9-10). Diotrephes's motives and actions were based on selfishness. Thus, wrote John, he "loves to be first" (3 John 9*a*).

THE THIRTEENTH SUPRACULTURAL PRINCIPLE

Christian leaders who receive their financial support from the church they serve must be on guard against a selfishness that causes them to refuse to share financial help with other Christian leaders who are in need (3 John 5, 8).

Unfortunately, there are "Diotrepheses" in churches today—pastors who become self-oriented and refuse to support other Christian leaders and organizations simply because they want more for themselves. True, there must be balance here. It is not right for a church to increase its missionary budget and neglect to care for the financial needs of those who are ministering in that particular church. Oftentimes this mentality on the part of a church board or missionary committee actually becomes a stumbling block to the pastor who is struggling financially.

The other side of this issue, however, is when pastors develop a self-oriented approach to church finances and stand in the way of helping others. To do so is to violate the very heart of the Christian message. It is an ultimate form of hypocrisy. May God give us more spiritual leaders like Gaius and fewer like Diotrephes.

38

Revelation

Whether or not Revelation was the last book written in the New Testament canon does not invalidate the fact that its focus is on the end times. Revelation is unique in that it is the only piece of New Testament literature devoted exclusively to prophecy. Little is said about material possessions except in the short letter written to the church in Laodicea (see map on p. 348). What is said stands as an appropriate conclusion to what the New Testament has to say about how a Christian should view and use his material possessions.

REVELATION 3:17-18

You say, "I am rich; I have acquired wealth and
do not need a thing." But you do not realize that
you are wretched, pitiful, poor, blind and naked.
I counsel you to buy from Me gold refined in the fire,
so you can become rich; and white clothes to wear,
so you can cover your shameful nakedness;
and salve to put on your eyes, so you can see.

EXPOSITION

The church in Laodicea is the last of the seven churches mentioned in Revelation. Though I do not hold dogmatically to the theory that the seven churches forecast the development of the church throughout history, I cannot deny the fact that there appears to be a chronological unfolding of one basic truth—that is, the imminence of Christ's return grows more prominent in the exhortations that are given from church to church (see Rev. 2:5, 16, 25; 3:3, 11, 20). Christ's final exhortation to the church in Laodicea seems to be related to the grand culmination of history with His return: "Here I am! I stand at the door and knock" (3:20*a*).

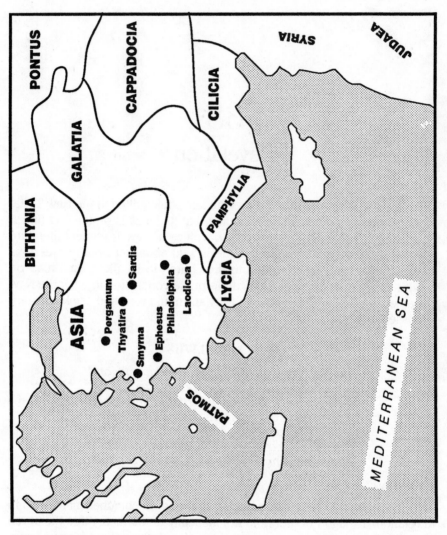

The Provinces of Asia Minor and the Seven Churches of Asia

The state of this final church is one that reflects a materialistic mind-set that has become conformed to the world's system. Jesus Christ made clear that it is possible to be lulled into complacency and a carnal state by cultural affluence. Again and again throughout this study, we have encountered warnings against this possibility. What is most dangerous, this can happen to Christians without their being aware of what is actually taking place.

Jesus pointed out that the Christians in Laodicea needed three things: gold, clothing, and eye salve. Gold symbolizes *faith* (1 Pet. 1:7). White garments symbolize true righteousness and *holiness* (Rev. 19:8). Salve for the eyes illustrates a *restored vision*—to be able to see clearly how materialistic they had become. In essence, Jesus was saying there is hope for churches who are Laodicean in nature. They can be restored and renewed.

THE FOURTEENTH SUPRACULTURAL PRINCIPLE

Christians must be on guard against self-deception and rationalization when they are living in an affluent society (Rev. 3:17-18).

This final principle from the book of Revelation is a fitting conclusion to our study. The apostle John was penning the very words that Jesus Christ spoke to him when he was in exile on the island of Patmos (1:9). In essence, Jesus was saying to Christians of all time that it is easy to be content with worldly wealth and to feel that we have everything we need. However, in reality we can have an abundance of material possessions but be "wretched, pitiful, poor, blind and naked" (3:17).

Unfortunately, this statement applies in a specific way to many Christians who live in twentieth-century American society. Never have we had more materially, but never have we given so little to the Lord's work. Ron Blue reports that "Sam Erickson of the Christian Legal Society once did a personal study of average charitable giving. His conclusion was that all Americans gave, on the average, 25 cents a day or $91 per year, and evangelical Christians gave an average of $1 a day or $365 per year."[1]

These statistics demonstrate that something is desperately wrong at "the heart" of American Christianity. Oftentimes, we listen to the Word of God being taught. We sing songs of praise. We claim to love God. But when it comes to giving, it appears that the majority of American Christians have "a form of godliness but" are "denying its power" (2 Tim. 3:5). Many of us are violating the Word of God, for we are not giving from our "firstfruits" systematically, regularly, and proportionately. If Jews under the Old Testament law gave an average of 23 percent of their annual income to do the work of God, how much should the average American Christian be giving in order to be a proportionate giver?

Specific Principles in Perspective from Part 7

1 TIMOTHY

1. All spiritual leaders in the church should be generous Christians who are willing to use their material possessions to serve those they shepherd and lead (3:2; Titus 1:6, 8).

2. Christians who occupy leadership roles in the church should be totally trustworthy when it comes to financial matters (3:2-3, 8; Titus 1:7-8).

3. The selection of people who receive consistent help from the church should be based upon specific scriptural guidelines (5:3-16).

4. Pastors and teachers who are hardworking, efficient, and productive in the ministry should be rewarded financially (5:17).

5. A Christian's first priority should be to focus on godliness and contentment rather than on riches, which often bring discontentment (6:6-10, 17-19).

TITUS

6. So-called Christian leaders who are teaching false doctrine and manipulating people in order to pursue dishonest gain should be silenced (1:10-11).

2 TIMOTHY

7. As the Day of Christ draws nearer, Christians should avoid the increasing tendency to intensify love for self, money, and pleasure (3:1-2*a*, 4*b*-5).

1 PETER

8. God allows periodic persecution to help Christians to put more emphasis on the spiritual and eternal dimensions of life rather than on the material and temporal (1:7, 18-19, 23-25*a*; 2:5, 11-12; 4:9; 5:2).

HEBREWS

9. All Christians are to show hospitality, not only to those believers in a specific local Christian community but to those whom they may not know personally (13:2, 5, 16).

2 PETER AND JUDE

10. Christians should be on guard against false teachers who are motivated by selfishness and greed and who exploit people with fabricated stories (2 Peter 2:3*a*, 14*b*; Jude 12*a*).

1 JOHN

11. Christians must be on guard against establishing false distinctions between what is "material" and what is "spiritual" (2:15-16).

2 JOHN

12. Christians should not support religious teachers and leaders who claim to be Christians but who deny that Jesus Christ came as God in the flesh (10-11).

3 JOHN

13. Christian leaders who receive their financial support from the church they serve must be on guard against a selfishness that causes them to refuse to share financial help with other Christian leaders who are in need (5, 8).

REVELATION

14. Christians must be on guard against self-deception and rationalization when they are living in an affluent society (3:17-18).

NOTE

1. Ron Blue, *Master Your Money* (Nashville: Thomas Nelson, 1986), p. 18.

Part 8

APPLYING BIBLICAL PRINCIPLES

This final section gives two perspectives. In chapter 39, all of the supracultural principles presented in this book and the basic biblical concepts accompanying these principles are outlined in chronological order as they appear in New Testament history. A practical question is posed with an evaluation scale to help apply each principle to local ministries.

In chapter 40, all of these principles are reorganized around twelve basic themes that emerge from an inductive study of these principles themselves. In addition, short captions are included with each principle for easy identification and communication.

These two chapters are designed to generate ideas for communicating these principles to others—in pulpit preaching and teaching, Sunday school classes, small discussion groups, board and committee meetings, and one-on-one discipling opportunities. Needless to say, what God says about material possessions and how Christians are to view and use them provides all of us with a vast amount of biblical content that can be communicated in a variety of teaching-learning situations.

39. Learning to Apply Supracultural Principles

40. A Systematic and Thematic Perspective

39

Learning to Apply
Supracultural Principles

Earlier it was stated that more is said in Scripture about material possessions and how Christians are to view and use them than about almost any other subject. A look at *all* of the supracultural principles that emerge from biblical functions, examples, and directives certainly verifies this conclusion.

Following are 126 *biblical concepts*, which include scriptural functions, examples, and directives that we have looked at in this study. Following each biblical concept is a *scriptural principle*, which—if correctly stated—is a supracultural truth that can be applied at any moment in history anywhere in the world. Finally, following each biblical concept and scriptural principle is a *practical question* to help Christians determine the degree to which their own local churches or ministries are practicing these principles.

A scale from one to ten helps evaluate the extent to which this principle is being applied. A "1" indicates the principle is being practiced "very little," and a "10" indicates the principle is being applied "very much." The numbers in between indicate degrees of application.

These scales can be filled out by church board members, pastors, other church leaders, finance committee members, Sunday school classes, or a whole congregation. Needless to say, all who participate will not only be evaluating local churches or ministries but will personally address the extent to which each is practicing these biblical principles himself.

PART 1: THE CHURCH IN JERUSALEM

1. *Biblical Concept.* The church in Jerusalem was "enjoying the favor of all the people" (Acts 2:47).

Scriptural Principle. As Christians use their material possessions in harmony with the will of God, it will encourage people to believe in Jesus Christ.

Practical Question. Are people in our community coming to know Jesus Christ because they see the believers in our church demonstrating unselfish and generous use of their material possessions to further the kingdom of God?

VERY LITTLE   VERY MUCH

1   2   3   4   5   6   7   8   9   10

2. *Biblical Concept.* "All the believers were one in heart and mind" (Acts 4:32).

Scriptural Principle. As Christians use their material possessions to meet one another's needs, it will create love and unity in the Body of Christ.

Practical Question. Are love and unity discernible in our church because believers are using their material possessions to meet one another's needs?

VERY LITTLE   VERY MUCH

1   2   3   4   5   6   7   8   9   10

3. *Biblical Concept.* The apostles' example (Acts 2:42).

Scriptural Principle. Spiritual leaders should model the way all Christians ought to use their material possessions.

Practical Question. Are the spiritual leaders in our church modeling the way all Christians should use their material possessions?

VERY LITTLE   VERY MUCH

1   2   3   4   5   6   7   8   9   10

4. *Biblical Concept.* "From time to time, those who owned lands and houses sold them, and brought the money from the sales and put it at the apostles' feet" (Acts 4:34-35).

Scriptural Principle. Christians should be willing to make special sacrifices in order to meet special material needs within the Body of Christ.

Practical Question. Do Christians in our church make special sacrifices to meet special material needs, particularly as they exist in our own local fellowship?

VERY LITTLE   VERY MUCH

1   2   3   4   5   6   7   8   9   10

5. *Biblical Concept.* "There were no needy persons among them. . . . The money from the sales . . . was distributed to anyone as he had need" (Acts 4:34-35).

Scriptural Principle. A primary motivating factor for consistent Christian giving should be to meet others' needs—particularly within the Body of Christ.

Practical Question. Are people in our church motivated to give because of human needs, especially within our local body?

VERY LITTLE   VERY MUCH
1   2   3   4   5   6   7   8   9   10

6. *Biblical Concept.* "Barnabas . . . sold a field he owned" (Acts 4:36).

Scriptural Principle. It is the will of God that Christians share their material possessions in order to encourage others in the Body of Christ.

Practical Question. Are individual Christians encouraging others in our church with their generous acts of love?

VERY LITTLE   VERY MUCH
1   2   3   4   5   6   7   8   9   10

7. *Biblical Concept.* The apostles gave Barnabas this new name to reflect his unselfish and generous spirit (Acts 4:36).

Scriptural Principle. Christians who are faithful in sharing their material possessions should be shown special appreciation.

Practical Question. Do we show special appreciation to those in our church who are faithful in sharing their material possessions?

VERY LITTLE   VERY MUCH
1   2   3   4   5   6   7   8   9   10

8. *Biblical Concept.* "Barnabas . . . brought the money and put it at the apostles' feet" (Acts 4:36-37).

Scriptural Principle. Christians need to be able to observe other believers who are faithful in sharing their material possessions.

Practical Question. Do the people in our church have opportunity to observe those believers who are especially faithful in sharing their material possessions?

VERY LITTLE   VERY MUCH
1   2   3   4   5   6   7   8   9   10

9. *Biblical Concept.* Barnabas contrasted with Ananias and Sapphira (Acts 4:34-36; 5:1-10).

Scriptural Principle. What Christians give should always be given to honor God and not themselves.

Practical Question. Do the people in our church give to honor God rather than themselves?

VERY LITTLE   VERY MUCH
1   2   3   4   5   6   7   8   9   10

10. *Biblical Concept.* God's punishment on Ananias and Sapphira (Acts 5:1-10).

    Scriptural Principle. God detests dishonesty, lack of integrity, and hypocrisy when it comes to giving.

    Practical Question. Is the giving in our church free from dishonesty, lack of integrity, and hypocrisy?

    VERY LITTLE   VERY MUCH
    1   2   3   4   5   6   7   8   9   10

11. *Biblical Concept.* Peter's questions to Ananias (Acts 5:4).

    Scriptural Principle. Though God wants all of His children to be generous, what Christians give should always be voluntary and from a heart of love and concern.

    Practical Question. Is the giving in our church motivated by concern for God and others and by a desire to see God's purposes fulfilled in the world?

    VERY LITTLE   VERY MUCH
    1   2   3   4   5   6   7   8   9   10

12. *Biblical Concept.* Organizing to meet the widows' needs (Acts 6:1-7).

    Scriptural Principle. It is God's will that every church have an efficient system for helping to meet the true material needs of others in the Body of Christ.

    Practical Question. Do we have an efficient and effective system for meeting the material needs of those in our church who are hurting financially?

    VERY LITTLE   VERY MUCH
    1   2   3   4   5   6   7   8   9   10

13. *Biblical Concept.* Seven men appointed to care for the widows (Acts 6:2-4).

    Scriptural Principle. Spiritual leaders in the church must at times delegate the administrative responsibilities to other qualified people who can assist them in meeting material needs.

    Practical Question. Do the spiritual leaders in our church (pastors, elders, etc.) look to other qualified people to help meet the material needs of others?

    VERY LITTLE   VERY MUCH
    1   2   3   4   5   6   7   8   9   10

14. *Biblical Concept.* The qualifications of those chosen to meet the widows' needs (Acts 6:3).

Scriptural Principle. Meeting the "spiritual needs" of people and meeting the "material needs" of people require the same high standard in terms of selecting leaders to meet these needs (Acts 6:3).

Practical Question. Do we require biblical qualifications for those who not only lead the church spiritually but for those who are selected to care for the material needs of people?

VERY LITTLE   VERY MUCH

1   2   3   4   5   6   7   8   9   10

General Principles from Part 1: The Church in Jerusalem

15. *Biblical Concept.* Example of the Jerusalem believers (Acts 2-6).

    Scriptural Principle. The way Christians use their material possessions is an important criterion for determining whether or not they are living in the will of God.

    Practical Question. Do the people in our church realize that the way in which they use their material possessions is an important way to determine the extent to which they are living in the will of God?

    VERY LITTLE   VERY MUCH

    1   2   3   4   5   6   7   8   9   10

16. *Biblical Concept.* Example of the Jerusalem believers (Acts 2-6).

    Scriptural Principle. It is by divine design that local churches provide the primary context in which Christians are to use their material possessions to further the work of God's kingdom.

    Practical Question. Do the people in our church financially support the ministry of our local fellowship?

    VERY LITTLE   VERY MUCH

    1   2   3   4   5   6   7   8   9   10

17. *Biblical Concept.* Example of the Jerusalem believers (Acts 2-6).

    Scriptural Principle. Christians should respond immediately to whatever portion of God's truth they have received.

    Practical Question. Are the people in our church responding according to what they already know about God's will in giving?

    VERY LITTLE   VERY MUCH

    1   2   3   4   5   6   7   8   9   10

18. *Biblical Concept.* Example of the Jerusalem believers (Acts 2-6).

    Scriptural Principle. The expectancy of the second coming of Jesus Christ should always be a strong motivational factor in the way Christians view and use their material possessions.

Practical Question. Are the people in our church motivated to give by the truth that Jesus Christ could come at any moment and require an accounting of how they used their material possessions?

VERY LITTLE   VERY MUCH

1   2   3   4   5   6   7   8   9   10

19. *Biblical Concept.* Example of the Jerusalem believers (Acts 2-6).

Scriptural Principle. As we obey God, He will clarify and help us understand His specific plans, enabling us to more and more live by faith and respond to His will.

Practical Question. Are the people in our church willing to trust God in their giving, realizing that He will give them more and more clarification as to how He wants them to use their material possessions?

VERY LITTLE   VERY MUCH

1   2   3   4   5   6   7   8   9   10

20. *Biblical Concept.* Example of the Jerusalem believers (Acts 2-6).

Scriptural Principle. God's plan for Israel in the Old Testament serves as a foundational model regarding the way Christians should view and use their material possessions today.

Practical Question. Does God's Old Testament model challenge the people in our church to give regularly, systematically, and proportionately?

VERY LITTLE   VERY MUCH

1   2   3   4   5   6   7   8   9   10

PART 2: THE TEACHINGS OF JESUS CHRIST

21. *Biblical Concept.* "Blessed are the poor in spirit for theirs is the kingdom of heaven" (Matt. 5:3).

Scriptural Principle. Having a lot of material things often makes it difficult for people to recognize and acknowledge their need of God in salvation.

Practical Question. Does affluence in our community make it difficult for those in our church to reach people with the gospel?

VERY LITTLE   VERY MUCH

1   2   3   4   5   6   7   8   9   10

22. *Biblical Concept.* "First go and be reconciled to your brother, then come and offer your gift" (Matt. 5:24).

Scriptural Principle. Material gifts are acceptable and "well pleasing" to God only when Christians have done their part to be in harmony with their brothers and sisters in Christ.

Practical Question. Do people in our church understand that their gifts are acceptable to God based upon their personal efforts to have a clear conscience in their relationships with other Christians?

VERY LITTLE								VERY MUCH	
1	2	3	4	5	6	7	8	9	10

23. *Biblical Concept.* "Give to the one who asks you, and do not turn away from the one who wants to borrow from you" (Matt. 5:42).

    Scriptural Principle. Christians should not only give to those who love them and care for them but also to those who may resent them and even try to harm them.

    Practical Question. Do the people in our church actually reach out and help in material ways those who may actually resent them or the message of Jesus Christ?

VERY LITTLE								VERY MUCH	
1	2	3	4	5	6	7	8	9	10

24. *Biblical Concept.* "But when you give to the needy, do not let your left hand know what your right hand is doing so that your giving may be in secret" (Matt. 6:3-4).

    Scriptural Principle. Christians should periodically check their motives to see if they are giving to glorify God or to glorify themselves.

    Practical Question. Do we encourage people in our church to periodically evaluate their motives for giving?

VERY LITTLE								VERY MUCH	
1	2	3	4	5	6	7	8	9	10

25. *Biblical Concept.* "Give us today our daily bread" (Matt. 6:11).

    Scriptural Principle. Christ wants Christians to pray for daily sustenance.

    Practical Question. Do the people in our church not only thank God for their material possessions but also ask Him to continue to meet their daily needs?

VERY LITTLE								VERY MUCH	
1	2	3	4	5	6	7	8	9	10

26. *Biblical Concept.* "Do not store up for yourselves treasures on earth ... but store up for yourselves treasures in heaven" (Matt. 6:19-20).

    Scriptural Principle. Whatever excess material possessions God enables Christians to accumulate should be used in creative ways to further the kingdom of God.

Practical Question. Do the people in our church use their excess material possessions in creative ways to carry out God's work in the world?

VERY LITTLE   VERY MUCH

| 1 | 2 | 3 | 4 | 5 | 6 | 7 | 8 | 9 | 10 |

27. *Biblical Concept.* "For where your treasure is, there your heart will be also" (Matt. 6:21).

Scriptural Principle. Christians can determine their true perspective toward material possessions by evaluating the consistent thoughts and attitudes of their hearts.

Practical Question. Do the people in our church focus their attention on their material possessions rather than on doing God's will in every respect?

VERY LITTLE   VERY MUCH

| 1 | 2 | 3 | 4 | 5 | 6 | 7 | 8 | 9 | 10 |

28. *Biblical Concept.* "No one can serve two masters. . . . You cannot serve both God and money" (Matt. 6:24).

Scriptural Principle. It is possible for a Christian to be in bondage to material possessions.

Practical Question. Are the people in our church in bondage to their material possessions?

VERY LITTLE   VERY MUCH

| 1 | 2 | 3 | 4 | 5 | 6 | 7 | 8 | 9 | 10 |

29. *Biblical Concept.* "But seek first his kingdom and his righteousness, and all these will be given to you as well" (Matt. 6:33).

Scriptural Principle. If Christians put God first in all things, He has promised to meet their material needs.

Practical Question. Are the people in our church putting God first in all things and trusting Him to then meet their material needs?

VERY LITTLE   VERY MUCH

| 1 | 2 | 3 | 4 | 5 | 6 | 7 | 8 | 9 | 10 |

30. *Biblical Concept.* "Therefore do not worry about tomorrow, for tomorrow will worry about itself" (Matt. 6:34).

Scriptural Principle. It is not the will of God that Christians be absorbed with worry about the future and how their material needs will be met.

Practical Question. Are the people in our church anxious and worried about their material needs?

VERY LITTLE   VERY MUCH

| 1 | 2 | 3 | 4 | 5 | 6 | 7 | 8 | 9 | 10 |

31. *Biblical Concept.* "And if anyone gives a cup of cold water to one of these little ones because he is my disciple, I tell you the truth, he will certainly not lose his reward" (Matt. 10:42).

    Scriptural Principle. God honors Christians in a special way when they meet the material needs of those who truly serve God.

    Practical Question. Do the people in our church understand that God will honor them in a special way when they meet the material needs of their spiritual leaders?

    VERY LITTLE   VERY MUCH
    1   2   3   4   5   6   7   8   9   10

32. *Biblical Concept.* "Honor your father and mother" (Matt. 15:4-6).

    Scriptural Principle. Christian children who are able should make sure that they care for their parents' physical needs.

    Practical Question. Do the grown children in our church take proper care of their parents if they have special material needs?

    VERY LITTLE   VERY MUCH
    1   2   3   4   5   6   7   8   9   10

33. *Biblical Concept.* "But many who are first will be last, and many who are last will be first" (Matt. 19:30).

    Scriptural Principle. God will reward Christians in His eternal kingdom on the basis of the degree of sacrifice involved in their giving.

    Practical Question. Do the people in our church understand that eternal rewards will be based upon the degree to which they make special sacrifices in sharing their material possessions to further God's work?

    VERY LITTLE   VERY MUCH
    1   2   3   4   5   6   7   8   9   10

34. *Biblical Concept.* "You give a tenth of your spices—mint, dill and cummin. But you have neglected the more important matters of the law —justice, mercy and faithfulness" (Matt. 23:23*b*).

    Scriptural Principle. Christians who give regularly and faithfully are invalidating the acceptability of their gifts to God when they neglect to love God and one another.

    Practical Question. Do the people in our church understand that their gifts are not acceptable to God when they do not love God and their brothers and sisters in Christ?

    VERY LITTLE   VERY MUCH
    1   2   3   4   5   6   7   8   9   10

GENERAL PRINCIPLES FROM PART 2: THE TEACHINGS OF JESUS CHRIST

35. *Biblical Concept.* The gospels.

Scriptural Principle. The truths that Jesus taught about material possessions are normative and supracultural.

Practical Question. Do the people in our church understand and obey Jesus' teachings about material possessions?

VERY LITTLE   VERY MUCH
1   2   3   4   5   6   7   8   9   10

36. *Biblical Concept.* The apostles' special revelation from the Holy Spirit (John 14:25-26).

Scriptural Principle. Christians must be careful not to evaluate subjectively what they believe is the Holy Spirit's leading when it comes to giving.

Practical Question. Do the people in our church realize that "inner promptings" to give certain amounts may be more motivated by selfish desires than by God's Holy Spirit?

VERY LITTLE   VERY MUCH
1   2   3   4   5   6   7   8   9   10

37. *Biblical Concept.* Jesus' parables.

Scriptural Principle. Christian leaders should develop an awareness of the economic structures and practices in every culture in which they are attempting to communicate God's truth in order to utilize these economic experiences to teach people spiritual truths.

Practical Question. Do the leaders in our church understand business philosophy and structures in our larger community and use illustrations from these business structures to relate spiritual truths to all of us?

VERY LITTLE   VERY MUCH
1   2   3   4   5   6   7   8   9   10

38. *Biblical Concept.* The apostles' example and personal experience.

Scriptural Principle. Spiritual leaders are responsible to teach believers in the church what God says about material possessions.

Practical Question. Do the spiritual leaders in our church teach our people God's will regarding how to view and use their material possessions?

VERY LITTLE   VERY MUCH
1   2   3   4   5   6   7   8   9   10

39. *Biblical Concept.* The Old and New Testament Scriptures (Mark 6:8-13; Luke 9:1-6).

Scriptural Principle. Economic policies for meeting the physical needs of Christian leaders who devote their full time to ministry must be built upon the totality of God's Word.

Practical Question. Have we developed our missionary support policy on a biblical theology of giving?

VERY LITTLE   VERY MUCH
1   2   3   4   5   6   7   8   9   10

40. *Biblical Concept.* The New Testament Scriptures (Matt. 19:28-29).

Scriptural Principle. Believers should be motivated to share their material possessions in hopes of receiving present blessings; however, they must realize that the most important perspective in Scripture involves eternal blessings and that their reward may not come in this life.

Practical Question. Are the people in our church primarily motivated to give by what they believe will be a financial return on this earth?

VERY LITTLE   VERY MUCH
1   2   3   4   5   6   7   8   9   10

41. *Biblical Concept.* The New Testament Scriptures.

Scriptural Principle. Christians today should apply the principles as taught by Christ and modeled by New Testament Christians, utilizing forms and methods that are relevant in their own particular cultures.

Practical Question. Has our church developed programs and patterns of giving based upon a biblical theology of material possessions?

VERY LITTLE   VERY MUCH
1   2   3   4   5   6   7   8   9   10

PART 3: MOVING BEYOND JERUSALEM

42. *Biblical Concept.* Persecution in Jerusalem (Acts 8:1-3).

Scriptural Principle. God sometimes allows difficulties and discomforts to come into Christians' experiences in order to refocus their priorities on eternal values.

Practical Question. Do I think that God has allowed difficulties to come into the lives of the people in our church to help refocus priorities on eternal values?

VERY LITTLE   VERY MUCH
1   2   3   4   5   6   7   8   9   10

43. *Biblical Concept.* Simon the sorcerer's desire to use Christianity to benefit himself financially (Acts 8:9-25).

Scriptural Principle. Wherever Christianity is active, some people will attempt to use the Christian message to benefit themselves.

Practical Question. Are there people in our local church or community that are using the message of Christianity primarily to benefit themselves?

VERY LITTLE   VERY MUCH

1   2   3   4   5   6   7   8   9   10

44. *Biblical Concept.* Simon the sorcerer compared with Ananias and Sapphira (Acts 8:9-25).

Scriptural Principle. God is sometimes more patient with uninformed people who are materialistic than He is with people who have more direct exposure to the truth.

Practical Question. Are self-serving people in our church taking advantage of God's patience and grace?

VERY LITTLE   VERY MUCH

1   2   3   4   5   6   7   8   9   10

45. *Biblical Concept.* Reaching the Ethiopian eunuch for Christ (Acts 8:26-40).

Scriptural Principle. Though it is often difficult for wealthy people to respond to the gospel, it is God's will that we reach these people, for they can influence great segments of humanity with both their social position and their material resources.

Practical Question. Are some in our church impacting people of prominence and wealth by reaching them with the gospel and then enabling these people to impact their own peers with the message of salvation?

VERY LITTLE   VERY MUCH

1   2   3   4   5   6   7   8   9   10

46. *Biblical Concept.* Reaching Cornelius and his household for Christ (Acts 10:1-48).

Scriptural Principle. It is God's will that Christians who have been blessed with material resources use their homes in special ways to offer hospitality to other believers.

Practical Question. Are the people in our church demonstrating hospitality to both Christians and non-Christians by using their homes to entertain, conduct Bible studies, and host other small group meetings?

VERY LITTLE   VERY MUCH

1   2   3   4   5   6   7   8   9   10

47. *Biblical Concept.* Philip the evangelist (Acts 8:5, 26, 40).

Scriptural Principle. God desires to use people with material resources who can give great segments of their time to the ministry while still providing for their families.

Practical Question. Do people in our church who are relatively well-to-do use their resources to enable them to devote large segments of time to ministry?

VERY LITTLE   VERY MUCH

| 1 | 2 | 3 | 4 | 5 | 6 | 7 | 8 | 9 | 10 |

48. *Biblical Concept.* Dorcas's benevolent acts of love (Acts 9:32-43).

    Scriptural Principle. God desires to use Christians who may not have an abundance of material possessions but who unselfishly use what they have, including their skills, to do the work of God.

    Practical Question. Do people in our church who have very little of this world's goods use their talents and abilities to serve others?

VERY LITTLE   VERY MUCH

| 1 | 2 | 3 | 4 | 5 | 6 | 7 | 8 | 9 | 10 |

49. *Biblical Concept.* Dorcas's benevolent acts of love (Acts 9:32-43).

    Scriptural Principle. Christians who are unselfish and benevolent become a unique verification to non-Christians that Jesus Christ is indeed the Son of God.

    Practical Question. Are the acts of benevolence and love by the people in our church impacting the non-Christian community with the gospel?

VERY LITTLE   VERY MUCH

| 1 | 2 | 3 | 4 | 5 | 6 | 7 | 8 | 9 | 10 |

50. *Biblical Concept.* Cornelius's conversion to Christ (Acts 10:1-48).

    Scriptural Principle. God's heart responds to non-Christians who are sincerely seeking to please Him and who express their sincerity through being generous with their material possessions.

    Practical Question. Are the people in our church in loving contact with unsaved individuals who are basically God-fearing and unselfish, in order to help them come to know Jesus Christ personally?

VERY LITTLE   VERY MUCH

| 1 | 2 | 3 | 4 | 5 | 6 | 7 | 8 | 9 | 10 |

51. *Biblical Concept.* The church in Antioch (Acts 11:19-30).

    Scriptural Principle. When Christians in a particular culture are excluded from social benefits because of their faith in Christ, other believers should set up some type of welfare system to take care of valid human needs.

Practical Question. Does our church help believers outside our own local fellowship who are in physical need and do not have access to sufficient resources to meet their needs?

VERY LITTLE   VERY MUCH

1   2   3   4   5   6   7   8   9   10

52. *Biblical Concept.* All the believers in Antioch (Acts 11:19-30).

Scriptural Principle. All Christians, according to their ability, should be involved in sharing their material possessions to carry on God's work in the world.

Practical Question. Is every believer in our church involved in sharing what he has to help others in need?

VERY LITTLE   VERY MUCH

1   2   3   4   5   6   7   8   9   10

PART 4: THE GENTILE CHURCH AND ITS EXPANDED MISSION

53. *Biblical Concept.* "The brother in humble circumstances ought to take pride in his high position" (James 1:9).

Scriptural Principle. Christians in the church who do not have a lot of material possessions should not feel inferior to those who have more.

Practical Question. Do most Christians in our church who do not have a lot of material possessions feel comfortable and accepted?

VERY LITTLE   VERY MUCH

1   2   3   4   5   6   7   8   9   10

54. *Biblical Concept.* "But the one who is rich should take pride in his low position because he will pass away like a wild flower" (James 1:10).

Scriptural Principle. Christians who have a lot of material possessions should demonstrate humility, realizing that their only true treasures are those they have stored up in heaven.

Practical Question. Do affluent Christians in our church demonstrate true humility in their relationships with their fellow Christians who do not have as much of this world's goods as they do?

VERY LITTLE   VERY MUCH

1   2   3   4   5   6   7   8   9   10

55. *Biblical Concept.* "Religion that God our Father accepts as pure and faultless is this: to look after orphans and widows in their distress" (James 1:27a).

Scriptural Principle. People who are in physical need have a special place in God's heart, and Christians who help meet these needs also have a special place in God's heart.

Practical Question. Do the people in our church understand the special place God has in His heart for those who have serious physical needs and for those who help meet these needs?

VERY LITTLE   VERY MUCH

1   2   3   4   5   6   7   8   9   10

56. *Biblical Concept.* "My brothers, as believers in our glorious Lord Jesus Christ, don't show favoritism" (James 2:1).

Scriptural Principle. Christians should never show favoritism toward people who have an abundance of material possessions; conversely, Christians should never be prejudiced against people who have few material possessions.

Practical Question. Are the Christians in our church free from showing favoritism to affluent people and at the same time free from prejudice against the poor?

VERY LITTLE   VERY MUCH

1   2   3   4   5   6   7   8   9   10

57. *Biblical Concept.* "In the same way, faith by itself, if it is not accompanied by action, is dead" (James 2:17).

Scriptural Principle. One of the most significant ways saving faith is tested as to its validity and reality is the way in which professing Christians view and use their material possessions.

Practical Question. Are the people in our church reflecting the reality of their conversion to Christ by being generous, unselfish Christians?

VERY LITTLE   VERY MUCH

1   2   3   4   5   6   7   8   9   10

58. *Biblical Concept.* "Instead, you ought to say, 'If it is the Lord's will, we will live and do this or that'" (James 4:15).

Scriptural Principle. All economic and financial planning should be done with an intense desire to be in the will of God in every respect.

Practical Question. Do the people in our church do all of their economic and financial planning with an intense desire to be in the will of God?

VERY LITTLE   VERY MUCH

1   2   3   4   5   6   7   8   9   10

59. *Biblical Concept.* "Now listen, you rich people, weep and wail because of the misery that is coming upon you" (James 5:1).

Scriptural Principle. Non-Christians who put their faith in material possessions and who abuse and misuse other people in order to accumulate wealth must be warned that they will eventually be judged severely by God Himself.

Practical Question. Has our church developed a way to sensitively communicate with unbelievers in our community that putting their faith and hope in material things will ultimately lead to disillusionment in this life and separation from God in the next?

VERY LITTLE   VERY MUCH

1   2   3   4   5   6   7   8   9   10

60. *Biblical Concept.* The teachings of the New Testament compared with James 5:1-3.

Scriptural Principle. Accumulating wealth brings with it specific temptations for both Christians and non-Christians.

Practical Question. Do the Christians in our church understand the subtle temptations that accompany the accumulation of material possessions?

VERY LITTLE   VERY MUCH

1   2   3   4   5   6   7   8   9   10

61. *Biblical Concept.* "Anyone who receives instruction in the word must share all good things with his instructor" (Gal. 6:6).

Scriptural Principle. Local church leaders whose primary ministry is teaching the Word of God should be given priority consideration in receiving financial support.

Practical Question. Do the people in our church consider it a priority in their giving to financially support their pastors who faithfully teach them the Word of God?

VERY LITTLE   VERY MUCH

1   2   3   4   5   6   7   8   9   10

62. *Biblical Concept.* "Therefore, as we have opportunity, let us do good to all people, especially to those who belong to the family of believers" (Gal. 6:10).

Scriptural Principle. Christians should plan ahead so they can be prepared to minister economically, first and foremost, to their fellow Christians who are in need but without neglecting non-Christians.

Practical Question. Do people in our church plan their giving so that they not only give regularly, systematically, and proportionately but also have funds set aside to meet emergency needs in carrying out God's work?

VERY LITTLE   VERY MUCH

1   2   3   4   5   6   7   8   9   10

PART 5: PAUL'S MISSION: THE SECOND JOURNEY

63. *Biblical Concept.* Paul's, Silas's, and Timothy's example (1 Thess. 2:9).

Scriptural Principle. Christian leaders should look to fellow Christians for financial support, not to the unbelievers they are attempting to reach with the gospel.

Practical Question. Does our church encourage members who are interested in missionary work to develop ministry and serving relationships with Christians before they seek financial support?

VERY LITTLE								VERY MUCH	
1	2	3	4	5	6	7	8	9	10

64. *Biblical Concept.* "Make it your ambition . . . to work with your hands . . . so that you will not be dependent upon anybody" (1 Thess. 4:11-12).

    Scriptural Principle. Christians should work hard to provide for their economic needs so that they are not criticized by unbelievers for being lazy and irresponsible.

    Practical Question. Do people in our church maintain a strong work ethic so as to be a good example to those in the community who do not know Christ?

VERY LITTLE								VERY MUCH	
1	2	3	4	5	6	7	8	9	10

65. *Biblical Concept.* "In the name of the Lord Jesus Christ, we command you, brothers, to keep away from every brother who is idle and does not live according to the teaching you received from us" (2 Thess. 3:6).

    Scriptural Principle. Christians should separate themselves from other Christians who are persistently irresponsible in not providing for their own economic needs.

    Practical Question. Do the leaders in our church apply principles of church discipline, in this case as it relates to Christians who are lazy and irresponsible?

VERY LITTLE								VERY MUCH	
1	2	3	4	5	6	7	8	9	10

66. *Biblical Concept.* "If a man will not work, he shall not eat" (2 Thess. 3:10*b*).

    Scriptural Principle. Christians who can, but do not, work for a living should not be given economic assistance.

    Practical Question. Are the people in our church cautious about financially helping people who may be taking advantage and, at the same time, practicing principles of love and caring for those who are truly in need?

VERY LITTLE								VERY MUCH	
1	2	3	4	5	6	7	8	9	10

67. *Biblical Concept.* "In the same way, the Lord has commanded that those who preach the gospel should receive their living from the gospel. But I have not used any of these rights" (1 Cor. 9:14-15a).

Scriptural Principle. Even though God has commanded that spiritual leaders be cared for financially by those they minister to, there are times when it is the part of wisdom for spiritual leaders to give up that right.

Practical Question. Are the spiritual leaders in our church committed to avoiding any activity that could be interpreted by unbelievers or immature Christians as taking unfair advantage of people financially?

VERY LITTLE   VERY MUCH
1   2   3   4   5   6   7   8   9   10

68. *Biblical Concept.* "On the first day of every week, each one of you should set aside a sum of money in keeping with his income" (1 Cor. 16:2).

Scriptural Principle. Christians should set aside a certain percentage of their income on just as regular a basis as they are paid in order to be able to systematically give to God's work.

Practical Question. Do all believers in our church set aside a portion of every paycheck to be given to the Lord's work?

VERY LITTLE   VERY MUCH
1   2   3   4   5   6   7   8   9   10

69. *Biblical Concept.* Paul's example (1 Cor. 16:3-4).

Scriptural Principle. Those who handle and distribute monies that are given to God's work should be above reproach in all respects and should be held accountable.

Practical Question. Are those who handle the money in our church accountable and above reproach in every respect?

VERY LITTLE   VERY MUCH
1   2   3   4   5   6   7   8   9   10

70. *Biblical Concept.* The example of the Macedonian churches (2 Cor. 8:1-2).

Scriptural Principle. Every local body of believers needs real-life examples of other churches that are positive models in the area of giving.

Practical Question. Are people in our church exposed to other churches who are positive models in the area of giving?

VERY LITTLE   VERY MUCH
1   2   3   4   5   6   7   8   9   10

71. *Biblical Concept.* "So we urged Titus, since he had earlier made a be-ginning, to bring also to completion this act of grace on your part" (2 Cor. 8:6, 10-11; 2 Cor. 9:3).

    Scriptural Principle. Christians need to be held accountable when they make financial commitments to God's work.

    Practical Question. Are all believers in our church held accountable when they make financial commitments to God's work?

    VERY LITTLE   VERY MUCH
    1   2   3   4   5   6   7   8   9   10

72. *Biblical Concept.* "But just as you excel in everything . . . see that you also excel in this grace of giving" (2 Cor. 8:7).

    Scriptural Principle. It is God's will that all Christians excel in the grace of giving.

    Practical Question. Do all of the believers in our church excel in their financial commitment to God's work?

    VERY LITTLE   VERY MUCH
    1   2   3   4   5   6   7   8   9   10

73. *Biblical Concept.* "For you know the grace of our Lord Jesus Christ, that though he was rich, yet for your sakes he became poor, so that you through his poverty might become rich" (2 Cor. 8:8-9).

    Scriptural Principle. God does not want Christians to respond to a com-mand to share their material possessions but, rather, to respond out of hearts of love that reflect sincere appreciation for His gift of salvation.

    Practical Question. Are all believers in our church giving to God's work primarily out of hearts of love rather than from a sense of obligation?

    VERY LITTLE   VERY MUCH
    1   2   3   4   5   6   7   8   9   10

74. *Biblical Concept.* "For if the willingness is there, the gift is acceptable according to what one has, not according to what he does not have" (2 Cor. 8:10-12).

    Scriptural Principle. God accepts and honors believers' gifts once they begin to give regularly and systematically, even though they may not be able to give as proportionately as they eventually will be able to once they have their economic lives in order.

    Practical Question. Do the believers in the church understand that, once they begin to give regularly and systematically, God honors their gifts based upon their willingness to give at that moment in their lives?

    VERY LITTLE   VERY MUCH
    1   2   3   4   5   6   7   8   9   10

75. *Biblical Concept.* "Our desire is not that others might be relieved while you are hard pressed, but that there might be equality" (2 Cor. 8:13-14).

    Scriptural Principle. It is not the will of God that some Christians cannot meet their physical needs while other Christians with abundance could help them in their time of need.

    Practical Question. Do people in our church who have abundance realize that they should be willing to share some of their excess with other Christians in crises who are unable to care for their physical needs at that particular time in their lives?

    VERY LITTLE   VERY MUCH
    1   2   3   4   5   6   7   8   9   10

76. *Biblical Concept.* Paul's example (2 Cor. 8:16-19, 22-24; 2 Cor. 9:3-4).

    Scriptural Principle. It is the will of God that no one particular Christian leader have to handle the financial needs of the Christian community alone.

    Practical Question. Do leaders other than our primary pastor help carry the burden for meeting the financial needs of our church?

    VERY LITTLE   VERY MUCH
    1   2   3   4   5   6   7   8   9   10

77. *Biblical Concept.* "Your enthusiasm has stirred most of them to action" (2 Cor. 9:2).

    Scriptural Principle. Christians who are generous will motivate other Christians to also be generous.

    Practical Question. Does our church stand out as an example in motivating other churches to be generous with their material possessions?

    VERY LITTLE   VERY MUCH
    1   2   3   4   5   6   7   8   9   10

78. *Biblical Concept.* "For if any Macedonians come with me and find you unprepared, we—not to say anything about you—would be ashamed of having been so confident" (2 Cor. 9:3-4).

    Scriptural Principle. Christians who make commitments financially should be on guard against embarrassing their spiritual leaders, as well as themselves, by being negligent in following through on their commitments.

    Practical Question. Do the people in our church maintain their financial commitments to the Lord so as not to be an embarrassment to themselves or our spiritual leaders?

    VERY LITTLE   VERY MUCH
    1   2   3   4   5   6   7   8   9   10

79. *Biblical Concept.* "So I thought it necessary to urge the brothers to visit you in advance and finish the arrangements for the generous gift you had promised" (2 Cor. 9:5a).

Scriptural Principle. God wants Christians to take a step of faith and trust Him to enable them to be able to give certain amounts of money based upon future earnings.

Practical Question. Do the Christians in our church include God in their financial planning, trusting Him to make it possible through future earnings to give regularly, systematically, and proportionately?

VERY LITTLE   VERY MUCH

| 1 | 2 | 3 | 4 | 5 | 6 | 7 | 8 | 9 | 10 |

80. *Biblical Concept.* "Then it will be ready as a generous gift, not as one grudgingly given" (2 Cor. 9:5b).

Scriptural Principle. Christians should organize and plan their giving in a systematic way so that they can give generously and not respond in a grudging fashion.

Practical Question. Do the Christians in our church give joyfully because the money is available through careful and systematic planning?

VERY LITTLE   VERY MUCH

| 1 | 2 | 3 | 4 | 5 | 6 | 7 | 8 | 9 | 10 |

81. *Biblical Concept.* "Remember this: Whoever sows sparingly will also reap sparingly, and whoever sows generously will also reap generously" (2 Cor. 9:6).

Scriptural Principle. Christians who are generous in their giving will receive generous blessings; conversely, Christians who are not generous in their giving will not receive generous blessings.

Practical Question. Do Christians understand the fallacy of prosperity theology but, at the same time, understand the true nature of the blessings God wants to bestow on those who are faithful in their giving?

VERY LITTLE   VERY MUCH

| 1 | 2 | 3 | 4 | 5 | 6 | 7 | 8 | 9 | 10 |

82. *Biblical Concept.* "Each man should give what he has decided in his heart to give, not reluctantly or under compulsion, for God loves a cheerful giver" (2 Cor. 9:7).

Scriptural Principle. Every Christian is ultimately responsible to give to God on the basis of his own heart decision.

Practical Question. Are the Christians in our church making decisions to give based upon internal motivation rather than simply from a sense of obligation?

VERY LITTLE   VERY MUCH

| 1 | 2 | 3 | 4 | 5 | 6 | 7 | 8 | 9 | 10 |

83. *Biblical Concept.* "And God is able to make all grace abound to you, so that in all things at all times, having all that you need, you will abound in every good work" (2 Cor. 9:8).

    Scriptural Principle. When Christians are faithful in their giving, God has promised to meet their needs.

    Practical Question. Do the people in our church believe that God will meet their physical needs if they are faithful in their giving?

    VERY LITTLE   VERY MUCH
    1   2   3   4   5   6   7   8   9   10

84. *Biblical Concept.* "You will be made rich in every way so that you can be generous on every occasion" (2 Cor. 9:11).

    Scriptural Principle. When Christians are generous, God has promised to enable them to continue to be generous.

    Practical Question. Are the believers in our church able to continue to give to God's work on a regular basis because they have already become faithful givers?

    VERY LITTLE   VERY MUCH
    1   2   3   4   5   6   7   8   9   10

85. *Biblical Concept.* "Your generosity will result in thanksgiving to God" (2 Cor. 9:11-13).

    Scriptural Principle. Generous Christians cause others to praise and worship God.

    Practical Question. Do other Christians praise and worship God because the believers in our church are faithful in their giving?

    VERY LITTLE   VERY MUCH
    1   2   3   4   5   6   7   8   9   10

86. *Biblical Concept.* "And in their prayers for you their hearts will go out to you, because of the surpassing grace God has given you" (2 Cor. 9:14).

    Scriptural Principle. People respect and love Christians who are unselfish and generous.

    Practical Question. Do the believers in our church understand that they will be greatly respected and loved by other believers if they become faithful givers?

    VERY LITTLE   VERY MUCH
    1   2   3   4   5   6   7   8   9   10

87. *Biblical Concept.* New Testament examples.

    Scriptural Principle. The local church is God's primary context for maintaining accountability in the area of material possessions.

Practical Question. Do the people in our church realize that one reason God ordained the local church is that they can be assured that the money they give is used in a responsible and God-honoring way?

VERY LITTLE   VERY MUCH

1   2   3   4   5   6   7   8   9   10

88. *Biblical Concept.* Paul's example.

Scriptural Principle. It is important that Christian leaders maintain a high level of communication in order to enable Christians to be obedient to God's will in the way they use their material possessions.

Practical Question. Have the leaders in our church developed a communication methodology that enables them to communicate efficiently and continually but sensitively about our responsibility to share material possessions?

VERY LITTLE   VERY MUCH

1   2   3   4   5   6   7   8   9   10

PART 6: PAUL'S MISSION: THE THIRD JOURNEY AND IMPRISONMENT

89. *Biblical Concept.* "Give everyone what you owe him: If you owe taxes, pay taxes; if revenue, then revenue" (Rom. 13:6-7).

Scriptural Principle. Christians should always be responsible and honest citizens in their own societies by paying all governmental taxes and revenues.

Practical Question. Are the people in our church faithful and honest in paying taxes and revenues to local, state, and federal governmental agencies?

VERY LITTLE   VERY MUCH

1   2   3   4   5   6   7   8   9   10

90. *Biblical Concept.* "Let no debt remain outstanding, except the continuing debt to love one another" (Rom. 13:8).

Scriptural Principle. Christians who owe money or goods should always pay what they owe.

Practical Question. Do people in our church pay money to those to whom they owe money?

VERY LITTLE   VERY MUCH

1   2   3   4   5   6   7   8   9   10

91. *Biblical Concept.* "For if the Gentiles have shared in the Jews' spiritual blessings, they owe it to the Jews to share with them their material blessings" (Rom. 15:27).

Scriptural Principle. All Christians have an obligation to support God's work in material ways.

Practical Question. Do the Christians in our church realize that they do have an obligation to give to God's work, even though God wants us to give out of willing and joyful hearts?

VERY LITTLE   VERY MUCH
1   2   3   4   5   6   7   8   9   10

92. *Biblical Concept.* "If you lend money to one of my people among you who is needy, do not be like a moneylender; charge him no interest" (Ex. 22:25).

Scriptural Principle. Christians must never take economic advantage of poor people, whether Christians or non-Christians.

Practical Question. Are people in our church taking advantage of poor people by lending them money in order to charge interest?

VERY LITTLE   VERY MUCH
1   2   3   4   5   6   7   8   9   10

93. *Biblical Concept.* "The wicked borrow and do not repay, but the righteous give generously" (Ps. 37:21).

Scriptural Principle. Christians who obey God's Word will be able not only to meet their own economic needs but also to help others who are in need.

Practical Question. Do the Christians in our church understand that, if they walk in the will of God, they will always be able to help meet the physical needs of those less fortunate than they are?

VERY LITTLE   VERY MUCH
1   2   3   4   5   6   7   8   9   10

94. *Biblical Concept.* The Old Testament example not to pay off debts during every seventh year (Deut. 15:1-3).

Scriptural Principle. Christians must set the example of being gracious to people who have borrowed money with good intentions and then have faced crises beyond their control that have made it difficult for them to make their loan payments on time.

Practical Question. Are the people in our church who have loaned money to others sensitive to their plight during times of crises that are beyond their control?

VERY LITTLE   VERY MUCH
1   2   3   4   5   6   7   8   9   10

95. *Biblical Concept.* "The rich rule over the poor, and the borrower is servant to the lender" (Prov. 22:7).

Scriptural Principle. Before Christians borrow money for any purpose, they should consider all of the circumstances and seek wisdom from others who can help them evaluate all aspects of the decision, including the risks involved.

Practical Question. Are believers in our church in debt because they have been influenced by a materialistic philosophy of life rather than a biblical approach to both accumulating and sharing their material possessions?

VERY LITTLE   VERY MUCH

1   2   3   4   5   6   7   8   9   10

96. *Biblical Concept.* "Do not be a man who strikes hands in pledge or puts up security for debts" (Prov. 22:26-27).

   Scriptural Principle. Christians who guarantee another person's loan based upon their own assets should make sure they are able to repay the loan without placing themselves in a position where they cannot meet other financial obligations.

   Practical Question. Do people in our church co-sign notes that could lead them to personal financial disaster, possibly devastating their families and negatively affecting their relationships with other Christians, with unbelievers, and with God Himself?

VERY LITTLE   VERY MUCH

1   2   3   4   5   6   7   8   9   10

97. *Biblical Concept.* "Let no debt remain outstanding" (Rom. 13:8).

   Scriptural Principle. Christians are out of God's will when they knowingly borrow money that they cannot pay back according to a predetermined agreement.

   Practical Question. Are people in our church unable to make debt payments because of irresponsible borrowing?

VERY LITTLE   VERY MUCH

1   2   3   4   5   6   7   8   9   10

98. *Biblical Concept.* Regular, systematic, and proportional giving (1 Cor. 16:2).

   Scriptural Principle. Christians are out of God's will when they cannot give God the "firstfruits" of their income because they have obligated themselves to pay off debts.

   Practical Question. Are Christians in our church unable to give regularly, systematically, and proportionately because of their debts?

VERY LITTLE   VERY MUCH

1   2   3   4   5   6   7   8   9   10

99. *Biblical Concept*. Philemon's example (Philem. 18).

    Scriptural Principle. Christians who put God first in their lives may open the door for people to take material advantage of them.

    Practical Question. Are Christians in our church willing to risk being taken advantage of in order to be obedient to God?

    VERY LITTLE   VERY MUCH
    1   2   3   4   5   6   7   8   9   10

100. *Biblical Concept*. Paul's communication model with Philemon (Philem. 14, 18-19).

    Scriptural Principle. Christian leaders should utilize methods of communication that create both a sense of obligation and a spirit of spontaneity and freedom.

    Practical Question. Do leaders in our church communicate in proper balance between giving out of obligation and giving spontaneously out of willing hearts?

    VERY LITTLE   VERY MUCH
    1   2   3   4   5   6   7   8   9   10

101. *Biblical Concept*. Paul's example and his relationship with Philemon (Philem. 20-22).

    Scriptural Principle. Christian leaders should not hesitate to ask for help when there is a need, both for others and for themselves.

    Practical Question. Do the people, and especially the leaders, in our church make it easy for our staff people to communicate their special economic needs through proper channels?

    VERY LITTLE   VERY MUCH
    1   2   3   4   5   6   7   8   9   10

102. *Biblical Concept*. Paul's experience in Ephesus (Acts 19:23-41).

    Scriptural Principle. Christians may face criticism or even retaliation when their commitment to do God's will conflicts with others' materialistic value systems.

    Practical Question. Are Christians in our church, but especially our spiritual leaders, willing to face criticism, and even some retaliation, from materialistically minded people because they are committed to teaching and practicing a biblical theology of material possessions?

    VERY LITTLE   VERY MUCH
    1   2   3   4   5   6   7   8   9   10

103. *Biblical Concept*. "He who has been stealing must steal no longer, but must work, doing something useful with his own hands, that he may have something to share with those in need" (Eph. 4:28).

Scriptural Principle. Christians should work hard to make an honest living, not only to take care of their own needs, but to help others in need.

Practical Question. Do the people in our church consider their vocational tasks an opportunity not only to make an honest living but to accumulate money to give to God's work?

VERY LITTLE   VERY MUCH
1   2   3   4   5   6   7   8   9   10

104. *Biblical Concept.* The slave-master example (Col. 3:23-24).

Scriptural Principle. Christian employees should work hard and serve their employers (both Christians and non-Christians) as if they are actually serving the Lord.

Practical Question. Do the people in our church perform their vocational tasks as if they were actually serving Jesus Christ?

VERY LITTLE   VERY MUCH
1   2   3   4   5   6   7   8   9   10

105. *Biblical Concept.* The master-slave example (Col. 4:1).

Scriptural Principle. Christian employers should always treat their employees fairly in every respect.

Practical Question. Do the Christian employers in our church treat their employees in the same way they would like God to treat them?

VERY LITTLE   VERY MUCH
1   2   3   4   5   6   7   8   9   10

106. *Biblical Concept.* "I thank my God every time I remember you" (Phil. 1:3-5).

Scriptural Principle. Christians who faithfully support God's servants in material ways create unusual joy in the hearts of those who receive their gifts.

Practical Question. Do the people in our church realize how much joy they create in their spiritual leaders' hearts when they are faithful in their giving?

VERY LITTLE   VERY MUCH
1   2   3   4   5   6   7   8   9   10

107. *Biblical Concept.* "In all my prayers for all of you, I always pray with joy" (Phil. 1:3-5).

Scriptural Principle. Christians who faithfully support God's servants in material ways enrich those servants' prayer lives by making prayer a joyful experience.

Practical Question. Do the people in our church realize the extent to which they enrich their spiritual leaders' prayer lives when they are faithful in their giving?

VERY LITTLE								VERY MUCH	
1	2	3	4	5	6	7	8	9	10

108. *Biblical Concept.* The example of Epaphroditus (Phil. 2:29-30).

Scriptural Principle. Christians who make special sacrifices to help meet the material needs of God's servants should be honored in special ways by others in the Body of Christ.

Practical Question. Have we developed a sensitive way to honor people in our church who have made special sacrifices to help meet other people's economic needs?

VERY LITTLE								VERY MUCH	
1	2	3	4	5	6	7	8	9	10

109. *Biblical Concept.* Paul's example with the Philippians (Phil. 4:11).

Scriptural Principle. God's servants should be open and honest about their material needs, but they should avoid any form of dishonesty and manipulation by playing on others' sympathy.

Practical Question. Are the people in our church able to discern when Christian leaders on television and radio, and even in some churches, are using manipulative and dishonest tactics to get people to give?

VERY LITTLE								VERY MUCH	
1	2	3	4	5	6	7	8	9	10

110. *Biblical Concept.* "I have learned the secret of being content in any and every situation" (Phil. 4:12).

Scriptural Principle. All Christians should learn to be content in the difficult times as well as in the prosperous times.

Practical Question. Are the believers in our church demonstrating contentment when they face difficult financial times?

VERY LITTLE								VERY MUCH	
1	2	3	4	5	6	7	8	9	10

111. *Biblical Concept.* "Not that I am looking for a gift, but I am looking for what may be credited to your account" (Phil. 4:14-17).

Scriptural Principle. Christian leaders who make their living in the ministry should serve Jesus Christ with the view that they are storing up treasures in heaven for those who support them financially.

Practical Question. Do the Christian leaders in our church realize they are storing up treasures in heaven, not only for themselves because of faithful service, but also for those who support them financially?

VERY LITTLE   VERY MUCH
1   2   3   4   5   6   7   8   9   10

112. *Biblical Concept.* "And my God will meet all your needs according to his glorious riches in Christ Jesus" (Phil. 4:19).

Scriptural Principle. God's promise to meet needs applies to the church as well as to individual believers in that church.

Practical Question. Do the people in our church understand that God desires to meet the needs of the whole church body, as well as individual needs within the body?

VERY LITTLE   VERY MUCH
1   2   3   4   5   6   7   8   9   10

PART 7: THE FINAL YEARS OF THE NEW TESTAMENT ERA

113. *Biblical Concept.* "Given to hospitality" (1 Tim. 3:2; Titus 1:6, 8).

Scriptural Principle. All spiritual leaders in the church should be generous Christians who are willing to use their material possessions to serve those they shepherd and lead.

Practical Question. Are our spiritual leaders selected on the basis of their commitment to be generous with their material possessions?

VERY LITTLE   VERY MUCH
1   2   3   4   5   6   7   8   9   10

114. *Biblical Concept.* Nonmaterialistic (1 Tim.3:2-3; Titus 1:7*a*-8).

Scriptural Principle. Christians who occupy leadership roles in the church should be totally trustworthy when it comes to financial matters.

Practical Question. Are our spiritual leaders selected on the basis of the biblical requirements that they not be "lovers of money" or those who "pursue dishonest gain"?

VERY LITTLE   VERY MUCH
1   2   3   4   5   6   7   8   9   10

115. *Biblical Concept.* Paul's guidelines for meeting widows' needs (1 Tim. 5:3-16).

Scriptural Principle. The selection of people who receive consistent help from the church should be based upon specific scriptural guidelines.

Practical Question. Have we set up a system in our church that will help those who are truly in need, while at the same time encouraging people to be responsible to meet their own needs?

VERY LITTLE   VERY MUCH

1   2   3   4   5   6   7   8   9   10

116. *Biblical Concept.* "The elders who direct the affairs of the church well are worthy of double honor, especially those whose work is preaching and teaching" (1 Tim. 5:17).

Scriptural Principle. Pastors and teachers who are hardworking, efficient, and productive in the ministry should be rewarded financially.

Practical Question. Does our church reward our spiritual leaders financially for their hard work, especially in teaching the Word of God?

VERY LITTLE   VERY MUCH

1   2   3   4   5   6   7   8   9   10

117. *Biblical Concept.* "For the love of money is the root of all kinds of evil" (1 Tim. 6:6-10; 17-19).

Scriptural Principle. A Christian's first priority should be to focus on godliness and contentment rather than on riches, which often bring discontentment.

Practical Question. Are the people in our church seeking to be godly rather than to accumulate wealth?

VERY LITTLE   VERY MUCH

1   2   3   4   5   6   7   8   9   10

118. *Biblical Concept.* "They must be silenced, because they are ruining whole households by teaching things they ought not to teach—and that for the sake of dishonest gain" (Titus 1:10-11).

Scriptural Principle. So-called Christian leaders who are teaching false doctrine and manipulating people in order to pursue dishonest gain should be silenced.

Practical Question. Do the people in our church make an effort to silence false teachers by not supporting them financially?

VERY LITTLE   VERY MUCH

1   2   3   4   5   6   7   8   9   10

119. *Biblical Concept.* "There will be terrible times in the last days. People will be lovers of themselves, lovers of money . . . lovers of pleasure rather than lovers of God" (2 Tim. 3:1-2*a*, 4*b*-5).

Scriptural Principle. As the Day of Christ draws nearer, Christians should avoid the increasing tendency to intensify love for self, money, and pleasure.

Practical Question. Do the Christians in our church realize that they can be easily influenced away from the will of God by the materialistic and hedonistic philosophies prominent in our culture today?

VERY LITTLE   VERY MUCH

1   2   3   4   5   6   7   8   9   10

120. *Biblical Concept.* "These have come so that your faith—of greater worth than gold, which perishes even though refined by fire—may be proved genuine and may result in praise, glory and honor when Jesus Christ is revealed" (1 Pet. 1:7, 18-19, 23-25a; 2:5, 11-12; 4:9; 5:2).

Scriptural Principle. God allows periodic persecution to help Christians to put more emphasis on the spiritual and eternal dimensions of life rather than on the material and temporal.

Practical Question. Do Christians in our church realize that God *does* allow difficulties to come into our lives in order to refocus our hearts on eternal values?

VERY LITTLE   VERY MUCH

1   2   3   4   5   6   7   8   9   10

121. *Biblical Concept.* "Do not forget to entertain strangers, for by so doing some people have entertained angels without knowing it" (Heb. 13:2, 5, 16).

Scriptural Principle. All Christians are to show hospitality, not only to those believers in a specific local Christian community, but to those whom they may not know personally.

Practical Question. Do Christians in our church make an effort to show hospitality to reputable believers they may know only by name and not personally?

VERY LITTLE   VERY MUCH

1   2   3   4   5   6   7   8   9   10

122. *Biblical Concept.* "In their greed these teachers will exploit you with stories they have made up" (2 Pet. 2:3a, 14b; Jude 12a).

Scriptural Principle. Christians should be on guard against false teachers who are motivated by selfishness and greed and who exploit people with fabricated stories.

Practical Question. Are the Christians in our church aware of the questionable fund-raising schemes that are used in today's Christian world?

VERY LITTLE   VERY MUCH

1   2   3   4   5   6   7   8   9   10

123. *Biblical Concept.* "Do not love the world or anything in the world" (1 John 2:15-16).

Scriptural Principle. Christians must be on guard against establishing false distinctions between what is "material" and what is "spiritual."

Practical Question. Have the Christians in our church learned to appreciate the things in this world that God has created for enjoyment and, at the same time, not to love those things in a lustful and prideful way?

VERY LITTLE   VERY MUCH

| 1 | 2 | 3 | 4 | 5 | 6 | 7 | 8 | 9 | 10 |

124. *Biblical Concept.* "If anyone comes to you and does not bring this teaching, do not take him into your house or welcome him" (2 John 10-11).

Scriptural Principle. Christians should not support religious teachers and leaders who claim to be Christians but who deny that Jesus Christ came as God in the flesh.

Practical Question. Have Christians in our church learned to discern when so-called spiritual leaders appear to be Bible-believing yet do not believe that Jesus Christ is truly God?

VERY LITTLE   VERY MUCH

| 1 | 2 | 3 | 4 | 5 | 6 | 7 | 8 | 9 | 10 |

125. *Biblical Concept.* Gaius's example compared with Diotrephes' (3 John 5, 8).

Scriptural Principle. Christian leaders who receive their financial support from the church they serve must be on guard against a selfishness that causes them to refuse to share financial help with other Christian leaders who are in need.

Practical Question. Are our spiritual leaders teaching and leading us to use some of our church income to help other Christian leaders and ministries?

VERY LITTLE   VERY MUCH

| 1 | 2 | 3 | 4 | 5 | 6 | 7 | 8 | 9 | 10 |

126. *Biblical Concept.* "You say, 'I am rich; I have acquired wealth and do not need a thing.' But you do not realize that you are wretched, pitiful, poor, blind and naked" (Rev. 3:17-18).

Scriptural Principle. Christians must be on guard against self-deception and rationalization when they are living in an affluent society.

Practical Question. Are the people in our church self-deceived by the materialistic philosophy that permeates our culture, causing them to rationalize away their selfishness and lack of generosity?

VERY LITTLE   VERY MUCH

| 1 | 2 | 3 | 4 | 5 | 6 | 7 | 8 | 9 | 10 |

40

A Systematic and Thematic Perspective

To this point we have looked at 126 supracultural principles that have emerged from God's unfolding revelation throughout New Testament history. Old Testament passages have been used to demonstrate continuity between God's plan for Israel and His plan for the church. Together, these principles form the essence of a biblical theology of material possessions.

All of these principles can be clustered around twelve basic themes. In turn, each cluster focuses on a "set of principles" that relate to each particular theme. As we look at the principles organized around these twelve subjects, note that the unfolding of biblical history also forms the chronological order in which these "clusters" appear. It is significant, but not surprising, that eight of these twelve themes appear in Part 1, in which we see the founding and expansion of the Jerusalem church. This observation alone points to the divine way in which God through the Holy Spirit unveiled His will in Scripture. More specifically, the first six themes and the initial principles unfold as the functions of the church in Jerusalem also unfold in Part 1:

TWELVE BASIC THEMES

1. *Reaching others with the gospel.* As Christians use their material possessions in harmony with the will of God, people will be encouraged to believe in Jesus Christ (Acts 2:47).

2. *Maintaining love and unity in the Body of Christ.* As Christians use their material possessions to meet one another's needs, love and unity are created in the Body of Christ (Acts 4:32).

3. *Modeling giving.* Spiritual leaders should model the way all Christians ought to use their material possessions (Acts 4:37).

4. *Meeting human needs.* Christians should be willing to make special sacrifices in order to meet special material needs within the Body of Christ (Acts 4:34-35).

5. *Giving with proper motives.* What Christians give should always be given to honor God and not ourselves (Acts 4:34-36; 5:4).

6. *Leadership responsibility and accountability.* It is by divine design that local churches provide the primary context in which Christians are to use their material possessions to further the work of God's kingdom (Acts 2-6).

The next three themes and the initial principles come from Part 2 as they are recorded in chronological order in Matthew's gospel:

7. *God's blessings for faithful giving.* Christ wants all Christians to pray for daily sustenance (Matt. 6:11).

8. *The problem of materialism.* It is possible for a Christian to be in bondage to material possessions (Matt. 6:24).

9. *Supporting Christian leaders.* God honors Christians in a special way when they meet the material needs of those who truly serve God (Matt. 10:42).

The next two themes and the initial principles appear first in Part 1, then in Part 6:

10. *God's specific plan for giving.* Christians must be careful not to evaluate subjectively what they believe is the Holy Spirit's leading when it comes to giving (John 14:25-26).

11. *Christians and the subject of debt.* Christians who owe money or goods should always pay what they owe (Rom. 13:8).

The final category, relating to the will of God, includes more overarching principles drawn from all sections of the study. However, the initial principles also emerge from Part 1:

12. *Giving and the will of God.* The way Christians use their material possessions is an important criterion for determining whether or not they are living in the will of God (Acts 2-6).

All of the additional scriptural passages and principles (114 to be exact) can be naturally clustered around these twelve basic concepts. Seen in this light, it becomes apparent that these remaining principles build upon the initial concepts. This process also verifies why it is helpful to first study these concepts as they appear sequentially in God's unfolding revelation. We are enabled to move from doing biblical theology to a more systematic approach with the assurance that we are truly representing what God has revealed for us over a process of time. Together these twelve profiles provide important areas for further thought, study, and application for our personal lives, our families, our churches, and other ministries.

THE FIRST PROFILE
REACHING OTHERS WITH THE GOSPEL

SHARING WHAT WE HAVE WITH OTHERS

1. *Encouraging faith* (principle 1). As Christians use their material possessions in harmony with the will of God, it will encourage people to believe in Jesus Christ (Acts 2:47).

2. *Serving enemies* (principle 23). Christians should not only give to those who love them and care for them but also to those who may resent them and even try to harm them (Matt. 5:42).

3. *Verifying truth* (principle 49). Christians who are unselfish and benevolent become a unique verification to non-Christians that Jesus Christ is indeed the Son of God (Acts 9:32-43).

PRACTICING A BIBLICAL WORK ETHIC

4. *Working hard* (principle 64). Christians should work hard to provide for their economic needs so that they are not criticized by unbelievers for being lazy and irresponsible (1 Thess. 4:11-12).

5. *Breaking fellowship* (principle 65). Christians should separate themselves from other Christians who are persistently irresponsible in not providing for their own economic needs (2 Thess. 3:6).

6. *Serving employers* (principle 104). Christian employees should work hard and serve their employers (both Christians and non-Christians) as if they are actually serving the Lord (Col. 3:23-24).

7. *Serving employees* (principle 105). Christian employers should always treat their employees fairly in every respect (Col. 4:1).

REACHING WELL-TO-DO PEOPLE WITH THE GOSPEL

8. *Ignoring God* (principle 21). Having a lot of material things often makes it difficult for people to recognize and acknowledge their need of God in salvation (Matt. 5:3).

9. *Penetrating culture* (principle 37). Christian leaders should develop an awareness of the economic structures and practices in every culture in which they are attempting to communicate God's truth in order to utilize these economic experiences to teach people spiritual truths (Jesus' parables).

10. *Understanding God's grace* (principle 44). God is sometimes more patient with uninformed people who are materialistic than He is with people who have more direct exposure to the truth (Acts 8:9-25).

11. *Reaching wealthy people* (principle 45). Though it is often difficult for wealthy people to respond to the gospel, it is God's will that we reach these people, for they can influence great segments of humanity with both their social position and their material resources (Acts 8:26-40).

12. *Understanding God's heart* (principle 50). God's heart responds to non-Christians who are sincerely seeking to please Him and who express their sincerity through being generous with their material possessions (Acts 10:1-48).

13. *Warning unbelievers* (principle 59). Non-Christians who put their faith in material possessions and who abuse and misuse other people in order to accumulate wealth must be warned that they will eventually be judged severely by God Himself (James 5:1).

PREPARING FOR NEGATIVE RESULTS

14. *Being vulnerable* (principle 99). Christians who put God first in their lives may open the door for people to take material advantage of them (Philem. 18).

15. *Enduring criticism* (principle 102). Christians may face criticism or even retaliation when their commitment to do God's will conflicts with others' materialistic value systems (Acts 19:23-41).

THE SECOND PROFILE
MAINTAINING LOVE AND UNITY IN THE BODY OF CHRIST

CREATING LOVE AND UNITY

1. *Achieving oneness* (principle 2). As Christians use their material possessions to meet one another's needs, it will create love and unity in the Body of Christ (Acts 4:32).

2. *Seeking forgiveness* (principle 22). Material gifts are acceptable and "well pleasing" to God only when Christians have done their part to be in harmony with their brothers and sisters in Christ (Matt. 5:24*b*).

3. *Avoiding invalidation* (principle 34). Christians who give regularly and faithfully are invalidating the acceptability of their gifts to God when they neglect to love God and one another (Matt. 23:23*b*).

4. *Winning respect* (principle 86). People respect and love Christians who are unselfish and generous (2 Cor. 9:14).

HONORING OTHERS WITHOUT SHOWING FAVORITISM

5. *Showing appreciation* (principle 7). Christians who are faithful in sharing their material possessions should be shown special appreciation (Acts 4:36).

6. *Accepting others* (principle 53). Christians in the church who do not have a lot of material possessions should not feel inferior to those who have more (James 1:9).

7. *Demonstrating humility* (principle 54). Christians who have a lot of material possessions should demonstrate humility, realizing that their only true treasures are those they have stored up in heaven (James 1:10).

8. *Avoiding favoritism* (principle 56). Christians should never show favoritism toward people who have an abundance of material possessions; conversely, Christians should never be prejudiced against people who have few material possessions (James 2:1).

THE THIRD PROFILE
MODELING GIVING

IDENTIFYING SPECIFIC MODELS

1. *Looking to leaders* (principle 3). Spiritual leaders should model the way all Christians ought to use their material possessions (Acts 2:42).

2. *Looking at believers* (principle 8). Christians need to be able to observe other believers who are faithful in sharing their material possessions (Acts 4:36-37).

3. *Looking to Israel* (principle 20). God's plan for Israel in the Old Testament serves as a foundational model regarding the way Christians should view and use their material possessions today (Acts 2-6).

4. *Looking at churches* (principle 70). Every local body of believers needs real-life examples of other churches that are positive models in the area of giving (2 Cor. 8:1-2).

UNDERSTANDING THE NEED FOR MODELS

5. *Providing encouragement* (principle 6). It is the will of God that Christians share their material possessions in order to encourage others in the Body of Christ (Acts 4:36).

6. *Motivating others* (principle 77). Christians who are generous will motivate other Christians to also be generous (2 Cor. 9:2).

7. *Causing worship* (principle 85). Generous Christians cause others to praise and worship God (2 Cor. 9:11-13).

8. *Serving others* (principle 113). All spiritual leaders in the church should be generous Christians who are willing to use their material possessions to serve those they shepherd and lead (1 Tim. 3:2; Titus 1:6, 8).

THE FOURTH PROFILE
MEETING HUMAN NEEDS

GUIDELINES FOR MOTIVATION

1. *Making sacrifices* (principle 4). Christians should be willing to make special sacrifices in order to meet special material needs within the Body of Christ (Acts 4:34-35).

2. *Meeting needs* (principle 5). A primary motivating factor for consistent Christian giving should be to meet others' needs—particularly within the Body of Christ (Acts 4:34-35).

3. *Touching God's heart* (principle 55). People who are in physical need have a special place in God's heart, and Christians who help meet these needs also have a special place in God's heart (James 1:27a).

4. *Providing equality* (principle 75). It is not the will of God that some Christians cannot meet their physical needs while other Christians with abundance could help them in their time of need (2 Cor. 8:13-14).

5. *Working to give* (principle 103). Christians should work hard to make an honest living, not only to take care of their own needs but to help others in need (Eph. 4:28).

GUIDELINES FOR METHODOLOGY

6. *Organizing well* (principle 12). It is God's will that every church have an efficient system for helping to meet the true material needs of others in the Body of Christ (Acts 6:1-7).

7. *Delegating responsibility* (principle 13). Spiritual leaders in the church must at times delegate the administrative responsibilities to other qualified people who can assist them in meeting material needs (Acts 6:2-4).

8. *Selecting leaders* (principle 14). Meeting the "spiritual needs" of people and meeting the "material needs" of people require the same high standard in terms of selecting leaders to meet these needs (Acts 6:3).

9. *Establishing priorities* (principle 32). Christian children who are able should make sure that they care for their parents' physical needs (Matt. 15:46).

10. *Showing hospitality* (principle 46). It is God's will that Christians who have been blessed with material resources use their homes in special ways to offer hospitality to other believers (Acts 10:1-48).

11. *Organizing socially* (principle 51). When Christians in a particular culture are excluded from social benefits because of their faith in Christ, other believers should set up some type of welfare system to take care of valid human needs (Acts 11:19-30).

12. *Withholding assistance* (principle 66). Christians who can, but do not, work for a living should not be given economic assistance (2 Thess. 3:10*b*).

13. *Sharing with discretion* (principle 109). God's servants should be open and honest about their material needs, but they should avoid any form of dishonesty and manipulation by playing on others' sympathy (Phil. 4:11).

14. *Proceeding cautiously* (principle 115). The selection of people who receive consistent help from the church should be based upon some specific scriptural guidelines (1 Tim. 5:3-16).

15. *Entertaining strangers* (principle 121). All Christians are to show hospitality, not only to the believers in a specific local Christian community but to those whom they may not know personally (Heb. 13:2, 5, 16).

THE FIFTH PROFILE
GIVING WITH PROPER MOTIVES

BASIC MOTIVES FOR GIVING

1. *Giving to honor God* (principle 9). What Christians give should always be given to honor God and not ourselves (Acts 4:34-36; 5:1-10).

2. *Giving generously but voluntarily* (principle 11). Though God wants all of His children to be generous, what Christians give should always be voluntary and from a heart of love and concern (Acts 5:4).

3. *Expecting Christ's return* (principle 18). The expectancy of the second coming of Jesus Christ should always be a strong motivational factor in the way Christians view and use their material possessions (Acts 2-6).

4. *Responding to God's grace* (principle 73). God does not want Christians to respond to a command to share their material possessions but, rather, to respond out of hearts of love that reflect sincere appreciation for His gift of salvation (2 Cor. 8:8-9).

DETERMINING PURE MOTIVES

5. *Avoiding hypocrisy and dishonesty* (principle 10). God detests dishonesty, lack of integrity, and hypocrisy when it comes to giving (Acts 5:1-10).

6. *Checking motives periodically* (principle 24). Christians should periodically check their motives to see if they are giving to glorify God or to glorify themselves (Matt. 6:3-4).

7. *Evaluating thoughts* (principle 27). Christians can determine their true perspective toward material possessions by evaluating the consistent thoughts and attitudes of their hearts (Matt. 6:21).

8. *Testing faith* (principle 57). One of the most significant ways saving faith is tested as to its validity and reality is the way in which professing Christians view and use their material possessions (James 2:17).

9. *Giving from the heart* (principle 82). Every Christian is ultimately responsible to give to God on the basis of his own heart decision (2 Cor. 9:7).

The Sixth Profile
Leadership Responsibility and Accountability

1. *Focusing the local church* (principle 16). It is by divine design that local churches provide the primary context in which Christians are to use their material possessions to further the work of God's kingdom (Acts 2-6).

2. *Teaching believers their responsibility* (principle 38). Spiritual leaders are responsible to teach believers in the church what God says about material possessions (Acts 2-6).

3. *Being accountable* (principle 69). Those who handle and distribute monies that are given to God's work should be above reproach in all respects and should be held accountable (1 Cor. 16:3-4).

4. *Sharing responsibility* (principle 76). It is the will of God that no one particular Christian leader have to handle the financial needs of the Christian community alone (2 Cor. 8:16-19, 22-24; 9:3-4).

5. *Maintaining a high level of communication* (principle 88). It is important that Christian leaders maintain a high level of communication in order to enable Christians to be obedient to God's will in the way they use their material possessions (Paul's example).

6. *Being direct though sensitive* (principle 100). Christian leaders should utilize methods of communication that create both a sense of obligation and a spirit of spontaneity and freedom (Philem. 14, 18-19).

7. *Being trustworthy* (principle 114). Christians who occupy leadership roles in the church should be totally trustworthy when it comes to financial matters (1 Tim. 3:2-3, 8; Titus 1:7a-8).

8. *Silencing the unqualified* (principle 118). So-called Christian leaders who are teaching false doctrine and manipulating people in order to pursue dishonest gain should be silenced (Titus 1:10-11).

THE SEVENTH PROFILE
GOD'S BLESSINGS FOR FAITHFUL GIVING

PRESENT BLESSINGS

1. *Giving daily provisions* (principle 25). Christ wants Christians to pray for daily sustenance (Matt. 6:11).

2. *Blessings for obedience* (principle 29). If Christians put God first in all things, He has promised to meet their material needs (Matt. 6:33).

3. *Providing for material needs* (principle 83). When Christians are faithful in their giving, God has promised to meet their needs (2 Cor. 9:8).

4. *Being able to be generous continually* (principle 84). When Christians are generous, God has promised to enable them to continue to be generous (2 Cor. 9:11).

5. *Being honored by others* (principle 108). Christians who make special sacrifices to help meet the material needs of God's servants should be honored in special ways by others in the Body of Christ (Phil. 2:29-30).

6. *Receiving God's blessings as a church* (principle 112). God's promise to meet needs applies to the church as well as to individual believers in that church (Phil. 4:19).

BOTH PRESENT AND ETERNAL BLESSINGS

7. *Being rewarded for sacrificial giving* (principle 33). God will reward Christians in His eternal kingdom on the basis of the degree of sacrifice involved in their giving (Matt. 19:30).

8. *Receiving both earthly and eternal blessings* (principle 40). Believers should be motivated to share their material possessions in hopes of receiving present blessings; however, they must realize that the most important perspective in Scripture involves eternal blessings and that their reward may not come in this life (Matt. 19:28-29).

9. *Receiving generous blessings for generous giving* (principle 81). Christians who are generous in their giving will receive generous blessings; conversely, Christians who are not generous in their giving will not receive generous blessings (2 Cor. 9:6).

THE EIGHTH PROFILE
THE PROBLEM OF MATERIALISM

WARNINGS AGAINST MATERIALISM

1. *Avoiding bondage* (principle 28). It is possible for a Christian to be in bondage to material possessions (Matt. 6:24).

2. *Avoiding those who take advantage* (principle 43). Wherever Christianity is active, some people will attempt to use the Christian message to benefit themselves (Acts 8:9-25).

3. *Avoiding unnecessary temptations* (principle 60). Accumulating wealth brings with it specific temptations for both Christians and non-Christians (James 5:1-3).

4. *Avoiding self-centered behavior* (principle 119). As the Day of Christ draws nearer, Christians should avoid the increasing tendency to intensify love for self, money, and pleasure (2 Tim. 3:1-2*a*, 4*b*-5).

5. *Avoiding self-deception and rationalization* (principle 126). Christians must be on guard against self-deception and rationalization when they are living in an affluent society (Rev. 3:17-18).

POSITIVE GUIDELINES

6. *Using excess creatively* (principle 26). Whatever excess material possessions God enables Christians to accumulate should be used in creative ways to further the kingdom of God (Matt. 6:19-20).

7. *Resting in God's faithfulness* (principle 30). It is not the will of God that Christians be absorbed with worry about the future and how their material needs will be met (Matt. 6:34*a*).

8. *Refocusing values* (principle 42). God sometimes allows difficulties and discomforts to come into Christians' experiences in order to refocus their priorities on eternal values (Acts 8:1-3).

9. *Learning to be content* (principle 110). All Christians should learn to be content in the difficult times as well as in the prosperous times (Phil. 4:12).

10. *Seeking to be godly* (principle 117). A Christian's first priority should be to focus on godliness and contentment rather than on riches, which often brings discontentment (1 Tim. 6:6-10).

THE NINTH PROFILE
SUPPORTING CHRISTIAN LEADERS

MOTIVATION FOR SUPPORTING CHRISTIAN LEADERS

1. *Being honored by God* (principle 31). God honors Christians in a special way when they meet the material needs of those who truly serve God (Matt. 10:42).

2. *Avoiding embarrassment* (principle 78). Christians who make commitments financially should be on guard against embarrassing their spiritu-

al leaders, as well as themselves, by being negligent in following through on their commitments (2 Cor. 9:3-4).

3. *Creating happiness in leaders' hearts* (principle 106). Christians who faithfully support God's servants in material ways create unusual joy in the hearts of those who receive their gifts (Phil. 1:3-5).

4. *Causing joy in prayer* (principle 107). Christians who faithfully support God's servants in material ways enrich those servants' prayer lives by making prayer a joyful experience (Phil. 1:3-5).

GUIDELINES FOR SUPPORTING CHRISTIAN LEADERS

5. *Considering the totality of Scripture* (principle 39). Economic policies for meeting the physical needs of Christian leaders who devote their full time to ministry must be built upon the totality of God's Word (Mark 6:8-13; Luke 9:1-6).

6. *Supporting those who teach* (principle 61). Local church leaders whose primary ministry is teaching the Word of God should be given priority consideration in receiving financial support (Gal. 6:6).

7. *Rewarding those who are productive* (principle 116). Pastors and teachers who are hardworking, efficient, and productive in the ministry should be rewarded financially (1 Tim. 5:17).

8. *Being on guard against false teachers* (principle 122). Christians should be on guard against false teachers who are motivated by selfishness and greed and who exploit people with fabricated stories (2 Pet. 2:3*a*, 14*b*; Jude 12*a*).

9. *Evaluating a leader's beliefs* (principle 124). Christians should not support religious teachers and leaders who claim to be Christians but who deny that Jesus Christ came as God in the flesh (2 John 10-11).

GUIDELINES FOR CHRISTIAN LEADERS

10. *Looking to Christians* (principle 63). Christian leaders should look to fellow Christians for financial support, not to the unbelievers they are attempting to reach with the gospel (1 Thess. 2:9).

11. *Giving up rights* (principle 67). Even though God has commanded that spiritual leaders be cared for financially by those they minister to, there are times when it is the part of wisdom for spiritual leaders to give up that right (1 Cor. 9:14-15*a*).

12. *Asking for help* (principle 101). Christian leaders should not hesitate to ask for help when there is a need, both for others and for themselves (Philem. 20-22).

13. *Serving to reward others* (principle 111). Christian leaders who make their living in the ministry should serve Jesus Christ with the view that they are storing up treasures in heaven for those who support them financially (Phil. 4:14-17).

14. *Guarding against selfishness* (principle 125). Christian leaders who receive their financial support from the church they serve must be on guard against a selfishness that causes them to refuse to share financial help with other Christian leaders who are in need (3 John 5, 8).

THE TENTH PROFILE
GOD'S SPECIFIC PLAN FOR GIVING

1. *Giving objectively* (principle 36). Christians must be careful not to evaluate subjectively what they believe is the Holy Spirit's leading when it comes to giving (John 14:25-26).

2. *Using material resources* (principle 47). God desires to use people with material resources who can give great segments of their time to the ministry while still providing for their families (Acts 8:5, 26, 40).

3. *Giving time and talent* (principle 48). God desires to use Christians who may not have an abundance of material possessions but who unselfishly use what they have, including their skills, to do the work of God (Acts 9:32-43).

4. *Giving willingly* (principle 52). All Christians, according to their ability, should be involved in sharing their material possessions to carry on God's work in the world (Acts 11:19-30).

5. *Planning ahead* (principle 62). Christians should plan ahead so they can be prepared to minister economically, first and foremost, to their fellow Christians who are in need but without neglecting non-Christians (Gal. 6:10).

6. *Giving regularly* (principle 68). Christians should set aside a certain percentage of their income on just as regular a basis as they are paid in order to be able to systematically give to God's work (1 Cor. 16:2).

7. *Being held accountable* (principle 71). Christians need to be held accountable when they make financial commitments to God's work (2 Cor. 8:6, 10, 11; 9:3).

8. *Giving immediately* (principle 74). God accepts and honors believers' gifts once they begin to give regularly and systematically, even though they may not be able to give as proportionately as they eventually will be able to once they have their economic lives in order (2 Cor. 8:10-12).

9. *Giving by faith* (principle 79). God wants Christians to take a step of faith and trust Him to enable them to be able to give certain amounts of money based upon future earnings (2 Cor. 9:5*a*).

10. *Giving joyfully* (principle 80). Christians should organize and plan their giving in a systematic way so that they can give generously and not respond in a grudging fashion (2 Cor. 9:5*b*).

11. *Being accountable in a local body* (principle 87). The local church is God's primary context for maintaining accountability in the area of material possessions.

12. *Giving responsibly* (principle 91). All Christians have an obligation to support God's work in material ways (Rom. 15:27).

THE ELEVENTH PROFILE
CHRISTIANS AND THE SUBJECT OF DEBT

1. *Paying debts regularly* (principle 90). Christians who owe money or goods should always pay what they owe (Rom. 13:8).

2. *Lending to help others* (principle 92). Christians must never take economic advantage of poor people, whether Christians or non-Christians (Ex. 22:25).

3. *Experiencing God's blessings* (principle 93). Christians who obey God's Word will be able not only to meet their own economic needs but also to help others who are in need (Ps. 37:21).

4. *Showing mercy in crises* (principle 94). Christians must set the example of being gracious to people who have borrowed money with good intentions and then have faced crises beyond their control that have made it difficult for them to make their loan payments on time (Deut. 15:1-3).

5. *Evaluating all risks* (principle 95). Before Christians borrow money for any purpose, they should consider all of the circumstances and seek wisdom from others who can help them evaluate all aspects of the decision, including the risks involved (Prov. 22:7).

6. *Being cautious regarding cosignatures* (principle 96). Christians who guarantee another person's loan based upon their own assets should make sure they are able to repay the loan without placing themselves in a position where they cannot meet other financial obligations (Prov. 22:26-27).

7. *Borrowing responsibly* (principle 97). Christians are out of God's will when they knowingly borrow money that they cannot pay back according to a predetermined agreement (Rom. 13:8).

8. *Putting God first* (principle 98). Christians are out of God's will when they cannot give God the "firstfruits" of their income because they have obligated themselves to pay off debts (1 Cor. 16:2).

THE TWELFTH PROFILE
GIVING AND THE WILL OF GOD

1. *Reflecting the will of God* (principle 15). The way Christians use their material possessions is an important criterion for determining whether or not they are living in the will of God (Acts 2-6).

2. *Responding immediately* (principle 17). Christians should respond immediately to whatever portion of God's truth they have received (Acts 2-6).

3. *Understanding God's will* (principle 19). As we obey God, He will clarify and help us understand His specific plans, enabling us to more and more live by faith and respond to His will (Acts 2-6).

4. *Obeying Jesus Christ* (principle 35). The truths that Jesus taught about material possessions are normative and supracultural (the gospels).

5. *Developing a specific plan* (principle 41). Christians today should apply the principles as taught by Christ and modeled by New Testament Christians, utilizing forms and methods that are relevant in their own particular cultures.

6. *Desiring to do God's will* (principle 58). All economic and financial planning should be done with an intense desire to be in the will of God in every respect (James 4:15).

7. *Excelling in giving* (principle 72). It is God's will that all Christians excel in the grace of giving (2 Cor. 8:7).

8. *Responding to government responsibilities* (principle 89). Christians should always be responsible and honest citizens in their own societies by paying all governmental taxes and revenues (Rom. 13:6-7).

9 *Refocusing priorities* (principle 120). God allows periodic persecution to help Christians to put more emphasis on the spiritual and eternal dimensions of life rather than on the material and temporal (1 Pet. 1:7, 18-19, 23-25*a*; 2:5, 11-12; 4:9; 5:2).

10. *Maintaining balance* (principle 123). Christians must be on guard against establishing false distinctions between what is "material" and what is "spiritual" (1 John 2:15-16).

Bibliography

Aune, David E. *The New Testament and Its Literary Environment.* Library of Early Christianity. Philadelphia: Westminster, 1987.

Barnett, Jake. *Wealth & Wisdom: A Biblical Perspective on Possessions.* Colorado Springs: NavPress, 1987.

Barrow, R. H. *The Romans.* Harmondsworth, Middlesex, England: Penguin, 1949.

Barth, Markus. *Ephesians: Introduction, Translation, and Commentary on Chapters 1-3.* Garden City, N.Y.: Doubleday & Co., 1974.

Beisner, E. Calvin. "How Much for How Many?" *Discipleship Journal* 49 (January/February 1989): 20.

Bellah, Mike. *Baby Boom Believers.* Wheaton, Ill.: Tyndale, 1988.

Bellah, Robert N., et al. *Habits of the Heart: Individualism and Commitment in American Life.* New York: Harper & Row, 1985.

Bettenson, Henry, ed. *Documents of the Christian Church.* 2d ed. London: Oxford University, 1963.

Blaiklock, E. M., ed. *The Zondervan Pictorial Bible Atlas.* Grand Rapids: Zondervan, 1969.

_____. *The Acts of the Apostles: An Historical Commentary.* The Tyndale New Testament Commentaries, vol. 5. Grand Rapids: Eerdmans, 1959.

Blue, Ron. *Master Your Money.* Nashville: Thomas Nelson, 1986.

Blue, Ron, and Judy Blue. *Money Matters for Parents and Their Kids.* Pomona, Calif.: Focus on the Family, 1988.

Brown, Raymond E. *The Churches the Apostles Left Behind.* New York: Paulist, 1984.

Bruce, F. F. *New Testament History.* Garden City, N.Y.: Doubleday & Co., 1972.

_____. *The Epistle of Paul to the Romans: An Introduction and Commentary.* The Tyndale New Testament Commentaries, vol. 6. Grand Rapids: Eerdmans, 1963.

_____. *Commentary on the Epistle to the Hebrews.* Grand Rapids: Eerdmans, 1964.

Buchanan, George Wesley. *To the Hebrews: Translation, Comment and Conclusions.* 2d ed. Garden City, N.Y.: Doubleday & Co., 1976.

Burkett, Larry. *Using Your Money Wisely: Guidelines from Scripture.* Chicago: Moody, 1985.

_____. *Answers to Your Family's Financial Questions.* Pomona, Calif.: Focus on the Family, 1987.

Burns, (S. J.) J. Patout, ed. and trans. *Theological Anthropology.* Sources of Early Christian Thought. Philadelphia: Fortress, 1981.

Cairns, Earle E. *Christianity Through the Centuries: A History of the Christian Church.* Rev. and enl. Grand Rapids: Zondervan, 1967.

Carson, Herbert M. *The Epistles of Paul to the Colossians and Philemon.* The Tyndale New Testament Commentaries, vol. 12. Grand Rapids: Eerdmans, 1960.

Chafer, Lewis Sperry, and John F. Walvoord. *Major Bible Themes.* Rev. ed. Grand Rapids: Zondervan, 1974.

Cohen, Shaye J. D. *From the Maccabees to the Mishnah.* Library of Early Christianity. Philadelphia: Westminster, 1987.

Cole, R. A. *The Epistle of Paul to the Galatians: An Introduction and Commentary.* The Tyndale New Testament Commentaries, vol. 9. Grand Rapids: Eerdmans, 1965.

_____. *The Gospel According to St. Mark: An Introduction and Commentary.* The Tyndale New Testament Commentaries, vol. 2. Grand Rapids: Eerdmans, 1961.

Cooper, John Charles. *The Joy of the Plain Life.* Nashville: Impact, 1981.

Cunningham, Agnes, ed. and trans. *The Early Church and the State.* Sources of Early Christian Thought. Philadelphia, Fortress, 1982.

Davies, W. D., and D. Daube, eds. *The Background of the New Testament and Its Eschatology.* Cambridge: University, 1956.

Davis, John Jefferson. *Your Wealth in God's World: Does the Bible Support the Free Market?* Phillipsburg, N.J.: Presbyterian and Reformed, 1984.

DeVries, LaMoine. "Samaria." *Biblical Illustrator* 15 (Winter 1989): 10-15.

Douglas, J. D., ed. *The New Bible Dictionary.* Grand Rapids: Eerdmans, 1962.

Drane, John W. *Early Christians.* San Francisco: Harper & Row, 1982.

Drumwright, Huber, Jr. *The Wycliffe Bible Encyclopedia.* Chicago: Moody, 1975.

Eerdman's Handbook to the History of Christianity. Grand Rapids: Eerdmans, 1977.

Eggleston, Lyle. "The Church That Learned to Give." *Moody Monthly* 88 (July/August 1988): 31-32.

Enns, Paul. *The Moody Handbook of Theology.* Chicago: Moody, 1989.

Fausset, A. R. *Job–Isaiah.* Vol. 3, *A Commentary: Critical, Experimental and Practical on the Old and New Testaments.* Grand Rapids: Eerdmans, 1948.

Ferguson, Everett. *Early Christians Speak.* Austin, Tex.: Sweet, 1971.

Financial Freedom. Men's Manual, vol. 2. Oakbrook, Ill.: Institute in Basic Youth Conflicts, 1983.

Finzel, Hans. *Help! I'm a Baby Boomer.* Wheaton, Ill.: Victor, 1989.

Foulkes, Francis. *The Epistle of Paul to the Ephesians: An Introduction and Commentary.* The Tyndale New Testament Commentaries, vol. 10. Grand Rapids: Eerdmans, 1963.

Froehlich, Karlfried, ed. and trans. *Biblical Interpretation in the Early Church.* Sources of Early Christian Thought. Philadelphia: Fortress, 1984.

Gapp, Kenneth Sperber. "The Universal Famine Under Claudius." *Harvard Theological Review* 28 (October 1935): 258-65.

Getz, Gene A. *Believing God When You Are Tempted to Doubt: The Measure of a Christian Based on James 1.* Ventura, Calif.: Regal, 1983.

_____. *Doing Your Part When You'd Rather Let God Do It All: The Measure of a Christian Based on James 2-5.* Ventura, Calif.: Regal, 1984.

_____. *Living for Others When You'd Rather Live for Yourself: Studies in Ephesians 4-6.* Ventura, Calif.: Regal, 1985.

_____. *Looking Up When You Feel Down: Based on Ephesians 1-3.* Ventura, Calif.: Regal, 1985.

_____. *The Measure of a Family.* Ventura, Calif.: Regal, 1976.

_____. *Pressing on When You'd Rather Turn Back: Studies in Philippians.* Ventura, Calif.: Regal, 1983.

_____. *Saying No When You'd Rather Say Yes: Making Choices Based on Titus.* Ventura, Calif.: Regal, 1983.

_____. *Sharpening the Focus of the Church.* Wheaton, Ill.: Victor, 1984.

_____. *Standing Firm When You'd Rather Retreat.* Ventura, Calif.: Regal, 1986.

Godet, Frederick Lewis. *Commentary on Romans.* Grand Rapids: Kregel, 1977.

Gonzalez, Justo L. *Faith and Wealth: A History of Early Christian Ideas on the Origin, Significance, and Use of Money*. San Francisco: Harper & Row, 1990.

Gower, Ralph. *The New Manners and Customs of Bible Times*. Chicago: Moody, 1987.

Grant, F. C. *The Economic Background of the Gospels*. New York: Russell & Russell, 1973.

Grant, Robert M. *Gods and the One God*. Library of Early Christianity. Philadelphia: Westminster, 1986.

Green, Michael. *Evangelism in the Early Church*. Grand Rapids: Eerdmans, 1970.

Guthrie, Donald. *The Pastoral Epistles: An Introduction and Commentary*. The Tyndale New Testament Commentaries, vol. 14. Grand Rapids: Eerdmans, 1957.

Hadas, Moses. *A History of Rome from Its Origins to 529 A.D. as Told by the Roman Historians*. Garden City, N.Y.: Doubleday & Co., 1956.

Heichelheim, Fritz M., Cedric A. Yeo, and Allen M. Ward. *A History of the Roman People*. 2d ed. Englewood Cliffs, N.J.: Prentice-Hall, 1984.

Hendriksen, William. *New Testament Commentary: Exposition of the Gospel According to Matthew*. Grand Rapids: Baker, 1973.

Hengel, Martin. *Property and Riches in the Early Church: Aspects of a Social History of Early Christianity*. Translated by John Bowden. Philadelphia: Fortress, 1974.

Hewitt, Thomas. *The Epistle to the Hebrews: An Introduction and Commentary*. The Tyndale New Testament Commentaries, vol. 15. Grand Rapids: Tyndale, 1960.

Hiebert, D. Edmond. *Wycliffe Bible Encyclopedia*. 2 vols. Chicago: Moody, 1975.

Hinson, E. Glenn, ed. and trans. *Understandings of the Church*. Sources of Early Christian Thought. Philadelphia, Fortress, 1986.

Hobbs, Charles R. *The Power*. New York: Harper & Row, 1987.

Hodge, Charles. *Commentary on the Epistle to the Romans*. Grand Rapids: Eerdmans, 1950.

Hoehner, Harold W. *Chronological Aspects of the Life of Christ*. Grand Rapids: Zondervan, 1981.

_____. *Chronology of the Apostolic Age*. Diss., the Graduate School of Dallas Theological Seminary, 1965.

Hughes, Philip E. *A Commentary on the Epistle to the Hebrews*. Grand Rapids: Eerdmans, 1977.

_____. *The New International Commentary on the New Testament: Paul's Second Epistle to the Corinthians*. Grand Rapids: Eerdmans, 1962.

Jeremias, Joachim. *Jerusalem in the Time of Jesus.* Translated by F. H. and C. H. Kay. London: SCM, 1969.

Johnson, Paul. *A History of Christianity.* West Hanover and Plympton, Mass.: Halliday, 1976.

Josephus, Flavius. *The Complete Works of Josephus.* Translated by William Whiston. Grand Rapids: Kregel, 1981.

Daily Life in Bible Times. Dallas: Wycliffe, 1988.

Kannengiesser, Charles, ed. *Early Christian Spirituality.* Sources of Early Christian Thought. Philadelphia: Fortress, 1986.

Keil, C. F., and F. Delitzsch. *The Pentateuch.* Vol. 1, *Commentary on the Old Testament.* Translated by James Martin. Grand Rapids: Eerdmans, 1973.

————. *Proverbs, Ecclesiastes, Song of Solomon.* Vol. 6, *Commentary on the Old Testament.* Translated by James Martin. Grand Rapids: Eerdmans, 1973.

Kugel, James L., and Rowan A. Greer. *Early Biblical Interpretation.* Library of Early Christianity. Philadelphia: Westminster, 1986.

Ladd, George Eldon. *A Theology of the New Testament.* Grand Rapids: Eerdmans, 1974.

Lange, John Peter. *Exodus. The Gospel According to Matthew. Romans and Corinthians. Galatians–Hebrews. James–Revelation.* Lange's Commentary on the Holy Scriptures, vols. 1, 8, 10-12. Edited and translated by Philip Schaff. Grand Rapids: Zondervan, 1969.

Latourette, Kenneth Scott. *A History of Christianity.* New York: Harper & Row, 1953.

Leckler, Gotthard Victor. *The Acts of the Apostles.* Lange's Commentary on the Holy Scriptures, vol. 9. Edited and translated by Philip Schaff. Grand Rapids: Zondervan, 1969.

Lightfoot, J. B. *St. Paul's Epistle to the Galatians.* 10th ed. London: Macmillan and Co., 1890.

Lindsay, Thomas M. *The Church and the Ministry in the Early Centuries: The Eighteenth Series of the Cunningham Lectures.* Minneapolis: James Family, 1977.

Malherbe, Abraham J. *Social Aspects of Early Christianity.* 2d ed., enl. Philadelphia: Fortress, 1983.

————. *Moral Exhortation, A Greco-Roman Sourcebook.* Library of Early Christianity. Philadelphia: Westminster, 1986.

————. *Social Aspects of Early Christianity.* Baton Rouge: Louisiana State Univ., 1977.

Martin, Ralph P. *The Epistle of Paul to the Philippians: An Introduction and Commentary.* The Tyndale New Testament Commentaries, vol. 11. Grand Rapids: Eerdmans, 1959.

Meeks, Wayne A. *The First Urban Christians: The Social World of the Apostle Paul.* New Haven: Yale, 1983.

————. *The Moral World of the First Christians.* Library of Early Christianity. Philadelphia: Westminster, 1986.

Mickelsen, A. Berkeley. *Interpreting the Bible.* Grand Rapids: Eerdmans, 1963.

Moll, Carl B. *The Psalms.* Lange's Commentary on the Holy Scriptures, vol. 5. Edited and translated by Philip Schaff. Grand Rapids: Zondervan, 1969.

Morris, Leon. *The Epistles of Paul to the Thessalonians: An Introduction and Commentary.* The Tyndale New Testament Commentaries, vol. 13. Grand Rapids: Eerdmans, 1956.

————. *The First Epistle of Paul to the Corinthians: An Introduction and Commentary.* The Tyndale New Testament Commentaries, vol. 7. Grand Rapids: Eerdmans, 1958.

Murray, John. *The New International Commentary on the New Testament: The Epistle to the Romans.* 2 vols. Grand Rapids: Eerdmans, 1965.

Nash, Ronald H. *Poverty and Wealth: The Christian Debate over Capitalism.* Westchester, Ill.: Crossway, 1986.

Norris, Richard A., ed. and trans. *The Christological Controversy.* Sources of Early Christian Thought. Philadelphia: Fortress, 1980.

Olford, Stephen F. *The Grace of Giving.* Grand Rapids: Baker, 1984.

Orr, James, ed. *The New International Standard Bible Encyclopedia.* 5 vols. Grand Rapids: Eerdmans, 1955.

Peters, George W. *A Theology of Church Growth.* Grand Rapids: Zondervan, 1981.

Peters, George N. H. *The Theocratic Kingdom of Our Lord Jesus, the Christ, as Covenanted in the Old Testament and Presented in the New Testament.* 3d ed. 3 vols. Grand Rapids: Kregel, 1972.

Pfeiffer, Charles F., Howard F. Vos, and John Rea, eds., *Wycliffe Bible Encyclopedia.* 2 vols. Chicago: Moody, 1975.

Pfeiffer, Charles F., and Howard F. Vos. *The Wycliffe Historical Geography of Bible Lands.* Chicago: Moody, 1968.

Ramsay, William M. *An Historical Commentary on St. Paul's Epistle to the Galatians.* New York: G. P. Putnam's Sons, 1900.

Richard, Ramesh P. "Application Theory in Relation to the New Testament." *Bibliotheca Sacra* 143 (July–September 1986).

Rusch, William G., ed. and trans. *The Trinitarian Controversy.* Sources of Early Christian Thought. Philadelphia: Fortress, 1980.

Ryrie, Charles C. *Biblical Theology of the New Testament.* Chicago: Moody, 1959.

————. *Balancing the Christian Life.* Chicago: Moody, 1969.

Saucy, Robert L. *The Church in God's Program.* Chicago: Moody, 1972.

Schroeder, Wilhelm J. *Deuteronomy.* Lange's Commentary on the Holy Scriptures, vol. 2. Edited and translated by Philip Schaff. Grand Rapids: Zondervan, 1969.

Silva, Moises, ed. *Has the Church Misread the Bible?* Foundations of Contemporary Interpretation, vol. 1. Grand Rapids: Academia, 1987.

Sparks, Jack, ed. *The Apostolic Fathers.* Nashville: Thomas Nelson, 1978.

Stambaugh, John E., and David L. Balch. *The New Testament in Its Social Environment.* Library of Early Christianity. Philadelphia: Westminster, 1986.

Stibbs, Alan M. *The First Epistle of Peter: A Commentary.* The Tyndale New Testament Commentaries, vol. 17. Grand Rapids: Eerdmans, 1959.

Stott, John R. W. *The Epistles of John: An Introduction and Commentary.* The Tyndale New Testament Commentaries, vol. 19. Grand Rapids: Eerdmans, 1964.

Stowers, Stanley K. *Letter Writing in Greco-Roman Antiquity.* Library of Early Christianity. Philadelphia: Westminster, 1986.

Swetmon, Bill R., *A Giving Heart: A Handbook on Christian Stewardship.* Nashville: Gospel Advocate, 1986.

Tasker, R. V. G. *The General Epistle of James: An Introduction and Commentary.* The Tyndale New Testament Commentaries, vol. 16. Grand Rapids: Eerdmans, 1956.

————. *The Gospel According to St. Matthew: An Introduction and Commentary.* The Tyndale New Testament Commentaries, vol. 1. Grand Rapids: Eerdmans, 1961.

————. *The Gospel According to St. John: An Introduction and Commentary.* The Tyndale New Testament Commentaries, vol. 4. Grand Rapids: Eerdmans, 1960.

————. *The Second Epistle of Paul to the Corinthians: An Introduction and Commentary.* The Tyndale New Testament Commentaries, vol. 8. Grand Rapids: Eerdmans, 1958.

Tenney, Merrill C. *Interpreting Revelation.* Grand Rapids: Eerdmans, 1957.

————. *New Testament Survey.* Grand Rapids: Eerdmans, 1953.

————. *New Testament Times.* Grand Rapids: Eerdmans, 1965.

Thomas, W. H. Griffith. *St. Paul's Epistle to the Romans.* Grand Rapids: Eerdmans, 1946.

Tidball, Derek J. *Skillful Shepherds: An Introduction to Pastoral Theology.* Grand Rapids: Zondervan, 1986.

Tierney, Brian. *The Middle Ages.* Sources of Medieval History, vol. 1. 3d ed. New York: Alfred A. Knopf, 1978.

Unger, Merrill F. *Unger's Bible Dictionary.* Chicago: Moody Press, 1957.

Verner, David C. *The Household of God: The Social World of the Pastoral Epistles.* Dissertation Series, Society of Biblical Literature, no. 71. Chico, Calif.: Scholars, 1983.

Vine, W. E. *An Expository Dictionary of New Testament Words.* Old Tappan, N.J.: Fleming H. Revell, 1940.

Virkler, Henry A. "Applying the Biblical Message: A Proposal for the Transcultural Problem." In *Hermeneutics: Principles and Processes of Biblical Interpretation.* Grand Rapids: Baker, 1981.

Vischer, Lukas. *Tithing in the Early Church.* Translated by Robert C. Schultz. Philadelphia, Fortress, 1966.

Webster's Ninth New Collegiate Dictionary. Springfield, Mass.: Merriam-Webster, 1986.

Wilkinson, L. P. *The Roman Experience.* New York: Alfred A. Knopf, 1974.

Willingale, A. E. *The New Bible Dictionary.* Grand Rapids: Eerdmans, 1962.

Womer, Jan L., ed. and trans. *Morality and Ethics in Early Christianity.* Sources of Early Christian Thought. Philadelphia: Fortress, 1987.

Yankelovich Monitor Report, 1987.

Zockler, Otto. *The Proverbs of Solomon.* Lange's Commentary on the Holy Scriptures, vol. 5. Edited and translated by Philip Schaff. Grand Rapids: Zondervan, 1969.

Zuck, Roy B. "Applications in Biblical Hermeneutics and Exposition." In *Walvoord: A Tribute*, edited by Donald K. Campbell. Chicago: Moody, 1982.

General Index

Abrahamic Covenant, 113
Achaian Christians, 258-59
    their model in giving, 55
Acts 6 Group, 16
Affluence, problems of, 168-69
Agape Love Feast, 52
American Christians, 100, 333-34
American economic opportunities, 178
Angels at ascension, 72
Apostles, the
    after church scattered, 123
    and the upper room, 31
    basis of motivation, 73
    death of, 118
    foundation of the church, 108
    Jesus' promises to, 71
    limited knowledge of, 72, 194
    position in kingdom, 72
    progressive knowledge of, 73
    their priorities, 48
    their sacrifice, 69
    their fishing business, 69
    their missionary tour, 70, 95, 115-16
Apostles' Teaching, 43
    and the gift of teaching, 63
    in the book of Acts, 61
    Matthew's personal experience, 69-70

Peter's witness, 71-72
relationship to Jesus' teaching, 43, 61-63, 75
their testimony in Jerusalem, 69
their witness regarding Judas Iscariot, 70-71
Aramaic speaking community, 124-25
Artemis, idol of, 291
Authors quoted
    Bruce, F. F., 335, 338
    Burkett, Larry, 276-77
    Chafer, Lewis Sperry, 117
    Cole, Alan, 99
    Delitzsch, F., 269-70
    Drumwright, Huber, Jr., 158
    Enns, Paul, 22, 27, 165
    Fausset, A. R., 274
    Foulkes, Francis, 297
    Gapp, Kenneth, 146
    Godet, Frederick Lewis, 259
    Goldberg, Louis, 142
    Gonzalez, Justo, 21
    Hendricksen, William, 81, 101, 103
    Hewitt, Thomas, 336
    Hiebert, D. Edmond, 73
    Hodge, Charles, 259
    Hoehner, Harold, 58, 145

Scripture Index

Moody Press, a ministry of the Moody Bible Institute,
is designed for education, evangelization, and edification.
If we may assist you in knowing more about Christ
and the Christian life, please write us without obligation:
Moody Press, c/o MLM, Chicago, Illinois 60610.